# HARALAMBOS AND HOLBORN
# SOCIOLOGY
## THEMES AND PERSPECTIVES

# AS- and A-level
# STUDENT HANDBOOK
## accompanies the sixth edition

**Martin Holborn and Peter Langley**

Collins

Published by HarperCollins *Publishers* Limited
77–85 Fulham Palace Road
Hammersmith
London W6 8JB

For free online support visit:
www.haralambosholborn.com

©2004 Martin Holborn and Peter Langley
10 9 8 7 6 5 4 3

British Library Cataloguing in Publication Data
A catalogue record for this publication
is available from the British Library

ISBN-13 978-0-00-717947-3

ISBN-10 0-00-717947-2

Commissioned by Thomas Allain-Chapman
Edited by Louise Wilson
Text and cover design and typesetting by Patricia Briggs
Printed and bound by Imago

Browse the complete Collins catalogue at:
www.collinseducation.com

# CONTENTS

# ACKNOWLEDGEMENTS

The Publisher and authors would particularly like to thank Pam Law, Ruth Moores and Steve Chapman for their substantial and invaluable contribution to this book. The AQA-style questions were written by Pam Law and Ruth Moores, and the OCR-style questions by Steve Chapman. Thanks are also due to Fionnuala Swann for revising the OCR questions and writing the Health question, and to Danny Matthews for editorial assistance.

# USING THIS STUDENT HANDBOOK

Each chapter of the *Student Handbook* consists of five elements.

## 1 Specification map

Specification grids show you how each chapter relates to the AQA and OCR specifications. The complete specification for each topic is provided in the chapter that most closely reflects its content. Where a chapter covers part of a module, this is indicated.

## 2 Essential notes

These summarize key issues, arguments and studies in an accessible and simple way. The material included has been selected from the main book because of its relevance to the A-level specifications. The essential notes can be used as a record of your course, for revision or as a reminder of the content of the main book.

## 3 Test your knowledge and understanding

A series of carefully chosen multiple-choice questions at the end of each chapter aims to make you think, as well as simply testing your knowledge. Try answering a few after you have covered each part of a chapter or work through them all as a form of revision. Correct answers are provided at the end of the book.

## 4 Develop your analysis and evaluation skills

You are given a number of statements or questions that reflect key debates in each chapter and that are often the focus of exam questions. The exercises then direct you to the key sociologists who take particular positions in the debate.

## 5 Practice exam questions

Each chapter ends with sample exam questions written by senior examiners from AQA and OCR. The questions are annotated to show how you can use each chapter in the AS or A2 exams, provide guidance on exam technique and give you a clear idea of what will be expected of you in the exams.

## Specifications

An understanding of the major sociological perspectives is important across all aspects of both AQA and OCR specifications, especially at A2 level.

**Parts of modules covered** (NB *Socialization, culture and identity* is a theme running through the AQA specification)

| Specification | Specification details | | Coverage |
|---|---|---|---|
| **OCR** AS: The Individual and Society | **Introducing the individual and society** | ■ The role of values, norms and the agents of socialization in the formation of culture <br> ■ Learning social roles. How expected patterns of behaviour regulate social life | These issues are covered in the section on culture and society (p. 1). |
| **AQA** A2: Theory and Methods | | ■ Consensus, conflict, structural and social action theories | Sociological theories are introduced on pp. 2–3. |
| | | ■ The concepts of modernity and post-modernity in relation to sociological theory | These concepts are dealt with on pp. 1–3. |

For more detailed specification guidance visit www.haralambosholborn.com

## Essential notes

### CULTURE AND SOCIETY

Ralph Linton (1945) sees culture as the way of life shared by members of a society. It is learned and is a vital part of human society. Cultures vary from society to society. For example, some societies have practised geronticide (the killing of old people). Tasmanian Aboriginals, for example, sometimes left the old to die.

- **Socialization** is the process through which you learn a culture, and it continues throughout life.
- **Primary socialization** is the first phase, usually taking place in the family.
- **Peer groups** (groups of a similar age and status), the education system and occupations are important agents of secondary socialization.
- **Socialization** is essential for participation in human society; humans who have not been socialized – e.g. the wolf-children of Midnapore (see p. ix of the textbook) – find it very difficult to adapt to human society.
- **Values** are general guidelines about what is considered good and desirable or bad and undesirable in a society. In contemporary Britain, widely held values include acquiring material possessions, honesty, and so on. In Sioux society, generosity was a key value.
- **Norms** are specific guides to action that derive from general values. Norms define when, for example, it is acceptable to remove clothes. Norms are regulated by negative **sanctions** (punishments) and positive sanctions (rewards).
- **Statuses** are social positions, such as doctor, teacher, student, wife, man, member of an ethnic group, teenager and so on. Some statuses are **ascribed** (given

to you and largely fixed), e.g. statuses of male and female; others are **achieved** (they result from your own actions), e.g. different job statuses.
- Each status has social **roles** attached to it that specify appropriate behaviour for the status (e.g. the roles of teacher and pupil). Roles make behaviour reasonably predictable, but people do not always conform to them.

### THE DEVELOPMENT OF HUMAN SOCIETIES

Some sociologists see societies as having gone through broad **developmental stages**, such as premodern, modern and postmodern.

#### Premodern societies

Anthony **Giddens** (1997) distinguishes three types:

- Hunting-and-gathering societies based on hunting animals and gathering fruit and vegetables.
- Pastoral and agrarian societies in which animal herding and settled agriculture have developed.
- Non-industrial civilizations such as the Aztecs, Ancient Egyptians, Greeks and Romans.

#### Modern industrial societies

These started developing in the late eighteenth and nineteenth centuries. **Lee and Newby** (1983) identify four key features:

- **Industrialism** – the Industrial Revolution started in the late eighteenth century. It greatly increased human productive power and reduced the degree to which nature shaped social life.

- **Capitalism** involved the employment of labour for wages and businesses based upon making profits.
- **Urbanism** resulted in populations being increasingly concentrated in towns and cities.
- **Liberal democracy** eventually replaced monarchical rule, giving people a say in how society was run.

The above changes have been seen as creating **modernity**, which involves a belief in the ability to plan, achieve progress and solve problems using science and technology. Some see sociology as closely involved with modernity.

## Postmodernity

**Postmodernity** is claimed by some sociologists to be replacing modernity.

- Postmodernity tends to involve a loss of faith in science and rationality, a loss of belief in progress and increased scepticism about any theories that claim to be able to produce a better future.
- Some non-rational beliefs (such as New Age beliefs) have become more popular. According to some postmodernists, the changes are linked to a post-industrial (service- or information technology-based) economy.

To some postmodernists, older theories of society have become outdated, but other sociologists question the value of theories of postmodernity.

## THEORIES OF SOCIETY

## Functionalism

Leading functionalists include Emile **Durkheim** (1858–1917) and Talcott **Parsons** (1902–79).

- Originally functionalists borrowed ideas from biology. They saw each part of society as having a **function** (a purpose or a job it does) like each part of the body (e.g. the government of a society is like a human's brain).
- Functionalists see society as having a **structure**, with key institutions performing vital functions, and roles directing people in how to behave.
- They identify the functions of each part of the structure – e.g. the family socializes the young and produces a shared culture.
- Institutions are there to meet the basic needs or **functional prerequisites** of society – e.g. producing food and shelter for people.
- A **value consensus** (shared beliefs about right and wrong) helps society to run smoothly and to integrate the different parts.

## Conflict perspectives

Conflict perspectives argue that there are differences of interest between groups in society (what is good for one group is bad for another). This creates the potential for conflict between groups. There are a range of conflict theories.

## Marxism

**Marxism** is based upon the work of Karl Marx (1818–83), though it has been adapted by later writers.

- Marx argues that societies result from humans getting together to produce food.
- The **forces of production** (the technology used to produce things) shape social relationships.
- The economic system consisting of the forces and **social relationships of production** forms the infrastructure of society.
- The **infrastructure** shapes other parts of society such as the government, family life, the education system and religion – collectively known as the **superstructure**.
- Most societies are based upon **exploitation** of some groups by others. Those who own the **means of production** (such as the land, factories, raw materials or capital) exploit those who work for them, and who lack the means to produce things themselves.
- Contemporary societies are seen as **capitalist** societies in which the owners of capital are dominant.
- Capitalists (the **bourgeoisie**) exploit their workers (the **proletariat**) by paying them less in wages than the wealth created by their work. Capitalists accumulate profits (or **surplus value**) and get richer and richer.
- In capitalist societies, the **ruling class** owns the means of production. It tries to use the superstructure (e.g. the government, legal system, religion and the mass media) to persuade workers that society is fair and just, in order to prevent workers from rebelling against their exploitation. If it succeeds, **ruling-class ideology** is dominant and creates **false class consciousness** (a mistaken belief that society is fair) amongst workers.
- Eventually workers will come to realize that they are being exploited and will overthrow capitalism and create a communist society.
- In **communism** the means of production (land, factories, etc.) will be communally owned, so there will be no ruling class, no exploitation and much less inequality than in capitalism

## Feminism

There are different versions of feminism but all see society as divided between men and women.

- Feminists tend to see women as exploited by men, and society as patriarchal or male-dominated.
- Examples of **patriarchy** include men monopolizing high-status and well-paid jobs, doing less housework than women and holding the most senior positions in politics.
- Most feminists tend to see women as having shared interests, and believe that progress towards ending patriarchy is possible.
- **Difference feminists** argue that different groups of women may have different interests, and that not all women are equally exploited.
- Many feminists criticize sociology (particularly older sociology) as being **malestream**: that is, written by men, largely about men and from a masculine viewpoint.

## Interactionism

Unlike **macro theories** (which look at society as a whole, e.g. Marxism and functionalism), interactionism (a **micro theory**) looks at social behaviour in smaller groups.

■ Interactionists stress the importance of meanings – the way people interpret the behaviour of others.
■ **Meanings** develop during interaction as people try to get a feel for the intentions behind other people's actions.
■ Humans possess a self-concept, or idea, of what sort of person they are.
■ **Self-concepts** develop in response to the reactions of others. You end up thinking of yourself in the same way as others think of you.
■ Like functionalists, interactionists believe that roles exist, but they see them as much more **flexible** and negotiable. For example, married couples develop their own interpretations of the roles of husband and wife.
■ Society is seen as more fluid, less rigidly fixed, than in macro theories.

## Postmodernism

Postmodernist perspectives have developed since the 1980s.

■ Some versions see important changes taking place in society.
■ Other versions question the ability of conventional sociology to produce worthwhile theories of society.
■ Some postmodernists argue that social behaviour is no longer shaped by factors such as class, gender, ethnicity and different types of socialization. It is now simply a question of **lifestyle choice**.
■ Some postmodernists argue that sociological theory can never objectively describe the social world.
■ **Lyotard** (1984) criticizes all grand or general theories, and many postmodernists stress that everybody's viewpoint on society is equally valid.

## VIEWS OF HUMAN BEHAVIOUR

There are three main views of human behaviour, which underlie different approaches to producing sociological data.

## Positivism

■ Positivists believe that human behaviour can be **objectively** measured.
■ Direct **observation** can produce objective data, and only that which can be observed should be studied.
■ Human behaviour is shaped by **external stimuli**.
■ Sociologists should use **natural science** methods.
■ **Statistical data** can be produced which can be used to uncover **cause-and-effect relationships** between two or more things.

## Social action perspectives

■ Social action perspectives argue that sociology is not like the natural sciences because it involves the study of **conscious** human beings.
■ Humans interpret the **meaning** of things before reacting and do not react passively to external stimuli.
■ In order to explain behaviour, sociologists need to examine what is going on inside people's heads – these **internal meanings** cannot be directly observed.
■ Proponents of social action approaches include Max Weber (1864–1920) and the interactionists.

## Phenomenology

■ Phenomenologists deny that any objective **classification** of the social world is possible.
■ All **categorization** is subjective: statistics are simply based upon personal opinions (e.g. whether a death is a suicide).
■ Without factual data, causal explanations of human behaviour cannot be produced.
■ Sociologists can only really study the factors that influence the way people categorize the world (i.e. what makes them decide that a death is a suicide or that a particular action is a crime).

## SOCIOLOGY AND VALUES

Positivists believe that an **objective**, unbiased, value-free sociology is possible, but many sociologists argue that it is not. They argue that a researcher's values (or personal beliefs about right and wrong) are bound to influence what they study, how they study it and how they interpret the data.

■ Functionalism has often been seen as supporting the status quo and opposing change because it views all institutions as having useful functions. It is therefore seen as having a **conservative ideology**.
■ Marxism advocates change in order to remove exploitation and oppression. It can therefore be seen as having a **radical ideology**.

## The sociological imagination

Some sociologists, such as **Giddens** (1977, 1979, 1984), argue that different perspectives should be combined and that both **social structure and social action** are important for understanding society.

C. Wright Mills (1959) advocates a similar approach. He argues that links should be made between **public issues** (such as unemployment) and **personal troubles** (such as the experience of the unemployed individual).

## TEST YOUR KNOWLEDGE AND UNDERSTANDING

1 Socialization is:
 a Mixing with other people
 b Influencing other people
 c Learning how society expects you to behave
 d Beliefs about right and wrong

2 An example of a value in British society would be:
 a A belief in the superiority of the English football team
 b A belief that honesty is desirable
 c A belief in UFOs
 d A belief in the theory of evolution

3 An example of an ascribed status is:
 a The status of a taxi driver
 b The status of being a good footballer
 c The status of having passed a degree
 d The status of being a woman

4 A norm is:
 a A specific guide to acceptable behaviour in a social situation
 b Being normal
 c A belief in right and wrong
 d A position in society and the behaviour associated with it

5 The central feature of modernity is:
 a A belief in the ability to achieve rationally planned progress
 b A lack of faith in science
 c A strong belief in religion
 d The key importance of information technology

6 Postmodernity involves which two of the following?
 a The revival of non-rational beliefs
 b The dominance of manufacturing industry
 c Scepticism about theories which claim to be able to create the perfect society
 d Faith in science

7 Which one of the following perspectives is most likely to see institutions in society as being useful?
 a Functionalism
 b Marxism
 c Feminism
 d Interactionism

8 Which one of the following theories sees the exploitation of women as a key feature of society?
 a Functionalism
 b Marxism
 c Feminism
 d Interactionism

9 Which one of the following theories sees the exploitation of the working class as a key feature of society?
 a Functionalism
 b Marxism
 c Feminism
 d Interactionism

10 Which one of the following theories is a micro theory?
 a Functionalism
 b Marxism
 c Feminism
 d Interactionism

11 Which one of the following theories emphasizes lifestyle choice?
 a Functionalism
 b Marxism
 c Feminism
 d Postmodernism

12 Which one of the following theories emphasizes the importance of the self-concept?
 a Marxism
 b Feminism
 c Interactionism
 d Postmodernism

13 Which one of the following theories emphasizes the difficulty of categorizing the social world?
 a Marxism
 b Social action perspectives
 c Positivism
 d Phenomenology

14 Which one of the following theories emphasizes the importance of following objective, scientific methods?
 a Interactionism
 b Positivism
 c Phenomenology
 d Social action perspectives

15 Objective means the same as:
 a Value-laden
 b Value-free
 c Valueless
 d Valuable

# DEVELOP YOUR ANALYSIS AND EVALUATION SKILLS

## Is Britain a modern society?

**Background:** to sociologists the idea of modernity does not simply mean contemporary, it refers to a particular phase in the development of society. This phase is characterized by the importance of industry, a capitalist system, urbanization and liberal democracy. It can be contrasted with the idea of pre-modern and postmodern societies. There is no question of Britain being pre-modern anymore, but some sociologists do consider it to be postmodern.

| **Yes** | **No** |
|---|---|
| ■ The development of human societies (pp. 1–2) | ■ Theories of society – functionalism, Marxism and postmodernism (pp. 2–3) |
| ■ Modernity, postmodernity and postmodernism (pp. 1–2) | |

**Top tip:** Britain might be considered postmodern to the extent that any of the following are true: a loss of faith in science, pessimism about the idea of progress, belief in non-rational ideas and a service or information-based economy replacing an industrial one.

## Do all societies share a basic consensus about norms and values?

**Background:** A basic problem in sociology concerns how societies can stick together without people being in constant conflict and the society disintegrating. Functionalists think the answer lies in the existence of a generally shared agreement about right or wrong and how people should behave. They believe that this value consensus allows people to cooperate and this benefits everybody. However, Marxists believe that, before communism at least, all societies have conflict between classes and feminists believe there is a basic conflict between men and women. A combination of distorted beliefs (or ideology) and force is used to prevent or control conflict rather than any genuine agreement about values.

| **Yes** | **No** |
|---|---|
| ■ Functionalism (p. 2) | ■ Marxism (p. 2) |
| | ■ Feminism (p. 2) |

**Top tip:** Think about whether people really do believe the same things are right and wrong. Examples of controversial issues include abortion, eating meat and the invasion of Iraq. Do different political parties and different religions share the same values?

## Is sociology a scientific subject that should use scientific methods?

**Background:** Scientific subjects tend to have higher status than other subjects and so some sociologists have wanted their discipline to be seen as scientific. Positivists claim that sociology can use exactly the same methods as natural science and can be objective in finding the causes of things that happen in society. Social action perspectives disagree, arguing that human behaviour is shaped by the meanings and motives in people's heads, which are subjective and cannot be studied scientifically. Phenomenologists also deny sociology can be scientific because they believe that all data is based on subjective classifications and there are no hard facts about the social world.

| **For** | **Against** |
|---|---|
| ■ Positivism (p. 3) | ■ Social action approaches (p. 3) |
| | ■ Phenomenology (p. 3) |

**Top tip:** The sociology of suicide is a good example to use to illustrate the different viewpoints and is discussed in the methodology chapter (see pp. 197–198).

# Chapter 1

# SOCIAL STRATIFICATION

Textbook pp. 1–91

## Specifications

NB *Social differentiation, power and stratification* is a theme running through the AQA specification

| Specification | Specification details | | Coverage |
|---|---|---|---|
| **AQA** A2: Stratification and Differentiation | ■ Different ways of measuring social class, and the relationship between occupation and social class. | | Marxist, Weberian, functionalist and feminist sociologists all have something to say about these debates (pp. 7–8). |
| | ■ Different theories of stratification. | | The key theories are examined on pp. 7–8. |
| | ■ Differences in life-chances by social class, ethnicity, gender and age. | | These are covered in the chapters on 'Race', Ethnicity and Nationality (pp. 37–8) and Sex and Gender (pp. 26–7). Other chapters, notably Education (pp. 156, 160–2, 162–5), Health (pp. 64–6) and Poverty and Social Exclusion (pp. 48–9) contain detailed accounts of differences in life chances. |
| | ■ Different explanations of changes in the class structure, and the implications of these changes. | | Covered on pp. 8–17. |
| | ■ The nature, extent and significance of patterns of mobility. | | See the section on social mobility in capitalist societies (pp. 15–16). |
| **OCR** A2: Social Inequality and Difference | **The dimensions of workplace inequality** | ■ Contemporary changes in the distribution of wealth and income. | Covered on pp. 8–9. |
| | | ■ Contemporary workplace inequalities. The impact of changes in the workplace on class, ethnic and gender inequality. | See the section on changes in the British stratification system on p. 8–17. Relevant material also in chapter 10 (pp. 137–9). |
| | | ■ Workplace change and its impact on class formation and identity. | Pages 8–17 cover the main changes in the class structure. |
| | **Poverty as a dimension of inequality** | ■ Concepts and measures of poverty. | See the section on the definition and measurement of poverty in chapter 4 (pp. 45–6). |
| | | ■ Contemporary trends in poverty in terms of class, gender and ethnicity. | See the section on official statistics on social exclusion in chapter 4 (pp. 48–9). |
| | | ■ The underclass debate; theories of culture and poverty | See the section on the underclass and poverty in chapter 4 (pp. 50–1). |
| | **Explanations of inequality and difference** | ■ Concepts of class. Material and cultural class-based explanations of inequality; neo-Marxist and neo-Weberian. | The major theories of class are covered on pp. 7–8. The sections on gender and social class (p. 16) and 'Is Britain a meritocracy?' (p. 16) are also relevant. |
| | | ■ Feminist theories. Economic and cultural theories of gender inequalities. The restructuring of gender identities. | Feminist and other explanations of gender inequalities are covered in chapter 2, pp. 24–6. This chapter also contains material on changing gender identities (pp. 27–8). |
| | | ■ Definitions of race and ethnicity. Material and cultural theories of ethnic inequalities. Ethnic identities and their impact on inequality. | Material on 'race' and ethnicity can be found in chapter 3. Definitions of race are discussed on p. 33, theories of ethnic inequalities on pp. 33–4 and 37–8, and ethnic identities on pp. 35–6. |

**Parts of other modules covered**

| | | Coverage |
|---|---|---|
| **AQA** AS: Wealth, Poverty and Welfare | ■ Different definitions of poverty and wealth and income. | Definitions of wealth and income are covered on pp. 8–9. |
| | ■ Different explanations of the distribution of poverty, wealth and income between different groups. | Explanations of the distribution of wealth and income are covered on pp. 7–9. |
| **OCR** AS: The Individual and Society | ■ The meaning of class identities. Their impact on social behaviour. | Covered on pp. 9–15 and 16–17. |

For more detailed specification guidance visit **www.haralambosholborn.com**

# INTRODUCTION

**Social inequality** refers to any differences that result in some people having more socially valued characteristics than others. Degrees of power, prestige and wealth may be significant.

**Social stratification** refers to a situation in which people are divided into distinct groups ranked at different levels. The Hindu caste system is an example – different castes have different levels of status depending on their supposed degree of religious purity.

Those at different levels in a stratification system may develop a common **subculture** or way of life.

**Social mobility** refers to movement between strata.

**Status** in stratification systems can be **ascribed** (given at birth, e.g. the caste system) or **achieved** (resulting from what you do, e.g. class systems).

**Life chances** are your chances of getting socially desirable things (e.g. money, education, longevity), and are affected by your place in the stratification system.

Stratification systems have sometimes been based on what were thought to be natural inequalities or **biological differences** (e.g. apartheid in South Africa assumed that whites were superior to blacks). However, sociologists see such views as rationalizations to legitimate the position of powerful groups.

# A FUNCTIONALIST PERSPECTIVE

## Parsons – stratification and values

Parsons (1964) sees all societies as having a value consensus – a general agreement about what is desirable and valuable (or undesirable). Whatever these values, individuals will be ranked in accordance with them.

Stratification is **inevitable** as all societies have some values and will make judgements.

In complex industrial societies, planning and organization require some individuals to have more **authority** than others.

Stratification unites people because it derives from **shared values**.

## Criticisms

Critics argue that many values are not shared and that stratification can be highly divisive.

## Davis and Moore – role allocation and performance

Davis and Moore (1967, first published 1945) argue that all societies share certain functional prerequisites. One of these is **role allocation** – ensuring that roles are filled and performed effectively and conscientiously by properly trained people.

Some jobs are more **functionally important** and some people have more **ability** than others.

To match the most able to the most important jobs, and to ensure that tedious, unpleasant or dangerous jobs are filled, a **rewards system** is needed.

The better-rewarded will form a higher stratum. This process is **inevitable**, **universal** (found in all societies) and **beneficial** because it helps society to function better.

## Criticisms

Melvin Tumin (1953) argues that:

1 Many low-paid and even unskilled jobs are just as vital as higher-paid or more skilled jobs.
2 There is a greater pool of talent than Davis and Moore assume.
3 Training is a pleasant experience and does not require extra rewards to persuade people to undertake it.
4 Stratification systems can demotivate those at the bottom.
5 Stratification systems do not provide equality of opportunity and tend to prevent those from lower strata achieving their potential.
6 Stratification systems encourage 'hostility, suspicion and distrust'.

# A MARXIST PERSPECTIVE

According to Marx:

- All stratified societies have two major classes: a **ruling class** and a **subject class**.
- The ruling class owns the **means of production** (land, capital, machinery, etc.), and the subject class does not.
- The ruling class **exploits** the subject class.
- The ruling class uses the **superstructure** (e.g. legal and political systems) to legitimate (justify) its position and prevent protests by the subject class.
- In capitalist societies the main classes are the **bourgeoisie** (the capitalist class that owns the main means of production – capital) and the **proletariat** (the working class that has to sell their labour to survive).
- The bourgeoisie exploits the working class through the system of **wage labour**. Capitalists pay wages to workers, but make a profit (**surplus value**) because they pay workers less than the value of what they produce.
- **Capitalism** is the newest type of class society but it will also be the last. Eventually it will be replaced by a **communist** society in which the means of production (land, capital, factories, machinery, etc.) will be communally owned.

The **transition to communism** will not be straightforward because it requires **revolutionary action** by the proletariat. However, the bourgeoisie uses the superstructure (e.g. the media, education system, and political and legal systems) to suppress the proletariat by creating **false class consciousness** (which means that workers do not realize that they are being exploited). Eventually, though, **class consciousness** will develop – workers will realize that they are being exploited and will rise up to change society.

Class consciousness will develop because:

- There is a basic **contradiction** in capitalist societies between the interests of workers and capitalists.
- Workers will become concentrated in large factories, making it easier to communicate with one another and organize resistance.
- Workers' wages will decline in relation to the growing wealth of capitalists, in order to maintain profits. There will be a **polarization** of classes, with the rich getting richer and the poor poorer, making inequalities more obvious.
- **Skill divisions** between workers will be reduced as new technology is introduced, resulting in a more homogeneous and united working class.
- The **petty bourgeoisie** (small capitalists such as shopkeepers) will be unable to compete and will sink into the proletariat.
- Capitalist economies are unstable, and **economic crises** and periods of high unemployment will cause growing resentment.
- Workers will join together to form unions, political parties and revolutionary movements as class consciousness grows, enabling them to overthrow capitalism and replace it with communism.

### Criticisms

Many other theories and much of the research we will look at offer evaluation of the Marxist perspective.

## A WEBERIAN PERSPECTIVE

Max Weber (1864–1920) accepted some of Marx's ideas but rejected others.

Weber argued that classes develop from people's **market situation** (their situation in relation to buying and selling things, including their labour power) in market economies.

Weber differs from Marx in a number of ways:

- Like Marx he saw a basic division between those who have considerable **property** (and can live off the proceeds) and those who do not – the **propertyless** – who have to sell their labour. However, there are also significant differences within the two groups as well as between them.
- Within the propertyless group there are some who can sell their labour for a higher price (those with scarce but sought-after skills such as professionals and managers). They have an advantaged market situation compared to other groups of workers. Unlike Marx, Weber therefore believed that different **occupational groupings** could form classes.
- Weber saw no evidence of a polarization of classes. Instead he thought that the middle class of white-collar workers in bureaucracies would expand.

- Weber did not believe that a revolution by the proletariat was likely.
- He thought that some, but not all, power came from wealth.
- He argued that class was not the only basis for group formation. Status groups (groups of people who enjoyed similar levels of status or respect in society) could also be formed. **Status groups** might be based on ethnicity, age, nationality, gender, etc., and tended to share similar lifestyles. Class and status could be closely linked (for example, ethnic minorities might be excluded from highly-paid jobs in a society), but this was not always the case. Status groups often cut across class divisions (e.g. members of the gay community).
- Organized groups which seek to exercise political power or influence those with power are called **parties** by Weber. Parties may be political parties (e.g. the Labour and Conservative parties) or they may be pressure groups. They may be based on class (e.g. the 'old' Labour Party), status groups (e.g. Gay Rights organizations) or neither (e.g. Greenpeace).

## CHANGES IN THE BRITISH STRATIFICATION SYSTEM

### Changes in the occupational structure

- During the twentieth century the proportion of manual workers and personal service workers fell steadily from over three-quarters of all employees to well under a half, while the proportion of **non-manual workers** rose from under a quarter to over a half.
- **Manufacturing industry** declined, particularly in the last quarter of the twentieth century, while service industries grew.
- **Private sector** service jobs have increased rapidly over recent years.
- **Women**, especially married women, now form a bigger proportion of the workforce, but women are more likely to work part-time and are concentrated in intermediate and junior non-manual jobs.

### The changing distribution of income

Income has an important effect on **life chances**. Official statistics measure income in a variety of ways:
- **Original income** refers to all income apart from state benefits.
- **Gross income** includes state benefits.
- **Disposable income** deducts tax and national insurance.
- **Final income** includes the value of benefits such as healthcare, which are not given in cash.

Government figures show that the poorest 20% of the population receives less than half the average final income, while the richest 20% receives nearly twice the average. However, taxes and benefits do equalize and redistribute income to some extent.

The Royal Commission on the Distribution of Income found that there was some **redistribution of income** away from the richest groups between 1949 and 1979, but middle-income groups benefited most. From 1979 to 1997 changes in taxation and benefits under Conservative governments generally benefited the well-off at the expense of the poor. Since 1997, government policies have tended to favour those in low-paid work.

Overall, income inequalities declined in the twentieth century but not enough to eradicate class differences.

### The changing distribution of wealth

- There are no direct measures of the distribution of wealth, but surveys and data on the value of the estates of those who have died give some indication of wealth distribution.
- Wealth can be defined in different ways: **marketable** wealth includes only things that can be sold; **non-marketable** wealth includes the value of pensions, etc.
- Available figures suggest that wealth inequalities narrowed from 1900 to the early 1990s, widened throughout the 1990s.
- Wealth remains quite highly **concentrated**: in 1999 the richest 1% of the population owned 23% of all marketable wealth, and the richest 10% owned 54%.
- The proportion of people in Britain owning **shares** has increased in recent years, but shares make up a declining proportion of personal wealth (15% in 1995), and most people only have small shareholdings.

## THE UPPER CLASS

### Westergaard and Resler – a Marxist view

In 1975 **Westergaard and Resler** (1976) put forward a Marxist view that there was a **ruling class** in Britain consisting of the richest 5–10% of the population, whose position came from the ownership of capital. Private share ownership was highly concentrated in this minority group.

The ruling class was made up of company directors, top managers, higher professionals and senior civil servants, many of whom were big shareholders.

### Saunders – a New Right view

Peter **Saunders** (1990) puts forward a New Right view of the upper class. He agrees with much of what Westergaard and Resler say about the concentration of wealth, but he sees this group as an **influential economic elite** rather than a ruling class.

Most big companies are run by managers with only small shareholdings in the company. Much wealth is not privately held but is in pension schemes, insurance policies, etc., meaning that most people have a stake in capitalism.

Saunders claims that the economic elite do not have most of the power – power is decentralized. Class divisions have weakened and a ruling class no longer exists.

### Scott – Who Rules Britain?

John **Scott** (1982, 1991, 1997) is influenced by Marxism, elite theory and Weber.

Scott sees Britain as retaining an **upper/ruling class** but it is much changed since the nineteenth century.

- The upper class evolved from nineteenth century interlocking **networks** of landowners, financiers and manufacturers.
- During the twentieth century, family-controlled companies became less common (though important ones remain) and **joint stock companies** developed. Furthermore, professional **managers** took a greater role in running companies.
- A **capitalist class** persists. The ownership of property for use (e.g. housing) has become more widespread, but the ownership of property for power (e.g. stocks and shares, privately owned businesses, etc.) remains highly concentrated.
- The decisions of big companies and big financial institutions are controlled by a network of managers and directors who often have directorships in many companies (**interlocking directorships**). This capitalist class comprises around 0.1% of the adult population.
- The policies of all governments (even Labour ones) are strongly influenced by the interests of the capitalist class, and governments cannot go against the interests of capitalists without risking grave economic problems.

### Sklair – the global system and the transnational capitalist class

Leslie **Sklair** (1995) argues that **globalization** and the global system have produced a **transnational capitalist class** associated with major transnational corporations. Members of this class are not loyal to particular countries; they see their interests in terms of the capitalist system as a whole.

#### Criticisms

Sklair underestimates the importance of finance capitalists and the continuing power of nation-states, but he may be right to add a transnational dimension to ruling-class theory.

Elite theory and pluralism provide alternative views (see chapter 9, pp. 123–4).

## THE MIDDLE CLASSES

Marx's ideas on the middle class have influenced later research.

Marx argued that classes would be increasingly polarized between the bourgeoisie and the proletariat. The small business people/self-employed (the petty bourgeoisie) would sink into the proletariat.

Marx recognized the growing number of white-collar workers but said little about their significance. Many critics of Marx argue that there is a growing middle class, which undermines his theory of two polarizing classes.

**Weber**, however, believed that there was a middle class, with superior **life chances** to the working class and a more advantaged **market situation** (they had skills and qualifications which were in demand, which allowed them to command higher wages than the working class).

The conventional way to distinguish between the middle class and the working class is to equate them with **non-manual and manual workers**. However, the idea that non-manual workers make up the middle class can be **criticized**:

1 Unlike Marxist and Weberian theories, it has little theoretical basis.
2 Non-manual workers are a diverse group which may overlap with other classes.

## THE UPPER MIDDLE CLASS

Until the 1980s the **petty bourgeoisie** of self-employed and small employers declined in line with Marx's theory. However, from the 1980s it increased.

### The professions

- The **professions** grew from around 4% of those employed in 1900 to 13% of men and 11% of women by 1996.
- Professionals are employed both in growing **private businesses** and in the welfare state.
- They can be divided into **lower professions** (e.g. teachers, social workers, nurses) and **higher professions** (doctors, lawyers, accountants, etc.).
- **Savage** *et al.* (1992) distinguish between professions and **welfare professions**.
- Professionals generally have above-average incomes, but higher professionals/non-welfare professionals are particularly well paid. Both tend to have greater security and more fringe benefits than most other workers.

### The functionalist perspective on the professions

**Functionalists** such as Bernard Barber (1963) see professional jobs as having distinctive attributes:

- Possession of a body of specialist knowledge.
- Concern for the interests of the community.
- Control of behaviour through a code of ethics.
- High rewards and prestige, reflecting their contribution to society.

#### Criticisms of functionalism

1 Many have criticized the professions – e.g. lawyers have been accused of mystifying the law; teachers have been attacked for allowing underachievement, Harold Shipman murdered many of his patients. **Illich** (1975) accuses doctors of hiding the damaging effects of the environment.
2 Weberians and Marxists provide alternative views.

### The Weberian perspective on the professions

**Parry and Parry** (1976) believe that professions serve their own interests rather than community interests.

- They restrict entry to the profession in order to limit the supply of qualified workers in order to ensure they get high wages.
- **Professional associations** tend to protect and defend the image of the profession rather than protecting the public.
- Professional associations ensure that their members have a **monopoly**, thus protecting their interests.
- Professionalism is seen as a **market strategy** designed to maximize the security and rewards of a particular job, not as a characteristic of particular types of work.
- Higher professions get paid more than lower professions simply because they have achieved **monopoly status** (e.g. doctors and the BMA compared to teachers and their unions).

### Macdonald – the professional project

**Macdonald** (1997) argues that groups of workers undertake what he calls the **professional project** – they organize to get their work accepted as professional using techniques such as **social closure** (excluding others), establishing their own jurisdiction and attaining respectability.

### Professions as servants of the powerful

C. Wright **Mills** (1951) suggests that professions increasingly serve the **interests of the powerful** rather than their own interests. Professionals are largely employed by the rich or by large corporations and have to serve those who pay them.

### The deskilling of professions

**Braverman** (1974) argued that professional work was being **deskilled** (the skill was being removed from it) as the work was increasingly controlled by the powerful.

### The declining independence of the professions

Several sociologists have pointed to the **declining independence** of professionals. For example, **Johnson** (1972) argues that accountants have to be loyal to their company above their profession.

### The Ehrenreichs – the professional-managerial class

The **Ehrenreichs** (1979) do not see professions as a separate group. They put forward a neo-Marxist view that there is a distinct **professional-managerial class** making up 20–25% of the population.

They see this class as carrying out vital functions for capitalism:

- Organizing production.
- Controlling the working class.

- Promoting ruling-class ideology.
- Developing a consumer goods market.

There is **conflict** between this group and the working class, because the professional-managerial class serve the interests of the ruling class, and the working class sometimes resist their control.

### Criticisms

1 Marxists such as E.O. **Wright** (1978) do not see this group as a distinctive class but merely as intermediate strata.
2 **Weberian** theorists see the middle classes in terms of market situation rather than the functions they perform for capitalism.

## THE LOWER MIDDLE CLASS

This group includes clerical workers, secretaries and shop assistants.

According to the **proletarianization thesis** (supported by Marxists) this group has been proletarianized – they have become working-class.

Harry **Braverman** (1974) argues that they have been **deskilled** – e.g. clerical workers have gone from a virtual managerial role to doing very routine work.

**Weberians** tend to argue that the lower middle class remains distinct from the working class.

David **Lockwood** (1958) argues that the lower middle class has:

1 A better **market situation** than the working class, with higher wages, job security and promotion prospects.
2 A better **work situation**, working closely with managers and not being closely supervised.
3 A superior **status situation**: their work has more prestige than manual work.

**Stewart, Prandy and Blackburn** (1980), in a study of large firms, argue that most male clerical workers remain middle-class because their jobs are often stepping-stones to junior management positions.

**Crompton and Jones** (1984) are critical of the Weberian views above. They argue that:

1 Most clerical workers are female and their promotion prospects are much lower than those of men.
2 Many supposed managerial positions to which clerical workers are promoted are themselves routine.
3 Clerical jobs have been deskilled and are now proletarian, whatever the prospects for individuals holding those positions.

**Marshall, Newby, Rose and Vogler** (1988), in their survey of 1,770 British people, found no evidence of deskilling or loss of autonomy at work among clerical workers. However, they found that **personal service workers** (who are largely female) had very little control or autonomy at work, and they could be regarded as working-class.

## MIDDLE CLASS OR MIDDLE CLASSES

### Giddens – the middle class

**Giddens** (1973) uses a Weberian perspective to claim that the middle class form a single group, with educational qualifications and the ability to sell their mental labour power.

### Goldthorpe – the service and intermediate classes

**Goldthorpe** (1980) is also a Weberian but he distinguishes between a **service class** (larger employers, professionals, managers) and an **intermediate class** (clerical workers, small proprietors, technicians, etc.). The service class form a higher class of employees, who get increments on their salary and have pension rights and promotion prospects.

In later work Goldthorpe divides the middle class up according to whether they are **employed, employers** or **self-employed.**

### Criticisms

Goldthorpe has been criticized for:

1 Failing to identify a difference between managers and employers and professionals.
2 Disagreeing with the Marxist view that big employers constitute a ruling class.

### Roberts, Cook, Clark and Semeonoff – the fragmented middle class

**Roberts** et al. (1977) conducted a study of class images among 243 white-collar workers and distinguished four groups:

1 Those with middle-range, middle-class incomes had an image of society in which most people were middle-class (**middle-mass image**).
2 Small employers saw themselves as squeezed between a small upper class and a large mass of ordinary workers (**compressed middle-class image**).
3 Professionals tended to see society as a finely graded ladder of opportunity.
4 Clerical workers saw themselves as working-class (**proletarian image**).

**Roberts** et al. conclude that the **middle class is fragmented.**

### Criticisms

This study is based on a small, all-male sample and includes only the subjective views of individuals rather than objective differences in their positions.

### Abercrombie and Urry – the polarizing middle class

**Abercrombie and Urry** (1983) see the middle class as increasingly polarized between proletarianizing routine white-collar workers and professionals and managers with advantaged market and work situations.

### Savage, Barlow, Dickens and Fielding

Savage *et al.* (1992) claim that the middle class can possess three different types of asset:

1 **Property assets**, which are owned in particular by the petty bourgeoisie.
2 **Organizational assets** – held, for example, by managers with jobs in large organizations.
3 **Cultural assets** – deriving from educational attainment and credentials – which are particularly concentrated amongst professionals.

Members of the middle class use their different types of asset to help their children gain middle-class positions.

These different types of asset can lead to differences of interest and **division** in the middle class.

In recent years another line of division has opened up between **public sector professionals** and better-rewarded **private sector professionals**, managers and the petty bourgeoisie.

Different middle-class groups tend to adopt different **lifestyles**:

■ Public sector professionals tend to have a relatively healthy, ascetic lifestyle.
■ Well-paid private sector professionals have a more extravagant postmodern lifestyle.
■ Managers and civil servants have an undistinctive lifestyle.

### Evaluation

This study may underestimate the power and influence of managers and oversimplify lifestyle differences. However, it does highlight important sources of division and discuss the changing nature of the middle classes.

### Derek Wynne

Derek Wynne (1998) uses the ideas of **Pierre Bourdieu** (see pp. 14–15) in identifying divisions within the middle class on a private housing estate. Managers and professionals on the estate developed different lifestyles.

**Managers** largely gain middle-class status through the possession of **economic capital** and many base their lifestyle around drinking.

**Professionals** owe their middle-class status more to **cultural capital** and base their lifestyle more around taking part in sport.

Differences in leisure activity reflect differences in class background, education and occupation but differences in **consumption** patterns are increasingly important and these are starting to have the biggest role in shaping class.

### Criticisms

Wynne's own research seems to suggest that class background remains more important than lifestyle choice in creating class differences.

## THE WORKING CLASS

The working class tend to receive lower wages, enjoy less job security and receive fewer fringe benefits than the middle class.

They have significantly poorer **life chances**, such as lower life expectancy.

The issue of whether the working class share a distinctive **lifestyle** has been controversial.

In the 1960s, David **Lockwood** (1966) identified a group that he called **proletarian traditionalists**, who lived in close-knit working-class communities (e.g. coal miners) and exemplified traditional working-class culture. The main features of the culture were:

■ Loyalty to workmates.
■ Spending leisure time with workmates.
■ A belief in pursuing goals collectively rather than individually.
■ A **fatalistic** attitude to life (a belief that life chances depend on luck).
■ A present-time orientation with an emphasis on **immediate gratification** (i.e. enjoy yourself now).
■ A tendency to see class in terms of a division between 'us' (working people) and 'them' (the rich and powerful).
■ **Segregated conjugal roles**, with men as the main breadwinners and women as home-makers.

These characteristics are diametrically opposed to supposed **middle-class values** such as individualism, a belief in deferred gratification (planning for the future), an image of society as a status hierarchy with opportunities for individuals, and joint conjugal roles.

Marx predicted an expanding and increasingly homogeneous and **class-conscious** working class, but some sociologists have argued that the working class is becoming smaller, more **fragmented** and less class conscious.

■ Less than half the workforce now comprises manual workers, and in 2001 only 22% of men and 8% of women were employed in manufacturing. Traditional male manual work has declined most rapidly (e.g. shipbuilding, mining, mechanical engineering).
■ New technology, the growth of more skilled work in high-technology companies and the increased employment of women may have fragmented the working class.
■ Members of the working class may be less likely to see themselves as part of a united working class.

However, **Beynon** (1992) argues that we are not witnessing the 'end of the industrial worker'. Rather:

■ Some manufacturing jobs have shifted abroad.

- Many so-called service sector jobs are actually related to production (e.g. working in McDonald's).
- Subcontracting redefines work such as cleaning factories as service sector work.

Thus, the working class remains bigger than statistics suggest.

## EMBOURGEOISEMENT

This theory, first advocated in the 1950s by **Kerr et al.** and **Bernard**, suggested that well-paid **affluent workers** were becoming middle-class in terms of attitudes and lifestyle. If true this would undermine Marx's theory of an increasingly united and class-conscious working class.

**Goldthorpe, Lockwood, Bechhofer and Platt** (1968a, 1968b, 1969) investigated the theory in a study of affluent manual workers and white-collar workers in Luton in the 1960s. They found:

1 Although affluent workers earned as much as routine white-collar workers they had inferior conditions of work and a **poorer market situation** (e.g. fewer promotion prospects).
2 They retained a collectivist outlook but support for unions was no longer based on unconditional loyalty. **Instrumental collectivism** (collective action if it would improve wages) had replaced solidaristic collectivism (based on strong loyalty).
3 Both affluent workers and white-collar workers had adopted a **privatized, home-centred lifestyle**, but the manual workers did not mix socially with the white-collar workers.
4 Most saw society in terms of a **pecuniary model**, in which position was largely determined by income.
5 They continued to be Labour voters, but for instrumental reasons rather than loyalty.

Goldthorpe et al. concluded that affluent workers made up a new working class of **privatized instrumentalists**, located between the traditional working class and the middle class.

Fiona **Devine** (1992) returned to Luton in the late 1980s to see how things had changed. She found that workers:

1 Continued to support unions but remained instrumental collectivists.
2 Continued to choose largely working-class friends and retained fairly traditional conjugal roles.
3 Still had a pecuniary model of society.
4 Retained fairly left-wing political views, but some were disillusioned with the Labour Party, and some intended to vote Conservative.

Devine concluded that they were less individualistic than the affluent workers in Goldthorpe et al.'s study, and she felt that they had retained significant features of traditional working-class attitudes and lifestyle.

**Marshall, Newby, Rose and Vogler** (1988) conducted a large survey on class in Britain in the 1980s, and found

evidence of some **sectionalism, instrumentalism and privatism**. But they argued that these characteristics were nothing new – they dated back to the nineteenth century – and they therefore denied that there had been any major change in the working class.

### Divisions in the working class

Ralph **Dahrendorf** (1959) in the 1950s argued that the working class was increasingly divided by **skill level**, with a growing proportion of skilled workers anxious to maintain higher wages and status. He claimed that there had been a 'decomposition' of the working class.

Roger **Penn** (1983) studied cotton and engineering industries in Rochdale between 1856 and 1964 and found that skill divisions had long existed, and there was no evidence that they were becoming much more significant.

Ivor **Crewe** (1983), on the other hand, claims that there is an increasing division between a growing **new working class** and a shrinking **old working class**. The new working class:

- Live in the south.
- Are not union members.
- Work in private industry.
- Own their own home.
- Tend to vote Conservative.

The old working class, in contrast, live in other areas of the country, are union members and council tenants, work in the public sector, and tend to vote Labour.

However, **Marshall et al.** (1988) found that class continued to have more influence on voting than the **sectoral divisions** identified by Crewe.

**Warwick and Littlejohn** (1992) studied mining communities in the 1980s and found some divisions between the more successful workers, who were able to buy their council houses, and the less successful who suffered from unemployment. However, these divisions were based on **economic differences** not level of skill.

### Class consciousness

While **Marx** predicted growing **class consciousness**, the evidence suggests that it is not happening.

In **Goldthorpe et al.**'s 1960s study of affluent workers in Luton, and in more recent social surveys, most of the working-class subjects see wage inequality as necessary. The Luton workers saw little direct conflict of interest between themselves and managers. However, this and other studies have found that workers still tend to agree with statements such as 'big business has too much power'.

Thus some sociologists believe that the **seeds of class consciousness** are still there. **Devine** found that 1980s Luton workers, conscious of inequality and injustice, still looked to unions and the Labour Party to tackle such issues, but they had little faith that they could achieve much.

Sociologists such as **Blackburn and Mann** (1975) argue that the working class show **inconsistencies and contradictions** in their views. They experience exploitation and subordination at work, which encourage class consciousness, but the mass media and the ideology of the dominant class undermine class consciousness.

**Marshall** *et al.* also found **contradictory beliefs**: many of the working class in their sample were aware of injustice and inequality but were ambivalent about taking steps to reduce inequality. Overall Marshall *et al.* found considerable potential for class consciousness, in terms of seeing society as unfair, but they criticized the Labour Party for failing to mobilize and harness this sense of dissatisfaction.

## THE LOWER STRATA

Some sociologists have argued that there is a class underneath the working class. This class is often referred to as the **underclass**.

### Murray – the underclass in America and Britain

Charles **Murray** (1989) puts forward a **cultural view** of the underclass. He argues that, in America and more recently in Britain, there is a growing underclass defined in terms of behaviour and attitudes. It includes:

- **Single parents.**
- The **unemployed** who did not want to work.
- Those making a living from **crime.**

In America, a large proportion of the underclass is black.

The underclass reject values such as honesty and hard work. **Welfare payments** allow people to become single parents, and children lack the role-model of a hard-working father, thus perpetuating underclass attitudes.

### Criticisms

1 This cultural theory neglects economic divisions.
2 It ignores structural factors which might cause lack of economic success – e.g. lack of employment opportunities, the decline of manual work.
3 It blames the disadvantaged for their problems (see pp. 50–1 for further criticisms).

### Giddens – the underclass and the dual labour market

**Giddens** (1973) has a more economic theory of the underclass. He sees them as workers who tend to find jobs in the **secondary labour market** (low-paid, insecure jobs with few prospects). Employers tend to recruit women and ethnic minorities into such jobs, partly because of discrimination and prejudice.

The underclass have more radical views than the working class who are in secure employment.

### Criticisms

Kirk **Mann** (1982) argues that there is no clear dividing line between the primary (secure, well-paid work) and secondary labour markets.

He claims that Giddens fails to give a convincing explanation of why women and ethnic minorities are in secondary employment (see pp. 39–40 for a discussion of ethnicity and the underclass).

### Gallie – the heterogeneity of the underclass

Gallie (1988, 1994) argues that the underclass is too heterogeneous to be seen as a single class. He found big differences in the employment situations of women and members of ethnic minorities, and points out that there is a big flow into and out of unemployment.

The underclass also includes diverse age groups, and they often have different interests. They are therefore unlikely to develop shared consciousness.

Gallie found no evidence that the long-term unemployed were resigned to being without work and little evidence of a political split between the working class and the underclass.

However, Gallie does think that the **long-term unemployed** may form a distinct group

### Runciman – the underclass as claimants

W.G. **Runciman** (1990) sees the underclass as consisting of those reliant upon **benefits**, with little chance of being able to participate in paid employment. This places them in a different economic situation from even low-paid workers.

### Criticisms

1 **Dean and Taylor-Gooby** (1992) criticize Runciman for failing to take into account the large numbers who escape from reliance upon benefits. This makes any supposed underclass highly unstable.
2 **Dean** argues that the term underclass is used imprecisely in a variety of ways, often with the implication that the disadvantaged are to blame for their problems. He therefore argues that it should no longer be used.

## CLASS IDENTITY AND CULTURE

### Pierre Bourdieu

Bourdieu (1984) sees **cultural** aspects of class as being as important as **economic** aspects. Economic, **cultural** and **lifestyle** factors interact to shape your life chances.

There are four types of capital related to class.

1 **Economic capital** consists of wealth and income.
2 **Cultural capital** includes educational qualifications and knowledge of the arts. In the latter sense there are different levels of cultural capital:
  a **Legitimate culture** is held by dominant classes and is seen as good taste, e.g. classical music.

b **Middlebrow culture** is held by middle classes.
c **Popular taste** held by lower classes and seen as having little value, e.g. pop music.
Cultural capital also relates to **lifestyle** and **consumption**, e.g. the foods you eat.

3 **Social capital** consists of social connections and friendships.
4 **Symbolic capital**, similar to status, concerns reputation.

Different types of capital can be used to achieve upward mobility. Sometimes one type of capital can be used to gain another, e.g. economic capital can be used to pay for private education to gain cultural capital.

Groups whose position is based on different types of capital tend to develop a different **habitus**. The habitus consists of the different ways a group perceives the world and the different tastes and perceptions they have. The habitus of a group changes over time.

### Criticisms

1 Some see the theory as underestimating individual choice by assuming that people tend to conform to their habitus.
2 Bourdieu may neglect the importance of institutions such as the welfare state in shaping class.

### Simon Charlesworth – a phenomenology of working-class experience

■ **Charelsworth** (2000) studied working-class life in Rotherham.
■ The **habitus** of the working class was reflected in the way they dressed, their comportment and nights out.
■ Lacking symbolic and cultural capital life is a daily struggle which creates a **culture of necessity**.
■ Education plays a crucial role in encouraging people to devalue themselves

### Beverley Skeggs – Formations of Class and Gender

■ **Skeggs** (1997) studied working-class women on caring courses in an FE college.
■ The women lacked economic, cultural, social and symbolic capital.
■ The women sought to **disidentify** themselves from the working class by trying to show that they were respectable, responsible and by avoiding being seen as 'tarts' or 'sluts'.
■ However, they wanted to be seen as desirable to maximise their value in the 'marriage market'.

### Conclusion

These studies suggest that class continues to exert a strong influence on people's lifestyle and life chances through the interaction of cultural and economic aspects of class.

## SOCIAL MOBILITY IN CAPITALIST SOCIETY

■ **Open societies** allow social mobility (movement between strata) whereas closed ones do not.

■ **Achieved status** means that your status depends upon what you do.
■ **Ascribed status** means that your status is based upon who you are (e.g. kinship, gender, ethnicity, class background).
■ Sociologists such as **Parsons** see industrial societies as increasingly open and based on achieved status.
■ **Intragenerational mobility** refers to mobility within one generation – e.g. a person being promoted at work.
■ **Intergenerational mobility** refers to mobility between generations – it is measured by comparing the occupational statuses of parents and children.

### Glass – social mobility before 1949

In 1949 **Glass** did the first British study. It found low rates of **long-range mobility** (movement across several strata) and high rates of **self-recruitment** (recruitment of the children of class members) in the highest class.

### Criticisms

Glass's research methods have been criticized for using an unrepresentative sample which failed to reflect the growing number employed in white-collar occupations.

## THE OXFORD MOBILITY STUDY

In 1972 the Oxford Mobility Study provided more up-to-date and reliable data.

It divided the class structure into three main groups: the service class (highest), the working class (lowest) and an intermediate class.

It found higher rates of **long-range mobility** than Glass's study and high rates of **absolute mobility** (the total amount of social mobility). This was largely due to a considerable expansion of the service class, creating more room at the top of the stratification system. There were high rates of **upward mobility**.

However, **relative mobility** chances (the chances of those from different backgrounds achieving particular positions) remained unchanged. Thus children from the service class were much more likely to achieve positions in the service class than children from the working class. **Kellner and Wilby** (1980) summarize this as the **1:2:4 rule of relative hope** – for every child from the working class who ends up in the top class, two achieve this from the intermediate classes and four from the service class.

### Trends since the Oxford Mobility Study

**Goldthorpe and Payne** (1986) used data from British election studies to show that from 1972 to 1983 relative mobility chances stayed about the same, despite further growth of the service class.

At the very top of the stratification system there is evidence that mobility is low. **Elite self-recruitment** tends to take place, whereby elite positions are filled by the children of those already in the elite.

The **National Child Development Study (NCDS)** (1997) found that 55% of sons stayed in the working class (compared to 57% in the Oxford study). However, there was more chance of working-class sons getting service-class jobs than in the Oxford study (26% as opposed to 16%).

### Gender and mobility

- Most studies of mobility have used the class of the main breadwinner (usually a man) to determine the class of family members.
- **Goldthorpe and Payne** argue that other ways of determining the class of women (e.g. using their own jobs) make little difference to the overall findings of mobility studies.
- Anthony **Heath**, however, found that women from service-class backgrounds were more likely to be **downwardly mobile** than men from this class, while women from working-class backgrounds were more likely to be upwardly mobile than men. Heath believes that overall this disadvantages women rather than men.
- The NCDS (1997) also found that women from service-class background were less likely than men from this background to maintain their class position. Women were more likely than men to be upwardly or downwardly mobile to the intermediate class.

## IS BRITAIN A MERITOCRACY?

A **meritocracy** is a social system in which life chances are based on merit.

### Saunders – Unequal but Fair?

Peter **Saunders** (1996) argues that Britain is meritocratic.

- There is considerable **upward mobility** from the working class.
- Differences in the chances of those from different classes being upwardly mobile largely stem from inherited differences in terms of **intelligence, talent and motivation**.
- Saunders used data from the NCDS to claim that intergenerational mobility rates were higher than suggested in other studies and that class differences in mobility could be explained in terms of differences in ability and effort.

#### Criticisms

1 Saunders ignores the unemployed and those in part-time work.
2 Measured intelligence might itself be the result of class differences rather than inherited characteristics. Measures of effort (such as levels of absenteeism) might be related to the effects of labelling, ill-health, etc., which are class-related.
3 **Marshall and Swift** (1986) argue that Saunders has misinterpreted the figures and that, even when factors such as effort and intelligence are taken into account,

working-class children still do considerably worse than middle-class children.
4 **Savage and Egerton** (1997) examined the NCDS and found high rates of mobility but big differences in opportunities. For example, in the service class, 75% of high-ability sons and 67% of high-ability daughters ended up in the service class, compared to 45% of high-ability sons and 28% of high-ability daughters from the unskilled working class.

## GENDER AND SOCIAL CLASS

The position of women in the class structure was neglected in many early studies – women were often assumed to simply have the same class as their husbands. However, increasingly this has been disputed. There are a number of viewpoints:

1 Frank **Parkin** (1972) argues that the life chances of women are largely determined by the position of the male breadwinner in a family.
2 **Britten and Heath** (1983) disagree, pointing out that there are an increasing number of **cross-class families** in which women have a better-paid, higher-status job than men.
3 **Goldthorpe** (1983) largely agrees with Parkin, arguing that the family is the **unit of class analysis**. However, he does concede that the class of the family should be taken from the head of household. This is usually the man, but it can be the woman – e.g. in single-parent households or where the woman has more commitment to paid employment than the man.
4 Michelle **Stanworth** (1984) argues that men and women should be placed in classes as individuals according to their jobs, not as members of families.
5 **Rose and Marshall** (1988) found that **class fates** (e.g. mobility chances) were more affected by the class of individuals, while **class actions** (e.g. who you voted for) could be better predicted by the family's class.

## CONTEMPORARY THEORIES OF STRATIFICATION

### The death of class?

The **postmodernists Pakulski and Waters** (1996) claim that class is losing its significance.

- People no longer feel that they belong to classes, and supposed classes include a big variety of people.
- New **cleavages** are more important in shaping people's social and political beliefs than class.
- Towards the end of the twentieth century, stratification became based on **cultural differences** rather than economic ones.
- **Lifestyle and identity** have become more important than economic differences – e.g. your status is more to do with the décor of your house than the job you have.
- Some low-paid jobs (e.g. in the media) have higher status than better-paid jobs.

- As a result, stratification systems are more **fragmented and fluid** than previous class systems; it is easier to change status than it once was.

Pakulski and Waters explain the death of class in terms of:

1 The increasing importance of educational qualifications in shaping status.
2 The declining importance of privately owned property compared to property owned by organizations.
3 A wider distribution of wealth, giving more people greater lifestyle choices and more opportunity to choose what they consume according to their taste.
4 **Globalization**, which has reduced the importance of class inequalities within countries.
5 The growth of new politics based around non-class issues such as ethnicity and religion.

## Criticisms

1 Harriet **Bradley** (1997) argues that Pakulski and Waters have no consistent definition of class.
2 They ignore the extent to which economic class differences still affect what people can afford and therefore what lifestyle choices they can make.
3 **Marshall** (1997) argues that they are highly selective in the arguments and evidence they use and tend to neglect evidence that economic class inequalities are still a major factor in shaping people's lives.

## *Ulrich Beck – Risk Society*

Beck (1992) believes societies have moved from **simple modernity** to **reflexive** or **late modernity**.

- In **simple modernity** most conflict is about the distribution of **wealth**.
- In **reflexive modernity** technology increases production and reduces material need, making class divisions less important.
- There is increasing concern with **risk** created by science and technology rather than material need.
- Risks are associated with obesity from processed foods, the possibility of nuclear accidents and toxins in the environment.
- All social classes are subject to these risks, not just lower classes.
- Late modernity involves **reflexivity** or reflection on these risks.
- People experience risk as individuals, and society becomes **individualized** as class identities become weaker.

## Criticisms

1 **Scott** (2000) argues that wealth does enable you to avoid some risks.
2 Beck may underestimate the extent to which wealth still shapes life chances.
3 Beck ignores empirical research which shows that class still shapes identity.

## *Westergaard – the hardening of class inequality*

John **Westergaard** (1995, 1997) argues that, far from disappearing, class inequalities are hardening.

He sees class in Marxist/Weberian terms as determined by a person's position in the economic order.

- There is strong evidence of increasing inequality:
- In Britain the highest-paid 10% of white-collar workers had a 40% increase in real wages from 1980 to 1990, while the poorest 10% of manual workers had no rise in pay.
- From the 1970s to the 1980s the share of all income earned by the richest 20% of households increased from 37% to 44%, while the share of the poorest 20% of households fell from 10% to 7%.
- Privately owned wealth was becoming more concentrated in the hands of a few in the 1980s.
- The power of big business has been growing as a result of **privatization** and the adoption of **free-market policies**.

Westergaard sees the reasons for these changes as lying in government policies and the growth of **transnational corporations**.

He accepts that **lifestyle and consumption** have become increasingly related to **identity**. However, he sees these as strongly influenced by economic differences such as wage inequality.

**Gender divisions** tend to reinforce class inequality. In middle-class families, the man and the woman may have well-paid jobs, whereas few working-class families benefit from one partner's higher white-collar salary.

**Ethnic divisions** are closely related to class, with some ethnic minorities tending to be concentrated towards the bottom of the stratification system.

Westergaard accepts that **class consciousness** may have declined but he partly attributes this to the Labour Party's failure to express and mobilize dissatisfaction in society.

Class consciousness has the potential to revive, as surveys show continued dissatisfaction with inequality in British society.

## TEST YOUR KNOWLEDGE AND UNDERSTANDING

1 Which one of these is an example of achieved status?
   a The high status of whites in South Africa before the abolition of apartheid
   b The high status of men in some societies
   c The high status of cabinet ministers in British government
   d The high status of hereditary peers in Britain

2 False class consciousness involves:
   a Making less money than other people
   b Being aware you are being exploited
   c Being unaware of where the true interests of your class lie
   d Becoming revolutionary

3 In Weber's sociology, your class position is determined by:
   a A combination of whether or not you own property and your position in the labour market
   b Your position in the labour market alone
   c Whether you own property
   d Your status

4 Which two of these statements describe changes in the British occupational structure during the twentieth century?
   a An increasing proportion of paid jobs were held by women
   b The proportion employed in manufacturing increased
   c The proportion of people employed in manual work increased
   d White-collar employment grew

5 In 1999 the richest 10% of the British population owned what proportion of marketable wealth?
   a 10%
   b 42%
   c 54%
   d 64%

6 Which two of these statements describe the Weberian view of the professions?
   a The professions serve the public interest
   b The professions predominantly serve the interests of the rich and powerful
   c Professionalism can be seen as a market strategy
   d Professions largely serve their own interests

7 According to Savage, Barlow, Dickens and Fielding, a part-time university lecturer without a permanent contract would be a member of the middle class because they possessed:
   a Property assets
   b Organizational assets
   c Cultural assets
   d Personal assets

8 Which two of these developments did Marx predict would occur in the working class?
   a The working class would become more affluent
   b The working class would adopt middle-class lifestyles
   c The working class would eventually become aware that they were being exploited
   d The working class would get poorer in comparison with higher classes

9 Which one of these groups does Charles Murray not see as part of the underclass?
   a Pensioners
   b Single parents
   c Criminals
   d The work-shy

10 Which of these would be an example of social capital in Bourdieu's theory of class?
   a Having lots of friends.
   b Having a large bank balance.
   c Having a knowledge of classical music.
   d Knowing how to dress fashionably.

11 If the daughter of a coal miner becomes a manager this is an example of:
   a Intragenerational upward mobility
   b Horizontal mobility
   c Intergenerational upward mobility
   d Short-range intragenerational mobility

12 Which of these is not one of the reasons put forward by Pakulski and Waters for the 'death of class'?
   a Globalization
   b A wider distribution of wealth
   c The increased importance of qualifications in determining status
   d All workers enjoying good wages

13 Which two of the following statements accurately describe Ulrich Beck's theory?
   a We now live in simple modernity
   b Class is increasingly important as a source of identity
   c People from all backgrounds are concerned about risks
   d Class is less important than it used to be

14 According to John Westergaard, class differences are:
   a Staying much the same
   b Hardening
   c Reducing
   d Disappearing

15 Supporters of which two of these theoretical approaches are most likely to see Britain as meritocratic?
   a Marxism
   b The New Right
   c Functionalism
   d Weberian theories

# DEVELOP YOUR ANALYSIS AND EVALUATION SKILLS

## *Does social class still shape people's life chances and lifestyle?*

***Background:*** You need to define both lifestyle and life chances before answering this question using the introductory section (p. 7) and Weber's idea of a status group (p. 8). There are a number of approaches that suggest class is getting less important in shaping life chances and lifestyle, particularly those of the postmodernists Pakulski and Waters, and Ulrich Beck's idea of risk society. However, these have been criticized and can be countered with the ideas of Westergaard and studies of social mobility, as well as statistics that show continuing inequality of wealth and income. Bourdieu's work and studies of British class culture suggest that class continues to influence lifestyle.

| **Against** | **For** |
|---|---|
| ■ Pakulski and Waters (pp. 16–17)<br>■ Ulrich Beck (p. 17) | ■ Westergaard (p. 17)<br>■ Studies of social mobility, and income and wealth (pp. 8–9 and 15–16)<br>■ Bourdieu and studies of class culture (p. 14–15) |

***Top tip:*** You can argue that class is changing rather than ceasing to be important. There are lots of discussions in the chapter about changes in different classes – such as the embourgeoisement of the working class (p. 13), proletarianization of part of the middle class (p. 11) and Sklair's ideas on the globalization of the upper classes (p. 9).

## *Evaluate the Marxist theory of stratification.*

***Background:*** You should describe Marxist theory before evaluating it and then go on to discuss whether this nineteenth-century theory is still relevant. There is no shortage of issues to discuss. There are alternative theories of stratification to consider, such as those of Weber and postmodernists, as well as empirical questions about whether class divisions and class consciousness are as strong as they used to be. Before reaching a conclusion you need to consider whether a basic division between a ruling class and proletariat or working class remains.

| **Against** | **For** |
|---|---|
| ■ Weber (partially) (p. 8)<br>■ Postmodernism (pp. 16–17)<br>■ Weberian views of the middle classes (p. 11)<br>■ Arguments that the working class lacks class consciousness (pp. 13–14)<br>■ Risk society (p. 17) | ■ Marxist theory (pp. 7–8)<br>■ Westergaard (p. 17)<br>■ John Scott (partially) (p. 9)<br>■ Braverman (p. 10)<br>■ Some figures on the concentration of wealth (p. 9) |

***Top tip:*** You can also evaluate Marxism by considering whether it can really explain gender and ethnic inequality as well as class.

## *Stratification is an inevitable and desirable feature of human societies.*

***Background:*** This view is supported by functionalists, especially Davis and Moore. They see stratification as inevitable because of the need for role allocation, and desirable because it ensures the most able do the most important jobs. Parsons also sees it as inevitable and functional. Tumin is a particular critic of Davis and Moore. Marxist theory suggests stratification is not inevitable (because of communism) or desirable (because it is based on exploitation). The section on social mobility is useful for suggesting that some talent might be wasted by stratification.

| **Against** | **For** |
|---|---|
| ■ Tumin (p. 7)<br>■ Marx (pp. 7–8)<br>■ Some studies of social mobility (pp. 15–16) | ■ Davis and Moore (p. 7)<br>■ Parsons (p. 8) |

***Top tip:*** Treat the questions of whether stratification is inevitable and desirable as two separate issues, you might agree with one claim but not the other.

## AQA-STYLE STRATIFICATION QUESTION

### A2 Unit 6 Synoptic Paper

**Answer all parts of this question**

Total: 60 marks
1 mark=1 minute

Time allowed:
1 hour 30 minutes

**ITEM A**

In conventional class analysis two approaches dominate: Marxist and Weberian. Weberian theories see class position as partly determined by the job market and they suggest that higher classes in particular will try to exclude others from sharing their advantages by a process of closure of opportunities. This, it could be argued, might explain the position of women and certain ethnic groups.

In Marxist theory, class position is determined by people's relationship to the means of production, either as owners, or as non-owners who can only survive by selling their labour power. Those who neither own the means of production nor sell their labour power (such as children, some women, the elderly/retired, the unemployed, the disabled/ill) have no class position other than by their association with someone in paid labour.

**Comments on the question**

- This is a synoptic question, which links theoretical and methodological issues to the topic
- What might be different today compared with 100 years ago? See p. 9 on share ownership for one answer

**[a]** Discuss briefly how Marxist theories of class might create problems in measuring class today. [8 marks]

**Advice on preparing your answer**

- See pp. 7–8 for the relevant theory and apply your knowledge of methodology to this problem – e.g. class consciousness and/or the difference between people's occupation and their perception of their class
- Interpret the item to show how this occupational-based theory has difficulty dealing with certain groups
- Consider ownership – e.g. see p. 9 on measuring assets

**Comments on the question**

- This is a **synoptic** paper so you should show knowledge from different areas of the specification
- This could mean **actions** of the in-group to prevent others from joining them, or **attitudes** learned by a group which prevent them from thinking they can join the group concerned
- Focus must be on these groups and you could suggest there are differences between ethnic groups and groups of women

**[b]** Examine how closure of opportunities might explain the social position of women and certain ethnic groups.

[12 marks]

**Advice on preparing your answer**

- **Actions**
  1 Entry qualifications apply for certain professions, see p. 10
  2 Unwritten barriers exist, such as the ability of public schools to dominate certain professions, see Haralambos and Holborn, pp. 552–4
  3 Chapter 3, pp. 24–7 and chapter 4, pp. 36–7 will be of use here
  4 Subtle (and sometimes illegal) processes such as sex and race discrimination can be both individual and institutional, and direct and indirect

- **Attitudes**
  1 Cultural hegemony and stereotypes (chapter 13, especially p. 183)
  2 Fatalism (p. 12) and hidden curriculum (chapter 11, p. 153)

**Comments on the question**

- Look at theories and evidence in support of the ideas, and against them
- To get the maximum marks you do need to show that you have considered all four aspects
- Again remember that this is a synoptic paper and you can bring in evidence from many parts of the specification
- 20 marks are for knowledge; 20 marks are for analysis and evaluation

[c] Examine the view that stratification is inevitable and beneficial to both individuals and society. [40 marks]

**Advice on preparing your answer**

- Define stratification, see p. 7
- Outline the arguments that see it as inevitable and beneficial, i.e. Parsons, Davis and Moore (p. 7)
- Remember to look at both the total society and the possible benefits for all individuals (maybe the security of 'knowing their place')
- Now consider the arguments and evidence against inevitability (Marx, Weber and others, see pp. 7–8), against it being beneficial to society (Tumin, p. 7), and against it being beneficial to individuals (see Tumin, Marxists, feminists, etc.)

# OCR-STYLE SOCIAL STRATIFICATION QUESTION

## A2 Synoptic Unit 2539: Social Inequality and Difference

**Answer all parts of this question**

Total: 90 marks
1 mark = 1 minute

Time allowed:
1 hour 30 minutes

### ITEM A

Adonis and Pollard argue that a new social class has emerged in Britain, a professional and managerial elite which they refer to as the 'Super Class'. This group is made up of both males and females and is based on the old professions who have made their fortunes in the City. The Super Class tend to intermarry and therefore earn combined super-salaries. They can be distinguished from the rest of society by their consumption patterns, which revolve around nannies and servants, second homes, exotic holidays, private health and pension schemes and private education for their children.

### ITEM B

Social class distribution by Registrar General's category, economically active population (%)

| Class | Occupation | 1971 | 1981 | 1991 |
|-------|------------|------|------|------|
| I | Professional | 4 | 4 | 5 |
| II | Managerial | 18 | 22 | 28 |
| IIINM | Skilled non-manual | 21 | 22 | 23 |
| IIIM | Skilled manual | 28 | 26 | 21 |
| IV | Semi-skilled | 21 | 19 | 15 |
| V | Unskilled | 8 | 7 | 6 |

Source: extracted from Mark Kirby, *Stratification and Differentiation*, Macmillan, 2000, p. 9

**Comments on the question**

- Everything you need is in Item A. Do not be tempted to go beyond it
- Identify only. Don't waste time offering an explanation
- No more, no less

**[a]** Using only Item A, identify two characteristics of the 'Super Class'. [6 marks]

**Advice on preparing your answer**

- Don't lift material word for word from the items. Be prepared to put the information into your own words
- Focus on salaries and consumption

---

- No more, no less
- Identify only. There is no need to offer an explanation for these patterns

**[b]** Using only Item B, identify two patterns shown by the data in the table . [6 marks]

- Always look closely at how data in tables, graphs, etc. are organized
- Focus on maior patterns and trends

---

- Don't offer any more
- This question is asking you to explain why a problem has come about
- Clearly distinguish between the two problems identified

**[c]** Identify and explain two problems facing sociologists trying to measure the distribution of wealth.
[12 marks]

- This a synoptic question. It is demanding some knowledge of methodology

---

- This a synoptic instruction and means you should dip into a couple of other topics for the evidence as well as taking material from your notes on this unit
- Outline means describe. There is no need to offer an explanation

**[d]** Using your wider sociological knowledge, outline the evidence that suggests that social class is still very important today. [22 marks]

---

- Describe the main points and concepts that make up the theory and any evidence that supports it
- You can mention other theories but these should be offered as evaluative alternatives to whatever theory you choose to focus on
- Assess means weigh up the arguments for and against the theory. Try to be balanced rather than one-sided

**[e]** Outline and assess one sociological explanation of class inequality.
[44 marks]

# Chapter 2

# SEX AND GENDER

Textbook pp. 92–151

## Specifications

**Parts of modules covered** (NB *Social differentiation, power and stratification* is a theme running through the AQA specification)

| Specification | Specification details | | Coverage |
|---|---|---|---|
| **OCR** AS: The individual and society | ■ The meaning of gender. The process of gender-role socialization. | | Gender is defined on p. 23. Gender role socialization is the focus on p. 24. |
| **OCR** A2: Social inequality and difference | ■ Feminist theories. Economic and cultural theories of gender inequalities. The restructuring of gender identities. | | Feminist and other explanations of gender inequalities are covered on pp. 24–6. For changing gender identities see pp. 27–8. |
| **OCR** A2: Power and control/Popular culture | **Cultural representations, power and difference** | ■ Femininity and the culture industries; the social construction of femininity, romance and the treatment of the female body as a commodity; the influence of ethnicity and social class.<br>■ Masculinity and the culture industries; male identity, mass media, fashion and consumption; the influence of ethnicity and social class. | The section on feminism and the future (pp. 27–8) covers recent changes in femininity. There is also a discussion of gender representations in the media in chapter 13, p. 185–6. Masculinity is the focus on p. 28. |

For more detailed specification guidance visit **www.haralambosholborn.com**

## Essential notes

## INTRODUCTION

Some sociologists describe mainstream sociology as **malestream sociology** to indicate that it is male-dominated.

**Pamela Abbot** and **Claire Wallace** (1997) identify six feminists criticisms of malestream sociology.

■ Most research has been about **men**.
■ Studies using all-male samples are often **generalized** to everybody.
■ Women's issues such as **housework** and **childcare** have been neglected.
■ Studies of women tend to be distorted and **sexist**.
■ Variables such as class have been seen as more important than sex and gender.
■ Malestream sociology ignores the pervasive nature of **patriarchy**.

Dr Robert **Stoller** (1968) defines sex in terms of physical differences between **males** and **females**: sex organs, secondary sex characteristics and hormones. These differences mean that women can bear and suckle children whereas men cannot.

Stoller defines **gender** in terms of the psychological and cultural differences between what is defined as **masculine** and **feminine** in particular societies.

This implies that differences between men and women in terms of behaviour and social roles are at least partly social and cultural rather than **biological**.

## SEX AND GENDER DIFFERENCES

Many have argued that differences between males and females are biologically based. They have claimed that higher amounts of **testosterone** and other **androgens** in males make them more aggressive.

However, critics point out that most of the research to support this is based on animal experiments and the results may not be applicable to humans. **Archer and Lloyd** (2002) argue that aggression in boys has more to do with 'masculine values' of **reputation and honour'** than to do with testosterone levels, although cultural and biological factors interact.

The theory of **brain lateralization** suggests that the left hemisphere of the brain – specializing in verbal and language skills – is dominant in females, while the right hemisphere – specializing in visuo-spatial abilities – is dominant in males. This could explain differences in male and female aptitudes and interests.

However, research findings in this area are contradictory, and both males and females can be very able in areas where the other sex is supposed to have more ability.

## SOCIOBIOLOGY

**Sociobiologists** explain behaviour in terms of **reproductive strategies** and the desire to pass on your genes to children. The best strategy for women is to seek the most suitable partners since a woman can bear only a limited number of children. The best strategy for men is to get as many women pregnant as possible. This is held to explain differences in male and female behaviour.

Critics point out that this approach cannot explain homosexuality or celibacy. **Oakley** (1972) argues that it cannot explain societies such as the Trobriand Islands where women take the lead in sexual relationships.

## BIOLOGY AND THE SEXUAL DIVISION OF LABOUR

From a study of 224 societies, the functionalist George Peter **Murdock** (1949) argues that a **sexual division of labour** develops, in which men do the hunting and heavy work and engage in warfare, while women do the gathering, cooking, repairing clothes and carrying water. This results from practical reasons: men are stronger and are not burdened by pregnancy and nursing children.

Talcott **Parsons** (1955) argues that women are more suited to **expressive roles** such as the socialization of children, because they give birth and are naturally closer to children.

John **Bowlby** (1953) argues that children are psychologically damaged by the absence of the natural mother, or mother substitute, during their early years (**maternal deprivation**).

Ann **Oakley** (1974) rejects these views, arguing that the division of labour between men and women is based on **culture** not biology. She points out:

- There are many societies which are exceptions to the general rule, e.g. amongst Mbuti Pygmies there are no specific sex roles.
- In contemporary societies such as China and Cuba a lot of heavy work is done by women.
- The **mother-housewife role** is a cultural construction. Evidence shows that children do not have to be cared for by their mothers to grow up well-adjusted.

## THE SOCIAL CONSTRUCTION OF GENDER ROLES

Many sociologists argue that males and females learn to be masculine and feminine – their roles are **socially constructed**. Oakley sees gender role socialization taking place through:

- **Manipulation** – e.g. dressing girls in 'pretty' clothes.
- **Canalization** – e.g. directing boys and girls towards different toys.
- **Verbal appellations** – e.g. telling boys they are strong and girls they are pretty.
- **Exposure to different activities** – e.g. getting girls to help with domestic tasks.

The mass media reinforce stereotypes of masculinity and femininity.

**Kessler and McKenna** (1978) point out that in some societies there is a third gender, the **berdache** (found amongst native American tribes). The berdache are 'men' who dress and act in feminine ways and are considered neither male nor female.

Anne **Fausto-Sterling** (2000) believes that **dualistic** views of sex (you are either male or female) are misleading and lead to unnecessary operations on **transgendered** people. However, cultural and biological systems interact, for example by affecting the neural connections in the brain, to produce particular **gender systems**.

## GENDER INEQUALITY

Feminist theories try to explain inequalities and differences between men and women and suggest what should be done about them. There are several broad approaches.

- **Radical feminism** – Radical feminists believe that women are exploited by, and subservient to, men. Society is **patriarchal**, or male-dominated. Men are the ruling class and women the subject class. Radical feminists explain the inequality in various ways, some seeing **biology** as the cause, others seeing **culture** or **male violence** as more important. Female supremacists see women as superior to men, while **female separatists** believe that women should stay completely independent of men.
- **Marxist and socialist feminism** – Marxist and socialist feminists see the **capitalist system** as the main source of women's oppression and stress the importance of the exploitation of women as paid and unpaid workers. Some would like to see a communist society established.
- **Liberal feminism** – This perspective is associated with **equal rights** campaigners, who want **reforms** to improve women's position, rather than revolution. They often attribute inequality to **sexism**, discrimination and sex role **stereotyping** and socialization.
- **Black feminism** – Black feminists believe that 'race'/ethnic differences between women have been neglected by white feminists, and they stress the particularly deprived position of black women. **Brewer** argues that **class**, **race** and **gender** combine to give black women multiple sources of deprivation.

## THE ORIGINS OF GENDER INEQUALITIES – FEMINIST VIEWS

Feminists adopting different approaches have tried to explain how gender inequalities originate.

Shulamith **Firestone** (1970) argues that the **sexual class system** is the most fundamental form of stratification. The **biological family** results from women being burdened by pregnancy, childbirth, breastfeeding and menstruation. They become dependent on men and **power psychology** develops, which maintains female oppression.

Critics point out that in some societies women seem less disadvantaged by biology than in others (see Oakley, p. 24).

Ortner (1974) sees female oppression as cultural. Because women give birth they are defined as closer to nature than men, who are seen as more **cultural**. Culture is seen as superior to nature.

Coontz and Henderson (1986) criticize Ortner, arguing that not all societies see culture as superior to nature.

## THE ORIGINS OF GENDER INEQUALITIES – MARXIST AND SOCIALIST PERSPECTIVES

Engels argued that gender inequality had a **materialist** base. The **monogamous** family only developed once herding of animals replaced hunting and gathering. Men used monogamous marriage to control women's sexuality so that they could identify their own biological children and pass down their herds of cattle to them.

However, Engels's theory is not based on sound empirical evidence.

Coontz and Henderson also provide a materialist explanation. They argue that men became dominant due to the practice of **patrilocality**, whereby a wife went to live with her husband's family. This tended to mean that men gained control of women's labour and the wealth they produced.

## GENDER AND INDUSTRIALIZATION

This view does not follow a particular feminist perspective, but sees gender inequality as originating from the Industrial Revolution. Oakley (1981) argues that women became disadvantaged because of the creation of the **mother-housewife role** in the nineteenth century. Children were gradually banned from the workplace in the new mines and factories, leaving women at home to care for them. Unable to earn their own living, women became dependent on men.

However, the importance of the mother-housewife role may have declined in the late twentieth century with more women working.

## GENDER IN CONTEMPORARY SOCIETIES – RADICAL FEMINIST PERSPECTIVES

The radical feminist Kate Millett (1970) argues that modern societies are patriarchal and there are many sources of patriarchy.

- **Biology** plays some part through superior male strength and the use of violence (though this is now more psychological than real).

- **Ideological factors** and socialization are important.
- **Sociological factors**, such as the woman's role as mother in family life, also contribute.
- Women have a **caste-like status** which means that even higher-class women are subordinate to men.
- **Educational and economic inequalities** hold women back.
- **Myth and religion** are used to justify male dominance.
- **Psychology** plays a part since women interiorize patriarchal ideology.
- **Rape, sexual violence and the use of force** underpin male power.

Critics such as Rowbotham (1979) question the usefulness of a vague term like patriarchy. Rowbotham also denies that all men exploit all women.

## GENDER IN CONTEMPORARY SOCIETIES – MARXIST AND SOCIALIST PERSPECTIVES

- **Engels** argued that men retained power because of access to work, particularly well-paid work, and he expected inequalities to reduce once women returned to work.
- Marxist feminists such as **Benston** (1972) argue that women are used as a **reserve army of labour**, benefiting capitalism by keeping wages low. They are a relatively docile, easily exploited workforce.
- **Hartmann** (1981) argues that capitalism might create low-paid jobs and a reserve army of labour, but this does not explain why women occupy these positions. She argues that **patriarchy** provides the key. Men maintain their control over women by exploiting their labour and denying them access to jobs that pay a living wage, so that they stay dependent on their husbands.

## WALBY – THEORIZING PATRIARCHY

Sylvia **Walby** (1990) provides both a theory of patriarchy, mixing a variety of feminist theories, and an assessment of how much women's lives have improved.

She argues that there has been a move from **private patriarchy** (the exploitation of women in the home) to **public patriarchy** (the exploitation of women outside the home).

She identifies six **structures of patriarchy:**

- **Paid employment** – here Walby acknowledges some reduction in inequality, with women having more access to paid employment. However, the gap in wages between the sexes has only narrowed slightly. Walby sees lack of well-paid work as the most important factor discouraging women from taking paid employment.
- **Household production** continues to be based on patriarchal relations of production, with men benefiting from women's unpaid labour. However, women are doing more paid work, and relaxed divorce laws make it easier to escape from exploitative marriages.

Some women – e.g. some black women who are exploited at work – may see family life as preferable to paid employment. Marriage brings material benefits for some women, but violence for others.

- **Culture** continues to differentiate between males and females, but **sexual attractiveness** has replaced domesticity as the key feature of femininity. This has increased women's freedom in some ways, but it has also subjected them to degrading pornography and sometimes sexual violence.
- **Heterosexuality** is a patriarchal structure, but it has changed. Women have more freedom to engage in sex outside marriage, but sexual double standards still applaud male promiscuity while promiscuous women are seen as 'slags'.
- It is not clear whether **violence** against women has increased. While the police take domestic violence against women more seriously than they used to, violent husbands are still rarely convicted.
- The **state** has become less discriminatory but still remains **patriarchal**, **capitalist** and **racist**. For example, single mothers continue to be treated badly.

Overall, the changes indicate a shift from private patriarchy (women exploited as mothers and housewives) to public patriarchy (women exploited as workers and sex objects). However, the nature of patriarchy varies by social group – e.g. Muslim women are more constrained by private patriarchy than other groups.

In later work Walby detects a **generational difference**, with younger women experiencing gains in areas such as sexual freedom, educational opportunities and paid employment. However, poorly qualified young women and single parents suffer considerable disadvantages, and most elite positions continue to be male-dominated.

### Evaluation

Jackie **Stacey** (1993) praises Walby for an 'all-encompassing' approach but criticizes her for using the idea of structure rather loosely and ignoring the subjectivity of women.

Anna **Pollert** (1996) attacks the use of the term **patriarchy** in general. It usually involves a circular argument: it is used both as a description and as an explanation of inequality between the sexes. Pollert argues that capitalism is a system with an internal dynamic, but that patriarchy is not. She prefers empirical studies of how class, gender and ethnicity relate to one another, rather than theorizing about patriarchy.

## POSTMODERNISM, SEX AND GENDER

- **Postmodern feminism** generally rejects the idea that all women share the same interests and their position can be explained in terms of a single theory.
- It emphasizes **differences** between groups of women – e.g. between lesbian and heterosexual women, women from different classes and ethnic groups, and women of different ages.
- Postmodern feminists celebrate difference.

- They reject the idea of **progress**, seeing it as a product of male rationality, and therefore they reject the idea of a single path to female liberation.
- They argue that women's position can be improved by **deconstructing** (taking apart and criticizing) **masculine language and thinking**.
- They attack the male way of thinking of women as the '**other**' (as different from and inferior to men).
- By allowing the **voices** of different women to be heard, the idea of women as an inferior 'other' can be broken down.

### Criticisms

- Sylvia **Walby** (1992) criticizes postmodern feminism for losing sight of the importance of inequality and the degree to which the experience of oppression and inequality gives women shared interests.
- Postmodern feminists tend to neglect important areas such as male use of violence to maintain power and gender inequalities at work.

## GENDER AND PAID EMPLOYMENT

In 1970 the **Equal Pay Act** legislated that women should be paid the same as men for doing the same or broadly similar work. In 1984 an amendment stipulated that women should get equal pay for work of equal value.

The **1975 Sex Discrimination Act** made discrimination on the grounds of sex illegal in employment, education and the provision of goods and services.

Despite these Acts and some improvements in the position of women in Britain, women remain disadvantaged at work.

- The **proportion of the labour force** who are women has risen considerably. In 1961 women made up 32% of the labour force; by 2001 about the same number of men and women were in employment.
- In 2001 more than five out of six **part-time workers** were women.
- The proportion of **married women** who work has risen most rapidly.
- Women continue to be **less well paid** than men. In 1970 women working full-time earned 63% of the average full-time male wage; by 1999 they were still only getting 81.6% of the average male wage.
- **Vertical segregation** continues – i.e. women have fewer of the higher-status jobs.
- **Horizontal segregation** – i.e. where men and women tend to have different types of job – also continues. Women tend to be employed in areas such as personal services, administration, hotels and restaurants. Most routine clerical and secretarial workers are women, as are most primary teachers. Men tend to dominate in areas such as manufacturing, construction and transport. There are more men in higher professions and more women in lower professions, particularly welfare professions.
- Women have made progress in some professions, such as medicine. However, they still hold few **elite positions**.

There are a number of explanations for gender inequalities at work:

■ **Human capital theory** suggests that women are less valuable to employers than men because they are less committed to work and more likely to take career breaks to raise children. This gives employers less incentive to promote women and invest in their training.

However, a study by Peter **Sloane** (1994) found that gender continued to influence pay even when qualifications and experience were taken into account.

The **dual labour market theory** of **Barron and Norris** (1976) distinguishes:

■ The **primary labour market** of well-paid, fairly secure jobs with prospects.
■ The **secondary labour market** of poorly paid, insecure jobs with few prospects.

Employers try hard to attract and retain **primary workers**, who are seen as key to the success of their enterprises, but **secondary workers** are seen as easily replaced. It is difficult to transfer from the secondary to the primary labour market, and women tend to be concentrated in the secondary sector. This is due in part to employer sexism but also to factors such as lack of unionization.

**Beechey** (1986) criticizes the theory because:

■ Some women in crucial, skilled jobs (e.g. working in textiles) still get low pay.
■ Women are promoted less than men even when employed in primary sector jobs.
■ **Marxists** such as **Braverman** (1974) argue that women's work has been **deskilled** as employers seek to cut costs by taking the skill out of much of the work. Clerical and service sector work, predominantly done by women, has been deskilled.

However, critics of Braverman suggest that the skills required for some jobs have changed or increased rather than decreased, and women often get low pay even when doing skilled jobs.

Another Marxist-influenced theory sees women as a cheap **reserve army of labour**, brought in during economic booms but thrown out during slumps. This creates flexibility for capitalists and depresses overall wage levels. According to **Beechey**, women tend to be in the reserve army because: they are often not in unions; they may be prepared to work for less if their wage is a second income; they are seen as combining work with domestic responsibilities.

However, this theory cannot explain horizontal segregation, and the continued growth of female employment suggests that women are not being used as a temporary, reserve army of workers.

■ Linda **McDowell** (1992) applies **post-Fordist** theory to female employment. Post-Fordism suggests that there has been a move away from mass production to more **flexible production** of specialist products. Businesses keep a core of highly skilled workers, but most other workers are temporary or part-time, or work is contracted out to other firms. Women tend to be concentrated in the more flexible jobs, particularly part-time work, although some have benefited from gaining **core jobs**.

Research by **Lovering** (1994) found evidence to support this theory in some companies but not in others, suggesting that post-Fordist trends affect only some workers.

■ Some feminists stress the role of **male trade unionists** in restricting women's opportunities. **Walby** (1986) argues that in some areas (e.g. engineering) trade unions have used exclusion to disadvantage women, while in industries such as textiles, women have been disadvantaged by confinement to certain lower-paid areas of work. Low-paid work ensures that women are more likely to take on domestic responsibilities than men.

■ **Radical feminists** see **patriarchy** rather than capitalism as the main cause of female disadvantage. **Stanko** (1988) argues that **sexual harassment** in the workplace is used to keep women in their place. Men use their power in the workplace to protect their position. Women in jobs such as bar and secretarial work are **sexualized** and are not taken as seriously as workers or candidates for promotion.

Lisa **Adkins** (1995) goes further, arguing that **sexual work** has become integral to many women's jobs. In service sector jobs where women have contact with men they are expected to engage in **sexual servicing**: looking attractive, engaging in sexual banter, tolerating sexual innuendo and so on.

■ Damian **Grimshaw** and Gill **Rubery** (2001) believe the pay gap between men and women has stopped narrowing because:
  - **Sub-contracting** and **performance-related pay** have depressed women's wages in the public sector.
  - Women continue to do most of the **part-time work**.
  - **Fragmented organizations** make it hard to enforce equal pay laws.
  - Women tend to be excluded from **informal networks** of male-dominated management.
  - **Individualization** of pay has disadvantaged women.

## FEMINISM AND THE FUTURE

**Feminism** had considerable influence on sociology in the 1970s and 1980s and, arguably, had some influence on social changes. In the 1990s questions were raised about feminism's future prospects.

■ In 1992 Susan Faludi argued that there had been a **backlash** against feminism. This backlash claimed that feminism had gone far enough – it had achieved equality for women, but it had made their lives unhappy. For example, women pursuing careers and neglecting family life tended to suffer health problems, to become infertile and so on. Faludi sees these arguments as unfounded. She argues that major **inequalities** remain. In the USA and Britain men still earn considerably more than women, and Faludi points to research which shows that married women are more likely to be depressed and unhappy than single women with careers.

- **Postfeminists** argue that the feminism of the 1970s and 1980s is outdated because it sees all women as sharing the same interests and ignores the **diverse interests** of different groups of women. No one project can liberate all women. Ann **Brooks** (1997) welcomes this development, arguing that it has high-lighted the particular issues surrounding **women of colour and lesbians.**
- Natasha **Walter** (1998) believes there is still much that feminists need to change. She believes that postfemi-nists place too much emphasis on **political correctness** and **language** and neglect continuing problems of **inequality** which affect all women. Women still tend to suffer from problems such as **low pay**, lack of **child-care**, the **dual burden** of paid employment and domes-tic labour, **poverty** and **domestic and sexual violence.** To Waters feminism needs to return to the **mainstream** of British politics.
- Imelda **Whelehan** (2000) believes that there is evidence of **retrosexism** in the **laddish culture** of much of the popular media. The idea of the **singleton** – the ageing **ladette** getting too old to have children – plays upon women's fears of being without a man. Popular culture creates the myth of liberation for women through **girl power** while disguising the continuing existence of **oppression** and **discrimination.**
- Germaine **Greer** (2000) denies that women have been liberated by increased **lifestyle choice**. Often this involves an obsession with physical **beauty**, a desire to drink as much as men, and a requirement to be **promiscuous**, all of which makes women more **depen-dent** on men, not more **independent**. Women cannot be themselves as they still have to act in the ways men want them to.

## MASCULINITY

In much early sociology men were simply taken as the norm, while women were different and their behaviour therefore needed explaining. More recently, attention has shifted to focus on the distinctive characteristics of masculinity and how **masculinity** affects society.

- David **Gilmore** (1990) argues that masculinity is, in part, **socially constructed**. What is considered mascu-line varies from society to society. **Biological differ-ences** between men and women may be exaggerated or altered by society. In most societies men are seen as **impregnators, providers and protectors.** They perform important roles for society, taking **risks** in order to ensure that society survives. Men who succeed in these roles gain high status.

However, in a minority of societies masculinity is very different. In **Tahiti**, men tend to be timid and passive –

there is no warfare and, with a plentiful food supply, no need for men to face danger. Amongst the **Semai** of Malaysia all violence and aggression are taboo and there is little difference between the behaviours expected of men and women.

Gilmore's work can be criticized for being based on **functionalist** analysis and for exaggerating the degree to which men protect and provide for women.

- Victor **Seidler** (1989, 1994) sees masculinity in Western societies as being based on **Enlightenment** thinking. The Enlightenment (seventeenth- to eighteenth-cen-tury science and philosophy in Europe) attacked emo-tion and superstition and emphasized an **objective, detached and scientific** approach. Men became associ-ated with these characteristics, while women were seen as more emotional and closer to nature.
- **Connell** (1995) argues that masculinity develops from both **biology and culture**, which should be seen as fused together. He argues that masculinity can take a variety of forms. These forms develop and change – some decline, and some become more prominent.

**Hegemonic masculinity** is the dominant form of masculinity in any society. In contemporary Western societies, white middle-class heterosexual masculinity tends to be dominant. It tries to maintain dominance over subordinate groups, e.g. gay men. However, it is always subject to challenge, and alternative masculini-ties may exist alongside it without being fully accepted. In his research Connell found four groups of men in which there was evidence of a crisis in the gender order:

- The first group wish to 'live **fast, die young**'. These young working-class men engaged in an exaggerat-ed form of masculinity which involved an accep-tance of violence. It involved hostility towards homosexuals, but also an element of contempt towards women. It was largely based on hegemonic masculinity, but Connell sees it as a form of **protest masculinity** which is a reaction against poverty and educational failure.
- Another group were involved in the **environmental movement**, which emphasizes equality and cooper-ation rather than competitiveness. The men were consciously opposed to elements of hegemonic masculinity.
- The '**very straight gays**' were homosexual but gener-ally acted in ways that were typical of conventional masculinity. However, they tended towards more egalitarian relationships with partners than is typi-cal of heterosexual hegemonic masculinity.
- **Men of reason** were part of hegemonic masculinity. They were professionals who saw men as more rational than women.

Connell concludes that the nature of masculinity is **contradictory** and **constantly changing**. He is not optimistic about the prospects for transforming masculinity, but he believes there will continue to be challenges to hegemonic masculinity.

## TEST YOUR KNOWLEDGE AND UNDERSTANDING

1 According to Robert Stoller's distinction between sex and gender, which two of the following would be sex rather than gender characteristics?
   a The difference between male and female sex organs
   b The possession of different levels of hormones by men and women
   c The tendency for men to do more of the heavy work
   d The tendency for women to appear more emotional than men

2 Which two of the following types of behaviour does sociobiology have trouble explaining?
   a Promiscuity in men
   b Coyness in women
   c Homosexuality
   d Celibacy

3 Gender role socialization refers to:
   a The process by which boys and men and girls and women learn how society expects males and females to behave
   b The way boys and girls socialize with one another
   c The biological differences between males and females
   d The different roles of men and women in society

4 Which one of the following types of feminist places most stress on economic factors in explaining gender inequality?
   a Radical feminists
   b Socialist feminists
   c Liberal feminists
   d Black feminists

5 Which one of the following types of feminist tends to believe that gender inequality can be successfully addressed through equal rights legislation and changing attitudes?
   a Radical feminists
   b Socialist feminists
   c Liberal feminists
   d Black feminists

6 Anna Pollert criticizes the concept of patriarchy for which two of the following reasons?
   a Men are not dominant in society
   b It involves the confusion of description and explanation
   c Gender relations are not a system in the sense that capitalism is
   d The term patriarchy is used in too many different ways

7 Which one of the following is a criticism of postmodern feminism?
   a It neglects language
   b It ignores difference
   c It neglects inequality
   d It emphasizes violence too much

8 By 1999 what percentage of the male wage did women earn?
   a 61%
   b 71%
   c 81%
   d 91%

9 Which one of the following theories suggests that women are particularly likely to be thrown out of work during a recession?
   a Dual labour market theory
   b The reserve army of labour theory
   c The deskilling theory
   d The post-Fordist theory

10 According to Grimshaw and Rubery which TWO of the following have helped to maintain the gender gap in pay?
   a The reduction in unemployment.
   b Rising educational qualifications for women.
   c Sub-contracting in the public sector.
   d The individualization of pay.

11 Postfeminism emphasizes:
   a The variety of interests held by different groups of women
   b The importance of the men's movement
   c The end of gender roles
   d The end of gender inequality

12 Which one of the following is not mentioned by David Gilmore as a traditional role for men?
   a Impregnator
   b Provider
   c Protector
   d Politician

13 According to Bob Connell, the most dominant type of masculinity in any society is called:
   a Ruling-class masculinity
   b Dominance masculinity
   d Elite masculinity
   d Hegemonic masculinity

14 Which one of the following statements would Bob Connell be most likely to disagree with?
   a The nature of masculinity is constantly changing
   b Culture alone shapes masculinity
   c There is something of a crisis in the gender order
   d Some groups of men emphasize cooperation rather than competitiveness

15 Which TWO of the following does Imelda Whelehan believe are evidence of sexism making a comeback?
   a Lad culture
   b The importance of fashion
   c Films about the singleton woman
   d Domestic violence

## DEVELOP YOUR ANALYSIS AND EVALUATION SKILLS

### Can inequality between men and women be explained by the concept of patriarchy?

**Background:** You need to define patriarchy before answering this question. It can simply be defined as male domination in society (see pp. 25–6) but note that it is a rather imprecise term and might be used in different ways by different types of feminists. Give an indication of the views of different types of feminists (radical, Marxist, socialist, liberal, black and postmodern). Most tend to approve of the use of the term patriarchy but postmodern feminists see it as too sweeping. Sylvia Walby is useful for refining the concept (pp. 25–6) and Stacey and Pollert are useful for criticising it (p. 26).

| **Against** | **For** |
|---|---|
| ■ Stacey and Pollert (p. 26) | ■ Radical feminists (p. 25) |
| ■ Postmodern feminists (p. 26) | ■ Sylvia Walby (pp. 25–6) |
| ■ Marxist and socialist feminists (partly against) (p. 25) | ■ Marxist and socialist feminists (partly in favour) (p. 25) |
| ■ Black feminists (partly against) (p. 24) | ■ Black feminists (partly in favour) (p. 24). |

**Top tip:** Think about whether the idea of patriarchy is more a description than an explanation of inequality. Marxist and socialist feminists see capitalism as playing a part, as well as patriarchy, while black feminists see racism as important as well.

### Differences between men and women stem from biology rather than culture.

**Background:** You could start by discussing Stoller's distinction between sex and gender (p. 23). Biological arguments include discussions of hormones, brain lateralization, sociobiology, Murdock's study of 224 societies and the arguments of Bowlby and Parsons. You can criticize many of these views and you should discuss the opposing view that gender is socially constructed. Oakley's work is particularly useful here. Nearly all feminists (except Firestone) also see culture as more important than biology. Fausto-Sterling offers a possible conclusion.

| **Against** | **For** |
|---|---|
| ■ Oakley (p. 24) | ■ Sex differences (pp. 23–4) |
| ■ Feminist perspectives (apart from Firestone) (pp. 24–5) | ■ Biology and the sexual division of labour (p. 24) |
| | ■ Firestone (pp. 24–5) |

**Top tip:** Connell's work on masculinity (p. 28) is also very useful for answering this question.

### Men are responsible for women's low wages.

**Background:** At the start it is useful to establish that there are still wage differences between men and women and to note that both vertical and horizontal segregation still exist (pp. 26–7). Radical feminists tend to blame this situation on men. Stanko and Adkins best represent the view expressed in the question, blaming low female pay on patriarchy, sexual harassment and the sexualization of work. Walby tends to blame male trade unionists for the situation. On the other hand, more structural explanations attribute the situation to impersonal economic forces such as the operation of the labour market. Examples of this sort of approach include theories of the dual labour market and post-Fordism. Marxist theories of deskilling and the reserve army of labour see capitalism as most important.

| **Against** | **For** |
|---|---|
| ■ Reserve army of labour and deskilling (p. 27) | ■ Stanko (p. 27) |
| ■ Dual labour market theory (p. 27) | ■ Adkins (p. 27) |
| ■ Post-Fordism (p. 27) | ■ Walby (p. 27) |

**Top tip:** Grimshaw and Rubery (p. 27) could be useful for a conclusion as they mention both structural factors and men (through informal networks) as playing a role.

# AQA-STYLE SEX AND GENDER QUESTIONS

The questions below are examples of where you might be able to use sections of this chapter to answer questions from other areas of the specification. It is worth remembering that Sex and Gender is part of one of the underlying core themes and thus will come into every part of the specification.

## AS Unit 2: Work and Leisure

**Comments on the question**

- Give reasons
- Which laws might you consider?
- This could mean different things: equality of wages, of promotion and training opportunities, of retirement rights
- Other factors outside might explain why they remain unequal in employment

**(a)** Explain why changes in the law might not bring about equality in employment between men and women. [20 marks]

**Advice on preparing your answer**

- See p. 26 for the Acts referred to.
- Consider cultural differences between men and women (p. 24)
- Consider patriarchy (p. 25) and its effects (pp. 25–6)
- Notice that not all women and not all men are in the same position

## A2 synoptic Unit 6: Stratification

Notice that although the question is very similar to the one above, different skills and information will be needed to answer it.

**Comments on the question**

- This requires that you bring some evaluation to your reasoning
- This question does not have the same tight focus on employment. You should draw on your synoptic understanding from other modules you have studied
- What is meant here? Is it equality of opportunity or equality of outcome or both? You should discuss this briefly
- This is the focus, but it is worth remembering that differences of age, class and ethnicity may interact as well

**(b)** Critically examine the reasons why changes in the law may not bring about equality between men and women. [40 marks]

**Advice on preparing your answer**

- A quick look at the nature/nurture debate
- Gender in contemporary societies (p. 25–6)
- The role of patriarchy (p. 24–5)
- Discrimination (pp. 26–7)
- Hegemonic masculinity (p. 28)
- In order to fully answer the question you would need to draw on other areas, e.g.:
  1 Women in the family (chapter 8)
  2 Women in education (chapter 11)
  3 The role of the mass media and self-identity (chapters 12 and 13)

# OCR-STYLE SEX AND GENDER QUESTION

## AS Unit 2532: The Individual and Society

**Answer all parts of this question**

Total: 60 marks
1 mark = 1 minute

Time allowed:
1 hour

### ITEM A

Jonathan Rutherford believes that the traditional definition of masculinity is under increasing threat because a number of changes have undermined male dominance of the economy and family. Working-class masculinity has been threatened by the decline of manual work. which has resulted in high levels of male unemployment. The male roles of breadwinner and head of household have been challenged by working women. Confusion and anxiety about male identity may be responsible for increasing levels of suicide among young men.

**Comments on the question**

- The reasons are in the data. There is no need to go beyond this
- Make sure that you explain the reason you have identified – perhaps with an example
- Make sure that the examiner can clearly see two reasons
- Don't offer more than two points

[a] Using Item A only, identify and briefly explain two reasons why the traditional model of masculinity is under threat. [8 marks]

**Advice on preparing your answer**

- Don't lift the material word for word from the item. Try to put it into your own words

- Go beyond simply providing a list. Explain using examples
- No more, no less
- Don't ignore this crucial instruction

[b] Identify and briefly explain two masculine identities that exist in modern UK society, other than the traditional model of masculinity. [8 marks]

- The section on masculinity (p. 28) will be useful here

- This means 'describe'
- This means you should briefly weigh up any arguments/ evidence for or against the ways you identify

[c] Outline and briefly evaluate two ways in which males are socialized into masculine norms and values. [18 marks]

- The section on gender role socialization on p. 24 will help you with this task
- Focus on agents of socialization

- This means that you need to look at arguments against the view as well as arguments and evidence that support it
- They may not be experiencing any such thing, i.e. you might want to conclude that masculinity and femininity are still quite traditional in character

[d] Discuss the view that masculinity and femininity may be experiencing gender transformation. [26 marks]

- Don't forget to discuss both

# Chapter 3

# 'RACE', ETHNICITY AND NATIONALITY

Textbook pp. 152–235

## Specifications

Parts of modules covered (NB *Social differentiation, power and stratification* is a theme running through the AQA specification)

| Specification | Specification details | Coverage |
|---|---|---|
| **OCR** AS: The Individual and Society | ■ The meaning of ethnic identities. Their impact on social behaviour.<br>■ The meaning of national identities. The role of institutions in shaping and reinforcing national identity. | Ethnic identities covered on pp. 35–6; national identities on pp. 38–9. |
| **OCR** A2: Social Inequality and Difference | ■ Definitions of race and ethnicity. Material and cultural theories of ethnic inequalities. Ethnic identities and their impact on inequality. | Definitions of race are discussed on p. 33; theories of ethnic inequalities on pp. 34, 35–80; ethnic identities on pp. 35–6, 38–9. |

For more detailed specification guidance visit **www.haralambosholborn.com**

## Essential notes

## INTRODUCTION

There has been a long history of racism and racial or ethnic conflict. Examples include the enslavement of Africans, anti-Semitism in England, the slaughter of Jews in Nazi Germany, ethnic cleansing in the former Yugoslavia, conflict between Protestant and Catholic ethnic groups, attacks on asylum seekers in Britain and so on.

## 'RACE'

Biological theories of 'race' connect phenotype (physical appearance) with genotype (genetic differences).

■ Michael Banton (1987) argues that the term 'race' was not used in English until 1508. Before that everyone was assumed to be descended from Adam and Eve. This was a monogenesist theory – i.e. everybody had the same origin.
■ In the eighteenth and nineteenth centuries polygenetic theories developed. These held that there were different 'races' with different origins. They divided people into different groups such as Caucasian, Mongolian, Malay, American (native American) and Ethiopian (black African).
■ Drawing on the theory of evolution, Herbert Spencer (1971), argued that different 'races' had evolved to different degrees, with Aborigines amongst the least evolved and white Europeans amongst the most evolved.
■ The geneticist Steve Jones (1991, 1994) argues that there are no clear dividing lines between different 'races'. Although there are genetic differences between groups, humans are a very homogeneous species. Genes for skin colour are not linked to other genes, and there are big genetic differences between people of the same supposed 'race'. To Jones, 'race' is simply a social definition since societies use widely differing definitions and there is no genetic justification for distinguishing 'races'.
■ Richardson and Lambert (1985) argue that 'race' has no biological basis, but the belief that 'races' exist has important social consequences. In particular, doctrines of racial superiority (the belief that particular 'races' are superior to others) influence behaviour. They criticize the doctrine of racial superiority, pointing out that at different stages of history a wide variety of societies with different 'races' have been the most dominant or technologically advanced, and they conclude that 'race' is a social construct – it is concerned with what people make of physical differences rather than the differences themselves.

## MIGRATION AND 'RACE' RELATIONS

Some sociologists see the effects of migration as central to understanding race relations.

### Migration to Britain

John Richardson (1985) points out that for many centuries Britain has had migration from diverse areas, and it has long had an ethnically diverse population. One example of migration took place with the Norman Conquest, and there was considerable Jewish immigration in the 1870–1914 period, and Polish immigration during the Second World War.

In the 1950s and 1960s there was substantial immigration to Britain from the New Commonwealth, particularly African-Caribbean immigration from the West Indies, and Asian immigration from India, Pakistan and, in the 1970s, East Africa. This migration became politically controversial, with politicians such as Enoch Powell arguing that it would lead to racial violence. **Immigration laws** were progressively tightened, with the 1962 Commonwealth Immigrants Act and the 1971 Immigration Act. Many commentators, such as **Pilkington** (1984), argue that such Acts were racially **discriminatory** since they allowed more white than non-white immigration.

A 1988 Act made it difficult for families of non-white immigrants to come to Britain, and the 1993 Asylum and Immigration Act tightened up rules on people applying for **political asylum** in Britain. In 1999 the Immigration and Asylum Act introduced **vouchers** rather than cash payments for asylum seekers and it encouraged the dispersal of asylum seekers to different parts of Britain. These measures were criticized in the **Parekh Report** because they made asylum seekers feel stigmatized and isolated. The 2002 Nationality Immigration and Asylum Bill proposed repealing these measures and concentrating asylum seekers in large centres, but this too has proved controversial.

Commentators such as **Cohen** argue that such changes have made it difficult for those who are genuinely being persecuted to come to Britain. **Skellington and Morris** (1992) see immigration laws as discriminatory against black and Asian people. They point out that:

- A great deal of white immigration is allowed, e.g. from European Community countries.
- Britain was a net exporter of people for much of the twentieth century, so arguments that Britain is becoming overcrowded as a result of immigration are spurious.

Britain's non-white **ethnic minority population** is comparatively small. The 2001 census found that 2% of the British population described themselves as black, while 3.6% described themselves as Indian, Pakistani or Bangladeshi. In total 4,635,296 people saw themselves as belonging to an ethnic minority out of a total population of 58,789,194 – 7.9% of the population.

## Migration and assimilation

The **immigrant-host model** examines race relations in terms of the relationship between an immigrant minority and a host majority.

It is often assumed that the immigrant minority will gradually be **assimilated** into the host majority.

As in **functionalist** theories of **value consensus**, the host majority are often assumed to have a shared culture. And as in functionalism, an evolutionary process of adaptation is assumed to take place.

## *Park – race relations and migration*

Robert **Park** (1950) of the **Chicago School** first put forward this sort of approach in the 1920s and 1930s. He argued that there was a process of **interracial adjustment** following migration.

Initial **competition** and **conflict** would usually give way to **accommodation** (in which groups learn to live together) and **assimilation** (in which the different racial groups merge with minority groups, gradually blending into the majority group).

Park acknowledged that some conflict could remain.

## *Patterson – Dark Strangers*

In a study of first-generation immigrants from the West Indies to Brixton, Sheila **Patterson** (1965) found that some accommodation between the two communities had taken place, and she anticipated that, as with the Irish, assimilation would eventually take place.

## *Richardson and Lambert – a critique of the immigrant-host model*

**Richardson and Lambert** (1985) criticize the immigrant-host model:

- Concepts such as accommodation and assimilation are too vague and hard to apply to actual situations.
- Assimilation may not be desirable: some prefer the diversity of a **multicultural society**.
- The model ignores the existence of racism as a barrier to developing harmonious relationships.
- **Conflict theorists** criticize it for wrongly assuming there is a consensus in host societies.

## *Castles and Kosack – a Marxist view*

The Marxists **Castles and Kosack** (1973) see migration in terms of the international capitalist system:

- From colonial times, many Third World countries have been used as a source of cheap, easily exploited labour.
- In Europe and elsewhere, migrant workers continue to be exploited as a **reserve army of labour**.
- 'Race prejudice' against the migrant workers develops among the working class, who see the new workers as a threat to their jobs. This prevents a united working class from developing **class consciousness**.

## *Castles and Miller – **The Age of Migration***

In more recent work **Castles and Miller** (1993) argue that the scale of international migration has led to increasing **cultural diversity** in most states.

Minority groups have increasingly sought to maintain their culture and identity. In many places this has led to greater acceptance of a **plurality** of cultures.

However, in some countries which have experienced little migration in recent years there is the danger of **exclusionary nationalism** (the former Yugoslavia is an example).

# ETHNICITY

The idea of **ethnicity** places emphasis on **culture** rather than the biological differences implied by the term 'race'.

Unlike immigrant-host models there is no assumption that there will be greater integration or assimilation between ethnic groups.

## Defining ethnicity

- Milton **Yinger** (1981) defines an ethnic group in terms of a real, or perceived, difference between one group and others, in some combination of 'language, religion, race... ancestral homeland... culture'. It involves participation in 'shared activities built around their (real or mythical) common origin or culture'.
- John **Richardson** (1990) also sees ethnicity as based upon cultural differences. He criticizes 'racial' categories, arguing that biological differences are not clear cut.

However, there are problems with the term ethnicity:

- Many ethnic groups are subdivided.
- Different aspects of culture, such as language, territorial origin and religion, can produce conflicting categories.

**Ethnographic studies** of ethnicity examine the culture and lifestyle of ethnic groups.

## Studies of British Asians

Roger and Catherine **Ballard** (1977) studied Punjabi Sikhs in Leeds. They found:

- A strong desire to maintain the distinctive features of Sikh culture in the first generation. This was partly based on the **'myth of return'** (the belief that they might one day return to the Punjab).
- A greater interest in materialism and educational achievement in the second generation.
- Children developed **multiple presentations of self**. They retained an attachment to their parents' culture while acting in more Westernized ways outside the home.
- While racism played some part in shaping behaviour, the preferences of Sikhs themselves were also important. In later work, **Ballard** (1990) emphasized the differences between groups of British Asians:
- Sikhs tended to come from richer areas than Muslims and had been more economically successful in Britain.
- **Cultural factors** – such as Muslim wives being less likely to take paid employment than Sikh wives – played some part.

**Tehmina N. Basit** (1997) interviewed a sample of British Muslim girls, their parents and some teachers in two schools in East England. She found:

- The girls and parents had a strong sense of Asian identity but also saw themselves as British.
- Most families maintained strong **contacts with kin** in Asia but most of the girls felt they would not feel comfortable living in Asia.

- The parents had a stronger **Asian identity** than their children.
- The girls adopted elements of both British and Asian culture.
- Teachers tended to have rather **stereotypical views** about the Asian girls which did not reflect reality. For example, the girls were more motivated to get good qualifications and jobs than teachers realized.

## Pryce – West Indians in Bristol

Ken **Pryce** (1979) studied West Indians in Bristol in the 1970s.

He found a variety of **subcultures** in the West Indian community, split between two main types of response to life in Britain:

1 The **expressive-disreputable orientation** involved rejection of a white society that was perceived as hostile and racist.
2 The **stable, law-abiding orientation** involved acceptance or at least grudging toleration of white society.

Pryce's study shows how ethnic groups can develop different subcultures resulting from different responses to **racism and exploitation**. The more politically aware young West Indians are continuing a tradition of **anti-colonial struggle** which started in the Caribbean.

## Explanations of ethnicity

James **McKay** (1982) looks at explanations for the existence of ethnicity.

- **Primordial explanations** suggest that humans naturally divide the world into people similar to themselves ('us') and people who are different ('them'). McKay criticizes this approach because it cannot explain variations in the strength of ethnic attachments or changes in ethnic identity.
- **Mobilizationist explanations** see ethnicity as actively created rather than an inevitable product of being human. People use **ethnic symbols** and ethnicity to further their own ends. McKay sympathizes more with this approach but argues that it fails to explain the emotional strength of ethnic attachments. He believes that the two approaches should be combined.

In some ethnic groups, primordial attachments are strong (e.g. amongst Basque Nationalists); in other groups, ethnicity is more symbolic and based upon mobilization (e.g. Irish people living outside Ireland who take part in a St Patrick's Day parade).

Thomas Hylland **Eriksen** (2002) believes that ethnic groups only exist through their differences with other groups being seen as **socially significant**. He believes that ethnic identities can be **mobilized**. For example he describes a study of a Croatian village in which the rise of nationalism during the war in **Bosnia** in 1996 strengthened Serb, Croat and Muslim identities.

Ethnic identity can be actively **achieved** through peoples' efforts, but there is also an element of **ascription**. People are **socialized** into ethnic groups and develop 'a shared system of communication' which cannot be changed at will.

### Brown – the causes of ethnic conflict

Michael **Brown** (1997) examines the causes of ethnic conflict:

1 **Systemic explanations** explain conflict in terms of the nature of the overall security system. For example, conflict between ethnic groups in the former Yugoslavia could be seen as resulting from the break-up of a powerful, centralized state which kept ethnic conflict in check.
2 **Domestic explanations** involve the ability of states to deal with the concerns of different ethnic groups. Sometimes states themselves encourage hostility to ethnic groups to distract attention from the failings of the government.
3 **Perceptual explanations** consider how distortions, myths and false histories can encourage hostility to an ethnic group.

Conflict is most likely where groups who have hostile perceptions of one another live in close proximity without a strong centralized authority to keep them in check. The break-up of the Soviet Union has led to many such conflicts.

More optimistically Brown suggests that **ethnic conciliation** is possible.

### Ethnicity – an evaluation

The idea of ethnicity has certain strengths:

1 The ethnicity approach gets away from the biological determinism of 'race'.
2 It avoids the assumption of eventual assimilation of the host-immigrant model.
3 It recognizes the part ethnic groups play in actively shaping their own lifestyles.
4 It also tends to support multiculturalism.

However, it also has a number of weaknesses:

1 Marxists believe that it ignores social structure.
2 Some commentators believe that it neglects the importance of racism.
3 Some theories of globalization question whether there are still clear distinctions between ethnic groups.

## RACISM

Approaches which stress the importance of racism tend to be particularly concerned with:

- Constraints placed on 'racial'/ethnic groups by discrimination.
- Inequalities between such groups.

They tend to be less concerned with cultural differences.

Key terms are:

- **Prejudice** – learned beliefs or values which make people biased against a group.
- **Discrimination** – actions that disadvantage people because of prejudice.
- **Racism** – this word has been used in a variety of ways and has a comparatively recent origin. John Rex (1986) sees racism as 'deterministic belief systems about the differences between ethnic groups'. To John **Solomos** (1993) racism is not just a question of beliefs but also involves discrimination on the basis of racist beliefs.
- **Cultural racism** refers to widespread racist beliefs in a particular culture rather than views held by individuals.
- **Institutional racism** is a controversial term, but it most commonly refers to partly unconscious racism which results from the way institutions are organized or the culture that operates in them. The Stephen Lawrence Inquiry (**MacPherson Report**, 1999) defined it as 'The collective failure of an organization to provide an appropriate and professional service to people because of their colour, culture or ethnic origin.' However, it has also been defined in terms of the inequalities between ethnic groups which result from state policy (the structural Marxist view) and in a variety of other ways.

The idea of institutional racism has been criticized:

1 Many see it as poorly defined.
2 **Miles** criticizes approaches that suggest that institutional racism is simply 'what white people do'.
3 The definition of institutional racism in terms of inequality between groups ignores the possibility that other factors (such as cultural differences) might play a part in creating inequality.

However, it does draw attention to the way in which the policies of some institutions disadvantage ethnic minorities, whether or not there is any conscious discrimination.

### The extent of individual racism

Various attempts have been made to measure the extent to which individuals in Britain are racist.

- The *British Social Attitudes Surveys* found, between 1983 and 1991, a reduction in those who were 'very prejudiced' (from 4% to 2%) and a small reduction in those who were 'a little prejudiced' (from 31% to 29%).
- The *British Social Attitudes Survey 2000* found that 44% of people thought that immigrants take jobs away from British-born people, 34% said that equal opportunities had gone too far and 28% described themselves as racially prejudiced.

A problem with these sorts of studies is that they only measure the racism that people admit to. Furthermore, they only measure individual racism, saying nothing about cultural or institutional racism.

## Racial harassment

Some studies look at the extent of racism actually experienced by people.

- The **Policy Studies Institute (PSI) survey** published in 1997 estimated that every year 1% of ethnic minority members in Britain were subject to racially motivated attacks; about 2% had property damaged for racial reasons; and about 11–12% experienced racial abuse or insults.
- The *British Crime Survey* (2000) found 60% of Asians and 51% of blacks were worried or fairly worried about racially motivated attacks compared to 12% of whites.

## Solomos and Back – racism and popular culture

John **Solomos** and **Les Back** (1996) have studied racism in popular culture. They argue that there is a long history of racist imagery in British culture.

- British **Imperial propaganda** in the nineteenth and early twentieth centuries used images such as John Bull and Britannia which were connected with the notion of white British people civilizing the world.
- In the 1930s there was concern in the popular media about sex between white and non-white people.
- In the 1950s the sheer number of black people entering Britain was portrayed as a problem.
- In the 1960s black people were portrayed as **welfare scroungers**.
- In the 1970s **muggings and riots** were associated with African-Caribbeans.
- By the late 1980s there was more apparent acceptance in the popular media of black and Asian people in Britain, and there were more **multicultural images** – e.g. in Benetton's advertising.

Solomos and Back see some progress taking place but argue that racist elements remain in popular culture. For example, black people are sometimes still discussed in the popular media in terms of sexual attractiveness rather than in terms of achievement (e.g. Linford Christie's 'lunchbox').

# INEQUALITIES BETWEEN ETHNIC GROUPS IN BRITAIN

Various government statistical sources provide useful data on inequalities between ethnic groups in Britain. The **Labour Force Survey of 1998-2000** showed that:

- 41% of white men were in the highest two social classes compared to 47% of Indian men, 44% of Chinese men, 33% of Black men, 31% of Pakistani men and 23% of Bangladeshi men.
- Patterns were different among women where 41% of Chinese women, 34% of white women, 34% of black women, 33% of Indian women and 29% of Bangladeshi/Pakistani women had jobs in the top two classes.
- A **Cabinet Office Report** in 2000 showed big differences in earnings between ethnic groups with white men

earning twice as much as Bangladeshi men. Some of the differences in pay were related to qualifications but racism played some part in explaining them as well.

- Statistics on **expenditure** show that whites spend more than all other ethnic groups.
- Nevertheless some members of ethnic groups have been very successful and **Heidi Safia Mirza** suggests that the achievements of black women in Britain tend to be underestimated.

# THEORIES OF RACISM

## Cox – a Marxist theory

Oliver **Cox** (1948) puts forward a Marxist theory. He argues that racism developed with capitalism and served as a justification for the exploitation of slave workforces in colonies. However, critics have argued that racism exists outside capitalist systems.

## The Birmingham Centre for Contemporary Cultural Studies – a neo-Marxist theory

The **Birmingham Centre for Contemporary Cultural Studies** argues that racism predates colonialism, and that colonialism is only one factor influencing racism. **Economic factors** are important but specific **historical and cultural factors** also shape racism, as do the **resistance and struggle** of ethnic minorities.

Following this approach, **Lawrence** (1982) argues that the 1970s saw the development of a '**new racism**' in Britain. Racism was no longer based on explicitly portraying non-white people as inferior but on portraying their cultures as a threat to the integrity of British culture.

## Gilroy – There Ain't No Black in the Union Jack

Paul **Gilroy** (1987) examined both racism and ethnic minority cultures. He discusses the process of **race formation** in which interaction within and between ethnic minorities and whites shapes the identity of different groups.

Gilroy agrees that there is a **new racism** based on perceived cultural threats to the supposed British way of life. It emphasizes **ethnic absolutism** – the idea that ethnic minority cultures are completely alien to white British culture.

However, Gilroy argues that there is increasing overlap. For example, black and white **youth culture** and music overlap and incorporate elements from different sources. There are therefore some grounds for optimism about a future decline of racism.

## Islamophobia, British Asians and racism

- In recent years, particularly since the 9/11 terrorist attacks in the USA (2001) there has been a particular interest in racism directed against Muslims.
- This sort of racism has been termed **Islamophobia**.

The **Runnymede Trust** (1997) defined Islamophobia as 'unfounded hostility towards Islam'. It distinguished open and closed views of Islam.

- **Open** views could be critical of Islam but were sensitive to differences within Islam and could be critical of non-Islamic religions as well.
- **Closed** views see Islam as inferior and uncivilized and are based more on prejudice than evidence.

**Edward Said** (1995) explains hostility to Islam in terms of the idea of Orientalism.

- **Orientalism** consists of a set of views about the Orient developed amongst writers, politician and intellectuals in European and other Western countries.
- It developed as a **discourse** which justified Western intervention in Eastern countries.
- It is **essentialist** – seeing essential differences between the Occident (West) and the Orient (East), and ignoring the big differences between counties in these hemispheres.
- In *Covering Islam* (1997) Said shows how the Western **media** presented critical and stereotypical views of Islam in the 1990s.

**Claire E. Alexander** (2000) claims that media coverage of fights in London exaggerated the violence involved; falsely claimed that these were based strictly on racial divisions, and helped to create a **myth** that **Asian gangs** were a new and significant social problem.

## NATIONALISM AND IDENTITY

### Nationalism

Many commentators believe that there has been a recent revival of nationalism, despite many predictions that it would decline.

- Benedict **Anderson** (1983) sees nationalism as different from racism in that you can become a member of a nation whereas you cannot become a member of a different race.
- Robert **Miles** (1989) and others see close connections between race and nationalism, with racist ideas often used to justify the supposed superiority of people from particular nations.
- Miles sees a central feature of nationalism as a desire for a particular group to have a **sovereign nation-state**, i.e. an independent state.

### McCrone – The Sociology of Nationalism

David **McCrone** (1998) distinguishes between **civic nationalism** and **ethnic nationalism**:

- **Civic nationalist** sentiments are based upon being a member of a particular nation-state, such as the USA, which includes diverse ethnic groups.
- In **ethnic nationalism**, perceived membership of an ethnic group unites people – e.g. Serbs and Croats in the former Yugoslavia.

McCrone goes on to explain how four different types of nationalism emerged:

1 Nationalism in the **modern nation-state** – this type of nationalism emerged in countries such as the UK, France and the USA. The nation-state developed with the economic changes of capitalism and the Industrial Revolution, but the building of nationalist identities sometimes exploited existing ethnic and cultural groupings.
2 Nationalism emerged in many countries which were colonies, as they struggled for independence and sought to become **post-colonial societies**.
3 **Neo-nationalism** is found in independence movements in Western societies, such as the Basque country and Scotland. It tends to develop in areas with strong economies and a strong civil society.
4 **Post-communist nationalism** exists in some areas which used to be part of the Soviet Union, and in other areas of Eastern Europe. With the decline of strong centralized authority, groups with particular national and ethnic identities sought to establish national homelands for themselves, and some fought over particular territories.

### Cohen – British nationality and identity

Robin **Cohen** (1994) discusses British nationality and **identity**. He argues that there is no clear dividing line between being British and not being British. For example, the Scottish and Welsh and people in former colonies may to different extents identify themselves as British or distance themselves from being British.

There is also some overlap between European and American identities and being British, which means that defining who is alien – i.e. non-British – is not clear cut.

### Hall – new ethnicities

The complexity of national identity is reflected in the emergence of **new ethnicities**.

Stuart **Hall** (1996) sees new ethnicities in terms of the development of **new identities** in black cultural politics in Britain.

These new identities stress the great variety of differences between people. People see themselves and are seen by others not just in terms of ethnicity but also in terms of age, religion, sexuality, class and gender.

Hall also argues that there is increasing **hybridization** with the merging and overlapping of different identities. **Globalization** and **migration** have led to increasingly diverse populations living in particular areas and therefore different cultures influencing one another.

In some areas the response has been **ethnic absolutism**, based on trying to maintain **ethnic purity** and hostility to members of other groups – e.g. **ethnic cleansing** in the former Yugoslavia.

Hall sees ethnic absolutism and nationalism as major threats in a globalizing world.

## Modood – new ethnicities and identities

Some evidence of changing ethnic identities in Britain is provided by survey research carried out by **Modood et al.** (1997).

- This found that by the mid-1990s most British Caribbeans and South Asians thought of themselves *both* as British and as members of ethnic minorities.
- Older Caribbeans and South Asians born outside the UK identified more with their country of origin than younger generations born in Britain.
- There were considerable variations in people's sense of identity in all ethnic groups.

## Back – new ethnicities and urban culture

Research by Les **Back** (1996) on two London council estates found a mixture of **racism** and the development of **new ethnicities**.

- On one estate a number of white youths adopted elements of black youth culture and felt they had as much in common with some black people as with white people.
- Some young black people had a strong sense of British citizenship.

## Modernity, postmodernity, racism, ethnicity and identity

- Zygmunt **Bauman** (1989), a postmodernist, links **modernity** to racism. He argues that modernity made the Holocaust (the mass extermination of Jews and other groups in Nazi Germany) possible.
  1 **Bureaucratic planning** made mass extermination possible.
  2 Modern **organizational discipline** was used to control the individuals who carried out the exterminations.
  3 The existence of modern **nation-states** allowed Jews to be seen as outsiders.
  4 Modern **scientific rationalism** was used to 'prove' the inferiority of Jews.

- Davis **Goldberg** (1993) blames modernity for creating racism. He argues that there was no racism in premodern societies.
  1 Modernity brought a new **liberal conceptual order** in which people thought of themselves as rational individuals rather than the subjects of God.
  2 Non-Western people whose lands were colonized began to be defined as less than rational by Western liberals and scientists, leading to the development of racism.
  3 Non-Westerners were regarded as '**others**' and seen in terms of racist and stereotypical images.

Goldberg believes that the development of **postmodernism** – in which people have more mixed, varied and insecure identities – makes it possible that racism might decline.

- Ali **Rattansi** (1994) argues that under postmodernism two processes might undermine racism:
  1 **Decentring the subject** rejects the view that people have a strong and unambiguous sense of identity.
  2 **De-essentialization** rejects the view that there are fundamental or unchanging differences between societies or groups of people.

With more **fluid identities** it becomes hard to maintain rigid, racist views because there are no longer clear distinctions between groups of people.

- Kenan **Malik** (1996) criticizes postmodern theories.
  1 He argues that the **Enlightenment** philosophy on which modernity was based saw humans as equal and provided the theoretical basis for liberating people.
  2 It was not modernity as such which caused racism but the inequality produced by **capitalism**. The working class was the first group to be seen as 'racially' inferior, and only later did racism become applied to people from different ethnic groups.
  3 Malik believes that **modern** ideas about the equality of humans are a more positive way of tackling racism than the **postmodern** idea of simply accepting difference. This is because groups who are different may also be or become very unequal.

## ETHNIC MINORITIES IN THE LABOUR MARKET AND STRATIFICATION SYSTEM

A number of attempts have been made to explain the tendency for people from (some) ethnic minorities to get lower pay and to have lower-status jobs.

## Discrimination in the labour market

**Discrimination** is one possible explanation.

**Brown and Gay** (1985) used bogus job applications to measure the extent of racial discrimination by employers in the 1980s. They found evidence that more than a quarter of employers discriminated against ethnic minority applicants by denying them job interviews.

In the 1990s survey by the **Policy Studies Institute**, substantial minorities amongst ethnic groups (e.g. 28% of Caribbean people) claimed to have been denied a job because of their race or religion.

## Ethnic minorities as an underclass

Some sociologists have seen ethnic minorities as making up an underclass.

- Charles **Murray** (1984) argued that in the USA there was a growing **black underclass** made up of single mothers, young men unwilling to work, and criminals. Their problems stemmed from their **culture** which was characterized by dependency. Welfare payments made single parenthood possible and encouraged **dependency** on benefits rather than earned income. However, Lydia **Morris** (1994) points out that there is no automatic entitlement to benefits for the unemployed in the USA.

■ An alternative view of the underclass in the USA is put forward by William Julius **Wilson** (1987).

1 He sees blacks and Hispanics living in inner cities as making up an underclass, but because of **disadvantage** rather than because of cultural differences.

2 A combination of **racism** and lack of skills has held these groups back, and their lack of economic success has reinforced racial stereotypes.

3 Successful blacks and Hispanics have moved out of the inner cities, leaving the least successful behind.

4 Wilson suggests that the term underclass should be abandoned because it has been used by some to unfairly blame the disadvantaged for their problems. He prefers the term **ghetto poor** which has no such connotations.

■ In 1973 **Giddens** argued that there was an **ethnic minority and female underclass** in Britain, as a result of structural problems such as low skills and discrimination.

■ John **Rex** and Sally **Tomlinson** (1979) studied the area of Handsworth, Birmingham, in the late 1970s and found evidence of an **ethnic minority underclass**. They found that blacks and Asians were concentrated in **secondary labour market** jobs – those with few prospects and little security. For example, a high proportion worked in metal or metal goods manufacturing but only a low proportion in the better-paid vehicle manufacturing sector.

## Marxist approaches

■ An alternative view is put forward by Marxists such as **Castles** and **Kosack** (1973).

1 From a study of immigrant groups in various European countries, they acknowledge that such groups are concentrated in low-paid and low-status work

2 In Britain this is mostly due to **discrimination**. However, in France, Germany and Switzerland many members of ethnic minorities are **migrant workers** who lack citizenship rights. Here restrictive laws and regulations prevent them from getting better work.

3 Castles and Kosack see immigrants as a **reserve army of labour** – easily hired and fired – who are needed to cope with the booms and slumps of capitalist economies. They see them as the most disadvantaged group in the working class rather than as a separate underclass.

■ The Marxists Annie **Phizaklea** and Robert **Miles** (1980) see ethnic minorities as one faction in the working class. The working class has always contained different factions – e.g. males and females and skilled and unskilled workers.

■ Andrew **Pilkington** (1999) questions all of the above theories which see ethnic minorities as forming a distinct stratum below or at the bottom of the working class.

1 He points out that substantial proportions of all ethnic minorities have non-manual jobs. African Asian men are more likely to be in high status employment than white men.

2 Although ethnic minorities overall have lower pay and lower-status jobs, there is a great deal of overlap and no evidence of ethnic minorities as a whole forming an underprivileged stratum.

3 Over time all ethnic minority groups have made greater gains in the labour market than whites.

4 Bangladeshis and Pakistanis remain the most disadvantaged. There is polarization within these groups between the successful and unsuccessful.

## Conclusion

Heidi **Mirza** (1992) highlights the success of some black women in Britain. She argues that a range of factors (such as class, background, gender, age and cultural difference, as well as ethnicity) need to be examined in order to understand the labour market.

# TEST YOUR KNOWLEDGE AND UNDERSTANDING

1 Saying that 'races' are socially defined means:
a Races are genetically different
b A race is simply what a particular society sees as a race
c There is considerable overlap between races
d Races do not exist

2 Which one of these statements is not a criticism of the biological theory of 'race'?
a Skin colour is only linked to a small number of genes
b Humans are a genetically relatively homogeneous species
c There are big genetic differences between people of the same supposed 'race'
d There are distinct, genetically different racial groups which can be identified through skin colour

3 Which one of these statements about the immigrant-host model is not true?
a The model assumes that the hosts have a shared culture
b The model sees assimilation as unlikely to happen
c The model sees accommodation as part of the process of adaptation
d The model was first developed at the University of Chicago

4 Which one of these statements is true?
a The idea of ethnicity places more emphasis on culture than on genetics
b There are always clear dividing lines between ethnic groups
c Ethnic groups are based on the locality where the groups live
d Ethnic groups are homogeneous

5 Which two of the following are strengths of the ethnicity approach?
a It stresses the importance of racism
b There are clear distinctions between ethnic groups
c It avoids biological determinism
d It sees ethnic minorities as active agents

6 Which TWO of the following statements describes the findings of Basit's research on British Asian girls?
a Families had few contacts with kin in Asia.
b The girls combined elements of British and Asian culture.
c The girls did not see themselves as being at all British.
d Teachers often had stereotypical views abut Asian girls.

7 Which one of the following is an example of institutional racism?
a A widespread belief that an ethnic group is inferior
b Policing policies which disadvantage an ethnic group
c A member of the public shouting racial insults in the street
d An individual harassing somebody because of their 'race'

8 Which one of the following statements about ethnic minorities in he labour market is true?
a Chinese women have the lowest earnings of all ethnic groups.
b White men are the group most likely to be in the top two classes.
c Bangladeshis are more likely than other ethnic groups to have jobs in the lowest classes.
d All ethnic groups have similar levels of earnings.

9 Oliver Cox blames racism on:
a Ignorance
b Capitalism
c Patriarchy
d Migration

10 Who introduced the idea of Orientalism?
a The Runnymede Trust
b Claire Alexander
c Edward Said
d Robert Miles

11 Which one of these is not a phenomenon caused by globalization, according to Stuart Hall?
a Hybridization
b Ethnic absolutism
c A desire for ethnic purity
d The destruction of ethnic identities

12 Zygmunt Bauman can best be described as:
a A postmodernist
b A modernist
c A Marxist
d A feminist

13 Which one of these statements best describes the views of Kenan Malik?
a Modernity is responsible for racism
b Postmodernity will ensure equality between ethnic groups
c Modernity provides the potential basis for producing greater equality between ethnic groups
d Racism is confined to higher social classes

14 Which one of these writers sees the underclass as resulting from deficient culture and generous welfare systems?
a Anthony Giddens
b Charles Murray
c Lydia Morris
d William Julius Wilson

15 Andy Pilkington believes that ethnic minorities:
a Have achieved equality with whites in Britain
b Do not form a distinct underclass
c Are almost all living in poverty
d Have an inferior culture to whites

## DEVELOP YOUR ANALYSIS AND EVALUATION SKILLS

### Does biology produce distinct races and make some superior to others?

**Background:** There are two separate but linked parts to the question. You need to look at the biological arguments suggesting that genotype provides a biological basis for difference and the superiority of some 'races'. You can discuss monogenesist and polygenetic theories. Herbert Spencer is a useful advocate of the biological view. Steven Jones is a critic of the simple biological views and Richardson and Lambert attack the idea of racial superiority. The idea of ethnicity can be contrasted with the biological view.

| For | Against |
|---|---|
| ■ Polygenetic theories (p. 33) | ■ Jones (p. 33) |
| ■ Spencer (p. 33) | ■ Richardson and Lambert (p. 33) |

**Top tip:** Oliver Cox (p. 37) is interesting for suggesting that capitalism and colonialism produced biological theories of race.

### 'Both racism and inequalities between ethnic groups are dying out in Britain'. Discuss.

**Background:** You need to define racism (p. 36) (and point out there are different types) before answering this question. You will also need to identify different types of inequality and look at the evidence of whether these inequalities are declining. Work inequalities are covered in this chapter (pp. 39–40) but you can also look at issues of poverty (p. 49), education (pp. 162–5) and unemployment (p. 141). Evidence on the extent of racism is less precise but there is data on individual racism (p. 36) and plenty of studies of other forms of racism. The host-immigrant model suggests a decline in racism and conflict will take place progressively.

| For | Against |
|---|---|
| ■ Decline in individual racism (p. 36) | ■ Evidence of inequality (p. 37) |
| ■ Immigrant–host model (p. 34) | ■ Theories of racism (p. 37–8) |
| | ■ Evidence from other topic areas (see above) |

**Top tip:** The idea of Islamophobia suggests that racism may be shifting towards focusing on British Asians (pp. 37–8).

### 'Ethnicity is a more useful concept than racism' Discuss.

**Background:** You need to define both racism (pp. 36–7) and ethnicity (pp. 35–6) bringing out the point that neither is easy to define and there is no agreement on a correct definition. You also need to discuss the key differences between the concepts. In particular the idea of racism tends to see the position of ethnic minorities as shaped by external forces, whereas the idea of ethnicity puts more emphasis on the choices made by ethnic groups.

| For | Against |
|---|---|
| ■ Studies of ethnic groups (p. 35) | ■ The extent of individual racism and racial harassment (pp. 36–7) |
| ■ Explanations of ethnicity (pp. 35–6) | ■ Solomos and Black (p. 37) |
| ■ The strengths of the ethnicity approach (p. 36) | ■ Theories of racism (pp. 37–8) |
| | ■ Islamophobia (pp. 37–8) |
| | ■ The weaknesses of the ethnicity approach (p. 36) |

**Top tip:** You might want to conclude that you can't understand the situation of ethnic minorities without using both concepts. The work of Gilroy (p. 37) is an example of this.

# AQA-STYLE ETHNICITY AND RACE QUESTION

The questions below are from different parts of the specification but they are all parts of questions where you will be able to use knowledge from this chapter.

## AS Unit 2: Work and Leisure

**Comments on the question**

- This means look at from more than one point of view – does a viewpoint have evidence to back it up?
- Plural, so several reasons will be needed here
- Are all groups the same? Distinguish between them and consider whether male and female ethnic minority members are in the same position
- You might also need to look at chapter 10 to answer this question fully

**[a]** Examine the reasons for the continued discrimination of ethnic minority groups in the field of employment. [20 marks]

**Advice on preparing your answer**

- Start by explaining this term, see p. 36
- This chapter has several important points:
  1 Migration and conflict, p. 34
  2 Exclusionary nationalism, pp. 38
  3 Subcultural values, p. 35
  4 Racism, pp. 36–7
  5 Inequalities between groups, p. 37
  6 Reasons for racism from a variety of perspectives, pp. 36–7
  7 Underclass theory, p. 39 40

## A2 synoptic Unit 6: Stratification

**Comments on the question**

- Look at both sides of every argument you consider
- You should distinguish between different groups here
- This is the focus, not any other feature of life
- This means you shouldn't look at education for the answer here
- This is a fifth of your total marks, so only spend a fifth of your time, i.e. 18 minutes

**[b]** Briefly examine the reasons why ethnic minorities are still more likely to be receiving low pay than others with equal skills.

[12 marks]

**Advice on preparing your answer**

- This question is saying: 'If all else is equal why does discrimination occur?'
- The main answer will probably hinge on racism, so pp. 37–8 may be of great use here
- Consider the following types of racism: individual, institutional and cultural
- You could bring in ideas from:
  1 Communication and the media, chapter 13
  2 Work, unemployment and leisure, chapter 10
  3 Culture and identity, chapter 12

# OCR-STYLE 'RACE', ETHNICITY AND NATIONALITY QUESTION

## AS Unit 2532: The Individual and Society

| Answer all parts of this question |
|---|

Total: 60 marks
1 mark = 1 minute

Time allowed:
1 hour

### ITEM A

Les Back's research in 'Southgate', a council estate in South London, found that a new type of hybrid black-white ethnic culture was developing among young people. For example, Tony, who was a 17-year-old white male, had learnt to talk in the same way as local black people. Debbie, a white female, mainly had black friends. Although racism against black people had not disappeared from the area, both black and white youth shared racist ideas about the Vietnamese living in the area.

**Comments on the question**

- The characteristics are in the data; you will not be rewarded for going beyond this
- Make sure that the examiner can clearly see the two characteristics you have identified and explained – e.g. number them
- Go beyond simply supplying a list – explain using examples
- Don't offer more than two points

**[a]** Using Item A, identify and explain two characteristics of the new type of hybrid black/white ethnicity appearing among young people.

[8 marks]

**Advice on preparing your answer**

- Don't just copy the material from Item A. Try to put it into your own words

---

- No more, no less
- Make sure that two reasons are clearly seen by the examiner

**[b]** Identify and explain two reasons why some members of ethnic minority groups living in the UK may be reluctant to identify themselves as British. [8 marks]

- The section on Modood's research (p. 39) will assist you with this task
- Try to be very specific when talking about ethnic minority groups – e.g. are you talking about African-Caribbeans, Asians, etc.?

---

- This means describe the way
- Don't forget to do this
- This can be positive or negative
- Evaluation might focus on the fact that other agencies of socialization may be more important in shaping identity

**[c]** Outline and briefly evaluate two ways in which the workplace may shape the identity of some members of ethnic minority groups.

[18 marks]

- Workplace can be interpreted broadly to mean: the type of work people do; the occupational community to which people belong; the home as a workplace for full-time mothers, etc.
- You will find pp. 39–40 useful for answering this question
- Remember to be specific about ethnic minority groups

---

- This means that you need to look at arguments and evidence against the view as well as arguments and evidence that support it

**[d]** Discuss the view that what it means to be British is not clear cut. [26 marks]

- You will need to make clear what British identity is and how it is formed before you can discuss the view that it is not clearcut
- You do not have to accept the view – you might want to challenge it
- See p. 38 for some arguments that focus on this issue

# Chapter 4

# POVERTY AND SOCIAL EXCLUSION

Textbook pp. 236–289

Specifications

| Specification | Specification details | Coverage |
|---|---|---|
| **AQA** AS: Wealth, Poverty and Welfare | ■ Different definitions of poverty and wealth and income | Definitions of poverty are covered on pp. 45–6; definitions of wealth and income in chapter 1, pp. 8–9. |
| | ■ Different explanations of the distribution of poverty, wealth and income between different social group | Theories about the distribution of poverty are covered on p. 49; explanations of the distribution of wealth and income in chapter 1, p. 7–8. |
| | ■ Different explanations of the existence and persistence of poverty | Theories of poverty can be found on pp. 49–52. |
| | ■ Different solutions to poverty with particular reference to the role of social policy | Solutions to poverty are linked to theories and covered on p. 53. |
| | ■ The nature and role of public, private, voluntary and informal welfare provision | Some reference to welfare provision is included in the discussion of key explanations of poverty on pp. 49–53. |
| **Parts of other modules covered** | | |
| **OCR** A2: Social Inequality and Difference | ■ Concepts and measures of poverty.<br>■ Contemporary trends in poverty in terms of class, gender and ethnicity.<br>■ The underclass debate; theories of culture and poverty. | See the section on the definition and measurement of poverty on pp. 45–7. For contemporary trends see the section on official statistics on poverty and social exclusion on pp. 47–9. The underclass and poverty is covered on pp. 49–50. |

For more detailed specification guidance visit **www.haralambosholborn.com**

Essential notes

## THE DEFINITION AND MEASUREMENT OF POVERTY

Since studies of poverty began, researchers have been trying to establish a fixed standard against which to measure it. There are three main areas of controversy.

1 **Absolute** and **relative** poverty.
- Some writers argue that a common minimum standard of subsistence can be applied to all societies. Individuals without the resources to maintain a healthy life can be said to be in poverty.
- Supporters of the concept of **relative poverty** dismiss this idea. They believe that definitions of poverty must relate to the standards of a particular society at a particular time. The poverty line will vary according to the wealth of a society.

2 **Material** and **multiple deprivation** and **social exclusion**.
- Some sociologists assume that poverty consists simply of a lack of material resources – a shortage of the money required to maintain an acceptable standard of living.

- Others argue that poverty involves more than material deprivation. They see poverty as a form of multiple deprivation, involving additional factors such as inadequate educational opportunities, unpleasant working conditions and powerlessness. Today many writers prefer to use the term **social exclusion** to describe a situation where **multiple deprivation** prevents individuals from participating in social activities such as paid employment.

3 **Inequality** and **poverty**.
- From one point of view any society in which there is inequality is bound to have poverty. Those at the bottom will always be 'poor' and poverty could only be eliminated by abolishing all inequality.
- Most sociologists accept that some reduction in inequality is needed in order to abolish poverty but believe that it is possible to establish a **poverty line** – a minimum standard below which it is not possible to maintain an acceptable standard of living. Thus it would be possible to have a society with some inequality but where poverty no longer exists.

## ABSOLUTE POVERTY

The concept of absolute poverty involves a judgement of basic human needs. Most measures of absolute poverty are concerned with establishing the quality and amount of food, clothing and shelter deemed necessary for a healthy life.

Absolute poverty is also known as subsistence poverty since it is based on assessments of minimum subsistence requirements. This definition limits poverty to material deprivation.

Absolute poverty is usually **operationalized** (put into a form which can be measured) by pricing the basic necessities of life and defining as poor those whose income falls below this line.

### Criticisms of the concept of absolute poverty

The concept of absolute poverty has been widely criticized. It is based on the assumption that there are basic minimum needs for all people in all societies. The problem is that needs vary both within and between societies.

- **Within a society** – The nutritional needs of a bank clerk sitting at a desk all day are very different from those of a labourer working on a building site.
- **Between societies** – The Bushmen of the Kalahari Desert have very different nutritional needs from those of office workers in London.

The concept of absolute poverty is even more difficult to defend when it includes **cultural needs**. These needs vary from time to time and place to place, so that any attempt to establish a fixed standard is bound to fail.

## BUDGET STANDARDS AND POVERTY

The **budget standards** approach to measuring poverty calculates the cost of those purchases that are considered necessary to raise an individual or family out of poverty.

Seebohm **Rowntree** conducted three studies of poverty in York using this approach (1901, 1941, 1951).

### Rowntree – trends in poverty

Rowntree drew a poverty line in terms of a minimum weekly sum of money needed to live a healthy life. In the later studies he included extra items which were not strictly necessary for survival, such as newspapers and presents. He found that the percentage of the population in poverty dropped rapidly between 1899 and 1950.

Rowntree believed that increased welfare benefits would eventually eliminate poverty.

### Criticisms of Rowntree

- Rowntree's selection of necessities was based on expert views and ignored the customs of ordinary people.
- Rowntree's view that poverty was declining was challenged by later writers who adopted a relative definition of poverty.

### Bradshaw, Mitchell and Morgan – the usefulness of budget standards

The work of the **Family Budget Unit** (FBU) represents one attempt to develop the budget standards approach. On the basis of information provided by experts and consumer groups they worked out the cost of a 'low cost but acceptable (LCA) standard of living and a 'modest but adequate' (MDA) standard.

**Howard** *et al.* (2001) compared the cost of these budgets with Income Support levels. Although the situation had improved since 1998, in 2001 a family with two children under 11 were still only receiving 93% of the LCA standard.

### Evaluation

**Spicker** (1993) points out that people's quality of life is not solely determined by how they spend money. For example, living standards can be improved by the unpaid labour of family members. However, he does support the collection of data on what people actually spend rather than what experts say they should spend.

### Townsend – poverty as relative deprivation

Peter **Townsend** has carried out a number of studies on poverty and has played a major part in highlighting the continuing existence of poverty. He has also been a leading supporter of defining poverty in terms of **relative deprivation**.

Townsend believes that society determines people's needs – e.g. tea is not essential but members of British culture are expected to be able to offer visitors a cup of tea.

Townsend argues that relative deprivation needs to be thought of in terms of the resources available to individuals and households, and the way in which these resources affect participation in the community. Poverty involves an inability to participate in social activities that are seen as normal, such as visiting friends or relatives, having birthday parties for children and going on holiday.

### Poverty in the United Kingdom

Townsend used his definition of poverty to measure the extent of poverty in Britain. He used a **deprivation index** that included 12 items he believed to be relevant for the whole population, and he calculated the percentage of the population deprived of these items. They included:

- Not having had a week's holiday in the last year.
- Children not having had a friend over to play in the last month.
- Not having a refrigerator.
- Having gone through one or more days in the past fortnight without a cooked meal.
- Not usually having a Sunday joint.

On the basis of these calculations Townsend found that 22.9% of the population (12.46 million people) were living in poverty in 1968–9.

### Criticisms of Townsend's research

■ **Piachaud** (1981, 1987) claims that the index on which Townsend's statistics are based is inadequate. Going without a Sunday joint or eating salads may reflect cultural preferences rather than deprivation.
■ Townsend claims that he has identified a 'poverty line' – deprivation increases rapidly when income drops below a particular level. Piachaud rejects this view.
■ Piachaud argues that the implications of Townsend's definition of poverty are that poverty will remain as long as people behave in different ways – choosing to be vegetarian or not to go on holiday, for example.

### *Mack and Lansley – Poor Britain*

Joanna **Mack** and Stewart **Lansley** (1985) took note of many of the criticisms of Townsend's work in their study of poverty in Britain.

■ Their deprivation index included a question asking respondents whether they lacked a particular item through choice or necessity.
■ They selected the items in their deprivation index on the basis of asking respondents what they considered to be necessities in modern Britain.

They found poverty to be widespread, although on a lesser scale than Townsend. However, in a follow-up study (1990) they found that the numbers in poverty had risen significantly. Mack and Lansley believed that this increase was due to changes in the benefits system.

### *David Gordon et al. – Poverty and social exclusion in Britain*

Nine years after Mack and Lansley, this research (2000) adopted a similar approach. It considered:

■ whether people lacked a broad range of items because of low income.
■ the extent to which people were excluded from essential social activities.

They found that the percentage of households experiencing poverty had increased from 14% in 1983 to 24% in 1999. This was despite a big increase in living standards over this period. Gordon *et al.* provide two main explanations.

1 Despite the rise in average income, the income of the poorest households actually decreased over the period after allowing for inflation and housing costs. The incomes of the rich, however, grew rapidly, creating **growing income inequality** and a rise in relative poverty.
2 **The public's perceptions of necessities had changed.** In 1999 possession of a telephone and 'friends or family round for a meal' were both considered 'necessities' by over 50% of the sample for the first time.

### Criticisms of Mack and Lansley and Gordon *et al.*

■ The deprivation index was constructed by the public but the list they chose from reflected the researchers' **values** rather than a general **consensus**.

■ The researchers defined poverty as lacking three or more items from their list in the case of Mack and Lansley, two in the case of Gordon *et al.* A different definition would have produced very different results.
■ **Walker** (1987) points out that Mack and Lansley's method does not take into account the quality of items, only whether or not they exist.

## OFFICIAL STATISTICS ON POVERTY

Some countries, such as the USA, have an official poverty line, but Britain does not. Britain does, however, produce figures on low incomes.

### Low Income Families

Between 1972 and 1985 the government published figures on Low Income Families: those living at or just above the main means-tested state benefit. However, critics felt that the numbers in poverty depended on the political decisions of the government of the day. Increasing benefits would actually create more poverty!

### Households below average income

In 1988 these figures replaced those on Low Income Families. They measure the number of households receiving 60% of average income before and after housing costs. Figures are adjusted to take account number of children and household size. In 2000/1, a couple with children required a weekly income of £152, after housing costs, to avoid poverty.

Despite some criticisms, for example **Giles and Webb**'s (1993) argument that the figures simply measure income distribution rather than poverty, they are the most comprehensive official figures available.

### Trends in households below average income

■ According to the Child Poverty Action Group (Howard *et al.* 2001) there has been a major increase in poverty since 1979. Poverty increased from 9% of the population in 1979 to around 25% in 1999/2000. This is partly explained by increases in income inequality over this period.
■ However, over recent years numbers in absolute low income have fallen from 25% of the population to 17%.
■ One of the Labour government's stated aims is to reduce and eventually eradicate child poverty. The percentage of children living below poverty thresholds has declined from 34 to 31% between 1996/7 and 2000/2001 after housing costs (quoted in Sinclair, 2003). In 2001/2002 there was a further drop to 30% (Brewer *et al.* 2003). Despite this, Brewer *et al.* argue that the government would still miss its target of reducing poverty by 25% if the rate of reduction was not increased.

### *International comparisons*

■ **Poverty in the European Union** – Although there is no agreed method of measuring poverty, in 1995 the UK's poverty level was slightly above the EU average of 17%. The highest rates were in Portugal, Spain and Greece, the lowest in Denmark, Finland and the Netherlands.

- **Poverty worldwide** – In 1999 **Bradbury and Janti** (discussed in Howard *et al.* 2001) compared child poverty rates in 25 countries. They found that the UK had the third highest rate of child poverty, behind only the USA and Russia. The lowest rate was in the Czech Republic.

## SOCIAL EXCLUSION

In recent years some commentators have tried to broaden the issues surrounding deprivation by using the term **social exclusion** rather than poverty. The Labour government set up a Social Exclusion Unit in 1997. This aimed to encourage social inclusion by tackling social problems such as truancy and unemployment.

### Defining social exclusion

There is no agreed definition of social exclusion. **Burchardt *et al.*** (2002) describe it as a 'contested term'.

- **Byrne** (1999) differentiates between the terms 'social exclusion' and 'underclass'. He argues that social exclusion draws attention to the relationship between those who are excluded and those who are doing the excluding. The socially excluded cannot be seen as an underclass.
- Poverty refers to a lack of material resources whereas all definitions of social exclusion include a broader range of ways in which people may be disadvantaged or unable to participate in society. The socially excluded may include the unemployed, those who do not register to vote and isolated elderly individuals.

### Progressive and regressive views of social exclusion

The shift from discussion of poverty to social exclusion has been seen as both a **regressive** and a **progressive** step.

- **Nolan and Whelan** (1996) see it as a **regressive** step: a way of avoiding the issue of poverty and therefore avoiding any possibility of tackling income inequality
- **Lawson** (1995) sees it as a **progressive** step: tackling the problems of social exclusion would involve measures to deal with racism, to encourage a stronger sense of community and to combat sex discrimination.

**Byrne** supports what he calls '**strong**' definitions of social exclusion. These emphasize the importance of both material inequalities and inequalities of power. Tackling social exclusion would therefore require redistribution of income and radical changes in the structure of society. '**Weak**' definitions do not require any great increase in equality to tackle social exclusion.

The different definitions of social exclusion tend to reflect the political preferences of those who produce the definitions.

## OFFICIAL STATISTICS ON SOCIAL EXCLUSION

### Opportunities for all

**The Department for Work and Pensions** produces an annual report to monitor progress on tackling poverty and social exclusion. In 2002 the fourth annual report was published. The report identifies the following dimensions of poverty and social exclusion which often work together to reinforce social exclusion.

1 A lack of resources.
2 A lack of opportunities to work.
3 A lack of opportunities to learn.
4 Suffering health inequalities.
5 A lack of decent housing.
6 Disruption of family life.
7 Living in a disadvantaged neighbourhood.

The report uses 52 indicators to monitor social exclusion. Compared with 1996 the 2002 report found a worsening trend in only one indicator (the level of suicide and 'undetermined injury'). In 31 areas there had been improvements, in 11 there had been no significant change and in 9 there was insufficient data to determine a trend.

#### Problems with the DWP reports

1 **Sinclair** (2003) points out that the reliability of some of the findings can be questioned.
2 The report produces **no overall figures** for individuals experiencing poverty and social exclusion.
3 The selection of **indicators** changes between reports and there is no clear indication of why some are included and others excluded.

Alternative measurements of social exclusion tend to produce a less rosy picture of changes. However, the reports do show that Labour governments since 1997 have taken issues of poverty and social exclusion seriously. Their policies are evaluated on p. 53.

### Guy Palmer, Mohibur Rahman and Peter Kenway – Monitoring poverty and social exclusion

An alternative source on the extent of, and trends in, poverty and social exclusion is provided in this annual report. It differs from the DWP reports in the following ways:

- It uses a broader range of indicators.
- It is more critical of government policy.
- There is more data on which groups are experiencing what types of social exclusion.

#### Findings

- The report found 12.9 million people were below the threshold of 60% of median income, a fall of 300,000 from the previous year but still double the number of 20 years earlier.

- Useful progress had been made towards the government's target of cutting child poverty but the report questioned whether progress could be maintained at the same rate.
- Low wages continued to be a major cause of poverty and social exclusion.
- Educational outcomes were improving and deprived areas were sharing in that improvement.
- In terms of housing, central heating had become the norm and overcrowding was less common. However, the numbers in temporary accommodation had doubled.
- The figures on crime showed some progress with a decline in the number of burglaries.
- Little progress had been made on financial exclusion. For example, half of the poorest had no home contents insurance although they were the group most vulnerable to burglary.
- Despite falls in unemployment many were still experiencing social exclusion due to lack of paid employment.

## Evaluation

- The research is independent and not tied to government priorities.
- Careful justifications are given for choice of indicators.
- The report is still tied to using indicators for which government statistics exist.

### The social distribution of poverty and social exclusion

The chances of experiencing poverty are not equally distributed. Some groups are much more prone to poverty than others.

## Economic and family status

- Being in paid employment on a full-time basis greatly reduces the risk of poverty. **Retirement** and **unemployment** are both strongly associated with poverty.
- **Lone parenthood** leads to a high risk of poverty.
- Over a quarter of pensioner couples are poor, although some evidence suggests that the elderly are becoming less prone to poverty.

## Gender and poverty

More women than men were in poverty in 1999/2000. **Sinclair** (2003) suggests reasons for this:

- More women are likely to be **lone parents** than men.
- The majority of **single pensioners** are women.
- Women are more likely than men to be **unpaid carers**.
- Women are more likely than men to do **part-time work**.
- Female workers receive on average **lower wages** than men.

**Lister** (1995) argues that women are also more likely to have more responsibility for dealing with the effects of poverty because of their continued responsibility for most domestic labour.

## Ethnicity and poverty

Minority ethnic groups are more likely to experience poverty than other groups. **Howard** *et al.* (2001) suggest reasons for this:

- Members of ethnic minority groups tend to have much higher rates of **unemployment** than whites.
- Caribbeans and Africans have higher rates of **single parenthood** than other ethnic groups.
- Indians are more likely to suffer **disability** than other ethnic groups.
- People from ethnic minority backgrounds tend to receive **lower average** wages than whites.

**Alcock** (1997) argues that social exclusion resulting from **racism** is often as much a problem for ethnic minority groups as material deprivation.

## Poverty and disability

It has been estimated that nearly half of all disabled people live in poverty. The figure is high because:

- Most households containing a disabled person receive **no income from employment** so they are likely to rely on state benefits.
- Disabled people tend to have **high spending costs**.

# INDIVIDUALISTIC AND CULTURAL THEORIES OF POVERTY

The earliest theories of poverty placed the blame for poverty on the poor themselves. Those who suffered from very low incomes were unable or unwilling to provide for their own well-being. Although most sociologists reject these views, they are still popular with a minority of the general public.

### The New Right – the culture of dependency

The politics of the Conservative governments (1979–97) were influenced by the ideas of the **New Right**. A central plank of their policies was the claim that the welfare state was leading to a **culture of dependency**. Writers such as David Marsland have used this concept to help explain poverty.

## Marsland – poverty and the generosity of the welfare state

David **Marsland** (1996) claims that much research on poverty has exaggerated the extent of poverty in Britain, because relative definitions of poverty have confused poverty with inequality. In fact, steadily rising **living standards** have largely eradicated poverty.

For most people, low income results from the generosity of the welfare state. Marsland believes that **universal welfare provision** (the provision of benefits such as education and health services to all members of society regardless of whether they are on low or high incomes) has created an expectation that the state will look after people's problems – a culture of dependency.

## Criticisms of Marsland

Marsland ignores some important evidence such as the fact that the real incomes of the poorest have been falling.

**Jordan** (1989) claims that societies relying on **means-tested benefits** (welfare benefits that only go to the most needy) tend to develop a large underclass. If members of the underclass take low-paid jobs they lose benefits and end up worse off.

**Dean and Taylor-Gooby** (1992) interviewed social security claimants and found that their attitudes and ambitions were little different from those of other members of society. They wanted to earn their own living and would prefer not to have to rely on benefits. The study found little evidence of a dependency culture.

## The culture of poverty

Many researchers have noted that the lifestyle of the poor differs from that of other members of society. This observation has led to the concept of a **culture of poverty** (or, more correctly, a subculture of poverty), with its own norms and values.

The idea of a culture of poverty was first introduced by Oscar **Lewis** (1959, 1961, 1966) in the late 1950s. His fieldwork in Mexico led him to identify a particular **design for living** which had the following elements:

- Individuals feel **marginalized** and helpless.
- There is a high rate of **family breakdown**.
- There is lack of **participation** in social institutions.

These attitudes and behaviours are passed on to the next generation, making it very difficult to break out of poverty as members of the subculture are not able to take advantage of opportunities that may be offered.

## Criticisms of the culture of poverty idea

A great deal of research in both the developed and developing worlds has failed to identify a clear culture of poverty.

Recent qualitative research conducted by the **Joseph Rowntree Foundation** and summarized by Elaine **Kempson** (1996) provides support for the argument that no more than a small proportion of those on low income are part of a culture of poverty.

The studies found that many people looked very hard for work but encountered considerable barriers in their search for a job. Age, lack of skills, poor health and disability, for example, were all problems.

These kinds of barriers (known as **situational constraints**) may well be a more significant factor in keeping individuals on low incomes than a culture of poverty.

## THE UNDERCLASS AND POVERTY

In recent years the concept of an underclass has become widely used and increasingly controversial.

### Murray – the underclass in Britain

Charles **Murray** (1989, 1993) is an American sociologist who visited Britain in 1989 and 1993. He claimed that, like the USA, Britain was developing an underclass. This underclass did not just consist of the poorest members of society. It consisted of those whose lifestyles involve a 'type of poverty' characterized by what Murray calls '**deplorable behaviour**', such as refusal to accept jobs, delinquency and having illegitimate children.

Murray puts forward evidence in three areas to support his claim:

- **Illegitimacy** – Murray argues that illegitimacy is rapidly increasing, particularly among women from the lower social classes. The absence of a father means that illegitimate children will tend to 'run wild'. According to Murray, cohabitation does not provide the same stability as marriage.
- **Crime** – Murray associates the development of an underclass with rising crime. He argues that crime is damaging because it fragments communities. People become suspicious of each other and, as crime becomes more common, young boys start to imitate older males and take up criminal activities themselves.
- **Unemployment** – Murray does not see unemployment itself as a problem; instead it is the unwillingness of young men to take jobs that creates difficulties. Young men without jobs cannot support a family, so they are unlikely to get married when they father children, and the illegitimacy rate rises. In the absence of family responsibilities they find other, more damaging, ways to prove themselves – for example, through violent crime.

### Causes and solutions

Murray argues that the benefits system needs to be changed to get rid of **disincentives to marriage** and to discourage single parenthood. Single mothers can now afford to live on benefits and so males who father children are often isolated from the responsibilities of family life. To force pregnant women to marry, Murray advocates cutting benefits for unmarried women entirely.

### Critics of Murray

Murray's views have come under serious attack.

### Walker – blaming the victims

**Walker** (1990) argues that:

- Lone parenthood is often short-lived – most lone parents find a new partner in a relatively short time.
- Most of the so-called underclass have conventional attitudes. They want stable relationships and paid employment. It is not their values that prevent them from achieving their aims, but lack of opportunities.

### Heath – underclass attitudes

Anthony **Heath** (1990) collected data to test the claim that the attitudes of the underclass are different. Most of the evidence suggests that the majority of the underclass have **conventional aspirations**. They want jobs and happy marriages, but they are slightly less likely than other members of society to believe that people should get married before having children.

### Alcock – Murray's sweeping generalizations

**Alcock** (1994) points out that Murray'a sweeping generalizations about the negative effects of lone parenthood are unjustified. Two-parent families can also produce poorly socialized children.

### Blackman – the homeless and the underclass

Shane **Blackman** (1997) conducted an **ethnographic study** of the young homeless in Brighton. He argues against Murray's view that the underclass rejects society's values. What the young homeless needed was jobs and homes, not a different culture. Blackman sees members of the so-called 'underclass' as victims of society whose behaviour changes when they are given genuine opportunities to improve their situation.

## CONFLICT THEORIES OF POVERTY

The sociology of poverty has increasingly come to be studied within a conflict perspective. Conflict theorists argue that poverty continues to exist because society fails to allocate its resources fairly. To some extent conflict theorists disagree about the reasons why society has failed to eradicate poverty.

- Some regard poverty as the result of the failings of the welfare state.
- Others place more emphasis on the disadvantages faced by the poor in the labour market.
- Marxists believe that poverty is an inevitable consequence of capitalism.

### *Poverty and the welfare state*

Recent studies of relative poverty have found that those who rely on state benefits for their income are among the largest groups of the poor. However, it is widely assumed that the welfare state makes a major contribution to reducing poverty, and that it redistributes resources from the rich to the poor.

Many sociologists have challenged this view.

### Taxation

- **Giles and Johnson** (1994) show that tax changes between 1985 and 1995 made the richest better off and the poorest worse off.
- However, from 1997 the Labour government introduced tax credits for those on lower incomes. **Brewer, Clark and Goodman** (2002) calculate that the changes between 1997 and 2001 led to a gain of about 12% of net income for the poorest fifth of families, but just one per cent for the highest paid tenth of families.

### Wealth, poverty and social exclusion

The provision of welfare is one of the principal means that governments have of tackling poverty and social exclusion. However, some conflict theorists have questioned whether this is actually the case. In 1982 Julian LeGrand suggested that the better-off members of British society had benefited more from the welfare state than the poor. For example, the children of the middle classes were more likely to stay on at school and were more likely to go to university.

Although this analysis is now dated, there are some areas in which such conclusions can still be supported.

### Means-tested benefits

- **Piachaud and Sutherland** (2001) calculated that basic income support levels are not high enough to allow recipients to escape poverty.

### Education

- **Smith, Smith and Wright** (1997) identify a range of ways in which the poor are disadvantaged by educational policy, for example by cuts in the provision of free school meals.
- Critics of Labour education policy have argued that their policies tend to lead to those from richer backgrounds securing places in the most successful schools (see pp. 158–9).

### Housing

- **Ginsburg** (1997) notes that recent housing policy has been aimed at encouraging home ownership, while spending on new council houses has been restricted.

### Health

- **Benzeval** (1997) has found a growing health gap between the rich and poor in Britain.

Overall there is little evidence that government policies up to 1997 redistributed resources to the poor. However, according to **Hills** *et al.* (2002), Labour governments since 1997 have done more to tackle poverty and inequality than previous administrations.

## POVERTY, SOCIAL EXCLUSION, THE LABOUR MARKET AND POWER

Not all of those who experience poverty rely on state benefits for their income. A considerable proportion of the poor are employed, but receive wages that are too low to meet their needs. **Weberian** theories emphasize the concept of **market situation**: the ability of individuals to influence the labour market in their favour. Sociologists have put forward explanations to explain the market situation of the low paid.

1 There is increasing demand for specialist skills in advanced industrial societies. However, the

unemployed tend to be unskilled with low educational qualifications.

2 With increasing mechanization and automation, the **demand for unskilled labour** is contracting.

3 **Competition from Third World** manufacturers tends to force wages in Britain down.

4 Many low-paid workers are employed in **declining industries**. The narrow profit margins in these industries drive wages down.

### Post-Fordism, globalization and poverty

Enzo **Mingione** (1996) argues that increases in international poverty are linked to a shift from **Fordist** to **post-Fordist** production in the world economy.

This involves a decline in heavy industry and mass production and an increase in the service sector and more flexible production. This results in an increase in casual, insecure and temporary employment.

**Globalization** means that companies can move investment from country to country in search of cheap labour and freer trade. This makes more people vulnerable to poverty as jobs are less secure, and the increasing numbers of women in work mean that more families rely on two earners.

### Poverty and the capitalist system

**Marxists** believe that the poor are not a separate group in society but simply the most disadvantaged section of the working class. Marxists believe that poverty exists because it benefits the **ruling class**. It allows them to maintain the capitalist system and maximize their profits in the following ways.

■ Those whose services are not required by the economy, such as the aged and unemployed, must receive a lower income than wage earners. If this were not the case there would be little **motivation to work**.

■ **Low wages** help to reduce wage demands as workers tend to assess their incomes in terms of the baseline provided by the low-paid.

### Evaluation

With the increased emphasis on market forces, **Westergaard** (1994) argues that Marxist views are more relevant than ever. However, they are less successful than other conflict approaches in explaining why particular groups and individuals become poor.

### Burchardt, Le Grand and Piachaud – an integrated framework for explaining social exclusion and poverty

**Burchardt** et al. (2002) have put forward a 'framework for understanding social exclusion'. They argue that economic factors, behaviour and government policies are all important in causing social exclusion. All these elements need to be combined for a full understanding. A visual representation of their theory appears below.

### Brian Barry – social exclusion, poverty and social justice

**Barry** (2002) develops aspects of the approach outlined by Burchardt et al.

■ **Money**, or financial capital, is very important in determining whether or not people can participate in social activities.

■ Wider factors, such as **the provision of public services** are also important. For example, the availability of public transport.

■ Choices made by individuals are influenced by **circumstances**. For example, lack of job opportunities in area may depress motivation in education.

■ The rich exclude themselves through choice, for example by sending their children to **private schools**.

■ The wealthy also gain advantage through **social contacts** with other rich and influential people.

Barry sees social exclusion as influenced by individual choices, but these are shaped by constraints and wider social factors. He concludes that social exclusion cannot be tackled just by trying to deal with individual examples of the problem such as truancy. Some **redistribution of income** is necessary.

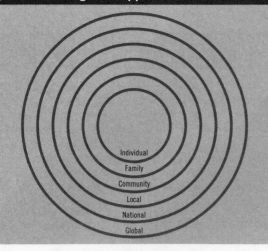

## Figure 4.1 **An integrated approach**

**Individual:** e.g. age, gender, race, disability; preferences, beliefs and values

**Family:** e.g. partnership, children, caring responsibilities

**Community:** e.g. school and physical environment, schools, health and social services

**Local:** e.g. labour market, transport

**National:** e.g. cultural influences, social security, legislative framework

**Global:** e.g. international trade, migration, climage change

Source: T Burchardt, J. Le Grand and D. Piachaud,
*Understanding Social Exclusion*, Oxford University Press, Oxford, 202, p.7

## POVERTY AND SOCIAL EXCLUSION – SOLUTIONS AND VALUES

### New Right solutions

After 1979 the Conservative governments of Margaret Thatcher and John Major were inspired by **New Right** ideas. They decided to:

■ Reduce welfare expenditure so that a more dynamic economy could be created. As the economy grew and living standards rose, wealth would **'trickle down'** to those on low incomes.
■ Move away from universal benefits in order to reduce the dependency culture which made people rely on state benefits.
■ Target resources to the poor so that benefits would only go to those in genuine need.

#### Criticisms of New Right policies

Most of the evidence included earlier in this chapter suggests that poverty actually worsened during this period. Carey **Oppenheim** (1997) found no evidence of a 'trickle-down' effect, although the government claimed that its policies had increased the income of the poorest 20% of the population.

### Welfare and redistribution as solutions to poverty

Some believe that the answer to poverty is to be found in improving welfare provision. Peter **Townsend** (1997) argues for a national plan to eliminate poverty. The plan might ultimately require the development of a kind of international welfare state. This might enable governments to:

1 Introduce limits on wealth and earnings and ensure adequate benefits for the unemployed.
2 Ensure that there was a link between benefits and average earnings.
3 Make sure that taxation was progressive.
4 Implement policies of job creation.

**Alcock** (1997) argues that state policies can help to avoid the need for redistribution of income and wealth by preventing individuals from falling into poverty or suffering from social exclusion.

### Marxist solutions

Because Marxists see poverty as simply one aspect of inequality, eliminating it involves a radical change in the structure of society.

**Westergaard and Resler** (1976) maintain that no substantial redistribution of wealth can occur until capitalism is replaced by **socialism**.

However, there is little prospect of a revolution occurring at the moment, and there is no evidence that the few remaining communist countries have eliminated poverty.

### 'New Labour' – 'A hand up, not a hand-out'

The 'New Labour' government which took office in Britain in 1997 claimed it had policies that would reduce poverty and social exclusion – what the poor needed was a 'hand up, not a hand-out'. In other words, they needed to be given the support they needed to help themselves rather than simply depending on state benefits. Another important aspect of their approach was to combine a concern with poverty with wider issues of social exclusion.

In general, its policies contained a novel mix of **contradictory ideologies**, influenced by both left-wing sociologists such as Peter **Townsend** and New Right thinkers such as Charles **Murray**.

### New Labour policies

Among the policies introduced were the following:

■ The launch of a **Social Exclusion Unit** designed to help the socially excluded reintegrate into society.
■ A strategy to reduce and eventually **eradicate child poverty** involving changing the tax and benefits systems to raise the incomes of low income households. A **minimum wage** was introduced in 1999 and new **Tax Credits** were introduced to boost the incomes of working parents.
■ Measures were introduced to encourage people back to work and cut unemployment. The **'Welfare to Work'** scheme focused on young people and another scheme on lone parents.
■ A number of government policies were designed to tackle **social exclusion**, such as setting up Education Action Zones, literacy and numeracy hours and after-school homework clubs. The New Deal for Communities provided extra resources for the most disadvantaged areas.

### Evaluation of New Labour policies

■ Stephen **Sinclair** (2003) believes the Labour Party is moving away from its traditional concern with the redistribution of wealth and income. Most of the benefits that have been increased above the level of inflation have been those targeted at groups such as children and the disabled who are unable to work.
■ Ruth **Levitas** (1998) detects a shift in the dominant values of the Labour party from a concern with poverty to a concern with social exclusion. Social exclusion is seen as involving greater social integration and social solidarity. This view owes much to the work of Emile Durkheim (see pp. 214–15). Levitas argues for a more more radical, egalitarian approach.
■ Robert M. **Page** (2002) is more supportive of New Labour. He argues that government policies have made significant improvements. He points to successes in reducing child poverty and to educational reforms which have reduced exclusions and improved literacy and numeracy.

## TEST YOUR KNOWLEDGE AND UNDERSTANDING

1 The view that individuals without the resources to maintain a healthy life can be said to be in poverty is based on which definition of poverty?
a Absolute definition
b Relative definition
c Multiple deprivation
d Social exclusion

2 In which year did Rowntree's first study of poverty take place?
a 1891       b 1901
c 1911       d 1921

3 What is meant by the budget standards approach to measuring poverty?
a Constructing a poverty line which is applicable to all societies
b Measuring how effectively households manage their budgets
c Using an absolute definition of poverty to measure it
d Measuring poverty by calculating the cost of purchases necessary to maintain a satisfactory minimum standard of living

4 Three of the following are criticisms of Mack and Lansley's and Bradshaw *et al.*'s research. Which is the odd one out?
a Their research only measures absolute poverty
b Their research does not take into account the quality of items in their deprivation index
c Different definitions of poverty would have produced very different results
d The public chose the items to be included in the deprivation index but the list from which they chose reflected the researchers' values

5 Which one of the following is not associated with the culture of poverty?
a Feeling of marginalization
b High rate of family breakdown
c Lack of participation in social institutions
d Situational constraints

6 Which one of the following can be considered to be a criticism of the idea of 'social exclusion'?
a It does not look beyond poverty as a simple lack of material resources
b It is difficult to define and measure with any accuracy
c It does not make us consider both the excluded and those who do the excluding
d It does not make policy-makers aware of the need to change social and economic structures

7 Three of the following are associated with a high risk of poverty. Which is the odd one out?
a Unemployment
b Retirement
c Lone parenthood
d Employment

8 Three of the following are reasons why women are more likely to be in poverty than men. Which is the odd one out?
a They are more likely to be lone parents
b They are more likely to work part-time
c They are more likely to have low educational qualifications
d They are more likely to be unpaid carers

9 Which one of the following has been responsible for eradicating most poverty in Britain, according to the New Right?
a The welfare state
b Rising living standards
c Means-tested benefits
d The culture of poverty

10 Which two of the following does Murray put forward as evidence for the existence of an underclass in Britain?
a Rising illegitimacy rate
b Rising standard of living
c Rising crime rate
d Rising level of welfare payments

11 Which of the following is not a New Labour policy initiative?
a Education Action Zones
b Welfare to work
c Action start
d Tax credits

12 Which one of the following statements are conflict theorists likely to agree with?
a Poverty is the result of individual inadequacy
b The welfare state has done much to eliminate poverty
c The welfare state has done very little to redistribute resources from the wealthy to the poor
d Poverty is the result of a culture of poverty

13 Three of the following are reasons why changes in the labour market have made people in Britain more vulnerable to poverty. Which is the odd one out?
a The decline in manufacturing industry
b Growth in high technology industries
c Increases in regional unemployment
d The decline of trade unionism

14 Marxists might well agree with three of the following statements. Which is the odd one out?
a The poor are merely the most disadvantaged section of the working class
b Low wages help to reduce wage demands in capitalist societies
c The welfare state 'contains' the demands of the working class
d It is possible for the welfare state to eliminate poverty

15 Which two of the following statements would the New Right be likely to agree with?
a Universal welfare benefits help create a dependency culture
b Means-tested benefits are socially divisive
c Reducing welfare expenditure makes the economy more dynamic and benefits the poor, as wealth will 'trickle down'
d The welfare state should redistribute wealth from the rich to the poor

## DEVELOP YOUR ANALYSIS AND EVALUATION SKILLS

### *Social exclusion is an important term in understanding deprivation in Britain.*

**Background:** The term 'social exclusion' broadens the issues around deprivation to include more than simply lack of material resources. Social exclusion may be used to refer to those who are not in employment, do not have educational opportunities, access to public transport and so on.

| *For* | *Against* |
|---|---|
| ■ Byrne – supports 'strong' definition of social exclusion (p. 48)<br>■ Lawson (p. 48) | ■ Byrne – opposes 'weak' definition of social exclusion (p. 48)<br>■ Nolan and Whelan (p. 48) |

**Top tip:** Contemporary studies of deprivation, such as the DWP reports and Palmer, Rahman and Kenway (see p. 48–9), include data on social exclusion as well as poverty. More recent theoretical accounts, including those of Burchardt, Le Grand and Piachaud and Barry (see p. 52), emphasize the importance of understanding the complex links between poverty and social exclusion.

### *The existence of an underclass is crucial in understanding poverty in Britain today.*

**Background:** The term 'underclass' has been used in a number of ways but is most associated with the American writer, Charles Murray. His views have been very influential in the creation of New Right ideas and policies. The underclass idea is also linked to the view that the welfare state has created a culture of dependency.

| *For* | *Against* |
|---|---|
| ■ Murray (p. 50)<br>■ Marsland (pp. 49–50) | ■ Walker (p. 50)<br>■ Heath (p. 51)<br>■ Alcock (p. 51)<br>■ Blackman (p. 51) |

**Top tip:** A key issue here is the extent to which those at the bottom of society have developed distinctive norms and values. Conflict theorists tend to see the poor as simply the most disadvantaged section of the working class.

### *Poverty cannot be abolished without major changes to social and economic structures.*

**Background:** This view represents a conflict approach to poverty. Conflict perspectives see the causes of poverty as lying in the way society is organized. From this perspective, poverty can be solved only if social resources are distributed more fairly. The most extreme version of this view comes from Marxists who see poverty as benefiting capitalism. Its elimination is dependent on the replacement of capitalism by socialism.

| *For* | *Against* |
|---|---|
| ■ Marxist views (p. 52)<br>■ Alcock (p. 53)<br>■ Westergaard and Resler (p. 53)<br>■ Barry (p. 52) | ■ New Right policies (p. 53)<br>■ Lewis – the culture of poverty (p. 50)<br>■ Murray (p. 50) |

**Top tip:** Many recent writers have some sympathy with the quotation above but accept that progress towards eliminating poverty can be made within existing social and economic structures (see Townsend, p. 53, for example). They point to the limited progress made by New Labour governments after 1997.

## AQA-STYLE WEALTH, POVERTY AND WELFARE QUESTION, AS UNIT 2

**Answer all parts of this question**

Total: 60 marks
1 mark = 1.25 minutes

Time allowed: 1 hour 15 minutes

### ITEM A

In Britain there is no official measure of poverty. However, those living on or below 50% of average income are often taken to be poor. The real incomes of this poor group have fallen in the last 20 years, while those of the top wage earners have increased. These changes not only produce greater inequality but can also give rise to problems of social exclusion.

### ITEM B

A major new piece of research on *Poverty and Social Exclusion*, published by the Joseph Rowntree Foundation (2000), produced some headline press coverage recently with the news that two million children in Britain went without some of the 'necessities of life'. Not only are these children members of low income families, but they go without two or more items that parents regard as necessary for living in a society such as Britain.

Source: Sue Middleton, 'Measuring poverty in Britain', *Sociology Review*, vol. 10, no. 3, February 2001

**Comments on the question**

■ The item gives you the context for this question

**[a]** Explain what is meant by 'real income'.

[Item A, line 3] [2 marks]

**Advice on preparing your answer**

■ The important word here is 'real', which has a very particular meaning in this context, so be sure to read carefully

■ The item gives you the context and some help in answering this question
■ No more – a waste of time; no less – you will fail to gain all marks

**[b]** Suggest **two** reasons why children are particularly vulnerable to poverty.

[Item B] [4 marks]

■ Write your answer as a list – you do not need to explain or develop your answer

**[c]** Identify three other groups of people who are prone to poverty apart from those mentioned in the items. [6 marks]

■ Select from a number of groups (see p. 49)
■ Do not include 'children', 'low income families' and those living on or below 50% of average income

- Do not forget the second part of this question
- This could be:
  1 A practical problem of using the measure
  2 The inappropriateness of the definition that gives rise to the measure

**[d]** Identify and explain one criticism for each of the two ways of measuring poverty mentioned in the items. [8 marks]

- Both these issues are discussed on pp. 45–6
- Select an appropriate point and apply to the measures in the item

- The question does not say that these have to be in current operation
- Make sure that you know what the term means (see p. 48)

**[e]** Examine social policies designed to prevent social exclusion. [20 marks]

- Different approaches to the problem are discussed on p. 53
- You must show how the policy will try to prevent the problem and how far it might be successful

- Use additional material to that contained in the items
- The plural tells you that you should examine more than one theory
- Any reference to this should recognize alternative definitions in the answer

**[f]** Using material from the items and elsewhere, assess sociological theories that argue that poverty is produced by structural inequality.
[20 marks]

- The link between inequality and poverty is explained on p. 45
- Structural theories adopt a relative view of poverty
- Examples of these theories: Field; conflict theories, pp. 51–2
- You can use individualistic and cultural theories (pp. 49–50) to show that structural theories do not explain every issue

# OCR-STYLE POVERTY AND SOCIAL EXCLUSION QUESTION

## A2 Synoptic Unit 2539: Social Inequality and Difference

**Answer all parts of this question**

Total: 90 marks
1 mark = 1 minute

Time allowed:
1 hour 30 minutes

### Item A

Percentages in poverty, by family type

| | % of group in poverty | | |
|---|---|---|---|
| | **1979** | **1995** | **1999** |
| Pensioner couples | 21% | 23% | 25% |
| Single pensioners | 12% | 32% | 37% |
| Couples with children | 8% | 23% | 24% |
| Single with children | 10% | 55% | 62% |
| Single without children | 7% | 23% | 22% |

### ITEM B

When Murray uses the term 'underclass' he is focusing on a certain type of poor person, defined not by his condition, e.g. long-term unemployed, but by his deplorable behaviour in response to that condition, e.g. unwilling to take the jobs that are available to him. Murray concludes that Britain has a growing population of working-aged healthy people who subscribe to a culture of welfare dependency, laziness and crime which is contaminating the life of entire neighbourhoods. Murray claims that these people are raising their children to see this way of life as normal.

## Comments on the question

- Do not go beyond the data in Item A
- There is no need to offer any explanations for these changes
- Make sure that you get the dates right
- Double-check any figures that you have used

**[a]** Using only the information in Item A, identify two main changes in the type of family in poverty in 1999 compared with 1979. [6 marks]

## Advice on preparing your answer

- To identify the 'main' changes, you should work out which two family groups were likely to experience poverty in 1979 and which two were likely to experience it in 1999
- Don't over-complicate the task

- No more, no less
- There is no need to offer an explanation for these characteristics
- There is no need to go beyond Item B for your answer

**[b]** Identify two characteristics of the underclass according to Item B.

[6 marks]

- Don't just compile a list. You must explain why what you have identified is a problem
- Scale means amount of poverty
- You must be clear in your understanding of this concept

**[c]** Identify and explain two problems in measuring the scale of poverty using relative definitions.

[12 marks]

- This is a synoptic question and you should use your knowledge and methodology to answer it
- Pages 45–7 may be useful in helping you to answer this question

- A synoptic instruction. As well as using material from this unit for this evidence, you should dip into two or three other areas that you have studied
- Describe the evidence only. There is no need to explain it

**[d]** Using your wider sociological knowledge, outline the evidence for the view that poverty has a significantly negative effect on the life-chances of individuals. [22 marks]

- Focus on data in the form of statistics or trends, and sociological studies of poverty and its effects
- You will find evidence in this resource, e.g.:
  1 Family poverty, p. 49
  2 The feminization of poverty, pp. 49
  3 Poverty and health, p. 64
  4 Education and poverty, pp. 156 and 158
- See p. 7 for a definition of this concept

- Describe the main features of the argument and its supporting evidence
- Examine specific evidence against the view, and describe alternative views if they are appropriate

**[e]** Outline and assess the view that the behaviour of an underclass is the main cause of poverty in the UK today. [44 marks]

- Item A may prove useful as an introduction
- Remember that you don't have to agree with the view
- See pp. 50–1 for an account of this view

## Specifications

| Specification | Specification details | | Coverage |
|---|---|---|---|
| **AQA** AS: Health | ■ Health, illness and disability as both social and biological constructs | | The section on defining health and illness (p. 61) is obviously relevant. Different theories (pp. 61–3) have things to say about the social construction of health and illness. Disability is covered on pp. 66–7. |
| | ■ Different explanations of the unequal social distribution of health and illness | | Health inequalities are discussed on pp. 64–6. |
| | ■ Different explanations of inequalities in the provision of, and access to, health care | | Different theories and models have something to say about these issues (pp. 61–6). |
| | ■ Different approaches to the study of mental health and illness | | Mental illness is covered on p. 67. |
| | ■ Different explanations of the role of medicine and the health professions | | Discussed in sections on models of health (pp. 63–4) and medicalization (p. 60). |
| **OCR** A2: Power and Control: Health | **The social nature of health and illness** | ■ The social construction of health and illness, mental health and disability. The importance of social reaction and labeling for identity. | The section on defining health and illness (p. 61) is obviously relevant. Different theories (pp. 61–3) have things to say about the social construction of health and illness. Disability is covered on p. 66–7 and mental illness on p. 67. |
| | | ■ Deviance, social control and the sick role. | The idea of the 'sick role' is associated with functionalism and this and alternative theories are discussed on pp. 61–3. The section on mental illness (p. 67) is also relevant. |
| | **Trends and patterns in health and illness** | ■ Problems of measuring health inequalities, including problems of measuring morbidity; health inequalities as a social artefact. | Covered on p. 64–5. |
| | | ■ Patterns, theories and explanations of health inequalities, according to social class, gender, ethnicity region and over time e.g. cultural, subcultural, social selection, social administration and structural explanations. | Health inequalities are discussed on pp. 64–6. |
| | **Medicine, power and control** | ■ The bio-mechanical model and the role of the medical professions: functionalist, Marxist, feminist, social action and postmodern critiques. | Discussed in sections on models of health (pp. 63–4). |
| | | ■ Medicine and the re-definition, control and regulation of the body, mind and sexuality (e.g. in relation to reproduction, abortion, mental illness). The ideological role of such definitions, with particular reference to gender and ethnicity. | Theories such as Marxism (pp. 61–2) and feminism (pp. 62–3) are relevant here, as is the section on medicalization (p. 63). Control and regulation of the mind is discussed in the section on mental illness (p. 67) and control and regulation of the body on p. 66. |

For more detailed specification guidance visit **www.haralambosholborn.com**

# DEFINING HEALTH AND ILLNESS

- The traditional **medical model** of health sees it as an **absence of disease**. Disease is present when the body diverges from **objective, scientific definitions** of the normal functioning of the human body. This approach uses a **negative definition** based upon the absence of problems to define good health.
- However, the **World Health Organization** uses a much broader definition, defining health as 'not merely an absence of disease, but a state of complete physical, mental spiritual and social well-being'. This approach uses a more **positive** definition which emphasizes the positive qualities which must be present for good health.
- Research into self-defined health amongst the population suggests that many people also use a **functional definition** of health which involves the ability to carry out normal, everyday activities.
- **Blaxter** (1983, 1990) found that different social groups defined health in different ways with younger males emphasizing the positive aspects of strength and fitness while younger females used a more functional definition.
- **Howlett** *et al.* (1992) found Asian ethnic groups favoured functional definitions of health while African-Caribbeans placed more emphasis on energy and strength.

# DISEASE AND ILLNESS

Evidence above suggests that the definition of health varies between social groups and is therefore **relative**. However, sociologists accept that there are objective medical conditions. Eisenberg (1977) distinguishes between:

- **Illness** – a physical state which is experienced as having an unpleasant impact, and,
- **Disease** – abnormal and harmful physical changes in the body.

Examples illustrate the relative nature of illness.

1 **Ackernecht** (1947) showed how a skin disease – **spirochetosis** – was so common amongst some indigenous South Americans that those without the disease were considered abnormal and the affected men were prohibited from marrying.
2 **L'Esperance** (1977) showed how nineteenth-century women could be defined as suffering from **hysteria** if they laughed or cried for 'no reason'. But it's not an actual disease; women were 'hysterical' if they tried to engage in non-traditional female roles outside the domestic sphere.
3 The history of the **NHS** in Britain suggests that as time has progressed people have come to expect higher standards of health and demanded treatment for a wider range of illnesses.

# THEORETICAL APPROACHES TO ILLNESS

## The functionalist perspective

**Talcott Parsons** (1951) argues that illness is socially defined in terms of the **sick role**. This is based upon two **rights** and two **obligations**.

- The rights are:
  1 The right to be exempted from normal **social obligations** such as work.
  2 The right to be absolved from **blame** – it is not their fault they are ill.
- The obligations are:
  1 The obligation to try to get **well**.
  2 The obligation to seek **medical help** for a condition.

The sick role is a type of **deviance** which can disrupt the smooth functioning of society. However, because of the obligations involved, it is likely to be a temporary state with the normal functioning of the individual and society being resumed as soon as possible.

There are a number of **criticisms** of this approach.

1 It is only useful for looking at **acute illness** and not **chronic illness** which have no short-term cure (e.g. asthma or diabetes) – however, Parsons argued that with chronic illness people are expected to manage their illness so that they can carry on with normal social roles.
2 **Friedson** (1970) argues that there are alternative roles to the sick role described by Parsons. Where a person is not expected to get better and faces death people are given unconditional access to the sick role. Where the illness is **stigmatized** (e.g. sexually transmitted diseases) the sickness is seen as being illegitimate: it is the person's fault and they are not given the rights associated with the sick role.
3 Many people who are ill do not consult doctors, and **Scambler** *et al.* (1981) show that people are more likely to consult friends and relatives about illness than doctors.
4 **Bryan Turner** (1995) argues that Parsons ignores the fact that medical consultations may be **a site of conflict** between the different interests of doctors and patients.
5 **Waitzkin** (1971) supports Parsons' general theory but argues that the sick role can be used to allow some **deviance** which avoids greater conflict which can seriously harm society. During the Vietnam War many better-educated men were able to avoid conscription to the US army which reduced political opposition to the war from higher classes.

## The political economy perspective

This approach is influenced by **Marxism**, and argues that medicine serves the interests of the powerful.

**Navarro** (1986) sees medicine as benefiting **capitalism**.

1 It maintains a workforce that is healthy enough to work to help capitalists make profits, and defines illness as an inability to do this.
2 It has an **ideological function** of masking differences in health caused by inequality as it portrays illness as the result of bad luck or irresponsible behaviour. According to **Doyal and Pennell** (1979) much ill health is the result of capitalism, e.g. it is caused by tobacco companies, pollution and work-related accidents and diseases.

3 To Navarro, **biomedical explanations** of illness predominate and emphasize the use of advanced drugs and technology. This produces large profits for capitalist drug and medical companies, disguises the real causes of illness in inequality, and exploitation and is much less effective than tackling the social causes of illness.

**Ellen Annandale** (1998) points out how highly profitable breast implants have continued to be used despite well-documented negative effects on health.

There are **criticisms** of the political economy approach.

1 **Hart** (1985) points out that capitalist societies have experienced large rises in **life expectancy**.
2 Hart argues that the criticisms of health care are more applicable to the USA than to some European countries that have free healthcare and strong laws to restrict the harmful activities of companies and protect workers.

**Navarro** accepts that there have been some health gains under capitalism, but argues that the gap in health between rich and poor has increased.

## POSTMODERN APPROACHES TO HEALTH

**Michael Bury** (1997) argues that improvements in health have led to the expectation of long and healthy lives in which people can plan their future. However, this is threatened by **chronic illness**. In a study of those diagnosed as suffering from rheumatoid arthritis he found that the diagnosis threatened people's identity causing a **biographical disruption** and leading them to review their lives. It also disrupted relationships with others because of the likelihood of increased dependence on others. The greater people's **physical, economic and relationship resources** the more they can retain a positive self-image.

**Gareth Williams** (1984) argues that over time the biographical disruption can be overcome with a **narrative reconstruction** which makes sense of how and why they got the disease, often blaming it on negative social experiences. This helps to repair the disruption and can 'realign present and past, self and society'.

**Carricaburu and Pierret** (1995) **criticize** the postmodern approach arguing that the response to disease reflects membership of particular **social groups** rather than individual biography. In a study of HIV-positive men, the gay men experienced a process of disruption more than the heterosexual men, as the diagnosis reinforced the gay men's perception of themselves as ill.

Similarly **Pound et al.** (1998) found that working-class men in the East End of London experienced strokes as just another crisis in their difficult lives and not as a biographical disruption.

## INTERACTIONIST PERSPECTIVES ON HEALTH AND ILLNESS

**Symbolic interactionists** tend to see illness as a form of socially defined deviance rather than as a disease.

**Tesh** (1988) studied **RSI** (Repetitive Strain Injury) amongst typists. He found that views on whether it constituted a disease varied.

1 **Employers** denied that it is a disease, blaming it on bad posture.
2 **Psychiatrists** argued that it is a psychological problem resulting from dislike of the work.
3 **Unions** claimed it is a common and serious real disease.

**Scambler** (1981) studied 79 women aged 16-44 and found that only one in 18 women who experienced symptoms of illness visited a doctor. **Freund and McGuire** (1991) use the phrase the **illness iceberg** to indicate that there is much more illness than is reported to doctors.

**Becker et al.** (1977) developed the health belief model to explain what influenced people to visit the doctor and to follow the advice provided by the doctor. They found that social factors are as important as medical factors. **Interaction** between the individual, doctors and others, and their perceptions of health and illness and the medical profession shape the process of consultation and treatment.

Interactionism has been **criticized** by **Day and Day** (1977) for ignoring socials factors such as inequality, pollution and stress which may cause ill-health.

## FEMINIST APPROACHES TO HEALTH

### 1 *Liberal feminism*

Liberal feminism explains inequalities in health between males and females in terms of the different **social roles** and **economic positions** of men and women. Liberal feminists have tended to see the medical professions as dominated by men who occupy most of the senior positions.

**Ellen Annandale** (1998) argues that from a radical feminist perspective, liberal feminism can be **criticized** for wrongly believing that minor changes can challenge **patriarchal domination of medicine**. They also see liberal feminism as wanting women to overcome the 'handicaps' of the female body and emotionality and therefore of wanting women to take on the worst features of being masculine.

### 2 *Socialist feminism*

Socialist feminists believe **capitalist patriarchal** society must be fundamentally changed to achieve equality between the sexes.

To **Lesley Doyal** (1995) capitalism defines female health in terms of the ability to **reproduce** the next generation of workers and being able to undertake **domestic tasks** and act as a **reserve army of labour**.

Doyal sees women's health as undermined by the **dual burden** of doing **paid work** as well as most of the **housework**. Women do more **caring** than men, suffer from physical and emotional damage from **sexual** abuse, and risk cervical cancer through sexual activity. They suffer more stress than men and can become dependent on prescribed drugs and tobacco to cope, harming their health in the long term.

In these ways health care **reproduces** the class, gender and ethnic **hierarchies** of patriarchal capitalism.

### 3 Radical feminism

Radical feminists argue that *all* women are exploited in a **patriarchal** society.

**Ehrenreich and English** (1978) believe **medicine** is used to **control women**. In the nineteenth century it was believed that women were naturally more frail than men and they needed to save their energy for reproduction. This justified the **exclusion** of women from a range of activities including higher education and sport.

**Graham and Oakley** (1986) argue that the **frames of reference** of male doctors see **pregnancy** as an entirely **medical** and potentially problematic event whereas women see it as a normal part of their lives and in terms of their social relationships. Doctors control pregnant women by putting women in a position of **passivity** (e.g. lying down to be examined) and by demanding information from them. Doctors reaffirm their superior status by using medical terminology and denying women information which might give them more control over the management of their pregnancy.

Radical feminism has been **criticized** for **essentialism** – seeing all women as essentially the same and ignoring differences between groups of women.

## MODELS OF HEALTH

### Traditional medicine

**Foster and Anderson** (1978) distinguish two types of traditional medicine.

1 **Personalistic systems** see sick people as the victims of a spirit wishing them harm although they often accept that accidents or disease can cause illness as well.
2 **Naturalistic systems** sees illness as a result of an individual lacking harmony with themselves. In ancient Greece illness was thought to be the result of an imbalance between four **humours**: black bile, yellow bile, blood and phlegm. Traditional Chinese medicine is based on reconciling the balance between **yin** (negative elements like cold and damp) and **yang** (positive elements like warmth and light).

### The biomedical model

This became the dominant model from the early nineteenth century. It has four key elements.

1 **Mind-body dualism** sees social factors as irrelevant in explaining illness which is seen as being a product of a malfunctioning of part of the body.
2 **Specific aetiology** looks for precise causes of illness such as bacteria and viruses.

3 The **mechanical metaphor** sees the body in terms of the role of each body part in the overall functioning of the organism, and categorizes diseases. Illnesses are diagnosed through symptoms which indicate the malfunctioning of part of the body and treated by trying to return particular body parts to normal functioning. Individual systems are emphasized rather than the totality.
4 Medicine is seen as an **objective science** using established scientific methods.

The biomedical model dominates contemporary health care to the exclusion of alternative models. However it has been criticized by sociologists.

- **Thomas McKeown** (1979) argues that improvements in health in England and Wales from the early eighteenth century were very largely the result of improved **nutrition and hygiene**. Developments in medicine such as the introduction of immunization and improved medical techniques have played a much smaller part in rising life expectancy.
- Most people do not see their own health exclusively in terms of the biomedical model. For example, a study by **Blaxter** (1983) found that working-class women understood that factors such as **stress, poverty and poor environment** were important as specific biological causes of illness.

### Medicalization

Some critics of the biomedical model and the medical profession believe that medicine involves **social control** by extending what counts as illness.

- **Ivan Illich** (1976) argues that the medical profession actually harms people in a process known as **iatrogenesis**, where there is an increase in illness and social problems as a result of medical intervention.
  1 **Clinical iatrogenesis** involves serious side-effects of medical intervention which are often worse than the condition they were used to treat.
  2 **Social iatrogenesis** does harm by creating a passive and docile population who become reliant on the medical profession which prescribes drugs to help them cope with their life in society
  3 **Structural iatrogenesis** refers to the way that the medical profession reduces the ability of the population to face sickness, pain and death. These things are normal parts of life and ageing but people become unable to cope with them because of the claims and activities of medicine.
- **Marxists** such as **Navarro** (1980) link **medicalization** to the operation of an **oppressive capitalist system**. Medicine disguises the underlying causes of disease such as class inequality and poverty. Instead people see health as an individual problem.
- **Ehrenreich and English** (1978) believe that **women's bodies** have been **medicalized**. Menstruation and pregnancy have come to be seen as medical problems requiring intervention such as hysterectomies.
- **Conrad and Schneider** (1980) show how even **gambling** has been defined as an illness by the medical profession.

## PROFESSIONS AND POWER IN MEDICINE

This section concerns the status and power of doctors in society.

- **Millerson** (1964) follows the functionalist view of the profession in seeing professions as having certain traits which justify their high rewards and power in society. These traits are:
  1 The possession of **theoretical knowledge**.
  2 Having undergone a **specialized education**.
  3 Passing **examinations** in order to practise.
  4 Having an independent **professional body** which regulates behaviour.
  5 Being subject to a professional **code of behaviour**
  6 Serving the **public good** rather than personal interests.

**Critics** of the functionalist approach such as **Turner** (1995), argue that this view is an simply an **idealized image** of doctors which is promoted by the profession and it ignores the way in which professional bodies manipulate clients to obtain high rewards.

- **Eliot Friedson** (1970) puts forward a **Weberian** perspective. He argues that doctors obtain high rewards by using **social closure**. Entry to the profession is restricted by the professional body which limits the supply of qualified doctors to push up wages. The profession regulates itself, excludes other health care professionals from doing their work and justifies its wages by promoting the view that they are serving the **public good**.

- **Jamous and Peloille** (1970, and discussed in Turner 1995) argues that the medical profession maintains its position by ensuring **social distance** between itself and its clients. Prestige is maintained by mystifying the knowledge possessed by the professionals. Jamus and Peloille refer to this as the **indeterminacy/technicality ratio**.

- **Turner** (1995) argues that doctors dominate other medical professionals by using **indeterminacy**, as well as the following processes.
  1 **Subordination** involves forcing other professionals (such as midwives and occupational therapists) to carry out tasks delegated to them by doctors.
  2 **Occupational limitation** limits the range of activities other professionals are allowed to carry out.
  3 **Exclusion** prevents competing occupations from medical practice, e.g. homeopaths.

- From a **feminist** point of view, **Anne Witz** (1992) points out that most **subordinate** or excluded health care providers ((e.g. nurses or homeopaths) are **women**. This is because men use a **gendered exclusionary strategy** which blocks entry to the profession for women and a **gendered demarcatory** strategy to confine women to subordinate roles in health care.

Men established the medical specialism of obstetrics in order to gain control of the female midwifery profession. However, midwives **resisted** the domination of obstetricians and managed to retain control over 'normal' births.

- Increasingly in recent years the power of doctors has been challenged in the following ways.
  1 **Haug** (1973) believes that **de-professionalization** has taken place as a better-educated population makes it own choices, for example preferring herbal remedies to convectional medicine.
  2 **McKinlay and Arches** (1985) believe that **proletarianization** has taken place in the medical profession as the work of doctors in the NHS has become tightly controlled and regulated.
  3 **Carpenter** (1993) believes that other medical professions (such as nursing) have tried to **professionalize** themselves and increase their power in relation to doctors. For example, nurses are now allowed to prescribe a limited range of drugs.

## INEQUALITIES IN HEALTH

Health inequalities can be measured in different ways.

1 **Mortality rates** are the number of people dying over a period per 100,000 of the population.
2 **Standardized mortality rates** measure the relative chances of dying compared to the average mortality rate amongst 16-65 year olds which is represented by a figure of 100.
3 **Morbidity rates** measure rates of illness and disease.

### Studies of health inequality

- **The Black Report** (1980) was the first major British study of social class and morbidity and mortality rates. It found that higher social classes tended to show lower rates of mortality and morbidity.
- **The Acheson Report** (1998) showed continuing class inequality and a widening of class inequalities in health when comparing the highest and lowest classes.
  1 In the 1970s the **mortality rate** amongst men of working age in the lowest class was twice that of those in the highest class. By the 1990s it had increased to three times this level.
  2 The **life expectancy** of those in the highest class increased by two years between 1970 and 2000, compared to an increase of 1.4 years in the lowest class.
  3 Professional workers are much less likely than unskilled workers to suffer from a **limited longstanding illness** and the inequality in this regard has been increasing.
- **Shaw et al.** (1999) found that there were considerable **geographical differences** in mortality even when gender and class factors had been taken into account.

### Explanations for health inequalities

The following explanations have been used to explain class inequalities.

1 The **artefact explanation** suggests that the apparent rise in health inequality is misleading. **Illsley** (1986, 1987) argues that the emphasis on the relative decline in the health of the lowest class (class V) is misleading, because this class is small and shrinking in size. However, the

Acheson Report (1998) showed that health inequality was growing even when the top two classes (I and II) were compared with the bottom two classes (IV and V).

Other researchers have questioned whether the **Registrar General's Scale**, the class scheme on which these statistics are based, is a valid and reliable way of recording social class.

**Peter Saunders** (1993) argues that **consumption groups** have more influence on health inequality than on class, with those who own cars and homes enjoying better health than those who do not own these things.

2 The **direction of the relationship** between poor health and social class has been questioned. **Illsley** (1987) argues that those with poor health are more likely to be in lower social classes because they are less able to obtain and retain higher-class jobs than others as a result of their health problems.

However **Shaw et al.** (1999) suggest that the social and economic problems faced by lower classes *create* the health problems, rather than the other way round.

3 **Cultural explanations** suggest that the lifestyle of lower classes is more unhealthy than that of higher classes and this accounts for health inequalities.

Examples of **unhealthy cultural practices**, which are more common in the working class, include higher rates of smoking, greater consumption of fatty foods and lower consumption of fruit and vegetables. All these differences can lead to higher rates of cancer and heart disease.

This approach tends to blame lower classes for choosing an unhealthy lifestyle and suggests that **improved education** will solve the problems.

**Critics** of this explanation argue that risky behaviours cannot be seen as foolish lifestyle choices but are **rational responses** to class situation. **Graham** (1993) and **Graham and Blackburn** (1998) see smoking as a way in which working-class mothers try to cope with very stressful lives.

**Keith Patterson** (1981) argues that cultural explanations ignore the **underlying structure of society**. For example, poverty makes it difficult for lower classes to afford healthy foods, and capitalists promote unhealthy food through advertising in order to boost their profits.

4 **Materialist explanations** explain health inequality in terms of the **structure of society**. They see cultural differences which may be linked to poor health as shaped by inequalities in society. A range of arguments and studies support this approach:
- Manual workers suffer more **accidents at work** than non-manual workers.
- **Martin et al.** (1987) show a link between poor **housing and respiratory disease**.
- **Lobstein** (1995) found that healthy **diets** tend to be expensive and healthy food is more expensive in poor areas than in affluent areas.
- The **American Multiple Risk Factor** Intervention Trial (1996) showed that death rates were consider-

ably higher for lower social classes even when factors such as smoking, blood pressure and cholesterol levels were taken into account.
- **Doyal and Pennell** (1979) claim that the **capitalist desire for profits** explains health inequalities as it creates risks for workers and advertises and sells unhealthy products to consumers.

Materialist explanations have been refined by Shaw et al. (1999) who explain inequality in terms of the accumulation of disadvantages at crucial points in the **life course**, such as poor nutrition in childhood and job loss in adulthood.

5 **Putnam** (1995) argues that **social capital**, particularly **networks** of contacts, are important in understanding life chances.

**Wilkinson** (1996) accepts that the health of a population improves once a certain level of Gross Domestic Product is reached (around $5,000 per head). At this level an **epidemiological transition** improves mortality and morbidity rates. However, beyond this level, **income inequality** is far more important, with better health in countries with less income inequality. This is because countries with high levels of income inequality have greater **social divisions** and a **culture of inequality** in which there is less **trust** and **sense of community** and people develop less social capital.

**Scambler** (2002) **criticizes** Wilkinson for failing to spell out how a lack of social trust leads to ill health.

## Gender inequalities and health

Evidence from **self-report studies** suggests that women have higher rates of illness and restricted activity than men and suffer more depression. However, they tend to live longer than men. These patterns have been explained in a number of ways.

1 The **artefact explanation** suggests that women do not really suffer more ill-health, but are just more likely than men to perceive themselves as being ill. However, **MacIntyre** (1993) found that men are more likely than women to exaggerate their symptoms.
2 **Genetic explanations** may account for part of the difference in health between men and women. For example, **Waldron** (1983) suggests women have more resistance to heart disease.
3 **Social factors** are seen as most important by sociologists. These include:
- **Risk** – A higher death rate amongst 17-24 year old males than amongst females of the same age may be due to the greater willingness of males to engage in risky behaviour. **Lyng** (1990) suggests that male roles in society encourage them to engage in more edgework or risky behaviour.
- **Social deprivation** – **Miller and Glendinning** (1989) argue that lower wages and higher rates of poverty explain why women suffer more ill-health.
- **Female roles** – **Graham** (1984) argues that women spend less money on themselves than other family

members when allocating family budgets because of their **caring role** in society. **Popay and Bartley** (1989) argue that domestic labour can adversely affect women's health due to long hours and poor conditions.

## 'RACE' AND HEALTH

**Pearson** (1991) argues that there are inconsistencies in the way ethnic groups are defined, so date is unreliable. However there is clear evidence of some differences e.g. ethnic minorities of Indian, Pakistani or Bangladeshi origin have high rates of heart disease and those of Caribbean origin have high rates of stroke.

- **Nettleton** (1995) suggests that **genetic factors** play a part.
- **Cultural factors** have been suggested as differences, e.g. lack of vitamin D causing rickets amongst Asian ethnic minorities. However, **Ahmad** (1993) suggests that cultural explanations tend to ignore positive aspects of culture such as low rates of smoking and alcohol consumption amongst British Asians.
- **Material factors** – such as poorer housing, employment in hazardous occupations, higher rates of unemployment and lower wages – may account for some ethnic minority health disadvantages. In a study of Asian women in northern England, **Nettleton** (1993) found that the women felt their health was affected by isolation, the fear of racist attack and poor housing.

## THE BODY

### The body and late modernity

**Anthony Giddens** (1991) argues that in **late modernity** (see p. 218) the body is a crucial source of identity.

- People express themselves by **altering their bodies**, e.g. tattoos, piercing or cosmetic surgery.
- People have a sense of being able to see their bodies from the outside – **reflective mobilization**.
- An increased sense of **choice** creates uncertainty over how people want their bodies to be – the manufactured **uncertainty of everyday life**.
- Media images of 'perfect' bodies lead people to use drugs or diets which might affect health.
- There is also increased **choice in sexuality**.

According to **Featherstone** (1991) the body has become the focal point of a new emphasis on **consumption** and what **Turner** refers to as the **play ethic** which has largely replaced the **work ethic**.

### Foucault – The birth of the clinic

To **Foucault** (1971) peoples' beliefs about social reality are created by their actions and the way they talk about particular issues. He refers to this sense of reality as **discourse**.

- He describes discourses concerning health and illness as the **clinical gaze (le regard)**.
- In the late eighteenth century, new types of clinic in France introduced a new approach to medicine involving **clinical observation** and **physical examination**, particularly using the stethoscope.
- New classification systems for diseases developed that saw patients in terms of their bodies rather than as whole people. These developments were part of wider social and political changes in which there was increased **surveillance** of people's activities to establish greater state control over mass populations.
- Classifications in medicine helped to establish the distinction between the **normal** and the **deviant/ pathological**.
- These distinctions were **internalized** by the population who learned to control their own behaviour.
- In contemporary society this is reflected in people's willingness to monitor their own health.

**Armstrong** (1983) argues that in the twentieth century the **clinical gaze** was extended with dispensaries and the development of social science techniques to map the incidence of disease, and by the development of new specialisms, such as geriatrics and paediatrics.

## DISABILITY

**Vic Finkelstein** (1980) sees disability as a product of **capitalist society**.

Before industrial capitalism the disabled were simply part of the destitute population.

However, this group was not needed for machine-based factory work and they became a segregated and isolated group separated in **institutions**.

In the twentieth century there was a shift away from disability being seen as an **abnormality** to it being seen as a **sickness** which can be partially cured so people can return to employment.

**Oliver** (1990) argues that the **personal tragedy ideology** underpins the way disability is regarded.

Disability is seen as a personal tragedy that ruins peoples lives, rather than as a **social problem**. The alternative **social model of disability** sees the problems of the disabled as resulting from the failure of society to accommodate the needs of disabled people, rather than from the inherent problems caused by the disability.

From this viewpoint, **people with impairments** are **disabled** by the **prejudice of society**.

### Illness, blame and stigma

Some sociologists stress that illness is often seen as a **moral issue** rather than as a purely physical one.

**Helman** (1986) notes how patients often see 'colds' and 'chills' as the fault of their own carelessness whereas 'fever' and 'flu' are not seen as their own fault.

Within a **narrative of risk** people may be blamed for lung cancer because it is associated with smoking or AIDS because it is associated with sexual activity which may seen as irresponsible or immoral.

Erving Goffman (1968) showed how people with physical deformities suffered **stigma**.

- **Discrediting stigma** are clearly visible.
- **Discreditable stigma** are not as visible and people may try to hide them with **impression management**.

**Scambler and Hopkins** (1986) studied epileptics and how they tried to deal with their illness. They distinguished:

1 **Enacted stigma** – in which people suffered discrimination, and,
2 **Felt stigma** – in which people feared discrimination or had feelings of **shame**. People found ways of dealing with felt stigma such as **selective concealment** of their condition, **covering up** their condition completely, **medicalizing** their behaviour or **condemning the condemners** by challenging the attitudes of others through political movements.

**Hall** *et al.* (1993) studied the stigma of mental illness and found that significant minorities of the population wanted to avoid contact with the mentally ill.

**Philo** *et al.* (1996) found that 66% of all images of the mentally ill in the Scottish media were negative.

## MENTAL ILLNESS

1 Labelling theory
  - **Thomas Scheff** (1966) argues that there is no such thing as mental illness, it is simply a **label** applied to **deviant behaviour** which other people cannot understand.
  - People are **socialized** into **stereotypical views** on mental illness which is reinforced by the media.
  - **Erving Goffman** (1968) argues that the label of mental illness is used when it is in the interests of the **powerful** to use it. Once somebody is labelled mentally ill they are treated differently, reinforcing their behaviour. In *Asylums* (1968) Goffman found that people were often admitted to mental hospitals as involuntary patients when there was little evidence that they were suffering significant problems.
  - **Rosenhan** (1973) conducted research where several researchers were admitted to mental hospitals when they asked for voluntary admission as schizophrenics, even though they had no symptoms of **schizophrenia**. Their subsequent behaviour was often interpreted as evidence of schizophrenia and the staff paid little attention to what the patients said.
  - However, **Walter Gove** (1982) criticizes labelling theories of mental illness for **dismissing real and serious** mental problems as simply labels and for ignoring the fact that most medical staff are supportive and sympathetic.
  - **Miles** (1981), another critic of labelling theory, found that the label of mental illness tends only to be used as a last resort.

2 Foucault
  - **Foucault** (1971) argues that the concept of **madness** derived from an eighteenth-century emphasis on **rational and disciplined action**.
  - The emphasis on rationality led to undisciplined, irrational behaviour being defined as madness within the **dominant discourse of medicine**.
  - Mad people were seen as a **threat to the new rationality** and were separated from the rest of society in institutions where lepers were previously isolated from mainstream society.

3 Structural theories
  - **Structural explanations** of mental illness accept that mental illness exists but see it as resulting from structural factors such as **inequality**.
  - **Brown and Harris** (1978, 1989) found that depression amongst London women was caused by **stressful life events** and vulnerability factors (such as the lack of strong social networks). Working-class women were much more likely to suffer stressful life events than middle-class women because they had fewer material resources.
  - **Roger Gomm** (1996) has found that poorer people suffer more mental illness than people who are better off.

4 Gender and mental illness
  - **Women** are more likely than men to be diagnosed with mental illness, and six times more likely to be diagnosed with **depression**.
  - Such figures may reflect women's greater likelihood of seeking medical help.
  - However, **Brown** (1995) found that feelings of **entrapment and humiliation** are linked to depression, and these are linked to the roles of women, especially working-class women, in contemporary societies.
  - **Williams and Watson** (1996) adopt a **feminist perspective** blaming many of women's psychological problems on physical or **sexual abuse by men**.

5 Ethnicity and mental illness
  - In survey research, **Nazroo** (1997) found that British **African-Caribbeans** are more likely to receive treatment for **depression** than other ethnic groups are, and that people of **South Asian** origin have low rates of treatment for **depression**.
  - **Fernando** (2002) believes that such figures result from **cultural bias** in psychiatry which stem from a lack of understanding of cultural differences between ethnic groups.
  - Many argue that high rates of **deprivation** and the **experience of racism** explain higher rates of mental illness in some ethnic groups.
  - However, **Pilgrim and Rogers** (1999) suggest that deprivation and discrimination cannot explain the much higher rates of diagnosed mental illness amongst African-Caribbeans than amongst South Asians in Britain, as both groups suffer these problems.

## TEST YOUR KNOWLEDGE AND UNDERSTANDING

**1 Which of the following is a functional definition of an ill person?**
a A person who lacks physical and spiritual health
b A person who is not fit and strong
c A person who cannot carry out their normal social roles as a result of health problems.
c A person whose body is pathologically diseased

**2 Which of these is not part of the sick role according to Parsons?**
a The opportunity to miss work legitimately
b The right not to be blamed for being sick
c The obligation to seek medical help
d The chance to obtain sympathy from others

**3 The political economy approach is closest to:**
a A Marxist perspective
b A Weberian perspective
c A feminist perspective
d An interactionist perspective

**4 Which of the following examples would not support the political economy approach?**
a The use of patents by drug companies to ensure they can charge high prices for drugs
b The rising life expectancy in some capitalist countries
c The continuation of breast implant surgery despite the dangers
d The large numbers of accidents that take place at work

**5 According to Ivan Illich social iatrogenesis involves:**
a The reduced ability of the population to come to terms with illness and death
b The harm which results from a passive and docile population who rely on the medical profession
c The side-effects of medical intervention
d The increasing power of the medical profession

**6 A biographical disruption can best be defined as:**
a A medical diagnosis which forces a life review
b Death
c The inconvenience caused by a stay in hospital
d An acute physical illness

**7 Which of the following is an example of an interactionist study of health?**
a The Black Report
b Michael Bury's study of the effects of being diagnosed with a chronic illness
c Graham and Oakley's study of pregnancy
d Becker's study of visits to the doctor

**8 Which of the following best describes a socialist feminist view of health?**
a They see health care in Britain as patriarchal and as completely dominated by men
b They see health care in Britain as necessary for the smooth running of society
c They see health care in Britain as serving the needs of capitalists and men
d They see health care in Britain as reflecting gender roles

**9 Which of these is not an aspect of the biomedical model?**
a An emphasis upon environmental factors in causing illness
b Seeing the mind and body as separate entities
c Seeking specific causes for illnesses
d Using the mechanical metaphor

**10 Thomas McKeown believes that improvements in health in Britain since the early 18th century have largely been caused by:**
a Immunization
b Improvements in surgery
c Improvements in nutrition and hygiene
d Better diagnosis of illness

**11 The indeterminancy/technicality ratio refers to:**
a The exclusion of people who are not trained from practicing medicine
b The use of technical jargon to exclude women from medicine
c The use of technical jargon to mystify medicine
d The degree of choice that doctors have about the way that they practise medicine

**12 According to which of the following do consumption groups have more influence on health inequalities than class?**
a Lobstein
b Doyal and Pennell
c Anne Witz
d Peter Saunders

**13 Shaw *et al.* see class inequalities in health as being due to:**
a The way the statistics are calculated
b Differences in the possession of social capital
c An accumulation of disadvantages during a person's life
d Genetic differences between the classes

**14 According to Goffman discreditable stigma are:**
a Types of disability
b Physical deformities which may be hidden
c Infectious illnesses
d Easily visible deformities

**15 The view that the problems of disabled people results from society's unwillingness to accommodate their needs is called the:**
a Personal tragedy of disability
b The impediment theory of disability
c The labelling theory of disability
d The social model of disability

## DEVELOP YOUR ANALYSIS AND EVALUATION SKILLS

### 'Illness can be defined as a malfunctioning of the body'. Discuss.

**Background:** This quote puts forward a position that sociologists of health and illness would strongly disagree with. It describes the biomedical model, which tries to use an objective and scientific approach based around the ideas of mind–body dualism, specific aetiology and the mechanical metaphor. It can be contrasted with broader definitions, such as that of the World Health Organization, and attacked using evidence of the relative nature of illness. Parsons idea of the sick role, the political economy perspective, interactionism and feminist approaches all suggest that the definition of illness is influenced by society.

| For | Against |
|---|---|
| ■ Biomedical model (p. 63) | ■ Evidence of relative definitions (p. 63)<br>■ Parsons (p. 61)<br>■ Political economy perspective (pp. 61–2)<br>■ Interactionism (p. 62)<br>■ Feminism (pp. 62–3) |

**Top tip:** Foucault's work on discourse (pp. 66–7) is also useful for suggesting how social influences shape the definition of illness.

### Discuss the view that patriarchal capitalism causes ill-health.

**Background:** This view is strongly opposed to biomedical views of health and illness and combines the views of feminist and the political economy approach to health and illness. Writers from the political economy perspective agree that capitalism is a major cause of ill-health, while feminists agree that patriarchy is a major factor. However only socialist feminists would agree entirely with the view in the question. The biomedical model does not see social factors as important, and the social constructionist approach of interactionists sees illness more in terms of definitions produced during interaction. McKeown is best known for criticising the biomedical model, but his work also suggests the way that improvements within capitalism have reduced illness.

| For | Against |
|---|---|
| ■ Socialist feminism (pp. 62–3)<br>■ Radical feminism (partly) (p. 63)<br>■ Liberal feminism (partly) (p. 62)<br>■ Political economy approach (pp. 61–2) | ■ Biomedical model (p. 63)<br>■ Interactionism (p. 62)<br>■ McKeown (p. 63) |

**Top tip:** The question might suggest that there are class inequalities in health caused by capitalism (pp. 61–2), and gender inequalities in health caused by patriarchy (pp. 62–3), but it ignores ethnic inequalities, which may be caused by racism (p. 66).

### Discuss the view that the main function of medicine is social control.

**Background:** This view is supported by a range of radical writers who see medicine as part of an oppressive, capitalist system, a prop to patriarchy, and as doing more harm than good. Both Foucault and Illich, in different ways, see medicine as involved in social control. On the other hand, functionalist approaches see medicine and the professions as serving the interests of society, and Weberians tend to see medical practitioners as simply serving their own interests.

| For | Against |
|---|---|
| ■ The political economy approach (pp. 61–2)<br>■ Feminist approaches (pp. 62–3)<br>■ Illich (p. 63)<br>■ Foucault (p. 67) | ■ Parsons (p. 61)<br>■ Millerson (p. 64)<br>■ Weberian approaches (p. 64)<br>■ Arguments that doctors are losing power (p. 64)<br>■ Biomedical model (p. 63) |

**Top tip:** Labelling theories of mental illness (p. 67) are worth discussing as another possible example of medicine being used to control the population.

## AQA-STYLE HEALTH QUESTION

### AS Unit 1

**Answer all parts of this question**

Total : 60 marks

1 mark = 1.25 minutes

Time allowed: 1 hour and 15 minutes

### Item A

Health is a problematic concept. We all think we know what we mean when we say we are ill – but is health merely an absence of illness?

Illness itself is problematic: is it chronic or acute? Management of illness may vary upon type. Then there is the preventative versus curative argument. All these topics might influence policy decisions.

### Item B

In a recent survey of GP consultations interesting differences in health service use between different types of men were discovered. After age-standardising, 118 per 1,000 single men had consulted a GP in the last two weeks, compared with 128 per 1,000 married and cohabiting men and 156 per 1,000 separated, widowed and divorced men. There does seem to be some relationship between men's marital status and the state of their health. Irrespective of their (generally younger) age, single men seem to be healthier than men who have been married at some point; and of those who do get married, there is some evidence that those who remain married are healthier than those who, for whatever reason, do not.

There are also differences in GP consultation rates between minority ethnic groups; 22% of Bangladeshi men, 17% of Indian men and 16% of Black Caribbean men had consulted a GP in the two weeks prior to interview. Men in the Chinese, Irish and other minority ethnic groups had consultation rates similar to the figure for all men of 12%.

**Comments on question**

- This should be short, only two marks here

**[a]** Give a brief definition of health other than that in Item A. [2 marks]

**Advice on preparing your answer**

- Check the definition in Item A; make sure yours is different

- This is just asking for suggestions, keep it short

**[b]** Suggest two ways in which the treatment of illness might vary.

[4 marks]

- Item A contains types of illness and treatment, use these

- This asks for two elements, identification and a brief description
- Make sure you consider three different ways, no more, no less

**[c]** Identify and briefly describe three ways which might help prevent ill-health. [6 marks]

- This is a knowledge-based answer so little help from the Items directly

- Again there are two strands, do both
- Be careful, this asks for criticisms of the theory, do not waste time describing the theory, this will get no marks at all

**[d]** Identify and briefly describe two criticisms of labelling theory as an explanation of mental illness. [8 marks]

- Make sure you know what labelling theory is
- Check how it is applied to mental illness

- Examine here suggests knowledge, with a hint of evaluation, 14 of the marks are for knowledge
- Concentrate on ethnicity, though class and gender should also make a brief appearance
- Make sure you look at both health and illness

**[e]** Examine the ways in which ethnicity affects health and illness in modern Britain. [20 marks]

- There are a few pointers to men and ethnicity in Item B, but you need more information:
  - Rates of hospital admission
  - Mortality rates
  - Morbidity rates
  - Don't forget sex differences
  - Don't forget class differences
  - Spend most time on ethnicity but recognize that it is a complex concept

- Note the word assess: you need to look at several explanations (plural in the question) and evaluate them
- This question is specifically about use of health services
- The previous question was about health and illness, you need to be using different material here
- This is an AO2 question, only 6 marks for knowledge, 14 marks for analysis and evaluation

**[f]** Assess sociological explanations for the gender imbalance in the use of health services.
[20 marks]

- What is the gender imbalance?
  - Is it a true imbalance if you age-standardize?
  - Does class affect the gender imbalance?
  - What theories are there about this imbalance – feminist, Marxist, functionalist?
  - Is it a problem of statistics?
  - What evidence is there for any of the above theories?
  - What conclusion can you draw from the material you have used?

## OCR–STYLE HEALTH QUESTION

### A2 Unit 2536: Power and Control

Total: 60 marks
Time allowed: 60 minutes

**Comments on the question**

■ Make sure that you describe the view in detail with supporting evidence
■ Look at a range of arguments for and against the view
■ Try to give a balanced response (although in this question there is far more evidence to support the view than refute it – explain why this is).

[a] Outline and assess the view that health and illness are socially constructed. [60 marks]

**Advice on preparing your answer**

■ Spend ten minutes planning your response
■ Write an introduction that sets the scene, i.e. define 'socially constructed' and say why a debate has arisen about this.
■ See pp. 61–3 for views on the social construction of health
■ Criticisms are offered on p. 61
■ Finish with an evaluative conclusion based on the evidence – attempt to minimise personal bias.

# Chapter 6

# CRIME AND DEVIANCE

Textbook pp. 330–403

Specifications

| Specification | Specification details | Coverage |
|---|---|---|
| **AQA** A2: Crime and Deviance | ■ Different explanations of crime, deviance, social order and social control | Explanations are covered throughout the chapter. The only exception is the section on crime and official statistics on pp. 76–7. |
| | ■ The relationship between deviance, power and social control | Issues of power and control are dealt with in the section on the functionalist perspective (pp. 74–5). The final two sections on gender and ethnicity are also relevant (pp. 83–7). |
| | ■ Different explanations of the social distribution of crime and deviance by age, social class, ethnicity, gender and locality | Most of the sections on explanations of deviance suggest reasons why poorer people may be more likely to commit crime. The section on criminal statistics covers the issue of white-collar crime. There are specific sections on ethnicity and gender (pp. 83–7). |
| | ■ The social construction of, and societal reactions to, crime and deviance, including the role of the mass media | The introductory section explains how deviance is socially constructed (p. 74). Interactionist and neo-Marxist perspectives are also important (pp. 77–8 and 80). |
| | ■ The sociological issues arising from the study of suicide | The sociology of suicide is covered in the context of sociological methods in chapter 15 (pp. 197–8). |
| **OCR** A2: Power and Control/Crime and Deviance | ■ Defining crime and deviance, their social construction and relativity | The introductory section explains how deviance is socially constructed (p. 74). The interactionist perspective is particularly relevant here (pp. 77–9). |
| | ■ Social reactions to crime and deviance and their consequences, including the role of the mass media | Functionalist (pp. 74–5), interactionist (pp. 77–9), Marxist (p. 79) and neo-Marxist (p. 80–2) perspectives are of particular importance on this issue. |
| | ■ Measuring crime and the fear of crime; criminal statistics, self report and victim surveys | Covered in the section on crime and official statistics (pp. 76–7). |
| | ■ Patterns of crime and victimization by social profile; social class, ethnicity, gender, age and region | Most of the sections on explanations of deviance suggest reasons why poorer people may be more likely to commit crime. The section on criminal statistics covers the issue of white-collar crime. There are specific sections on ethnicity and gender and crime (pp. 83–7). |
| | ■ Theories and explanations of crime and deviance, e.g. structuralist, interactionist, feminist and realist approaches | Explanations are covered throughout the chapter. The only exception is the section on crime and official statistics on pp. 76–7. |
| | ■ Agents of social control and the role of law, the police, the criminal justice system, penal systems, the mass media and the state, criminalization and control | The role of agents of social control is referred to through much of the chapter. Of particular importance are the sections on key theories such as functionalism (pp. 74–5), interactionism (pp. 77–9), Marxism and neo-Marxism (pp. 79–82) and left and right realism (pp. 80–3). |
| | ■ Solutions to the problem of crime, the relationship between sociology and social policy | Left and right realism (pp. 80–3) both have something to say about solutions to crime. The section on marketization and globalization (p. 83) is also important. |

**Parts of other modules covered**

| OCR AS: Culture and socialization/Youth and culture | Youth and deviance | ■ Delinquency; the patterns and trends of delinquency according to social profile, for example class, gender and ethnicity. <br> ■ Gangs: territory, values, rituals and sanctions. <br> ■ Theories of delinquent subcultures, e.g. functionalist, Marxist and feminist accounts. | The work of Cicourel (p. 79) relates to the issue of social class and delinquency. See Alexander on the 'Asian gang' in chapter 3 (p. 38). Subcultural theories of deviance are discussed on p. 75. |

# INTRODUCTION

At its simplest, **deviance** is behaviour that does not follow the norms and expectations of a particular social group. There are three possible responses to deviance:

■ Deviance may be **positively sanctioned** (rewarded). For example, physicists who break the rules of their discipline and develop a new theory may be rewarded with a Nobel Prize.
■ Deviance may be **negatively sanctioned** (punished). For example, murderers deviate from the value society places on human life. Their behaviour generally results in widespread disapproval and punishment.
■ Deviance may be simply accepted without reward or punishment. For example, people with an obsession for collecting clocks are neither rewarded nor punished by others although they may be seen as a 'bit odd'.

# THE SOCIOLOGICAL STUDY OF DEVIANCE

In practice the sociological study of deviance is limited to deviance that results in negative sanctions. The most obvious forms of deviance are therefore:

■ **Crime**: activities that break the law and are subject to official punishment.
■ **Delinquency**: anti-social or criminal acts committed by young people.
■ Sociologists who study crime are often referred to as **criminologists**.

# DEVIANCE: A FUNCTIONALIST PERSPECTIVE

## The functions of deviance

A functionalist analysis of deviance looks for the source of deviance in the nature of society rather than in the biological or psychological nature of the individual. Although functionalists agree that social control mechanisms such as the police and the courts are necessary to keep deviance in check, many argue that a certain amount of deviance can contribute to the well-being of society.

**Durkheim** (1895) believed that:

■ Crime is an 'integral part of all healthy societies'. This is because individuals are exposed to different influences and will not all be committed to the shared values and beliefs of society.
■ Crime can be functional. All societies need to progress and all social change begins with some form of deviance. In order for change to occur, yesterday's deviance must become tomorrow's normality. Nelson **Mandela**, once imprisoned as a 'terrorist', eventually became president of South Africa.

■ Societies need both crime and punishment. Without punishment the crime rate would reach a point where it became **dysfunctional**.

Durkheim's views have been developed by A. **Cohen** (1966) who discussed two possible functions of deviance:

■ Deviance can be a **'safety valve'**, providing a relatively harmless expression of discontent. For example, prostitution enables men to escape from family life without undermining family stability.
■ Deviant acts can warn society that an aspect is not working properly – for example, widespread truanting from school.

## Merton – social structure and anomie

Robert K. **Merton** (1938) explains how deviance can result from the culture and structure of society. He begins from the functionalist position of **value consensus** – that is, all members of society share the same values. In the USA, members of society strive for the goal of success, largely measured in terms of wealth and material possessions. The means of reaching this goal are through talent, ambition and effort. Unfortunately, Merton argues, little importance is given to the means of achieving success. The result is an **unbalanced society** where winning is all and the 'rules' are not very important. This situation of 'normlessness' is known as **anomie**. Individuals may respond in different ways:

■ **Conformity** – The most common response is conformity. Conformists strive for success through the accepted channels.
■ **Innovation** – People from lower classes may have few qualifications and turn to crime to achieve material success.
■ **Ritualism** – Some people, particularly from the lower middle classes, may abandon the ultimate goal of wealth but continue to conform to the standards of middle-class respectability.
■ **Retreatism** – Retreatists are 'drop-outs' who have rejected both the shared value of success and the means provided to achieve it.
■ **Rebellion** – Rebels reject both goals and means but replace them with different ones. They wish to create an entirely new kind of society.

### Evaluation of Merton

1 **Taylor** criticizes Merton for failing to consider wider power relations in society – that is, who actually makes the laws and who benefits from them.
2 Merton assumes that there is a value consensus in American society and that people only deviate because of structural strain in society.
3 Merton's theory exaggerates working-class crime.
4 **Taylor**, **Walton** and **Young** (1973) argue that the theory cannot account for politically motivated crime where

people break the law because of commitment to a cause.

5 Merton has been defended by **Reiner** (1984) who believes that Merton's theory can be adapted to take into account most of these criticisms.

6 Merton's theory can be applied to some contemporary trends in crime. For example, **Savelsberg** (1995) argues that Merton's strain theory can help to explain the rapid rises in the crime rate in many post-Communist countries. Poland, for example, had its first free elections in 1989. Between 1989 and 1990 the official crime rate increased by 69%.

## STRUCTURAL AND SUBCULTURAL THEORIES OF DEVIANCE

**Structural theories** of deviance explain the origins of deviance in terms of the position of the individual in society. **Subcultural theories** of deviance explain deviance in terms of the subculture of a particular social group. Certain groups develop norms and values which are different from those held by other members of society.

### Cohen: the delinquent subculture

Albert **Cohen's** work (1955) modified Merton's position and combined both structural and subcultural theories of deviance. Cohen criticizes two aspects of Merton's theory of working class deviance:

1 Cohen argues that deviance is a **collective** rather than an individual response.
2 He also believes that Merton ignored **non-utilitarian crimes**. These are crimes that have no financial reward, such as vandalism and joy-riding.

Lower-working-class boys want success but cannot achieve their goals because cultural deprivation leads to educational failure and dead-end jobs. They suffer from status frustration and turn to criminal paths to achieve success. An alternative set of norms and values is adopted – a delinquent subculture – which reverses mainstream culture by valuing activities such as stealing, vandalism and truancy.

### Evaluation of Cohen

Box (1981) argues that Cohen's theory only applies to a minority of delinquents. The rest accept mainstream standards of success but resent being seen as failures and turn against those who they feel look down on them.

### Cloward and Ohlin – Delinquency and Opportunity

Richard A. **Cloward** and Lloyd E. **Ohlin** (1962) accept Merton's explanation of deviance in terms of the legitimate opportunity structure, but they argue that he failed to consider the **illegitimate opportunity structure**. Just as the opportunity to succeed by legitimate means varies, so does the opportunity to succeed by illegitimate means. For example, in one area there

may be a thriving criminal subculture, while in another area this subculture may not exist. Thus, in the first area, the adolescent has more opportunity to become a successful criminal.

Like Merton, Cloward and Ohlin believe that there is greater pressure on the working classes to deviate because they have less opportunity to succeed by legitimate means. They identified three possible responses to this situation:

1 **Criminal subcultures** emerge in areas of established organized crime where young people are exposed to deviant values and role models. In this situation young people have the opportunity to rise within the established criminal hierarchy.
2 **Conflict subcultures** develop in areas where there is little access to either legitimate or illegitimate opportunity structures. The response to this situation is often gang violence, which serves as a release from anger and frustration and as a means of achieving prestige in terms of the values of the subculture.
3 **Retreatist subcultures** are organized mainly around illegal drug use and occur because members have failed to succeed in both legitimate and illegitimate opportunity structures.

### Evaluation of Cloward and Ohlin

**Taylor, Walton and Young** (1973) criticize Merton, Cohen, and Cloward and Ohlin for assuming that everybody is committed to the success goal of achieving wealth. They point out that there are other possible goals and that some groups, such as 'hippies', make a conscious choice to reject conventional goals.

The marketization of capitalist societies has made these theories increasingly relevant. Nigel **South** (1997) believes that the British drug trade is largely based around 'disorganized' crime, which can be compared to Cloward and Ohlin's conflict subcultures, although some of it is based around professional criminal organizations and more closely resembles a criminal subculture. Many of the drug users themselves are part of a retreatist subculture.

## THE UNDERCLASS AND CRIME

### Murray – welfare, culture and criminality

Some sociologists have suggested that an **underclass** now exists which does not share the same values as other members of society. Charles **Murray** (1989) believes that the underclass is responsible for a large proportion of crime, and he blames welfare benefits which have made it possible for young women to become single parents and for young men to reject the idea that it is important to hold down a job.

### Inequality, the underclass and crime

Other sociologists reject Murray's '**New Right**' views but still believe that an underclass exists. **Taylor** (1997) argues that young, unskilled working-class males have been affected by increasing inequality and declining job prospects. Underclass criminal activity is the result of material deprivation rather than an unacceptable culture.

### Evaluation of underclass theories of crime

Many sociologists have questioned the idea that there is a distinctive underclass culture.

Most criticisms refer to the views of Charles Murray:

1 **Tham** (1998) compared welfare policies and crime rates in Britain and Sweden. During the 1980s and 1990s he found that crime increased more rapidly in Britain than in Sweden which had a more generous welfare state. He claims that crime rates are closely linked to levels of inequality.
2 **Mooney** (1998) argues that there is no link between single parenthood and criminality. Her research indicates that single parents are more likely to become the victims of crime than to become criminals themselves.

## CRIME AND OFFICIAL STATISTICS

Many theories of crime are based on the **official statistics** provided by government organizations such as the police and the courts. This information is often taken as an accurate measure of the total amount of crime. The data allows comparisons to be made between crimes, and with previous years. These statistics tend to show two main **trends**:

1 Some social groups appear to be more involved in crime than others. They are:
   ■ The working class
   ■ The young
   ■ Males
   ■ Some ethnic minorities
   These groups appear to be more likely to commit crimes than the middle class, the elderly, females and whites. Sociologists such as Merton and Miller have taken these statistics at face value and gone on to explain why these groups appear to commit a disproportionate amount of crime.
2 Crime rates in Britain remained low until the 1950s but have increased rapidly since then, although there was some decline in the mid-1990s. In recent years the vast majority of offences have been property offences. Often the release of crime figures receives widespread publicity and leads to concern that the country is experiencing a 'crime wave'.

**Maguire** (2002) points out that the official crime figures do not include all crimes. Many crimes are dealt with by other agencies such as the British Transport Police. These include tax evasion and benefits fraud.

### Unrecorded crime

Not all the crimes that take place are recorded by the police. For a crime to be recorded at least three things must happen:

1 Somebody must be aware that a crime has taken place.
2 That crime must be reported.
3 The police or other agency must accept that a law has been broken.

Some crimes, such as tax evasion, do not have an obvious victim, and it is these that are least likely to be reported. However, attempts have been made to estimate the amount of crime which victims are aware of but which is not reported to the police or not recorded as a crime by them.

### Victimization studies

In 1983 the Home Office published the first **British Crime Survey**. Since 2000 this survey takes place annually and represents an attempt to overcome the limitations of official crime statistics. Instead of relying on police records, it uses **victimization studies**. These involve asking individuals if they have been the victim of crime in the previous year, whether they reported the crimes and whether the police recorded them. These surveys reveal that the criminal statistics are highly unreliable.

Some of the key **findings** of the 2002 British Crime Survey are outlined below:

■ Less than half of all crimes are reported to the police. Reporting varies enormously according to the crime – 94% of vehicle thefts were reported, compared to just 33.1% of acts of vandalism and 25.7% of common assaults.
■ Most crimes are not reported because they are thought to be **too trivial** or it is felt that the police cannot do anything about them. Only a tiny minority were frightened of reprisals or of the police themselves.
■ Around 40% of all incidents reported to the police were not recorded as crimes. This was because the police judged the incident as too trivial, did not believe that it had taken place, felt that there was insufficient evidence to proceed, or the victim did not want them to pursue the matter.
■ In terms of trends in the overall crime rate, figures from the British Crime Surveys are broadly in line with the official police figures, with the overall crime rate beginning to fall in the mid 1990s.

Data from the British Crime Surveys are still not entirely reliable. **Croall** (1998) identifies four main problems:

1 Crimes can only be reported if victims are aware of them.
2 The results are limited by respondents' memory and their definition of events.
3 The survey is restricted to households so does not cover crimes committed against businesses or organizations.
4 The sample does not include people under 16.

So the findings of the British Crime Survey should be treated with caution. However, they are probably more reliable than the official statistics because they include so many crimes that are not reported.

## The characteristics of offenders – self-report studies

**Self-report studies** attempt to discover the characteristics of criminals. They use questionnaires or interviews and ask individuals to admit to the number and types of crime they have committed. The data can then be compared with official conviction rates to discover which types of offender are most likely to be convicted.

- Using data from 40 self-report studies from different countries, **Box (1981)** rejected the impression created by official statistics that working-class youths are more likely to engage in delinquency than middle-class youths.
- A more recent study by **Graham and Bowling (1995)** found that social class had no influence on whether young British males and females would admit to having committed offences, although the lower classes were more likely to admit to more serious offences.

### Evaluation of self-report studies

1 Individuals may wish to conceal their criminal acts. However, it is estimated that around 80% of those who reply do tell the truth.
2 It is likely that self-report studies identify more offenders than the official statistics.

## Bias in official statistics

Self-report studies indicate that there may be **police bias** against working-class delinquents. Support for this view is provided by **Chambliss**'s study (1973) of two American delinquent gangs:

1 The working-class **'roughnecks'** were viewed with suspicion and each of them was arrested at least once.
2 The middle-class **'saints'** were never arrested, although they carried out more serious delinquent acts than the 'roughnecks'.

Chambliss claims that the police do not take middle-class delinquency seriously – such activities are often dismissed as 'harmless pranks'.

## WHITE-COLLAR CRIME

Edwin **Sutherland** (1960) was the first sociologist to study 'white-collar crime'. He defines it as 'crimes committed by persons of high social status and respectability in the course of their occupations'.

David **Nelken** (2002) questions Sutherland's definition. White-collar crimes may be committed outside the course of occupations and some crime may be the responsibility of organizations or corporations (often called corporate crime) rather than individuals.

There are various types of white-collar crime.

- **Fraud and corruption** – One common type of fraud is **insider dealing**, in which shares in a company are bought by individuals who know that the company is about to be the subject of a takeover bid. Robert Maxwell was the owner of Mirror Group newspapers before his mysterious drowning in 1991. Maxwell had used money from the pension fund of Mirror Group employees to stave off the collapse of his business empire.
- **Personal harm** – According to **Streeter** (1997), in the late 1990s the effects of asbestos were killing 3,500 people per year. The actions which resulted in these deaths may not have been illegal but their consequences in terms of loss of life were extremely serious.
- **Politicians and officials** – Jonathan Aitken, a member of the last Conservative government, was found to have accepted hospitality at the Paris Ritz from Mohammed Al Fayed in return for asking questions in Parliament. He was later imprisoned for trying to cover this up.

A number of factors combine to reduce the apparent **extent** and seriousness of white-collar crime:

- White-collar crimes are difficult to detect as many do not have obvious 'victims'.
- In cases of bribery and corruption all those involved will benefit, so nobody is likely to report the offence.
- In cases where the victim is the public at large (such as misrepresentation in advertising) few members of the public have the expertise to realize that they are being misled, and government agencies do not have the resources to follow up more than a few cases.

Even if they are detected, few white-collar crimes lead to prosecutions. The power and influence of many of those involved mean that a **'blind eye'** is often turned or an 'official warning' given. Cases of professional misconduct are usually dealt with by the relevant professional association which may simply hand out a reprimand.

Official statistics probably significantly underestimate the extent of white-collar and corporate crime. As a result, crime is viewed as predominantly working-class behaviour.

## DEVIANCE – AN INTERACTIONIST PERSPECTIVE

Most of the theories considered up to this point have looked at the factors that supposedly direct the behaviour of deviants. This emphasis on the idea that deviants simply react to external forces is similar to a positivist position. **Interactionists** take a different approach. They examine:

- How and why particular individuals and groups are defined as deviant.
- The effects of such a definition on their future actions.

### Becker – labelling theory

#### The definition of deviance

Howard S. **Becker** (1963) suggests that there is really no such thing as a deviant act. An act only becomes deviant when others perceive it as such. He gives the example of a brawl involving young people:

- In a low-income neighbourhood this may be defined by the police as delinquency.

■ In a wealthy neighbourhood it may be defined as youthful high spirits.

The acts are the same but the meaning given to them is different. If youngsters are defined as delinquent and convicted, then they have become deviant. In other words they have been **labelled** as deviants.

### Possible effects of labelling

Once an individual or group is labelled as criminal, mentally ill or homosexual, others see them only in terms of that label. It becomes what Becker calls a **master status**. Labelling also causes the labelled group or individual to see themselves in terms of the label. This may produce a **self-fulfilling prophecy** in which the label actually makes itself become true.

Becker identifies a number of stages in this process:

1 The individual is labelled as deviant and may be rejected from many social groups.
2 This may encourage further deviance. A drug addict may turn to crime because employers refuse to give him/her a job.
3 Ex-convicts find it difficult to get jobs and may be forced to return to crime.
4 The **deviant career** is completed when individuals join an organized deviant group, thus confirming and accepting their deviant identity.
5 Now a **deviant subculture** may develop which includes norms and values which support their deviant behaviour.

### Young – labelling and marijuana users

Becker's approach is used by Jock **Young** (1971) in his study of 'hippie' marijuana users in London.

1 The police see hippies as dirty, lazy drug addicts.
2 Police action against marijuana users unites them and makes them feel different.
3 As a result they retreat into small groups.
4 **Deviant norms and values** develop in these closed groups. Hair is grown longer, clothes become more unconventional and drug use becomes a central activity.

Thus a **self-fulfilling prophecy** is created.

### Lemert – societal reaction – the 'cause' of deviance

Edwin M. **Lemert** (1972) distinguishes between **'primary' and 'secondary' deviance**.

Primary deviance consists of deviant acts before they are publicly labelled. Trying to find the causes of primary deviance is not very helpful because:

■ Samples of deviants are inevitably based only on those who have been labelled, and they are therefore unrepresentative.
■ Most deviant acts are so common that they are, in statistical terms, normal. Most males may at some time commit a homosexual act, engage in delinquency and so on.

The important factor in creating 'deviance' is the reaction of society – the public identification of the deviant. Secondary deviance is the response of the individual to that societal reaction.

### Labelling theory and social policy

Stephen **Jones** (2001) identifies two main policy implications of labelling theory:

1 As many types of behaviour as possible should be **decriminalized**. For example, in some countries, such as the Netherlands, cannabis has been effectively legalized.
2 When the law has to intervene, it should avoid giving people a **self-concept** in which they view themselves as criminals. For example, warnings and cautions could be used to deal with delinquents rather than placing them in institutions.

However, these policies became less popular during the 1990s. Recently the emphasis has been on the **'naming and shaming'** of offenders such as paedophiles and kerb-crawlers.

### Evaluation of the interactionist approach

Labelling theory enjoyed great popularity in the 1960s but provoked strong criticism in the 1970s. The key criticisms are as follows:

1 **Taylor, Walton and Young** (1973) argue that labelling theory is wrong in suggesting that deviance is created by the social groups who define acts as deviant. Some acts – such as premeditated killing for personal gain – will always be regarded as deviant in our society.
2 Many sociologists claim that the interactionist approach fails to explain why individuals commit deviant acts in the first place (primary deviance).
3 It is claimed that labelling theory is too **deterministic**. It assumes that, once a person has been labelled, their deviance will automatically increase. **Ackers** (1975) suggests that individuals might simply choose to be deviant, regardless of whether they have been labelled.
4 The interactionist approach fails to explain why some people are labelled rather than others and why some activities are against the law and others are not. It ignores the wider issue of the **distribution of power** in society.

Interactionists such as **Plummer** (1979) have strongly defended labelling theory against these criticisms. It is certainly true that the interactionist approach has had a significant influence on the sociology of deviance, particularly more recent approaches such as new left realism (see pp. 80–2).

## DEVIANCE – A PHENOMENOLOGICAL PERSPECTIVE

The phenomenological approach is similar to labelling theory as it concentrates on the process of labelling in enforcing the law. However, phenomenology focuses purely on the way in which some individuals and groups come to be labelled as deviant.

## Defining delinquency

Aaron **Cicourel** (1976) applies a phenomenological approach to understanding the treatment of delinquency in two Californian cities.

- The police use stereotypes of the 'typical delinquent' when selecting who to stop and question. They are more likely to stop juveniles in 'bad', low-income areas of town with high crime rates.
- Once arrested, the juvenile is more likely to be charged if they fit the picture of the 'typical delinquent': broken home, 'bad' attitude to authority, low-income background, ethnic minority etc.
- Middle-class juveniles were less likely to be charged with an offence. They were seen as 'ill' or temporarily straying form the correct path with a real chance of reform. Their parents were better able to present them as respectable and reasonable.
- Cicourel concludes that delinquents are produced by the agencies of social control.

## TRADITIONAL MARXIST PERSPECTIVES ON DEVIANCE

### Who makes the law? Who benefits?

- From a **Marxist perspective**, laws are made by the state which represents the interests of the ruling class.
- **Snider** (1993) notes that the capitalist state is often reluctant to pass laws that threaten the profitability of large businesses. Often the state has worked hard to attract large corporations and does not want to risk alienating them.
- **Pearce** (1976) argues that many laws which appear to benefit only the working class, in reality benefit the ruling class as well. Factory legislation protecting the health and safety of workers benefits capitalists by keeping workers fit for work and loyal to their employers.
- **Chambliss** (1976) suggests that much of what takes place in the creation of rules is '**non-decision making**'. Many issues – such as the way wealth is distributed – never reach the point of decision.

### Who breaks the law? Who gets caught?

- Marxists argue that crime is widespread in all parts of society. There are many examples of illegal behaviour by white-collar criminals and corporations (see p. 77).
- **Snider** (1993) argues that many of the most serious deviant acts in modern societies are **corporate crimes**. She claims that corporate crime costs more in terms of loss of money and life than crimes such as burglary and robbery.

### Why break the law? Why enforce the law?

Many Marxists see crime as a natural 'outgrowth' of capitalist society.

- **Chambliss** (1976) argues that the greed, self-interest and hostility generated by capitalist society motivate crimes at all levels within society. Members of all classes use whatever opportunities they have to commit crime.
- Given the nature of capitalist societies, crime is rational. **Gordon** (1976) argues that in a society where competition is the order of the day, individuals must fend for themselves in order to survive.

Gordon goes on to suggest that law enforcement in the USA supports the capitalist system in three main ways:

1 Individuals who commit crimes are defined as 'social failures' and seen as responsible for their actions. In this way blame and condemnation are directed at the individual rather than the capitalist system.
2 The imprisonment of selected members of the working class neutralizes opposition to the system. For example, American blacks are heavily over-represented amongst those arrested for street crimes such as robbery and aggravated assault.
3 Defining criminals as 'animals and misfits' provides a justification for their imprisonment. This keeps them hidden from public view and so the embarrassing extremes produced by the capitalist system are swept under the carpet.

### Evaluation of conventional Marxism

Marxist theories have come in for some heavy criticism:

1 **Feminists** have argued that Marxist theories ignore the importance of patriarchy in influencing the criminal justice system. Marxists have also been accused of neglecting the importance of racism in the enforcement of the law.
2 Crime has not been eradicated in **communist societies** based on Marxist principles.
3 Stephen **Jones** (2001) points out that capitalism does not always produce high crime rates. For example, in Switzerland the crime rate is very low.
4 Perhaps the distribution of power is not as simple as some Marxists suggest. Jones gives the example of insider trading (taking advantage of 'insider' knowledge to make huge profits on the stock exchange). This is illegal, which suggests that capitalists do not always get the laws they want.
5 '**Left realists**' (see pp. 80–2) believe that Marxists put too much emphasis on corporate crime. Other crimes, such as burglary, cause greater harm than Marxists imply. Their victims are usually working-class and the consequences can be devastating for them.
6 **Postmodern criminology** rejects Marxist criminology as being neither believable nor defensible (see p. 87).

Despite these criticisms, Marxism has been an influence on a number of critical perspectives on deviance. Some have drawn their inspiration from Marxism and can be referred to as neo-Marxist approaches. Others owe less to Marxism and are better defined as radical approaches.

## DEVIANCE – NEO-MARXIST AND RADICAL PERSPECTIVES

**Neo-Marxist** approaches to deviance are strongly influenced by Marxism but do not accept that there is a straightforward link between the structure of capitalist society and deviance.

### Taylor, Walton and Young – The New Criminology

In 1973, **Taylor, Walton and Young** published *The New Criminology*. This influential book criticized many existing theories of crime. The authors accept some key assumptions of Marxism but adopt a more liberal and tolerant view, influenced by labelling theory.

They outline what they call a **'fully social theory of deviance'**. The criminologist must consider the following aspects of deviance:

1 The way in which **wealth and power** are distributed.
2 The circumstances surrounding the **decision** of an individual to commit an act of deviance.
3 The **meaning** of the deviant act for the person involved. Was the individual 'kicking back' at society through an act of vandalism, for example?
4 The ways in which other members of society, such as the police, **respond** to the deviant act.
5 The reaction needs to be examined in terms of **the way in which society is organized**. Who has the power to make rules and decide how deviant acts should be dealt with?
6 The impact of the deviant label. This may have a variety of effects – the deviant may accept the label as justified, or they may ignore the label, or it may lead to greater deviance (see pp. 77–8).
7 Finally, criminologists need to look at the **relationship** between all these different aspects so that they can be fused into one complete theory of deviance.

### Evaluation of *The New Criminology*

*The New Criminology* has been criticized in a number of ways:

1 Feminists have criticized its concentration on male crimes.
2 Some 'new left realist' criminologists have accused it of neglecting the impact of crime on victims and romanticizing working-class criminals (see pp. 80–2).

In 1998, Paul **Walton** and Jock **Young** re-evaluated their earlier work. They accept some of the criticisms but argue that recent approaches such as 'realist criminology, feminist criminology and postmodern criminology are all committed to creating a more equitable and just society'. In that respect they are a continuation of the traditions of *The New Criminology*.

## LEFT REALISM

**Left realists** see their position as close to the British Labour party. Most left realists describe themselves as socialists and argue for reform of society rather than revolution. Left realism has developed since the 1980s and is particularly associated with **Jock Young**.

### The problem of crime

Left realists take the view that crime is a real problem which must be taken seriously, and they present a number of criticisms of previous criminology:

■ Some sociologists have tried to explain the huge rise in street crime since the Second World War by pointing to the unreliable nature of criminal statistics. Young (1993) argues that the rises have been so great that they cannot simply be explained by changes in reporting and recording.
■ Some sociologists have advanced the view that the chances of being a victim of street crime are minimal. However, **Lea and Young** (1984) point out that, while this is true, particular groups face high risks. These groups are the poor and deprived, ethnic minorities and inner-city residents. Those with low incomes also suffer more if they are robbed or burgled.
■ Left realists have carried out a number of **victimization studies** and found widespread fear of crime. Many people, particularly women, altered their behaviour to avoid becoming victims of crime.
■ **Lea and Young** attack the idea that offenders can sometimes be seen as promoting justice. They attack the image of the criminal presented in parts of *The New Criminology* as a type of modern-day Robin Hood.
■ While accepting that white-collar and corporate crime are commonplace and serious, left realists argue that recent criminology has concentrated too much on such crimes.
■ Left realists have acknowledged the importance of **under-reported and under-recorded crimes** such as sexual assaults and harassment, racially motivated attacks and domestic violence. They claim to take all crimes equally seriously.

### The explanation of crime

**Lea and Young** base their attempt to explain crime around three key concepts: relative deprivation, subculture and marginalization.

1 **Relative deprivation** – Deprivation will only lead to crime where it is experienced as relative deprivation. A group experiences relative deprivation when it feels deprived relative to similar groups or when its expectations are not met. In modern societies advertisers stress the importance of economic success and promote middle-class lifestyles and patterns of consumption. Rather like Merton (see p. 74), Lea and Young argue that rising crime is partly the result of rising expectations of high standards of living, combined with restricted opportunities to achieve this.

**2 Subculture** – Groups develop lifestyles to cope with the problem of relative deprivation, and subcultures can form as a result. However, these vary. Second-generation West Indian immigrants' subcultural solutions include the Rastafarian and Pentecostal religions as well as 'hustling' for money and street crime.

**3 Marginalization** – Marginal groups are those that lack organizations to represent their interests in political life. These groups tend to use violence and rioting as forms of political action. The key to avoiding marginality is employment, as workers have clearly defined objectives, such as higher wages. Young, unemployed West Indians do not have clearly defined aims or pressure groups to represent them. They feel a general sense of resentment which can lead to them taking to the streets and rioting.

## Dealing with crime

### Policing problems

**Kinsey, Lea and Young** (1984) argue that there are a number of flaws in policing:

- The **clear-up rate** is very low so the police are unable to deter criminals.
- The police spend little time actually investigating crime.
- The police rely on a flow of information from the public, but public confidence in the police is declining, particularly in inner-city areas and among members of ethnic minorities.
- Without the support of the public, the police have to resort to what the authors call **military policing** – stopping and searching large numbers of people or using **surveillance technology**. As a result, those who are not directly involved with the police come to see them as an alien force intent on criminalizing local residents – a process known as the **mobilization of bystanders**.

### Improving policing

Kinsey, Lea and Young argue that the key to police success lies in improving relationships with the community. To achieve this they recommend that:

- The public should have much more say in shaping police policy.
- The police should spend as much time as possible actually investigating crime.
- **Young** (1992) believes that certain areas are **over-policed** and others **under-policed**. In the former category are minor drug offences and under-age drinking. In the latter are racially motivated attacks, corporate crime, pollution and domestic abuse.

### Tackling the social causes of crime

**Young** (1992, 1997) does not believe that crime can be dealt with simply by improving the efficiency of the police. Left realists see the problem of crime as rooted in **social inequalities**. Young suggests:

- Improving leisure facilities for the young
- Reducing income inequalities

- Raising the living standards of poorer families
- Reducing unemployment and creating jobs with prospects
- Providing community facilities which enhance a sense of belonging

### The square of crime

Left realists believe that crime can only be understood in terms of the relationship between the four elements in the diagram below.

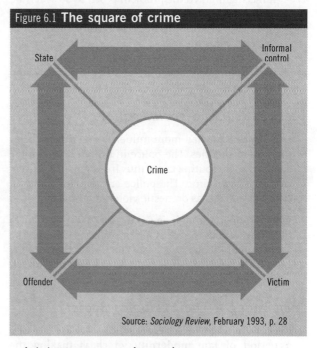

Figure 6.1 **The square of crime**

Source: *Sociology Review*, February 1993, p. 28

It is important to understand:

1 Why people offend
2 What makes the victims vulnerable
3 The factors that affect public attitudes and responses to crime
4 The social forces that influence the police

### Evaluation of left realism

Left realism has been criticized in a number of ways:

- **Hughes** (1991) argues that it fails to explain the causes of street crime. Left realists have not gathered empirical data about offenders' motives.
- Hughes also attacks left realism for its reliance on subcultural theory which has been heavily criticized (see p. 75).
- **Jones** (1998) argues that left realism fails to explain why some people who experience relative deprivation turn to crime while others do not.
- Jones also identifies flaws in the emphasis on victims. Left realists take victims' accounts of fear of crime at face value and never ask victims for their views about the causes of crime. They also only take into account the views of victims in urban areas where crime rates are high, thus giving a misleading impression of how harmful crime is.

- **Ruggiero** (1992) argues that left realists have neglected corporate and organized crime and that this type of crime cannot really be understood within the framework of their theory.
- However, **Hughes** also points out some strengths of left realism:
  - It has revived useful concepts such as relative deprivation.
  - It has promoted debate and theoretical development within sociology.
  - It has highlighted the problem posed by street crime for weaker members of society.
  - It has explored the position of victims much more than previous theories.
  - It avoids the worst excesses of both right- and left-wing approaches by neither glorifying nor attacking the police.

### Left realism and social policy

Left realism has had more influence on crime policies than other theories. The police in Britain now employ civilians to do routine tasks, thus freeing police officers to investigate crime. The police are also beginning to take crimes such as domestic violence seriously.

Labour's slogan 'Tough on Crime, Tough on the Causes of Crime' echoes the ideas of left realists. However, the reduction of inequality – a key factor underlying crime rates for left realists – has not been addressed as much as they would have liked.

### Jock Young – The Exclusive Society

Recently **Young** (1998) has argued that we are entering a period of **late modernity** which is making the problem of crime worse in a number of ways:

- Late modernity is characterized by great **uncertainty and instability** in areas such as family life and work, which make people feel less secure and stable.
- There is **less consensus about moral values**. Instead an increasing variety of subcultures claim that their values are legitimate.
- In the world of leisure there is an emphasis on **immediacy and personal pleasure**. People expect to be able to buy the consumer goods of their choice and to have lots of fun. At the same time there are fewer secure jobs and there is rising inequality. In these circumstances increasing numbers of people are likely to experience marginalization and relative deprivation.
- **Informal social controls** are becoming less effective as families and communities disintegrate.

A major reason for rising crime rates is the problem of **relative deprivation** (see p. 80). There are a number of reasons why this is significant.

1 Inequality has increased in recent years.
2 Marketization (see p. 83) places great emphasis on individual material success.

3 High levels of **cultural inclusion** (such as access to glamorous TV shows and advertising of designer brands) are combined with **social and economic exclusion**.
4 Many people feel they are not properly rewarded for their efforts at work.
5 The middle classes feel discontented because of their long working hours and they sense that other groups are now becoming part of the mainstream without necessarily making the sacrifices they have.
6 Everybody's feelings of relative deprivation are made worse because of the proximity of different social groups. For example, the excluded carry out much routine work for the middle classes such as working in shops and restaurants.

### Crime in the exclusive society

- **Crime becomes more widespread** – It is no longer confined to a deviant minority.
- **Crime becomes nastier** – There is an increase in hate crime such as racially motivated attacks.
- **The consensus of what constitutes crime breaks down** – For example, the boundaries of acceptable violence are disputed as in the debate about the smacking of children.

### Crime and social policy

Young believes that the Labour government's attempts to reduce crime by forcing truants to go to school and unemployed youth to work, and clamping down on anti-social behaviour, will not be a success because these policies are trying to recreate a 'golden age' of community with stable families and close communities. This does not exist any more. Young believes that a sense of relative deprivation will only be reduced if rewards in society are seen to be distributed more fairly. This would mean dealing with inherited wealth, discrimination on the grounds of race, sex and so on.

## RIGHT REALIST CRIMINOLOGY

### Wilson – Thinking About Crime

- James Q. **Wilson** (1975) denies that trying to get rid of poverty will lead to reductions in crime. This policy failed in the USA in the 1960s, and many poor people (for example, those who are elderly or sick) do not commit crimes.
- Wilson concentrates on street crime, which he believes the general public are most concerned about.
- He sees crime as the result of **rational calculation**. People will commit crime if the likely benefits exceed the likely costs. In reality the chances of getting caught for a particular crime are quite small. If offenders do not believe they are going to get caught, or if punishments take place long after offences, then even severe punishments will not deter people.
- **Strong communities** are an effective way of dealing with crime. People who are disgraced by their involvement in crime will lose their standing in the community. The problem is that crime itself undermines communities.

- Wilson and Kelling (1982) believe that it is crucial to try to maintain the character of neighbourhoods and prevent them from deteriorating. The role of the police is to clamp down on the first signs of undesirable behaviour. They should try to keep drunks, prostitutes, drug addicts and vandals off the street so that law-abiding citizens feel safe.

### Wilson and Herstein – Crime and Human Nature

Wilson and Herstein (1985) argue that some people are born with a predisposition towards crime. Their potential for crime is likely to be realized if they are not properly socialized. Where close-knit nuclear families are absent, effective socialization is unlikely.

Wilson and Herstein still believe that people have free will. Ultimately they choose whether to commit crime by weighing up the costs and benefits. Unfortunately it is too easy to live off welfare benefits, and the potential gains from crime are increasing as society becomes more affluent.

For many people the benefits of crime come to outweigh the costs, and the crime rate increases.

### Evaluation of right realism

Some aspects of right realist thinking have been influential. 'Zero tolerance' policing is based on the idea that it is effective to clamp down at the first sign that an area is deteriorating.

However, the views of Wilson and others have come under serious attack.

1 Matthews (1992) finds little evidence that tolerating broken windows and minor incidents has led to an increase in crime.
2 Jones (1998) argues that:
   - Factors such as lack of investment are far more important in determining whether a neighbourhood declines.
   - Concentrating attention on minor offenders would mean that more serious offenders would be more likely to get away with their crimes.
   - If some neighbourhoods were made more orderly then the disorderly and criminals would simply move their activities.
   - The biological approach ignores the role of inequality and unemployment in causing crime and neglects white-collar and corporate crimes.
   - Finally, despite the influence of right realist policies, the crime rate in the USA continues to rise.

## MARKETIZATION, GLOBALIZATION, INEQUALITY AND CRIME

Some sociologists are particularly critical of the increasing importance of market forces in Western capitalist societies and have analysed the impact this has had on crime.

### Taylor – The Political Economy of Crime

Ian Taylor (1997) is interested in how changes in the global economy and the ways in which some politicians have responded to these changes have affected crime.

### Marketization and opportunities for criminality

- The deregulation of financial markets has provided increased opportunities for crimes such as insider trading, where financiers use privileged knowledge to make a financial killing.
- Marketization has increased opportunities for crimes such as insurance fraud and false claims for subsidies from the European Commission.

### Changes in employment and unemployment

- Unemployment has become a more or less permanent feature of some areas. Lack of opportunity and hope leads some to turn to crime.
- Changing patterns of work have created more opportunities and incentives for criminal activity. Ruggiero, South and Taylor (1998) believe that subcontracting encourages the employment of people who are working illegally or in conditions or at wage levels that fail to conform to national laws.

### Materialism and inequality

Success is increasingly portrayed in terms of a lifestyle associated with expensive consumer goods. At the same time, inequalities have increased rapidly. Taylor sees crimes such as car theft as related to these changes.

### Drugs and globalization

- Taylor argues that there are few opportunities for young working-class men in cities such as Los Angeles which are suffering from deindustrialization. At the same time, the culture of entrepreneurship encourages many young blacks, who confront the additional problem of racism, to pursue illegitimate opportunities in the drugs business.
- For less successful, Third World countries, producing the crops from which drugs are derived requires little technology or investment and offers high profits.

## 'RACE', ETHNICITY AND CRIME

### The issue of 'race' and crime

- Croall (1998) argues that interest in 'race' and crime dates back to the nineteenth century when the Irish were portrayed as part of the 'dangerous classes'.
- Phillips and Bowling (2002) argue that in more recent years the issue returned to public attention because of the question of whether the over-representation of African-Caribbean people in prison was the result of their being more criminal than other groups or because of discriminatory treatment by the criminal justice system.

- Phillips and Bowling point out that Asians were usually seen as well-regulated because of close-knit communities and families. But by the 1990s they too were beginning to be seen as a problem. In 2001 'riots' involving Asians in Oldham, Burnley and Bradford led parts of the media began to develop an image of the 'Asian gang' (see p. 85).
- In the 1990s the **MacPherson Inquiry** into the racially motivated murder of the African-Caribbean teenager **Stephen Lawrence** and the failure of the police to bring his killers to justice, raised the issue of **institutional racism** (see p. 36) within the Metropolitan Police.

### The 'myth of black criminality'

- Paul **Gilroy** (1983) argued that black criminality was a myth. British Asians and African-Caribbeans originate from former colonies of Britain. Their struggle against British imperialism allowed these groups to learn how to resist exploitation. Demonstrations and riots represented resistance to a society that treated them unjustly.
- Gilroy claims that a myth of black criminality has been created as a result of the police's negative stereotypes. High levels of crime among ethnic minority groups are the result of police prejudice.

### John Lea and Jock Young – ethnic minority criminality

Lea and Young (1984) attack Gilroy for suggesting that the disproportionate number of black males convicted of crimes is the result of police racism. They argue that:

1 Most crimes are reported by the public, not uncovered by the police.
2 The crime rates for whites is slightly lower than that for Asians. If Gilroy is right, then the police can only be prejudiced against African-Caribbeans.
3 Statistics suggest that first-generation immigrants were highly law-abiding. It is hard to see how they could have passed down the tradition of 'anti-colonial struggle' to their children. What is more, many of the victims of the crimes committed by African Caribbeans are from the same ethnic group.

Lea and Young accept that police racism may exaggerate the ethnic minority crime rate, but believe there has been a real increase in the number of crimes committed by ethnic minorities. They believe that this is largely the result of relative deprivation, marginalization and the formation of subcultures.

The debate about the real incidence of crime among ethnic minority groups was based on limited evidence. It was only in 2000, in response to the MacPherson Inquiry, that the government first started publishing detailed statistics on ethnicity and crime. These will be examined later.

### Policing the Crisis – mugging, the state and law and order

The views of Gilroy are supported to some extent by Stuart **Hall** *et al.* (1979) in their explanation of the crime '**mugging**' in Britain in the 1970s.

The authors argue that there was a '**moral panic**' about crime and mugging in particular – a crime associated with black youth. (A moral panic is an exaggerated outburst of public concern over the morality and behaviour of a group in society.) Hall *et al.* found no evidence to indicate that the crime of mugging was new or increasing.

The moral panic over mugging could only be explained in the context of the problems facing capitalism at the start of the 1970s. Economic problems and industrial and social unrest meant that the **hegemony** (ideological domination) of the ruling class was under threat and it had to turn to force to control the crisis. Mugging was presented as a key element in the breakdown of law and order.

The moral panic over mugging helped capitalism in two ways:

1 The public was persuaded that society's problems were caused by 'immigrants' rather than the faults of the capitalist system.
2 The government was able to justify the use of force to suppress the groups that were challenging them.

The societal reaction to the threat of violence led to the labelling of large numbers of young blacks as deviants. Labelling helped to produce the figures that appeared to show rising levels of black crime, which in turn justified stronger police measures.

### Policing the Crisis – an evaluation

Given the range of issues the study deals with, it is not surprising that other sociologists have raised criticisms.

- **Downes and Rock** identify two weaknesses:
  1 The study claims that black street crime was not rising while at the same time arguing that it was bound to rise as a result of unemployment.
  2 The study fails to show how moral panic over mugging was caused by a crisis of British Capitalism.
- **Young** argues that the study provides no evidence that the public was panicking about mugging, not does it show that the public identified the crime with blacks. However, he also argues that it would have been quite rational if the public had been concerned about street crime.

### Studies of British Asian crime

Bowling and Phillips (2002) review a number of ethnographic studies of crime among British Asians.

Early studies linked a low crime rate among Asians with strong families and communities. For example, **Mawby and Batta** (1980) found that most Asians in Bradford were relatively poor and living in inner city areas. However, the study found they committed few crimes because the emphasis on *izzat*, or family honour, encouraged conformism. They were afraid of dishonouring the family name.

Desai found that young Asian men were taking a more aggressive stance in combating racist attacks. Some Bangladeshi boys were making a self-conscious attempt to counteract the image of themselves as weak and passive.

However, **Alexander** (2000) argued that the media image of a growing problem of Asian gangs was something of a myth. Although there was some violence in the area of South London covered by her study, it was greatly exaggerated by the media.

## Patterns of criminality

Black ethnic groups are over-represented in criminal statistics. For example, in 2000–2001 they made up only 1.8% of the population but 12.1% of the prison population.

Over the same period Asian ethnic groups were over-represented in terms of arrests and cautions. They made up 2.7% of the population but 4.4% of arrests.

White ethnic groups were less likely than others to be cautioned, arrested or imprisoned.

### Evidence of racism in the criminal justice system

The following sections are based on a review of evidence provided by **Bowling and Phillips** (2002).

### Policing and stops and searches

In 1999-2000 'black' people were five times more likely than whites to be stopped and searched. However, this may be partly because there are simply more members of ethnic minority groups in the urban areas where most stops are likely to take place.

The **Macpherson Inquiry** into the Stephen Lawrence case (1999) examined a range of evidence and it concluded that there was institutional racism in the police (see p. 36 for a definition of institutional racism).

### Arrests

In 1999–2000 about four times as many African Caribbean people were arrested as would be expected in terms of their proportion in the general population.

The difference was even greater in terms of imprisonment, with African Caribbeans having an imprisonment rate that is about six times that of whites.

### Prosecuting and sentencing

**Hood** (1992) found that, when other factors are taken into account, 'black' men were 5% more likely than white men to be given a custodial sentence. They were also given sentences which were on average three months longer than those of whites who had committed equivalent offences. The discrepancy was even greater among Asian men.

### Self-reported crime

Self-report studies have been used to try to discover whether the rate of offending among ethnic minority groups really is higher than among whites. Despite the methodological problems associated with this approach (see p. 77), the surveys have produced similar results: that official crime statistics exaggerate the extent of offending among ethnic minority communities.

## Race and victimization

There is clear evidence that most ethnic minorities are more likely to be victims of most crimes than whites are.

**Clancy et al.** (2001) argue that much of the difference in victimization can be explained in terms of social factors such as higher rates of unemployment among ethnic minorities and the younger age structure of those groups.

Since the Macpherson Inquiry, all incidents in which the victim believed there was a racial motive have been recorded as being racially motivated. In 1999–2000 the police recorded nearly 50,000 of these. Many more are not reported.

Data from the **British Crime Survey** indicates that there is increased fear of crime among ethnic minorities. This is compounded by their lack of faith in the ability of the criminal justice system to deal with racially motivated crimes.

## 'Race', ethnicity and crime – conclusion

**Bowling and Phillips** (2002) argue that black people are more likely to be criminalized. This in turn leads to greater social exclusion and therefore to a greater chance of criminalization – a vicious circle.

## GENDER AND CRIME

In 1977 Carol **Smart** put forward the following reasons to explain the neglect of women in criminology.

- Women tend to commit **fewer crimes** than men.
- Most crimes committed by women tend to be of a comparatively **trivial** nature.
- Sociology and criminology tend to be **dominated by men.**
- Traditional criminology is motivated by a desire to control problem behaviour. As women's behaviour is less of a problem than men's it has received less attention.

Official statistics indicate that women in all age groups appear to commit far less crime than men. This pattern has raised three main questions:

1 Do women really commit fewer crimes than men, are the figures misleading?
2 Is the proportion of crimes that are committed by women increasing, and is this linked to 'women's liberation'?
3 Why do some women break the law?

## Official statistics, criminality and gender

### Pollak – the 'masked' female offender

Writing in 1950, Otto **Pollak** argued that official statistics on gender and crime seriously underestimated female criminality. He argued that many crimes predominantly committed by females went unreported and unrecorded. Examples included shoplifting and prostitution.

He also gives reasons why there should be an under-recording of female crime.

1 The criminal justice system tends to be made up of men. Brought up to be chivalrous, they are usually lenient with female offenders.
2 More importantly, women are very good at hiding their crimes because they are used to deceiving men in matters such as revealing pain and sexual pleasure.

**Heidensohn** (1985) regards Pollak's work as based on an inaccurate stereotypical image of women. His work has little credibility today.

### Leniency towards female offenders: the 'chivalry' thesis

■ **Campbell** (1981) conducted a self-report study (see p. 77) and found that:
1 Female suspects were more likely than male suspects to be cautioned rather than prosecuted.
2 The rate of male:female juvenile offending was 1:1.33 rather than the official figure of 1:8.95.
■ **Hood** (1989) compared the sentencing of men and women and found that men were more likely to be given custodial sentences than women.

### Evidence against the 'chivalry' thesis

■ **Box** (1981) reviewed the data from self-report studies in Britain and the USA and concluded that the official statistics on gender and crime were fairly accurate.
■ **Farrington and Morris** (1983) conducted a study of sentencing in magistrates' courts. Although men received more severe sentences than women, the differences disappeared when the severity of offences was taken into account.
■ **Walklate** (1995) Believes that it is the female victim rather than the male suspect who ends up on trial in rape cases. Women have to establish their respectability if their evidence is to be believed.
■ In a study of domestic violence, **Dobash and Dobash** (1979) found that police officers were very unlikely to make an arrest in cases of domestic violence.

### Double standards in criminal justice

■ **Heidensohn** (1985) argues that the justice system is influenced by attitudes to gender in society as a whole. Women are treated more harshly when they deviate from norms of female sexuality. Sexually promiscuous girls are more likely to be taken into care than similar boys. On the other hand, courts may be reluctant to imprison mothers with young children.
■ **Carlen** (1997) argues that women are more likely to be sentenced according to the court's assessment of them as wives, mothers and daughters rather than the seriousness of their crimes.

## The causes of female crime

### Physiological causes

Some of the earliest attempts to explain female criminality were based on **biological theories**.

**Lombroso** (1895) compared the anatomical features of female criminals and non-criminals. He believed that male criminals could be identified by physical abnormalities such as having an extra toe or nipple. Few women had these features; therefore they were not '**born criminals**'.

Lombroso's work has long been discredited. However, biological theories have recently reappeared. **Moir and Jessel** (1997) explain some violent crime as being linked to **Prementstrual Syndrome** (PMS). Most sociologists, however, focus on social causes of female crime.

### Female crime and women's liberation

Fran **Adler** (1975) claimed that **women's liberation** had led to a new type of female criminal and an increase in women's contribution to crime. Women were taking on male social roles in both legitimate and illegitimate areas of activity. Instead of confining themselves to 'feminine' crimes such as shoplifting, women were getting involved in robbing banks, mugging and even murder.

Adler's views have proved to be very controversial. **Box and Hale**'s (1983) review of the debate concludes that it female crime has increased this is more likely to be due to unemployment and inadequate welfare benefits, Most female criminals are from lower-class backgrounds and are the least likely to have been touched by women's liberation.

### Carlen – women, crime and poverty

Pat **Carlen** (1985) conducted unstructured interviews with 39 convicted female offenders. She argues that working-class women have been controlled through the promise of rewards stemming from the workplace and family. When these rewards are not seen as worth the sacrifice, then criminality becomes a possibility.

### Female conformity

Frances **Heidensohn** (1985) attempts to explain why women commit fewer crimes than men. She argues that patriarchal societies control women more effectively than men, making it more difficult for them to break the law.

- **Control of women at home** – The time that women spend on housework and in caring for children means that they have little time for crime. Daughters are given less freedom than sons to come and go as they please.
- **Control of women in public** – Women often choose not to go out in public places because of fear of becoming a victim of crime or harassment. They also limit their behaviour in public for fear of being labelled a 'slag, slut or bitch'.
- **Control of women at work** – Women are usually controlled by male superiors at work and may be intimidated by various forms of harassment.

## MASCULINITIES AND CRIME

### *Messerschmidt – Masculinities and crime*

James W. **Messerschmidt** (1993) analyses why different groups of males turn to different types of crime in their attempts to be masculine.

### *Masculinities and crime in youth groups*

In order to achieve success white middle-class boys have to be subservient to schoolteachers. Outside the school they try to demonstrate some of the characteristics they repress within school. This may involve pranks, vandalism, minor thefts and excessive drinking. Such young men adopt an **accommodating masculinity**.

White working-class boys have less chance of academic success and tend to construct masculinity around the importance of physical aggression. They try to be tough and oppose the authority of teachers. Theirs is an **oppositional masculinity**.

Lower-working-class ethnic-minority boys do not expect to be able to hold down a steady job and support a family. They may use violence to express their masculinity, or they may become involved in more serious property crime than white working-class youths. This offers them some prospect of material success.

### Evaluation of Messerschmidt

**Jefferson** (1997) acknowledges the importance of Messerschmidt's work but points out that he fails to explain why particular individuals commit crimes rather than others. He tends to assume that all men in the same circumstances will be socialized to express their masculinity in the same ways.

Messerschmidt has also been accused of putting forward views that are rather stereotypical and negative towards men.

## POSTMODERNISM AND CRIMINOLOGY

**Smart** (1995) argues that traditional approaches to crime all adopt a version of positivism in the following ways:

- They try to find the causes of criminality.
- They try to find ways of eradicating crime.
- They assume that scientific methods are the best way of discovering the truth about crime.
- They believe that it is possible to find an overall theory to explain crime.

Postmodernists reject these traditional approaches to crime. They do not believe that crimes can be linked together and that common factors which cause them can be identified. They regard each criminal act as unique. They do not believe that it is possible to engineer reforms to improve society. Effective ways of dealing with crime must be local and individual.

### *Evaluation of postmodern approaches*

**Lea** (1998) believes that postmodernism has made a useful contribution to the study of the control of crime. In the postmodern world informal control mechanisms can come to dominate at the expense of the central state. Private security firms watch over shopping malls, and **closed-circuit TV (CCTV)** follows our movements around town and city centres. Security firms prevent undesirables from entering some estates. People are treated differently in different areas and seen increasingly as customers and consumers.

However, Lea also believes that postmodernism is regressive since it denies the possibility of being able to do anything to change unequal and unjust societies.

## SOCIOLOGY, VALUES AND DEVIANCE: WHOSE SIDE ARE WE ON?

- **Becker** (1970) is an **interactionist** sociologist. He believes that a value-free sociology is not possible. His sympathies lie with the '**underdog**' who is labelled by the agencies of social control.
- **Gouldner** (1971) takes a different, more radical view. He accuses interactionists of taking a liberal position which advocates cosmetic reform rather than radical change. In criticizing the agents of social control, labelling theorists like Becker fail to attack the real causes of deviance which lie in society itself.

Since the issues of crime, deviance and conformity are about basic ideas of right and wrong, it is hardly surprising that values influence this area of sociology to a great extent. Many of the theories examined in this chapter reflect how their authors think society ought to be arranged, as much as how they think it actually is.

# TEST YOUR KNOWLEDGE AND UNDERSTANDING

1 Which one of the following did Durkheim NOT believe?
   a Deviance acts as a safety valve for society
   b Deviance is dysfunctional for society
   c Deviance is inevitable in societies
   d All individuals are committed to shared values and beliefs

2 According to Merton, which one of the following is not a response to anomie?
   a Conformity
   b Innovation
   c Alienation
   d Ritualism

3 Three of the following are criticisms of Murray's view of the underclass and crime. Which is the odd one out?
   a The underclass do not share the same values as other members of society
   b Crime rates are not linked to generous welfare states
   c There is no link between single parents and criminality
   d There is no distinctive underclass culture

4 Which one of the following groups does not appear to be disproportionately involved in crime?
   a Men
   b African-Caribbean men
   c Asian men
   d The working class

5 Which one of the following crimes is likely to have high rates of reporting and recording?
   a Tax evasion
   b Burglary
   c Use of illegal drugs
   d Rape

6 Which one of the following is an example of white-collar crime?
   a Fraud
   b Burglary
   c Domestic assault
   d Murder

7 Three of the following are reasons why white-collar crime is under-represented in criminal statistics. Which is the odd one out?
   a It is not serious
   b It is often difficult to detect
   c There is often no direct victim
   d It is often dealt with informally

8 Which one of the following adapted well-known sayings is an accurate description of labelling theory?
   a All the world's a deviant
   b Deviance is in the eye of the beholder
   c To be or not to be a deviant
   d Deviants should be seen and not heard

9 Secondary deviance can be defined as which one of the following?
   a Less significant acts of deviance
   b The labelling of an individual as deviant
   c An act of deviance before it is publicly labelled
   d Deviance caused as a result of an individual or group being labelled

10 Which two of the following statements most closely reflect a Marxist view of deviance?
   a Laws reflect the interests of the powerful in society
   b Most crime is the responsibility of an underclass
   c Laws protect all members of society
   d Corporate crime is a serious problem which is ignored in most cases

11 Which one of the following measures to combat crime is most likely to be supported by right realists?
   a Reducing poverty
   b Zero tolerance policing
   c Increased leisure facilities for young people
   d Reducing inequality

12 Which of the following is not a possible reason why 'black' people are more likely than whites to be stopped and searched by the police?
   a The police have stereotypical views of 'black' people.
   b 'Black' people tend to live in urban areas where there is a higher police presence.
   c 'Black' people's fear of crime is greater than that of whites.
   d 'Black people are more likely to be on the streets after dark than other groups.

13 The 'chivalry thesis' is:
   a The idea that crimes committed by women tend to be trivial
   b The idea that women will be treated more leniently by the police and courts
   c The idea that women will be treated less severely by criminals
   d The idea that it is easier for women to become police officers and judges

14 Which one of the following statements would postmodernist criminologists support?
   a Sociology should try to identify the underlying causes of crime
   b Scientific methods are the best way of finding out about crime
   c Each criminal act is unique and cannot be fitted into general theories
   d It is possible to reform society to reduce crime rates

15 Which one of the following statements is closest to Becker's view?
   a Sociologists should be completely neutral
   b Sociologists should be on the side of law and order
   c Sociologists should deliberately take the side of the 'underdog'
   d Sociologists should take a radical view

# DEVELOP YOUR ANALYSIS AND EVALUATION SKILLS

## Do the origins of deviance lie in the individual's position in society?

**Background:** This view focuses on the structure of society as the major cause of deviant behaviour – it represents a structuralist perspective. Both functionalist and Marxist views can be described as structuralist, along with left realism with its focus on relative deprivation. Opponents of the structuralist position might argue that the cause of deviance lies within the individual. However, this view is seen as outdated in all but the most extreme criminal cases. A more popular alternative position is the interactionist approach – often referred to as labelling theory. This view holds that deviance is simply a 'label' that some people apply to the actions of others.

| For | Against |
| --- | --- |
| ■ Functionalist views: **a** Merton (p. 74), **b** Cohen (p. 75), **c** Cloward and Ohlin (p. 75)<br>■ Marxist and neo-Marxist views (pp. 79–80)<br>■ Left realism (pp. 80–2) | ■ Labelling theory (pp. 77–8) |

**Top tip:** The structuralist view can be extended to include explanations of gender and ethnic differences in crime which emphasize ethnic and gender differences in the way society is structured.

## Can official criminal statistics be trusted?

**Background:** Many early theories of crime were based on the assumption that official criminal statistics were an accurate reflection of the crime rate. However, the reliability of these figures has been questioned as many crimes go unreported and unrecorded. Alternative methods such as victimization and self-report studies have now been developed to reveal more of the 'dark figure' of crime.

| For | Against |
| --- | --- |
| ■ Crime and official statistics: unrecorded crimes (p. 76)<br>■ Crime and official statistics: white collar crime (p. 77)<br>■ Crime and official statistics Victimization studies (p. 76)<br>■ Crime and official statistics: self-report studies (p. 77) | ■ Left realism: the problem of crime (p. 80) |

**Top tip:** The sections on 'race', ethnicity and crime and gender and crime include debates about the accuracy of official crime figures. Although it is right to question the reliability of official figures, perhaps they should not be dismissed altogether. There are some crimes, for example burglary and car theft, where they are likely to be quite accurate.

## Is the criminal justice system more lenient towards women than men?

**Background:** Official statistics reveal that the crime rates of women are far lower than those of men. Some sociologists believe that one reason for this difference is the 'chivalry factor'. This means that agents of social control (usually men) treat women more leniently than men.

| For | Against |
| --- | --- |
| ■ Pollak (p. 86)<br>■ Campbell (p. 86)<br>■ Hood (p. 86) | ■ Box (p. 86)<br>■ Farrington and Morris (p. 86)<br>■ Walklate (p. 86)<br>■ Carlen (p. 86)<br>■ Heidensohn (pp. 86–7) |

**Top tip:** It is necessary to distinguish between different parts of the criminal justice process in dealing with this issue, such as police arrest rates and court sentencing. It is not possible to identify clearly one of these two positions as representing a feminist view, as feminist writers take a range of positions in this debate.

## AQA-STYLE CRIME AND DEVIANCE QUESTION

### A2 Unit 6 Synoptic Paper

| Answer all parts of this question | ITEM A |
|---|---|
| Total: 60 marks<br>1 mark =<br>1.5 minutes<br><br>Time allowed:<br>1 hour 30 minutes | The key to doing good quality research on a difficult topic such as armed robbery is trust. There are normally problems of access and of generating a suitable sample of offenders like these, but establishing trust in the research process is of paramount importance because it directly affects the quality and quantity of the information gathered from stigmatized, marginalized and excluded groups such as armed robbers.<br><br>Source: adapted from Roger Matthews, 'Doing research on armed robbery', *Sociology Review*, vol. 10, no. 3, February 2001 |

**Comments on the question**

■ Use the three descriptors of the group as the organizing principle and apply to show how trust may affect these

■ This question is testing your synoptic understanding of methods

**[a]** Examine how trust [Item A, line 2] can affect the quantity and quality of the information when studying any stigmatized, marginalized and excluded group.

[8 marks]

**Advice on preparing your answer**

■ Concerns about confidentiality may stop people giving any information

■ Box (p. 204) recognizes that these groups may tell you what you want to hear

■ This question is testing your synoptic understanding of theory and methods. The best answers might distinguish between the two terms

■ Note the negative phrasing of the question

**[b]** 'The personal and political sympathies of sociologists make it impossible to have a value-free sociology of deviance.' Discuss this view.

[12 marks]

■ A general debate can be found in chapter 14, p. 207

■ The application to this specific issue, with particular reference to Becker's commitment to the underdog and Gouldner's response, is set out on p. 87

- This question is testing your synoptic understanding of theory and the links between substantive areas of sociology
- Deviance occurs in all modules, including Families, Education, Work, Religion, Politics
- Criticisms and alternative views should be recognized
- Identify the quote as a functionalist perspective

**[c]** With reference to material from any part of the course, assess the view that deviance 'is a beneficial part of all healthy societies'.

[40 marks]

- The functions of deviance are outlined on p. 74
- Merton's theory (p. 74) recognizes that deviance can highlight where there are dysfunctions in society
- Political or religious deviance can bring about change
- Deviance of children in families and education can reinforce the norms and values of society
- It has been claimed that prostitution is a safety valve to protect the family
- Deviance provides work for social control and welfare agencies
- Functionalist ideas are criticized on pp. 74–5
- Alternative theoretical approaches are discussed in chapter 15 and would need to be used selectively to focus on the question

## OCR-STYLE CRIME AND DEVIANCE QUESTION

### A2 Unit 2536: Power and Control

**Answer all parts of this question**
Total: 60 marks 1 mark = 1 minute
Time allowed: 1 hour

### Comments on the question

- Make sure that your response is balanced – especially in terms of criticism of the view in the question
- Make sure that you describe the view in a detailed way with supporting evidence in the form of sociological theories and studies
- Assess the view by looking at both positive and negative aspects

**[a]** Outline and assess the view that criminal behaviour is a product of deviant culture.

[60 marks]

### Advice on preparing your answer

- This is an essay question. Spend at least 10 minutes putting together an essay plan
- An introduction is necessary to 'set the scene', i.e. to make clear what theoretical positions and sociological names produced the view in the question
- Begin by outlining the 'deviant culture' argument. The section on pp. 75–6 should be useful in helping you to summarize these arguments

Specifications

| Specification | Specification details | | Coverage |
|---|---|---|---|
| **AQA** A2: Religion | ■ Different theories of religion | | The main theories are discussed on pp. 93–4. |
| | ■ The role of religion as a conservative force and as an initiator of change | | The relationship between religion and social change is covered on pp. 94–6. The main theories (pp. 93–4) all discuss the effect of religion on society. |
| | ■ Cults, sects, denominations and churches and their relationship to religious activity | | Covered in the section on religious organizations (pp. 96–9). |
| | ■ Explanations of the relationship between religious beliefs, religious organizations and social groups | | These issues are also discussed on pp. 96–9. |
| | ■ Different definitions and explanations of the nature and extent of secularization | | Covered in the section on secularization (pp. 99–103). |
| **OCR** AS: Culture and Socialization/ Religion | **Religious institutions** | ■ Church, denomination, sect and cult. Their relationship to society and each other. | Covered in the section on religious organizations (pp. 96–9). |
| | | ■ New religious movements. Classifications and explanations of religious innovation and renewal. | Covered in the section on religious organizations (pp. 97–9). |
| | | ■ The appeal of religious institutions to 'spiritual shoppers'. | See the discussion of New Age movements on pp. 98–9, as well as the discussion of postmodernity and religion on pp. 98–9. |
| | **The influence of religion on the individual and society** | ■ The secularization debate; definitions and dimensions of secularization | Covered in the section on secularization (pp. 99–103). |
| | | ■ Religious fundamentalism; crises of meaning and the search for certainty | The issue of fundamentalism is discussed on p. 103. |
| | | ■ Religion and control; ethnicity; gender and sexuality | Feminist approaches are discussed on p. 94. |
| | **Religion and classical Sociology** | ■ Religion, ideology and conflict – Marxist theory in outline | Covered on pp. 93–4. |
| | | ■ Religion, stability and consensus – Durkheimian theory in outline | Covered on p. 93. |
| | | ■ Religion, social action and social change – Weberian theory in outline | See the section on religion and social change for an account of Weber's views (pp. 94–6). |

For more detailed specification guidance visit **www.haralambosholborn.com**

Essential notes

## DEFINITIONS OF RELIGION

Religious beliefs of some sort are present in every known society but their variety seems endless. Any definition of religion must encompass this variety. Two main approaches have been taken to defining religion.

1 **Functional definitions** – these define religion in terms of the functions it performs for society and individuals. *Example* – **Yinger**: 'a system of beliefs and practices by means of which a group of people struggles with the ultimate problems of human life' (quoted in Hamilton, 1995).

2 **Substantive definitions** – these are concerned with the content of religion. *Example* – **Durkheim** (1961) defined religion in terms of a distinction between the **sacred** and the **profane**. Sacred objects produce a sense of awe and respect, whereas profane objects do not.

## Evaluation

All definitions emphasize certain aspects of religion and ignore others. Functional definitions tend to be too inclusive (it is too easy to qualify as a religion); while substantive ones tend to be too exclusive (it is difficult to qualify as a religion).

## RELIGION – A FUNCTIONALIST PERSPECTIVE

**Functionalist** analysis is concerned with the contribution religion makes to meeting society's needs, such as social solidarity, value consensus, and harmony and integration between its parts.

### Emile Durkheim

- **Durkheim** (1912) argued that, in worshipping God, people are in fact worshipping society. Society is more important and more powerful than the individual, just as God is.
- Religion reinforces the shared values and moral beliefs – what Durkheim called the **conscience collective** – that hold society together. By defining these shared values as **sacred**, religion provides them with greater power.
- In worshipping society, people are, in effect, recognizing the importance of the social group and their dependence on it. In this way religion strengthens the unity of the group: it promotes **social solidarity**.
- Through acts of **collective worship**, members of society express, communicate and understand the moral bonds which unite them.

### Criticisms

1 Durkheim only studied a small number of Aboriginal tribes. It may be misleading to generalize from this small sample.
2 Most sociologists would not go as far as Durkheim in arguing that religion is, in fact, the worship of society.
3 **Hamilton** (1995) points out that Durkheim's theory may only be applicable to small non-literate societies. Modern societies are characterized by diversity.
4 Hamilton also argues that Durkheim overstates the degree to which common values influence individual behaviour. Often religious beliefs will conflict with dominant values.

### Bronislaw Malinowski

Like Durkheim, **Malinowski** (1954) uses data from small-scale, non-literate societies to support his ideas. He focuses on the role of religion in dealing with situations of **emotional stress** that threaten social solidarity. He identifies two sorts of events that may create this kind of stress:

1 Anxiety and tension tend to disrupt social life. Situations that produce these emotions include **crises of life** such as birth, puberty, marriage and death. Malinowski notes that in all societies these life crises are surrounded by **religious ritual**. At a funeral ceremony, for example, the social group unites to support the bereaved. The expression of **social solidarity** reintegrates society.
2 Actions that cannot be fully controlled or predicted also produce tension and anxiety. From his observations in the Trobriand Islands, Malinowski noted that such events were surrounded by ritual. Rituals reduce anxiety by providing confidence and a feeling of control.

### Criticisms

Malinowski has been criticized for exaggerating the importance of religious ritual in helping people to cope with situations of stress and uncertainty.

### Talcott Parsons

- **Parsons** argued that religious beliefs provide **guidelines for human action** and standards against which people's conduct can be evaluated. The Ten Commandments, for example, provide the basis for many social norms.
- Like Malinowski, Parsons sees religion as dealing with problems that **disrupt social life** – problems such as unforeseen, unpredictable events and situations of uncertainty.
- Another main function of religion for Parsons is to **make sense of all experiences**, no matter how meaningless or contradictory they appear. Religion provides a range of answers to questions about suffering, evil and so on.

### Criticisms of the functionalist approach

The functionalist perspective emphasizes the positive contributions of religion to society and ignores its **dysfunctional** aspects. Functionalism neglects the instances where religion can be seen as a divisive and disruptive force, as with Catholics and Protestants in Northern Ireland and Hindus and Muslims in India.

## RELIGION – A MARXIST PERSPECTIVE

To Marx (1963), religion is an illusion which eases the pain produced by exploitation and oppression. It is a series of myths that justify and **legitimate** the domination of the ruling class. As such it forms the basis of much **ruling-class ideology**.

Marx famously described religion as the **'opium of the people'**. Like a drug, it dulls pain and creates a dream world rather than bringing true happiness. It dulls the pain of oppression in the following ways:

- It promises a paradise of **eternal bliss** in life after death, making life bearable by giving people something to look forward to.

- Some religions make a **virtue of the suffering** produced by oppression. In particular, those who suffer poverty with dignity and humility will be rewarded in the afterlife. Religion thus makes poverty more tolerable.
- Religion can offer the hope of **supernatural solutions** to problems on earth. Anticipation of this future can make the present more acceptable.
- Religion often **justifies the social order** and a person's position within it. In this way social arrangements appear inevitable, and those at the bottom can accept and come to terms with their situation. In the same way, poverty and misfortune can be seen as a punishment for sin.

### Religion and social control

For Marxists, religion does not simply cushion the effects of oppression. It also acts as a mechanism of **social control**, keeping people in their place.

- By making unsatisfactory lives bearable, it discourages people from attempting to change their situation.
- By offering an illusion of hope in a hopeless situation, it prevents thoughts of overthrowing the system.
- By providing justifications for society, religion distorts reality and helps to produce **false class consciousness**. This blinds members of the oppressed class to their true situation.
- Ruling classes also adopt religious beliefs to justify their dominance to themselves and others.

### Evidence to support Marxism

There is considerable evidence to support the Marxist view of religion. Here are two examples.

1 There are many examples from history where ruling groups have used religion to justify their dominance. The **caste system** in traditional India was justified by Hindu religious beliefs; whilst in medieval Europe, kings and queens ruled by '**divine right**'.
2 **Bruce** (1988) points out that, in the USA, conservative Protestants – the '**New Christian Right**' – consistently support right-wing political candidates. Although they have had a limited influence on American politics, they have tended to defend the interests of the rich and powerful at the expense of other groups in the population.

### The limitations of Marxism

- Some evidence suggests that religion does not always legitimate power and that it can sometimes provide an **impetus for change** (see pp. 95–6).
- The fact that religion sometimes acts as an ideological force in the way suggested by Marx does not explain its existence.

### Maduro – the relative autonomy of religion

Some neo-Marxists deny that religion is always a conservative force. **Maduro** (1982) claims that religion can be **revolutionary**. Members of the clergy can develop revolutionary potential where oppressed members of the population have no outlet for their grievances. This has occurred in Latin America where some Catholic priests have criticized ruling groups and helped to organize resistance. This is known as **liberation theology** (see p. 96).

## GENDER, FEMINISM AND RELIGION

**Feminist theories** follow Marxist theories in arguing that religion can be an instrument of domination and oppression. However, unlike Marxism, they see religion as a product of **patriarchy** (see p. 24) rather than capitalism.

- **Armstrong** (1993) points out that women occupy a **marginal** position in most major religions. Although they have made gains in many areas of life, their gains in most religions have been very limited.
- Women continue to be excluded from key roles in many religions (although the Church of England finally allowed the **ordination of women priests** in 1992). This is despite the fact that women often participate in organized religion more than men.

### Women and resistance to religious oppression

Sociologists have come to acknowledge that women can no longer be seen as passive victims of religious oppression.

- **Badawi** (1994) notes that aspects of Islam are positive for women. For example, Islamic women keep their own family name when they get married.
- **Watson** (1994) examines the **veiling** of Islamic women. This practice is seen by many non-Muslim writers as a form of **social control**. However, Watson argues that veiling can have advantages for women in that it can reduce, or allow them to cope with, male oppression. For example, it reduces the possibility of **sexual harassment** and allows Muslim women to be judged for what they are rather than what they look like.

## RELIGION AND SOCIAL CHANGE

### Religion as a conservative force

Functionalists and Marxists have generally dismissed the possibility that religion can cause changes in society. They believe that religion acts as a **conservative force** and that it is changes in society that shape religion and not *vice versa*.

Religion can be seen as a conservative force in two senses.

1 Functionalists have claimed that it acts in this way because it promotes **integration** and **social solidarity**. In this way it facilitates the continued existence of society in its present form. Marx had similar views, although he saw religion as maintaining the status quo in the interests of the ruling class rather than those of society as a whole.

2 'Conservative' can also refer to traditional beliefs and customs. In some circumstances religion can support social change while at the same time promoting **traditional values**. This often occurs when there is a revival in **fundamentalist** religious beliefs.

## Conservatism, fundamentalism and social change

Recent years have seen the rise of fundamentalist religious beliefs in different parts of the world. **Taylor** (1987) defines **fundamentalism** as involving the following:

1 A group perceives a challenge to an ultimate authority, usually a god, in which they believe.
2 The group decides that the challenge cannot be tolerated.
3 They reaffirm their belief in the authority that is being challenged.
4 They oppose those who have challenged the established beliefs and often use political means to further their cause.

If fundamentalists are successful, they succeed in defending traditional values, but they also change society by **reversing innovations** that have taken place.

The most dramatic example of this process has been in Iran. During the 1960s and 1970s, **Iran** underwent a process of **liberalization**. Attitudes to women changed and there were good relations with the West. In 1979 the Iranian revolution took place, partly inspired by **Islamic fundamentalism**, and these changes were reversed.

In this case, religious beliefs contributed to producing revolutionary change. Religion did not act as a conservative force in one sense, but in terms of supporting traditional values, it did act as a conservative force.

## Changes in society and religion

Most sociologists agree that changes in society lead to changes in religion.

1 Talcott **Parsons** (1937, 1964, 1965), for example, believed that, as society developed, religion lost some of its functions (see p. 93).
2 **Marx** believed that changes in the economic base of society would lead to changes in the superstructure of society, including religion.
3 Supporters of the **secularization** idea think industrialization has led to changes which have reduced the importance of religion in society (see pp. 99–103).
4 Some sociologists have claimed that **globalization** and the advent of the **postmodern** world have produced changes in religion (see pp. 99 and 103).

## Max Weber – The Protestant Ethic and the Spirit of Capitalism

Both functionalists and Marxists emphasize the role of religion in promoting social integration and impeding social change. However, **Weber** (1930) argued that in some circumstances religion can lead to **social change**.

In his most famous book, *The Protestant Ethic and the Spirit of Capitalism*, Weber examines the relationship between the rise of a certain form of Protestantism known as **Calvinism** and the development of Western industrial capitalism.

Calvinist Protestantism originated in the seventeenth century. Calvin thought that there was a distinct group of the **elect** – those chosen to go to heaven – and that they had been chosen by God even before they were born. Those who were not among the elect could never gain a place in heaven.

This produced a **psychological problem** for Calvinists. They did not know whether they were among the elect. They suffered from an **uncertainty** about their status, and their behaviour was an attempt to convince themselves that they had been chosen to go to heaven.

### The Protestant ethic

The **Protestant ethic** enabled Calvinists to convince themselves that they were among the elect. The ethic was **ascetic**, encouraging abstinence from life's pleasures, a simple lifestyle and rigorous self-discipline. It produced individuals who worked hard in their careers or **callings**. Making money was a concrete indication of success in one's calling, and success meant that the individual had not lost grace in God's sight.

### The spirit of capitalism

Weber argued that underlying capitalism is the **spirit of capitalism** – a set of ideas, ethics and values. He claimed that ascetic Protestantism was a vital influence in the creation and development of the spirit and practice of capitalism, because the methodical and single-minded pursuit of a calling encourages the creation of wealth and restrictions on spending. This **accumulation of capital** produced the early businesses that expanded to create capitalist society.

### Evaluation

Weber's book has received both criticism and support.

1 It has been argued that Calvinism was strong in some parts of the world where capitalism did not develop until much later, such as Switzerland and Scotland. However, **Marshall** (1982) counters this by pointing out that Weber did not claim that Calvinism was the only factor necessary for the development of capitalism.
2 **Kautsky** (1953) argues from a Marxist perspective that early capitalism preceded and largely determined Protestantism. In his view, Protestantism became the **ideology** capitalists used to legitimate their position.
3 Another criticism questions the view that it was the religious beliefs of Calvinists that led to them becoming business people. Instead they devoted themselves to business because they were excluded from holding public office and joining certain professions by law.

## Religion and social change – conclusion

Many sociologists now accept that religion can be a force for change. **Nelson** (1986) points to a number of instances where religion has undermined stability or promoted change:

■ In **Northern Ireland**, Roman Catholicism has long been associated with Irish Republicanism.
■ In the USA in the 1960s the **Reverend Martin Luther King** played a leading role in establishing civil rights.
■ Also in the 1960s a number of radical groups emerged within the Roman Catholic church in Latin America. They preached **liberation theology**, arguing that it was the duty of church members to fight against unjust and oppressive right-wing dictatorships.
■ In Iran, **Islamic fundamentalism** played a part in the 1979 revolution.
■ The Roman Catholic church in Poland opposed the communist state and supported the free trade union **Solidarity**.
■ In South Africa, **Archbishop Desmond Tutu** was a prominent opponent of **apartheid**.

## Conservative or radical religion?

**McGuire** (1981) examines the factors that influence the type of role that religion plays in society. She identifies four main factors that determine the potential of religion to change society.

1 **Beliefs** – the beliefs of a particular religion will influence its role in society. For example, religions that emphasize adherence to strong moral codes are more likely to produce members who are critical of society and seek to change it.

2 **Culture** – in societies where religious beliefs are central to the culture, anyone wishing to produce change tends to use a religious legitimation for their actions. In Britain, however, religion plays a less central role, so it is less significant in justifying social change.

3 **Social location** – where an established church or other religious organization plays a major role in political and economic life, there is considerable scope for religion to have an impact on processes of change.

4 **Internal organization** – religions with a strong, centralized source of authority have more chance of affecting events.

# RELIGIOUS ORGANIZATIONS

Table 7.1 illustrates some of the key differences between the main kinds of religious organizations. However, some sociologists have suggested that these categorizations may be over-simplified when applied to contemporary societies.

## The church

■ **Bruce** (1996) argues that the concept of a **church** is primarily useful in describing pre-modern Christian societies. The development of **religious pluralism** (many different religious groups) in modern societies makes it difficult for the state to lend exclusive support to one religion because a single set of religious beliefs is no longer taken for granted and reinforced by all groups in society.
■ **Robertson** (1987) argues that there has been an increase in **church–state tensions** throughout the world. There is little room for religious concerns in the

| Table 7.1 **Comparing religious organizations: churches, denominations and sects** | | | |
|---|---|---|---|
| | **Church** | **Denomination** | **Sect** |
| Sociologist identifying these factors | Troeltsch (1931) | Niebuhr (1929) | Troeltsch (1931) |
| Example | Roman Catholic Church | Methodism | Jehovah's Witnesses |
| Social background of members | Members are drawn from all classes in society, although the upper class are particularly likely to join | Does not have universal appeal; not connected with the upper class | Connected with the lower classes |
| Relationship to state | Sometimes closely related to the state | Does not identify with the state and approves the separation of church and state | |
| Relationship to society | Churches accept and affirm life in this world | Members generally accept the norms and values of society | Members reject the values of the world that surrounds them |
| Demands on members | Members do not have to demonstrate their faith to become members of a church | Some minor restrictions may be placed on members – e.g. methodists are discouraged from drinking and gambling | Members may be expected to withdraw from life outside the sect. Deep commitment demanded from members |
| Tolerance | Often churches will jealously guard their monopoly of religious faith | Denominations do not claim a monopoly of religious truth and are tolerant of other religions | Sects tend to believe that they possess a monopoly of religious truth |
| Type of organization | A formal organization with a hierarchy of paid officials | Usually smaller than a church but still a formal organization with a hierarchy of paid officials | Central authority often rests with a charismatic leader whose special qualities persuade others to follow him |

world of international trade and diplomacy, so governments may come into conflict with the moral concerns of domestic churches.

## Denominations

**Stark and Bainbridge** (1985) are critical of the concept of a **denomination**. They claim that the division of religious organizations into separate types obscures rather than clarifies the differences between them.

## Sects

- **Bruce** acknowledges that **sects** can prosper in modern societies where people have more opportunity to form **subcultures**. Even with the greater toleration of contemporary societies, however, some sects may come into serious conflict with the wider society. In the 1990s there were a number of instances involving the deaths of sect followers – for example, the deaths of more than 80 **Branch Davidians** in the siege at Waco in Texas.
- **Wilson** (1982) argues that Troeltsch's description of sects (see Table 7.1) does not account for the increase in the number of sects in Europe and the USA in recent decades. Some of these **new religious movements** are examined in the next sections.

## Cults

Cults tend to be more **individualistic** than other organized forms of religion because they often lack a fixed set of beliefs. They tolerate other beliefs, and their own beliefs are often vague. They often have **customers** rather than members, and customers may have relatively little involvement with the organization once they have learned the basics. Many aspects of the **New Age** movement (see pp. 98–9) are based around cults.

# WALLIS – THE ELEMENTARY FORMS OF THE NEW RELIGIOUS LIFE

The development of a range of new religions in the 1970s led **Wallis** (1984) to categorize these as **new religious movements**. He divides new religious movements into three main groups based on their relationship to the outside world. He distinguishes between them according to whether the movement and its members reject, accommodate or affirm the world.

## World-rejecting new religious movements

- **World-rejecting** new religious movements have most of the characteristics of a **sect** described by Troeltsch.
- Their ideology is highly **critical** of the outside world, and the movement expects or seeks change.
- In order to achieve salvation, members are expected to have a sharp break from conventional life when they join the movement. Organizations of this type act as **total institutions**, controlling all aspects of their members' lives. As a result, they often develop a reputation for 'brainwashing' their members, since

families and friends find it hard to understand the change that has taken place in a member.

- Most are based around a **communal lifestyle**, and, as such, develop unconventional ways of living. The ill-fated Branch Davidians in Waco, Texas, are a case in point.

## World-accommodating new religious movements

- **World-accommodating** new religious movements are usually **offshoots** of an existing major church or denomination. For example, **Pentecostalist** groups are variants of Protestant religions.
- Typically these groups neither accept nor reject the world as it is, they simply live with it. They are concerned with religious rather than worldly questions.
- World-accommodating sects seek to restore the **spiritual purity** to a religion that they believe has been lost in more conventional churches and denominations. Pentecostalists, for example, hold that the belief in the Holy Spirit has been lost in other Christian religions.

## World-affirming new religious movements

- **World-affirming** new religious movements are very different from all other religious groups and may lack some of the features normally associated with a religion. However, these groups do claim to be able to provide access to **supernatural** or **spiritual powers**, and in that sense can be regarded as religions.
- Rather than rejecting existing society or existing religions, world-affirming groups accept the world as it is. They offer the follower the **potential** to be successful in terms of the dominant values of society by unlocking spiritual powers within the individual.
- Followers of world-affirming movements carry on normal lives and there is little social control over the members or customers.
- An example of a world-affirming new religious movement is **Transcendental Meditation** or TM. TM is based on the Hindu religion and was first introduced to the West in the late 1950s, achieving prominence when adopted by the Beatles in 1968. It is claimed that the meditation technique can provide '**unbounded awareness**' which can have beneficial effects for individuals and society.
- To Wallis, most world-affirming movements are cults, since, unlike sects, they tolerate the existence of other religions, have a rapid turnover of membership and are relatively undemanding on their followers.

### Evaluation

Wallis realizes that no religious group will conform exactly to his categories. He recognizes that some groups occupy the middle ground, incorporating elements of all three categories.

**Beckford** (1985) offers some criticisms of Wallis:

1 He argues that Wallis's categories are difficult to apply. It is not clear whether it is the teachings of the movement or the beliefs and outlooks of individual members that distinguish the different attitudes to the world.
2 Wallis pays insufficient attention to the **diversity of views** that exists within a sect or cult.
3 Beckford also questions the value of defining some groups as 'world-rejecting'. In his view, no group is able to reject the world altogether.

## REASONS FOR THE GROWTH OF SECTS, CULTS AND NEW RELIGIOUS MOVEMENTS

Religious sects and cults have existed for centuries, but the 1960s saw the growth of many new examples of these religious groups. This growth can be explained in terms of why individuals choose to join, or in terms of wider social changes. In fact the two explanations are linked, because social changes affect the number of people available as potential recruits.

### Marginality

**Weber** provided one of the earliest explanations for the growth of sects. He argued that they were likely to arise within groups that were **marginal** in society. Members of groups outside the mainstream of social life often feel that they are not receiving the rewards they deserve. Some sects offer explanations for the **disprivilege** of members and promise them a better future either on earth or in the afterlife.

In part, the growth of sects such as the **Black Muslims** in the USA in the 1960s was accomplished through recruitment from disadvantaged groups.

However, most of the members of world-rejecting sects in the 1960s and 1970s came from young, white, middle-class backgrounds. **Wallis** (1984) does not believe that this contradicts the marginality theory. Many of the recruits had become marginal in society because they were 'hippies, drop-outs, surfers, LSD and marijuana users'.

### Relative deprivation

**Relative deprivation** refers to subjectively perceived deprivation. In objective terms the poor are more deprived than the middle class, but in subjective terms certain members of the middle class may feel more deprived than the poor. They do not lack material wealth, but they feel **spiritually deprived** in a world they see as too materialistic, lonely and impersonal. They seek salvation in the sense of community offered by the sect.

### Social change

- **Wilson** (1970) argues that sects arise during periods of rapid **social change** when traditional norms are disrupted. He uses the example of the early **Methodist** movement, which had the characteristics of a sect. This grew up as the response of the urban working class to **industrialization**. In a situation of change and uncertainty, it offered the support of a close-knit community, clear norms and values, and a promise of salvation.
- **Bruce** (1995, 1996) believes that the weakness of conventional religions has encouraged some people to consider less traditional alternatives. As modern societies developed, faith in traditional forms of authority declined and denominations became popular. In contemporary secular societies, cults have become more popular because they require fewer sacrifices and less commitment than churches and sects.

### The growth of new religious movements

- **Wallis** (1984) argues that new religious movements were attractive to young people in the 1960s because they offered a more spiritual and caring way of life.
- **Bruce** (1995) sees the particular appeal of world-rejecting new religious movements as deriving from the failure of the youth '**counter-culture**' to radically change the world. Disillusioned young people sought their path to salvation through religion instead of peace and love.
- **Bruce** believes that world-affirming movements have grown because people find it difficult to gain satisfaction and a **sense of identity** from their work in contemporary societies. They no longer have a sense of calling to their work and may not identify strongly with their workmates. World-affirming movements offer a solution – they offer people both success and a spiritual element to their lives.

## THE NEW AGE

The term **New Age** has been applied to a range of ideas that started to become prominent in the 1980s. Although some of these beliefs were organized as new religious movements, in many cases they were not attached to any organization. Examples of New Age beliefs include:

- Interest in clairvoyance, contacting aliens, types of meditation and therapy
- Beliefs in magic, crystals, tarot cards, Feng Shui, astrology and witchcraft
- Participation in self-healing and natural or traditional remedies such as yoga and aromatherapy.

### The themes of the New Age

**Heelas** (1996) believes the key features of the New Age are:

1 A belief in **self-spirituality**. People have turned away from traditional religious organizations in their search for the spiritual and have begun to look inside themselves.
2 **Detraditionalization**: valuing personal experience above the authority that comes from traditional sources.
3 The belief that you can become **responsible for your own actions**. It emphasizes freedom to discover your own truth.

## Variations within the New Age

Heelas uses Wallis's typology of new religious movements to distinguish between different aspects of the New Age:

- **World-affirming** aspects can help you experience the best of the **outer world** – for example, to be more successful in business.
- **World-rejecting** aspects stress how to experience the best of the **inner world**, how to achieve spirituality and turn away from any concern with worldly success.
- Most New Age beliefs offer the **best of both worlds**, claiming you can be successful *and* spiritually fulfilled.

## The appeal of the New Age

**Drane** (1999) argues that the appeal of the New Age comes from the failure of the modern world to deliver personal satisfaction. He believes people in Western societies no longer trust institutions such as the medical professions and are disillusioned with the inability of churches to satisfy their craving for spirituality. Drane sees the popularity of the New Age as part of a move towards **postmodernity**.

However, Bruce and Heelas agree that the New Age can best be explained as a product of modernity.

**Bruce** claims that the New Age appeals to the middle classes working in 'expressive professions' who have an interest in human potential. Many aspects of the New Age are based on 'watered down' versions of Eastern religions such as Buddhism. However, unlike many of these, they emphasize the individual.

**Heelas** examines four ways in which modernity might link to the appeal of the New Age.

1 People have many roles but there is little overlap between those roles. They end up with a **fragmented identity** – the New Age offers ways of finding an identity.
2 **Consumer culture** creates dissatisfaction as people fail to achieve the perfection portrayed by advertisers. The New Age offers different ways of achieving perfection.
3 Following Bryan Wilson, Heelas argues that periods of rapid social change disrupt traditional norms and values, so people **seek certainty** in spiritual beliefs.
4 The **decline of conventional religion** leaves people without strong alternatives to the New Age.

## SECULARIZATION

### Support for the secularization thesis

Many classical sociologists believed that industrialization and the growth of **scientific knowledge** would lead to **secularization**, which can broadly be defined as the process of religious decline. Many contemporary sociologists have followed in their footsteps, arguing that modern societies are not compatible with the retention of a central role for religion. For example, **Wilson** (1966) defines secularization as 'the process whereby religious thinking, practice and institutions lose social significance'.

However, the concept of secularization is given different meanings by different sociologists. Steve **Bruce** (2002) says 'there is no one secularization theory. Rather there are clusters of descriptions and explanations that cohere reasonably well'.

## INSTITUTIONAL RELIGION

### Participation

Some researchers have measured the importance of religion in society in terms of **institutional factors** such as church attendance, membership and participation in religious ceremonies. Some of this evidence does point towards secularization but:

- The patterns vary between countries.
- The reliability and validity of the statistics are open to question.

### Church attendance in Britain

**Church attendance** figures show a continuing drop in attendance throughout the twentieth century, particularly in Anglican, Baptist, Catholic and United Reformed churches. In 1851 the 'Census of Religion' found just under 40% of the population attending church. In 2005 it is estimated that only 6.6% of the adult population will attend church (**Brierley**, 2001).

Attendance at special Christian ceremonies such as **baptisms** and **marriages** has also declined. In 1900, 73% of children were baptized; by 2000 the figure had dropped to 35%.

### Church membership in Britain

- Overall, there has been a decline in **membership** of religious organizations in the UK.
- Institutional Christian religions have declined most, while many non-Christian and smaller religions have gained members. Overall, the proportion of the population belonging to non-Christian religions doubled between 1975 and 2000 (**Brierley**, 2001).

### Religious participation in the rest of the world

- Rates of religious participation in the USA are **much higher** than those in Britain.
- **Barrett** (discussed in Brierley, 2001) estimates that 34.5% of the world population was Christian in 1990, declining only slightly to 33% by 2000. Christianity had declined in Europe but increased in Africa, Latin America and Asia.
- Globally there has been a big **increase in the proportion of Muslims** in the world and overall a decline in the proportion who are not religious.

These figures contrast with the apparent religious decline in Britain.

## Interpreting the evidence on participation and membership

Most of the long-term evidence on membership and attendance in Britain seems to support the secularization theory. Although recent years have seen a growth in smaller religious organizations, there is little doubt that fewer people attend a place of worship or belong to a religious organization. In the USA, however, the evidence seems to support those who question the secularization theory. In both cases, the **reliability** and **validity** of the statistics are open to question:

■ Nineteenth-century statistics pose problems because the methods of data collection do not meet today's standards of reliability.
■ Different criteria are used to record membership in different religions.
■ US statistics are based on survey evidence, and it has been suggested that more people claim to attend a place of worship than actually do.

The decline in church attendance in Britain can be interpreted in a number of different ways:

■ **Martin** (1969) claims that in the nineteenth century church-going was a sign of middle-class respectability to a greater extent than it is today.
■ Religion today may be expressed in other ways. It may have become **privatized**; people develop their own beliefs and see religious institutions as less important.

### Belief, churchgoing and atheism

Opinion poll data generally find that many more people retain religious beliefs than are members of religious organizations or regular attenders at places of worship. In 2000, 70% of people retained some sort of belief, while only 15% rejected the idea of a God or life force altogether.

However, **Bruce** (2001) points out that the results of a number of surveys show a strong weakening of religious beliefs. Nevertheless, in the **2001 Census**, 71.6% of people stated they were Christian, although the number of people who claimed to be 'Jedi' (0.7%) suggests that not everybody took the religion question entirely seriously.

Religious belief and participation may be the obvious place to look for evidence of secularization, but some theorists such as **Casanova** (1994), argue that that the role of religion in society is more significant in assessing whether secularization is occurring.

## Disengagement, differentiation and societalization

### Disengagement

Some sociologists have seen the truly religious society as one in which the church as an institution is very powerful in every aspect of society. A **disengagement** or withdrawing of the church from wider society is seen as secularization. **Martin** (1969) sees this view as concerned with decline in the power, wealth, prestige and influence of the church. In medieval Europe, the church and state were very close; today the church is hardly represented in government.

However, Martin points out that the church's contemporary concern with purely spiritual matters represents a purer form of religion, unblemished by secular concerns such as politics.

Casanova (1994) believes that religion is still important in public life. During the 1980s, religion was linked to political conflicts such as the conflict between Jews and Muslim Arabs in the Middle East and between Protestants and Catholics in Northern Ireland. Casanova does not reject the secularization theory, but he does argue that there has been a **deprivatization** of religion.

### Structural and social differentiation

An alternative to the view that disengagement equals secularization is provided by **Parsons** (1951, 1960, 1965). Parsons agrees that the church has lost many of its former functions. He argues that the evolution of society involves a process of **structural differentiation**: parts of the social system become more specialized and so perform fewer functions.

However, this process does not necessarily lessen the importance of social institutions. As we saw in a previous section (p. 93) Parsons argues that religious beliefs still give meaning and significance to life.

**Bruce** (1995) discusses what is essentially the same process, but he refers to it as **social differentiation**. He argues that social life in modern societies is dominated by the logic of capitalist production, with its emphasis on efficiency and profit. Religious faith is not significant.

### Societalization

**Bruce** (1995, 2002) uses the term **societalization** to refer to a process in which social life becomes **fragmented** and ceases to be locally based. The decline of communities in modern societies undermines religion in three ways:

1 Churches can no longer serve as the focal point for communities.
2 People's greater involvement with the broader society leads them to look more widely for services. They are less likely to turn to the local vicar or priest for support.
3 The cultural diversity of the society in which people live leads them to hold beliefs with less certainty.

### Religious pluralism

Some researchers imply that the truly religious society has one faith and one church. This picture is influenced by the situation in some small-scale societies, such as the Australian Aboriginals, described by Durkheim (see p. 93).

Modernization and industrialization tend to create a plurality of cultural and religious groups. This reminds individuals that their beliefs are a matter of **personal choice** and no longer part and parcel of their membership of society.

**Strong religion** (Bruce, 2002) which dominates people's lives cannot be widespread in a fragmented society. **Weak religion**, which is more a matter of personal choice and does not claim to be the only legitimate religion, is more suited to fragmented societies.

Some argue that **religious pluralism** is not incompatible with a society in which religion thrives. It is not necessary for everyone to share the same beliefs for religion to be important. Northern Ireland is a case in point.

Pluralism in modern societies stems from two main sources, which we will now examine:

■ The existence of different ethnic groups.
■ The growth of sects and cults.

### Ethnicity and religious diversity

**Bruce** (1996) acknowledges that certain ethnic groups retain strong religious beliefs. However, he does not see this as an argument against the secularization theory. He believes that religion remains strong because of its social importance rather than because of any deep religious convictions among members of the groups.

Bruce argues that religion tends to serve one of two main purposes for ethnic groups:

■ **Cultural defence** – where two communities are in conflict and they are of different religions, their religious identity becomes a way of asserting their ethnic pride. Bruce gives the example of Ian Paisley's **Democratic Unionist Party** in Northern Ireland. Only a tiny percentage of the population of Northern Ireland is a member of the religious group associated with the party, but many more support the party. This is because, according to Bruce, ethnic Protestants identify with the party's opposition to a united Ireland, not because of the religious convictions of the party's leaders.
■ **Cultural transition** – in this case religion is used as a resource for dealing with situations where people have to adjust their identity. For example, Asian and African-Caribbean migrants to Britain can use mosques, temples and churches as centres for their communities, and they can use their religion as a way of coping with the difficulties of being Asian or black and British.

Bruce believes that these processes keep religion relevant but do not create a religious society. **Brown** (1992) disagrees and sees '**ethnic defence**' as a key function of religion in the modern world.

There is certainly plenty of evidence that religion remains strong among many ethnic minorities. **Chryssides** (1984) argues that in Britain the religions of immigrant groups and their descendants have had three paths open to them:

1 **Apostasy** – religious beliefs are abandoned in a hostile environment.

2 **Accommodation** – religious beliefs are adapted to take account of the changed situation.
3 **Renewed vigour** – religion is asserted more strongly as a reaction to the hostility against it.

Examples of all three responses can be found, but the general pattern is one of accommodation and renewed vigour, with buildings being converted into mosques and religious practices being maintained or adapted.

### Sects, cults and secularization

The apparent vitality of sects (see pp. 97–9) seems to provide evidence against the theory of secularization.

■ **Greeley** (1972) believes that the growth of new religious movements represents a process of **resacrilization**: interest and belief in the sacred are being revived.
■ Since the 1980s, interest has grown in a range of beliefs such as tarot cards, astrology and traditional medicines. These sorts of ideas have been referred to as 'New Age'. Heelas (1996) regards the 'New Age' movement as significant. He points out that opinion poll evidence suggests substantial belief in reincarnation, horoscopes and flying saucers. Other sociologists see the growth of sects and new religious movements as evidence of secularization.
■ **Wilson** (1982) believes that sects are the last outpost of religion in societies where religious beliefs and values are of little significance.
■ **Bruce** (1995, 1996, 2002) argues that new religious movements recruit very small numbers compared to the decline in mainstream Christian religions. World-rejecting sects have affected the smallest number of people, while word-accommodating groups – who have the least influence on people's lives – have recruited the most.

### Secularization and the New Age

**Bruce** sees the growth of the New Age as posing little threat to the validity of the theory of secularization. He believes that New Age beliefs are weak and often temporary.

However, in a study of Kendal in the Lake District **Heelas** et al. (2001) found New Age beliefs to be quite significant in the lives of many people.

## The secularization of religious institutions in the USA

### Will Herberg – denominations and internal secularization

According to **Herberg** (1960), the main evidence for secularization in the USA is to be found in the decline of the religiosity of churches and denominations themselves. These organizations have compromised their religious beliefs to fit in with the wider society.

Herberg claims that the major denominations in America have undergone a process of secularization. They increasingly reflect the American 'way of life' rather than the word of God.

Herberg's general view has been supported by **Heelas and Seel** (2003). They claim that there has been a move away from traditional religions in the USA and a growth in the more **subjective religions** which allow considerable freedom to believers.

Herberg's argument has been challenged using the example of the New Christian Right in the USA.

### The New Christian Right

**Roof and McKinney** (1987) note the growth of conservative Protestant religions (sometimes called the New Christian Right) which seem to combine a serious commitment to religious teachings with a refusal to compromise religious beliefs. As such, they appear to contradict Herberg's claims.

**Bruce** (1988) argues that the New Christian Right has had very little impact. Very few of its members who have stood for national office have won their elections, for example. The only reason it gets so much attention, Bruce argues, is because its members are unusual for holding strong religious convictions in a secular world.

## RELIGION AND SOCIETY – DESACRILIZATION

A number of sociologists have argued that society has been undergoing a process of **desacrilization**, in which supernatural forces are no longer seen as controlling the world, and action is no longer directed by religious belief.

### Disenchantment

**Weber** provided one of the earliest statements of the desacrilization theory. He believed that modern societies are characterized by **disenchantment**: they are no longer charged with mystery and magic; the supernatural has been banished from society. Instead they are based on **rational action**: actions are based on deliberate and precise calculation and logic.

### Science and reason

**Bruce** (2002) stresses the importance of rationalization in undermining religious beliefs. Technological advances have given individuals a greater sense of control over the natural world and less need to resort to supernatural explanations. There are some things, such as life and death, which science and rationality cannot deal with. However, when people turn to God they do so as individuals and as a last resort after all the rational and scientific possibilities have been exhausted.

The theory of **postmodernism** suggests that societies have begun to move beyond the scientific rationality of modernity, partly because of a growing distrust of science. People are increasingly aware of the failures of science (such as the failure to find a cure for AIDS) and the damaging side-effects of science and technology (such as environmental damage).

## SECULARIZATION – INTERNATIONAL COMPARISONS

By concentrating on Britain and the USA, sociologists have taken a rather narrow view of social change and religion. **Martin** (1978) has looked at the changing role of religion in a range of societies. He finds different patterns of belief and participation in different societies.

- In predominantly Catholic countries such as Italy and Spain there tends to be more participation than in Protestant countries such as Britain.
- Religion is strongest in those modern industrial societies such as the USA where a plurality of ethnic groups express their cultural differences through participation in religion.
- In Islamic societies religious change varies from country to country. In Iran religious leaders gained political power after the 1979 revolution. However, in Turkey some see religion as a cause of 'backwardness' whilst others see it as the vital foundation for moral values.

**Bruce** (2002) argues that secularization applies only to pluralistic, democratic Western societies such as those found in Europe and North America. Such societies are fragmented and lack the strong communities needed to sustain religion as an important force in society.

### Religious revivals

**Kepel** (1994) claims that any trend towards secularization was reversed in *c.* 1975. Since then religious revivals have taken place around the world, often aimed at changing whole societies. Examples include Christianity in the USA and Europe, Judaism in Israel, and Islam throughout the world. However, Bruce (2001) believes that even Islamic fundamentalism is susceptible to the influence of modernization.

### Secularization – conclusion

#### Problems with proving or disproving secularization

As the views of sociologists such as Martin and Kepel illustrate, the theory of secularization has not been definitely proved or disproved. This is partly because different writers have used the term 'secularization' in different ways. This has led to confusion since writers discussing the process of secularization are often arguing about different things. **Glock and Stark** (1969) argue that researchers have not paid sufficient attention to defining religion and religiosity.

Contemporary theorists do pay more attention to the different aspects of secularization. Steve **Bruce** for example, a strong supporter of the theory of secularization, accepts that religion can remain an important part of individual beliefs, but he believes religion has lost its social and political significance.

### Casanova and types of secularization

**Casanova** distinguishes three aspects of secularization:

1 Secularization as **differentiation**. Secularization takes place when non-religious spheres of life become separate from religion.
2 Secularization as a **decline of religious beliefs**. Secularization occurs when fewer people participate in religion and hold religious beliefs.
3 Secularization as **privatization**. Religion stops playing a part in public life and does not try to influence people's lives.

To Casanova, it is only in the first sense that secularization has taken place. Religion no longer has a central position in modern societies but neither does it fade away.

## RELIGIOUS FUNDAMENTALISM

Samuel **Huntingdon** (1993) argues that sources of identity that are not religious have declined in significance. Religious movements, often labelled as 'fundamentalist', have developed in Western Christianity, Judaism, Buddhism and Hinduism as well as Islam. Most conflict in the world can now be related to religious differences.

Karen **Armstrong** (2001) argues that fundamentalist interpretations of Islam have become popular because of the failure of modernization and the constant interference of Western countries in the Islamic world in ways which damage Muslims but support Western interest. Thus political and economic factors are behind the clash between some Muslims and the West, not religious factors.

Anthony **Giddens** (1994) sees the growth of fundamentalist movements as a response to the way in which the contemporary world – what he calls '**high modernity**' undermines certainty. Fundamentalists, for example some Christian fundamentalists in the USA, simply assert that they are right through an appeal to traditional beliefs. They react against a **globalized world** by refusing to compromise or even consider that they might be wrong. Giddens believes that the different ethnic and religious groups who live in close proximity have to be more tolerant of one another if serious conflict is to be avoided.

# TEST YOUR KNOWLEDGE AND UNDERSTANDING

1 Which one of the following statements would a functionalist be most likely to agree with?
a Religion often causes social change
b Religion often causes conflict in society
c Religion reinforces shared values
d Religion is an ideological tool

2 Parsons would probably agree with three of the following statements. Which is the odd one out?
a Religion helps people to make sense of their experiences
b Religion helps deal with the problems that disrupt social life
c Religion has some dysfunctional aspects
d Religion provides guidelines for human action

3 Marx would probably agree with three of the following statements. Which is the odd one out?
a Religion acts as a mechanism of social control
b Religion is the opium of the people
c Religion is functional for society
d Religion creates false class consciousness

4 Which one of the following sociologists is most likely to believe that religion can play a role in changing societies?
a Weber
b Marx
c Parsons
d Durkheim

5 Many sociologists believe that religion is a conservative force in society. Which one of the following statements reflects this view?
a Religion is unlikely to be a key factor in causing social change
b Most religious believers are right-wing
c Religion is very powerful
d Religious fundamentalism is becoming increasingly popular

6 Which one of the following definitions best describes Weber's concept of the 'spirit of capitalism'?
a A set of values which encourage the accumulation of wealth
b A set of values which encourage a simple life and the avoidance of alcohol and other pleasures
c The view that capitalism is the best economic system
d A set of values based on Protestant beliefs

7 Three of these characteristics are associated with churches. Which is the odd one out?
a They are not usually linked to the state
b Members are drawn from all sections of society
c They accept and affirm life in this world
d Believers do not have to demonstrate their faith to become a member

8 Three of these characteristics are associated with sects. Which is the odd one out?
a They tend to reject the values of society
b Central authority often rests with a charismatic leader
c They are formal organizations with a hierarchy of paid officials
d Members are often expected to withdraw from conventional life

9 Three of the following would probably be considered examples of 'New Age' beliefs or actions. Which is the odd one out?
a Feng Shui
b Being a member of the Jehovah's Witnesses
c Having your tarot cards read
d Meditating

10 What is the name given to the process whereby the church withdraws from wider society?
a Structural differentiation
b Social differentiation
c Societalization
d Disengagement

11 Three of the following are characteristics of world-affirming new religious movements, according to Wallis. Which is the odd one out?
a They claim to provide access to spiritual or supernatural powers
b They are usually offshoots of a major church or denomination
c They offer followers the potential to be successful
d They tolerate the existence of other religions

12 One of the following statements about religious participation is false. Can you identify it?
a Church attendance is declining in Britain
b Church attendance is declining in the USA
c Non-Christian religions in Britain have gained members
d Christian religions in Britain have lost members

13 What term is used to describe a society containing a wide variety of religious groups?
a Cultural diversity
b Religious pluralism
c Ethnic diversity
d Privatization of religion

14 Bruce argues that when two communities are in conflict their religious identity can become a way of asserting their ethnic pride. What term does he use to refer to this?
a Cultural transition
b Cultural defence
c Cultural diversity
d Cultural pluralism

15 Which of the following statements is a definition of desacrilization?
a Supernatural forces are no longer seen as controlling the world
b There is a decline in sacred objects and symbols
c Secularization is occurring
d Conventional religions are losing support

# DEVELOP YOUR ANALYSIS AND EVALUATION SKILLS

## *Religion can cause change in society.*

***Background:*** Functionalists and Marxists share the view that religion is essentially a force acting for stability and against change in societies. Weber's classic studies of *The Protestant Ethic* and *The Spirit of Capitalism* are the starting point for arguments that religion can promote social change.

| *For* | *Against* |
|---|---|
| ■ Weber (pp. 95–6)<br>■ Nelson ( p. 96)<br>■ Maduro (p. 94)<br>■ Taylor on fundamentalism (p. 95) | ■ Durkheim (p. 93)<br>■ Malinowski (p. 93)<br>■ Parsons (p. 93)<br>■ Marx (pp. 93–4) |

***Top tip:*** McGuire (see p. 96) is useful in evaluating this debate in so far as she identifies specific factors that affect the role of religion in society, and avoids large scale generalizations.

## *Church membership and attendance statistics indicate a clear decline in religiosity.*

***Background:*** This statement represents one aspect of the secularization debate – the view that religion is losing its social significance. The view expressed does not indicate any particular church or country and the evidence does vary across the world and between religions.

| *For* | *Against* |
|---|---|
| ■ Decline in church attendance in UK (Brierley) (p. 99)<br>■ Decline in church membership in UK (Brierley) (p. 99)<br>■ Bruce: surveys show clear decline in religious beliefs (p. 100) | ■ Increase in non-Christian and smaller religions (p. 99)<br>■ Growth of New Age beliefs (pp. 98–9)<br>■ Doubts about reliability and validity of figures (p. 100)<br>■ Martin – religion in Victorian Britain (p. 100)<br>■ Rates of attendance and membership much higher in USA (p. 99)<br>■ Barrett: Christianity increasing in some countries. Big increase in proportion of Muslims (p. 99) |

***Top tip:*** A key issue here is the extent to which participation in formal religious organizations is a valid indicator of religiosity. It may be possible to go to church but not have strong religious feelings, while it is equally possible that people may have deep religious beliefs but do not attend church.

## *The growth of new religious movements and 'New Age' beliefs since the 1960s indicates a revival of religion.*

***Background:*** A variety of explanations have been put forward to explain the increase in these organizations and beliefs. This statement focuses on the social significance of this growth rather than the reasons for it.

| *For* | *Against* |
|---|---|
| ■ Greeley – resacrilization (p. 101)<br>■ Heelas – significance of New Age beliefs (p. 101) | ■ Bruce – small numbers in new religious movements (p. 101)<br>■ Wilson – religious pluralism indicates insignificance of religion (p. 101)<br>■ Drane: reflects move to postmodernity (p. 99) |

***Top tip:*** A key point is that although the numbers involved in these groups have grown, they are still very small. Although it is important to explain the terms 'new religious movements' and 'New Age', try not to spend too much time doing so, as this is not the main point of the question.

# AQA-STYLE RELIGION QUESTION

## A2 Unit 4, Part One

Answer the question in
Part One and one
question from Part Two

Total: 60 marks
1 mark = 1.5 minutes

Time allowed:
1 hour 30 minutes

### ITEM A

Church of England Sunday attendance has sunk to the lowest ever, according to Church statistics published in 1994. Even Christmas services were affected, with numbers falling by 7%, although church officials blamed poor weather and took some comfort from the fact that Easter services had become more popular.

Churchgoers' direct donations had increased by more than inflation and this was interpreted as a sign of a more committed membership.

**Comments on the question**

- There are many points you can pick up on from the item with careful and critical reading
- You must go beyond the information in the item to gain full marks

[a] Using material from Item A and elsewhere, examine some of the problems in measuring religious practice. [8 marks]

**Advice on preparing your answer**

- See pp. 99–100

- This requires that you demonstrate evaluation skills
- This means that you can use these and others
- Make sure that you understand and use this term correctly (see chapter 14, pp. 199–200)

[b] Discuss how far religious practices such as those in Item A are a valid indicator of religiosity.

[12 marks]

- Pages 99–100 looks at participation as a form of religious practice
- Other aspects of religiosity can be found on pp. 98–9

## A2 Unit 4, Part Two

Answer one question from this part

- Make specific criticisms of this material
- Suggest alternative evidence and arguments that would oppose this view
- The best answers will consider both these parts of the question
- Identify the source of this view as a Weberian one
- Better answers will see social change as a problematic concept

**Either**

Assess the evidence and arguments that religious beliefs can encourage social change.

[40 marks]

- Weberian views, p. 95
- Evidence for this, pp. 95–6
- Critique, p. 95
- Alternative views: Marxist, pp. 93–4; functionalist, p. 93

- You cannot successfully do this by writing two consecutive descriptive accounts. You need to identify similarities and differences in the two approaches
- Consider the following questions:
  1 What perspective do they adopt?
  2 What is the origin of religion?
  3 How does religion perform social control functions?
  4 What purpose does religion serve for individuals and society?
  5 What evidence can be used in support of or against each?
- A question that looks deceptively simple, but you need to be prepared!

**Or**

Compare and contrast functionalist and Marxist explanations of the role of religion in society.

[40 marks]

- You will need to analyse functionalist accounts (p. 93) and Marxist accounts (pp. 93–4), then use the answers to the questions opposite to write a short paragraph for each theory
- You can use other theories, e.g. Weber (p. 95), to show that they both fail to address change; and/or postmodernism

# OCR-STYLE RELIGION QUESTION

## AS Unit 2533: Culture and Socialization

**Answer both parts of this question**
Total: 45 marks, 1 mark = 1 minute
Time allowed: 45 minutes

### Comments on the question

- Make sure that the examiner can see that you have clearly identified two characteristics
- No more, no less
- Make sure that you develop an explanation of why or how what you have identified qualifies as a characteristic of secularization

[a] Identify and explain two characteristics of secularization. [15 marks]

### Advice on preparing your answer

- You will find a definition of this term on p. 99
- The section on pp. 99–103 includes material that will help you with this task

- Describe the view as fully as possible using supporting evidence in the shape of statistical data and sociological studies
- Consider arguments/evidence against the view and/or alternative view(s)

[b] Outline and assess the view that people join religious sects and cults as a way of coping with rapid social change.

[30 marks]

- Remember that this is only one view. Alternatives should be presented in your answer
- You should construct an introduction which defines sects and cults and which identifies where the view originates
- You will find information on the social change argument on pp. 98–9

# Chapter 8

# FAMILIES AND HOUSEHOLDS

Textbook pp. 464–537

## Specifications

| Specification | Specification details | | Coverage |
|---|---|---|---|
| **AQA** AS: Families and Households | ■ Different conceptions of the relationships of the family to the social structure, with particular reference to the economy and state policies | | Covered in sections on the main perspectives (pp. 109–11) and social policy (p. 117). |
| | ■ Changes in family and household structure and their relationship to industrialization and urbanization | | See the section on the family, industrialization and modernization (pp. 111–12). |
| | ■ Changing patterns of marriage, cohabitation, separation, divorce and childbearing and the diversity of contemporary family and household structure | | Most of these issues covered in sections on marriage and marital breakdown (pp. 116–17) and family diversity (pp. 112–14). |
| | ■ The nature and extent of changes in the family, with reference to gender roles, domestic labour and power relationships, and to changes in the status of children and childhood | | Gender roles, domestic labour and power are the focus of the section on conjugal roles (pp. 115–16). |
| **OCR** AS: Culture and Socialization/ Family | **The family and recent social change** | ■ Family concepts and definitions: kinship and households, nuclear and extended families | Basic concepts explained towards the start of the chapter (pp. 109–10). |
| | | ■ Recent demographic change: divorce, births, ageing population | Issues relating to marriage and divorce covered on pp. 116–17. Other demographic issues discussed as part of section on family diversity (pp. 112–14). |
| | | ■ Social policy and the family: family values debates. Policy towards families and children | Covered in sections on family diversity (pp. 112–14) and the family, politics and social policy (p. 117). |
| | **Diversity in families and households** | ■ Recent trends in family life; cohabitation, one-parent families, reconstituted families, dual career families, single-person households | See the section on family diversity (pp. 112–14). |
| | | ■ Dimensions of diversity; class, gender, ethnicity, lifestyle and location | Class differences are discussed in the section on family and industrialization (pp. 111–12), gender differences in conjugal roles (pp. 115–16), and ethnic diversity in the family diversity section (pp. 112–14). |
| | | ■ Explanations of family diversification, changing economic and domestic roles of men and women, changes in family obligations | The impact of changing roles of men and women is covered on pp. 115–16 while family obligations are discussed on p. 112. A more general explanation of family diversification can be found in the section on families, modernity and postmodernity on p. 117. |
| | **Power, inequality and family policy** | ■ The distribution of power between men and women in the family. Patriarchy, the domestic division of labour, decision-making | Covered in the section on conjugal roles (see pp. 115–16). |
| | | ■ The relationship between parents and children; changing conceptions of childhood, the legal status of children | Gender roles and childcare are discussed on p. 115. The social construction of childhood is covered in chapter 12 (p. 173). |
| | | ■ The dark side of family life: violence, child abuse and social policy | Critical views of the family are covered from Marxist and feminist viewpoints in particular (see pp. 110–11). |

For more detailed specification guidance visit **www.haralambosholborn.com**

# IS THE FAMILY UNIVERSAL?

## Variations in family structure

- The **nuclear family** – this is the smallest family unit and consists of a husband, wife and their dependent offspring.
- The **extended family** – this is a larger family grouping consisting of other members related by birth, marriage or adoption.

## Murdock: the family – a universal social institution

In 1949 **Murdock** looked at 250 societies and claimed that some form of family existed in each. He defined the family as a social group characterized by:

- Common residence
- Economic cooperation
- Reproduction
- Adults of both sexes, two of whom maintain a socially approved sexual relationship
- One or more children (own or adopted) of these adults

He concluded that the nuclear family is **universal**, either on its own or as the base unit within an extended family.

## Evaluation of Murdock

- Murdock's definition of the family includes at least one adult of each sex. However, many children, both today and in the past, have been raised in households that do not contain adults of both sexes.
- **Gough's** analysis (1959) of the Nayar society in India, before British rule was established in 1792, shows that women had several 'husbands' who took no responsibility for the care of their offspring.
- A significant proportion of black families in the West Indies, Central America and the USA are **matrifocal** (female-headed) families and do not include adult males.
- **Sheeran** (1993) argues that the 'female-carer core' is the most basic family unit. In Britain, for example, children usually have one woman who is primarily responsible for their care. This primary carer is not always the biological mother. It could be a grandmother, elder sister, aunt, adoptive mother or other female.
- **Gay and lesbian** households may well contain children, either from a previous heterosexual relationship or as the result of new reproductive technologies. **Callahan** (1997) argues that gay and lesbian households should be seen as families. If marriage were available, many gay and lesbian couples would marry, and their relationships are not significantly different from those in heterosexual households.

Whether the family is regarded as universal ultimately depends on how the family is defined. It may be a somewhat pointless exercise to try to find a single definition that embraces all the types of household and relationship that can reasonably be called families.

# THE FAMILY – A FUNCTIONALIST PERSPECTIVE

The analysis of the family from a functionalist perspective involves three main questions:

- What are the functions of the family for society?
- What are the functional relationships between the family and the wider social system?
- What are the functions of the family for individuals?

## Murdock – the universal functions of the family

**Murdock** (1949) argues that the family performs four basic functions for individuals and society and that these are applicable to all societies:

1. **Sexual** – essential for the continuation of the society
2. **Reproductive** – as for sexual
3. **Economic** – essential for survival (for example, the production and preparation of food)
4. **Educational** – essential for passing on the society's culture to the next generation

## Criticisms of Murdock

1. Murdock does not consider whether the above functions could be performed by other social institutions.
2. **Morgan** (1975) points out that Murdock presents the nuclear family as a totally harmonious institution. Later sections will question this view.

# PARSONS – THE 'BASIC AND IRREDUCIBLE' FUNCTIONS OF THE FAMILY

**Parsons** (1955, 1965) argued that the family retains two 'basic and irreducible' functions that are common to all societies. These are the **primary socialization of children** and the **stabilization of adult personalities**.

## Primary socialization

**Primary socialization** refers to socialization during the early years of childhood. The child's personality is moulded to absorb the central values of the society's culture. Parsons could think of no other social institution providing the warmth, security and mutual support necessary for the successful socialization of individuals.

## Stabilization of adult personalities

The emphasis here is on the marital relationship and the emotional security the couple provide for each other. This acts to balance out the stresses and strains of everyday life. The family also allows adults to 'act out' the childish parts of their personalities.

## Criticisms of Parsons

1. Parsons presents an idealized view of the family.
2. His picture is based largely on the American middle-class family. He ignores variations in families – for example, among different classes and ethnic groups.

3 Like Murdock, Parsons fails to explore alternatives to the family.

4 Parsons sees socialization as a one-way process and ignores the active role that children play in creating their own personalities.

5 Some contemporary perspectives argue that the family cannot be seen as performing functions on its own. It has to be seen in relation to other social institutions.

## MARXIST PERSPECTIVES ON THE FAMILY

### Engels – the origin of the family

Engels (1972, originally published 1884) attempted to trace the evolution of the family through time. The **monogamous nuclear family** developed to solve the problem of the inheritance of private property. Property was owned by males, who needed heirs to pass it on to. They needed greater **control over women** so the paternity of their offspring was certain. The monogamous family provided the most efficient device for this purpose.

### Zaretsky – personal life and capitalism

Zaretsky (1976) sees the family as a major prop to the **capitalist system**.

- The capitalist system is based on the **domestic labour** of housewives who reproduce future generations of workers.
- The family **consumes** the products of capitalism and this enables the bourgeoisie to keep profits up.

## FEMINIST PERSPECTIVES ON THE FAMILY

### The influence of feminism

Recently, **feminism** has had more influence on the study of the family than any other approach. Feminists have strongly criticized the effects of family life upon women.

Feminist approaches have:

- Introduced the study of areas of family life such as **housework** and **domestic violence**.
- Challenged established views about male dominance in families.
- Highlighted the economic contribution to society of women's domestic labour.
- Focused on **power relationships** within the family, in particular the ways in which men benefit from families at the expense of women.

At the same time, some recent feminist approaches have questioned the tendency of some feminists to make blanket condemnations of family life and have emphasized the different experiences of women in families.

### Marxist feminist perspectives on the family

**Marxist feminists** argue that the family and its exploitation of women serve the needs of capitalism.

- **Benston** (1972) points out that the husband's paying for the production and upkeep of the next generation weakens his bargaining power at work – he cannot go on strike because he has a family to support.
- **Ansley** (1972) argues that the emotional support of wives acts as a safety valve for the husbands' frustration that is caused by working within the capitalist system.

### Criticisms

1 Variations in family life – according to class and ethnic group, for example – are ignored.

2 **Morgan** (1975) points out that Marxist approaches often assume the existence of very traditional families – a type of family that is becoming less common.

3 **Marxist feminists** may exaggerate the harm done to women in the family. They are reluctant to concede that there may be positive elements to family life.

4 They also tend to portray women as the **passive victims** of exploitation.

### Radical feminist perspectives on the family

There are many types of radical feminism. **Bryson** identifies two characteristics they have in common:

1 Radical feminism is new, not adapted from existing theories.

2 It sees the oppression of women as the most significant aspect of a patriarchal and male-dominated society.

- **Delphy and Leonard** (1992) argue that the family is a **patriarchal** and **hierarchical** institution through which men dominate and exploit women. Wives may resist male domination but they find it difficult to escape from the patriarchal family.
- **Purdy** (1997) argues that women's disadvantages largely result from **childcare** responsibilities. She believes that there are many disadvantages of motherhood. It is expensive and a long-term commitment in terms of time and energy. She advocates a 'baby-strike'. Only then would men take women's demands for equality seriously.
- **Germaine Greer** (2000) argues that **wives** remain **subservient** to their husbands, although the increased divorce rate shows women accept this situation less. **Motherhood** can be rewarding, but it is not valued by society and mothers take the blame for many of society's problems. **Daughters** often suffer **sexual abuse** from male relatives. Greer concludes that women would be better off separated from **patriarchal families**.

### Criticisms

Many of the criticisms of Marxist feminism also apply to radical feminism.

### Liberal feminist perspectives on the family

**Jennifer Somerville** (2000) offers a more moderate assessment of women's position in contemporary societies.

- Somerville believes that many feminists fail to acknowledge the progress made by women in Britain.
- Women have more **opportunities** and **choices** open to them, and some men advocate greater **gender equality**.

- Many men do not live up to their responsibilities but most do not wish to live without a male partner.
- Feminists therefore need to adopt **principled pragmatism**, by which practical policies produce greater equality and change institutional arrangements based upon the idea of the male breadwinner.

## Criticisms

Somerville's claims are not backed up by detailed empirical evidence.

## Difference feminism

Neither **Marxist** nor **radical** feminism is very sensitive to differences between families. Both can be criticized for failing to acknowledge the variety of domestic arrangements and the range of effects family life can have.

Increasingly, feminists have begun to highlight these differences. These feminists have been referred to as **difference feminists**. Their work often has links with **postmodern** theories of the family

- **Nicholson** (1997) believes that there is a powerful **ideology** that supports **traditional families** but devalues other types. She believes that alternative families are often better than traditional ones for the women who live in them. Nicholson concludes that all types of family and household should be accepted because they could suit different women in different circumstances.
- **Calhoun** (1997) focuses on **lesbian families**. She argues that modern family life is characterized by choice, and lesbian and gay families are 'chosen families'. Calhoun believes that gay and lesbian relationships are just as much family relationships as those of heterosexual couples.

## Criticisms

1 Some difference feminists lose sight of the **inequalities** between men and women in stressing the range of choices open to people.
2 They also tend to neglect the common experiences shared by most women in families.

# THE FAMILY, INDUSTRIALIZATION AND MODERNIZATION

A major theme in the sociology of the family has been the relationship between the structure of the family and the process of **industrialization** (the move from an agricultural system to the mass production of goods in a factory system).

## The pre-industrial family

One form of **pre-industrial family** found in some traditional peasant societies is known as the classic extended family.

**Arensberg and Kimball's** study of Irish farmers (1968) found the basic family unit to be the **extended family**, consisting of a male head, his wife and children, his ageing parents who have passed the farm on to him, and any unmarried brothers and sisters. Together they work as a **unit of production**, producing the goods necessary for the family's survival.

Some people have argued that, as industrialization proceeds, the classic extended family breaks up and the **nuclear family** emerges as the predominant family form.

## Parsons – the 'isolated nuclear family'

**Parsons** (1959, 1965; Parsons and Bale 1955) argued that the **isolated nuclear family** is the typical family form in modern industrial society. It is isolated in the sense that relationships between the nuclear family and wider kin are a matter of choice rather than obligation. There are three key reasons for its suitability in industrial societies:

1 The **evolution** of society involves a process of **structural differentiation**. This means that institutions evolve that specialize in fewer functions. Specialist institutions such as businesses, schools and hospitals take over many of the functions of the family.
2 Parsons argued that there is a functional relationship between the isolated nuclear family and the **economic system**. In modern societies individuals are required to move to places where their particular skills are in demand. The isolated nuclear family is more suited to **geographical mobility** as it is not tied down with binding obligations to wider kin.
3 The isolated nuclear family is the best family form for societies where **status** is **achieved** rather than **ascribed** (fixed at birth). If adult children remained as part of an extended family unit, conflicts could arise if a son achieved a higher social position than his father, because within the family the father has a higher status.

## Criticisms of Parsons

**Cheal** (1991) is sceptical about what he calls the **modernist** view of the family advocated by **Parsons**, who argues that the nuclear family is well-adapted to modern societies and sees it in a positive light. Cheal argues that:

- There is nothing inevitable about modern institutions developing so that they function well together.
- Parsons makes over-generalized statements about the family that have not stood up well to the passage of time.

Detailed historical accounts of the development of the family have also cast doubt on Parsons' views.

## Laslett – the family in pre-industrial societies

**Peter Laslett** (1972, 1977) has studied family life and composition in pre-industrial England. For the period 1564 to 1821 he found that only about 10% of households contained kin beyond the nuclear family. His low figure may be due to:

- Short life expectancy
- Late marriage

Laslett found no evidence to support the view that the **classic extended family** was widespread in pre-industrial England.

## Anderson – household structure and the Industrial Revolution

Using data from the 1851 census, **Anderson** found that in Preston almost a quarter of households contained kin other than the nuclear family. The bulk of these extended families occurred among the poor.

Anderson suggests four reasons for this pattern:

1 In the absence of a **welfare state**, individuals were dependent on their kin in times of hardship.
2 The high death rate led to a large number of orphans who found a home with their relatives.
3 Additional members of a household lowered the share of the rent paid by each individual.
4 It was normal in factory towns for employers to recruit through kin.

## Young and Willmott – four stages of family life

In their book, *The Symmetrical Family* (1973), Young and Willmott suggest that the family has gone through four main stages. We will concentrate on their analysis of the working-class family and the first three stages.

### Stage 1 – The pre-industrial family

The **pre-industrial family** is a **unit of production**. It was gradually supplanted as a result of the Industrial Revolution. It did, however, continue into the nineteenth century and there are still some examples in farming families today.

### Stage 2 – The early industrial family

This type of family developed in the nineteenth century and reached its peak in the early twentieth century. The family ceased to be a unit of production and responded to the new industrial society by extending its **network** to include relatives beyond the nuclear family.

The early industrial family is still found in some well-established working-class communities and is documented in Young and Willmott's famous study *Family and Kinship in East London*.

### Stage 3 – The symmetrical family

By the early 1970s the stage 2 family had largely disappeared. The stage 3 family is **nuclear and home-centred**. Free time is spent doing chores and odd jobs, and leisure is mainly home-based. The **conjugal bond** between husband and wife is strong and they share work in the home. Young and Willmott use the term **symmetrical family** to describe the stage 3 nuclear family.

## Reasons for the rise of the symmetrical family

1 A reduction in the need for kinship-based support because of rising wages and the welfare state.
2 Increased geographical mobility.
3 Reduction in the number of children per family.

4 More amenities and entertainment in the home, making it a more attractive place.

## The 'Principle of Stratified Diffusion'

Young and Willmott believe that their theory of **stratified diffusion** explains many of the changes in family life. The theory states that what those at the top of the stratification system do today, those at the bottom will do tomorrow. The home-centred nuclear family began in the middle classes and eventually filtered down to the rest of society.

## Families and kinship in the 1980s and 1990s

In a comparison of attitudes to the family in 1986 and 1995, **McGlone** *et al.* (1996) argue that families remain very important to people in contemporary Britain.

■ Families remain an important source of help and support.
■ Family contacts are still maintained even though family members tend to live farther apart than in the past.
■ Differences between social classes remain significant, with the working class more likely to have frequent contact than the middle class.

The *British Social Attitudes Survey* (Park *et al.* 2001) found that only 10% of those who had a mother surviving saw her less than several times a year, and 61% of grandparents saw their grandchildren at least once a week.

## The dispersed extended and beanpole family.

Attempts have been made to characterize the contemporary family to take account of the continuing contacts between relatives.

■ **Willmott** (1988) claims that the **dispersed extended family** is becoming dominant in Britain. It consists of two or more related families who cooperate with each other even though they live some distance apart. Cars, public transport and telephones allow dispersed extended families to keep in touch.
■ **Julia Brannen** (2003) argues that contemporary family structure resembles a **beanpole**, as there are strong **intergenerational** links between parents and children across two, three or four generations, but **intragenerational** links (e.g. with siblings and cousins) tend to be weaker.

## FAMILY DIVERSITY

Leach (1967) calls the image of the happily married couple – a male breadwinner and a female carer/housewife – with two children, the **'cereal packet image'** of the family. This image is prominent in advertising.

However, recent research suggests that contemporary societies are characterized by a **plurality** of household and family types, so the idea of a typical family is misleading.

## Households in Britain

- There has been a steady decline in the proportion of British households consisting of **married couples with dependent children**, from 35% in 1971 to 23% in 2002.
- There has been a corresponding increase in **single-person households**.
- The proportion of **single-parent households** rose from 6% in 1971 to 10% in 2002..

## Types of diversity

Rhona and Robert Rapoport (1982) identify five types of family diversity in Britain:

1 **Organizational diversity** – There are variations in family structure, household type, patterns of kinship and differences in the division of labour in the household. There are also increasing numbers of reconstituted families – families formed after divorce and remarriage.
2 **Cultural diversity** – There are differences in the lifestyles of families of different ethnic origins and religious beliefs. (Ethnic diversity is discussed on p. 101.)
3 **Class diversity** – There are differences between middle- and working-class families in relation to child-rearing and adult relationships.
4 **Life-cycle diversity** – Differences result from the stage in the life cycle of the family. Newly married couples without children may have a different family life from those with dependent children, for example.
5 **Cohort diversity** – This refers to the periods at which the family has passed through different stages of the family life cycle. High rates of unemployment during the 1980s, for example, may have increased the length of time children lived with their parents.

In addition to these five aspects of diversity, **Eversley and Bonnerjea** (1982) argue that there are distinctive patterns of family life in different areas of Britain: **regional diversity**. In the 'sun belt' of southern England, for example, two-parent upwardly mobile families are typical, whilst in rural areas strong kinship ties are more common.

Allan and Crow (2001) see the trend towards diversity as being caused by:

- A rising **divorce** rate.
- A rise in lone-parenthood which partly reflects an acceptance that pregnancies do not have to be **legitimized** by marriage.
- Acceptance of **cohabitation** before marriage.
- Declining **marriage rates**.
- A growth in **stepfamilies**.

## Gay and lesbian families

**Gay and lesbian** households have become more common since the 1980s. **Weeks, Donovan and Heaphey** (1999) argue that gays and lesbians look on their households and even their friendship networks as 'chosen families'. They choose who to include in their families and negotiate their relationships.

## New reproductive technologies

**New reproductive technologies** such as **surrogate motherhood** add an entirely new dimension to family diversity. The implication is that biology will no longer restrict the possibilities for forming and enlarging families by having children.

## The increase in single-parent families

As mentioned earlier, single-parent families have become increasingly common in Britain. The figures must be interpreted with caution because they are only a snapshot and do not represent the changing family life of many individuals. Children may start their life in a single-parent family, but the single parent may well find a new partner, so the child will end up living with two parents.

## The causes of single parenthood

People who are married can become single parents by:

- **Divorce**
- **Separation**
- **Death** of a spouse

Single parents who have never married:

- May have been living with the parent of the child but have subsequently separated.
- May not have been living with the parent of the child when the child was born.

The rise in lone motherhood and fatherhood (about one in eight single-parent families are headed by a male) is closely linked to two factors:

1 Increases in the **divorce rate** (discussed on p. 116).
2 Increases in **births outside marriage**

**Allan and Crow** (2001) believe both these trends reflect an increased acceptance of diversity. **Brown** (1995) suggests that in previous eras 'shotgun weddings' (couples getting married to legitimate a pregnancy) were common. Now partners may choose to **cohabit** rather than marry. **Park et al.** use data from the British Social Attitudes Survey to show that younger age groups are much more accepting of births outside marriage than older age groups.

The **Rapoports** (1982) argued that the single-parent family was an important 'emerging form' of the family which is becoming accepted as a legitimate alternative to other family structures.

However, there is little evidence that a large number of single parents actively choose it as an alternative to dual parenthood. In a small-scale piece of research by **Burghes and Brown** (1995), all of the lone mothers in the sample aspired to forming a two-parent household.

## The consequences of single parenthood

Some have argued that single parenthood has become a serious problem for society. **Charles Murray** (1989), the **New Right** thinker, has gone so far as to claim that single parenthood has contributed to the creation of an anti-social underclass (see pp. 50–1).

Many sociologists disagree. **McIntosh** (1996) claims that lone mothers have been stigmatized and blamed for problems such as youth crime and unemployment.

However single parenthood is viewed, there is little doubt that it is associated with low living standards. The *General Household Survey* (2001) found that 51% of single-parent households had an income of £150 per week or less compared to 13% of married couples.

### Effects on children

- **McLanahan and Booth** (1991) review the findings of American studies, which seem to indicate that children are harmed by single parenthood – more likely to experience **poverty**, become **delinquent** or engage in **drug abuse**.
- However, as the authors themselves point out, these differences tend to stem from low income rather than the absence of a second parent.
- **Burghes** (1996) notes that some research indicates that children in families where parents divorce, start to do poorly in education before the divorce takes place. This may reflect the quality of the family relationships, of which divorce is only one aspect.
- **Cashmore** (1985) argues that it is often preferable for a child to live with one caring parent than with one caring and one uncaring parent. Single parenthood can also give women greater independence than they have in other family situations.

### Ethnicity and family diversity

Statistical evidence from the *Labour Force Survey* (2002) suggests that there are differences in household types among different ethnic groups.

- Black African and Black Caribbean families have much higher rates of **single-parenthood** than other groups. Rates among Indian families are very low with white and Pakistani/Bangladeshi families having rates near the average.
- Asian families are more likely to have **dependent children** in the household than the families of other ethnic groups.
- **One person households** are most common among black ethnic groups and least common among Pakistani/Bangladeshi ethnic groups.

### South Asian families

- **Ballard** (1982, 1990) has examined South Asian families in Britain.
- Many children had the experience of **two cultures**. They behaved in ways that conformed to the culture of wider society for part of the time, but at home conformed to their ethnic subculture.
- Although children expected to have some say in their marriage partner, they did not reject the principle of **arranged marriage**.

- Despite the distance involved, most families retained links with their village of origin in Asia.
- In Britain, close family ties remained. By living close together, people were able to retain strong family links.
- **Bhatti** (1999) found that ideas of *izzat*, or family honour, remained very strong, as did the roles of the traditional male breadwinner and female child-rearer.
- However, in a minority of families there were **generational clashes** especially where the sons sought to marry outside their own ethnic group.
- Overall, distinctive patterns of family life remained.

### West Indian families in Britain

- **Barrow** (1982) found that **mother-centred families** could rely less on the support of female kin than they could in the West Indies. However, equivalent networks did build up in areas with high concentrations of West Indians.
- **Berthoud and Beishon** (1997) identified a low emphasis on long-term partnerships, especially formal marriage. British African-Caribbean families had high rates of **divorce** and **separation** and were more likely than other groups to have children outside marriage. Nevertheless, over half of Caribbean families with children were married or cohabiting in long-term relationships.

### Ethnicity and family diversity – conclusion

The evidence suggests that immigrants and their descendants have adapted to fit British circumstances but have not fundamentally altered the relationships on which their traditional family life was based.

### Chester – the British neo-conventional family

In a strong attack on the idea that fundamental changes are taking place in British family life, **Robert Chester** (1985) argued that the changes have only been minor.

- If you look at the percentage of people rather than households, then nearly half the population still live in **nuclear family households**.
- It is inevitable that at any one time some people will not be members of nuclear family households. However, the vast majority of people still experience the **parent–children household** at some point.
- Chester accepts that many families are no longer 'conventional' in the sense that the husband is the sole breadwinner. He sees this type of family as a 'neo-conventional family' – little different from the conventional family apart from the increasing number of wives working for at least part of their married lives.

### Family diversity – conclusion

Since Chester was writing, there has been a slow but steady drift away from **nuclear families** in Britain. As the **Rapoports** argued in 1982, the amount of family diversity indicates increasing acceptance of alternative households and families. However, **Somerville** (2000) believes most people still aspire to conventional family life.

# THE CHANGING FUNCTIONS OF THE FAMILY

## The loss of functions

Many sociologists argue that the family has lost a number of its functions in modern industrial society. Institutions such as businesses, schools and welfare organizations now specialize in functions previously performed by the family.

## Functionalist views

Parsons (1955) maintains that the family still has a vital role in preparing its members to meet the requirements of the social system (see pp. 109–10).

Fletcher (1966) disputes the claim that some of the family's functions have been lost. He argues that the family has retained its functions and that these have increased in importance. The family is no longer a **unit of production**, but the modern home-centred family is a vital economic **unit of consumption** – for washing machines, DVD players and so on.

## Feminist views

Feminists disagree that the family has lost its economic function. They argue that much of the work that takes place in the family is not recognized as such because it is unpaid and usually done by women. (See pp. 110–11)

## Postmodernist and difference feminist views

These sociologists reject the view that there is any single type of family that always performs certain functions. With increasing **diversity**, some individual families and some types of family may be radical forces in society – for example, **gay and lesbian families**.

# CONJUGAL ROLES

A major characteristic of the **symmetrical family** – which **Young and Willmott** claimed was developing when they were writing in the 1970s – was the sharing of domestic work and leisure activities between spouses (see p. 112). Relationships of this type are known as joint conjugal roles, as opposed to **segregated conjugal roles**.

## Inequality within marriage

There is no generally accepted way of measuring inequality between husbands and wives. Different researchers have measured it in different ways. However, most find little evidence that inequality in marriage has been significantly reduced.

## Conjugal roles, housework and childcare

- Oakley (1974) argues that Young and Willmott's claim of increasing **symmetry** is based on inadequate methodology. Their conclusions were based on only one interview question which was worded in a way that could exaggerate the amount of housework done by men.
- Small-scale research in the 1970s by Oakley (1974) and Edgell (1980) found little sharing of household tasks.
- The *British Social Attitudes Survey* (1992) found more sharing of child-rearing than household tasks, although there was some movement towards a more egalitarian division of labour over time.
- Ferri and Smith (1996) used survey data to focus on childcare. In almost every kind of household – even where the woman had paid employment outside the home and the man did not – it was more common for the woman to take the main responsibility for childcare.

## Conjugal roles and hours worked

- Young and Willmott found that the differences between men's and women's work time in the home were not that great.
- Gershuny (1992, 1999) found that the husbands of working women continued to do less than half the total paid and unpaid work done by their spouses. However, although the '**dual burden**' of paid and domestic work remained for women, men seemd to make more effort to do housework when their wives were in paid work.
- Laurie and Gershuny (2000) found that over time there had been a slow drift towards men taking on more domestic responsibilities.
- Sullivan (1996) examined the allocation of leisure time. Although men did spend a little more time on socializing, sleeping, relaxing and eating than women, the difference was not great.

## Conjugal roles and power

- Edgell (1980) interviewed husbands and wives about decision making. He found that women tended to dominate in areas such as domestic spending and children's clothes, but men dominated in areas that were considered more important, such as moving house and overall finance.
- A more recent study by Hardill, Green and Owen (1997) found that although males dominated decision-making in most households, this was not the case in a significant minority of households.

## Conjugal roles – money management

- Pahl (1989, 1993) studied how couples manage their money. Just over a quarter of the couples in her study had a system of money management in which there was a fair degree of **equality**.
- Research by Vogler (1994) largely confirms Pahl's findings. She found an increase in the proportion of relationships with **egalitarian** financial arrangements but this proportion remained small.

## Conjugal roles – invisible and emotion work

- DeVault (1991) conducted a qualitative study on 'feeding the family'. She found that this aspect of domestic work involves a great deal of **'invisible' work** in planning and staging the meal. Again, it is women who are primarily responsible.

■ **Duncombe and Marsden** (1995) identify another invisible element of women's domestic work – emotion work. Many women in their study expressed dissatisfaction with their partner's emotional input into the relationship and the family. Most men did not acknowledge that **emotion work** needed to be done to make the relationship work. Women can end up doing a **triple shift**. Having completed their paid employment they not only have to do most of the housework, they also have to do the emotion work.

### Inequality within marriage – conclusion

A study of lesbian households by **Dunne** (1999) suggests that an equitable domestic division of labour can be achieved. However, it is hard to achieve in a culture that still differentiates so clearly between **masculinity** and **femininity**. The evidence indicates that women are still a long way from achieving **equality within marriage**. Husbands of wives with full-time jobs seem to be taking over some of the burden of housework, but the change is slow.

## MARRIAGE AND MARITAL BREAKDOWN

A number of threats to marriage have been identified, and this has led some commentators to express concern about the future of the family.

The threats fall into two main categories:

1 Threats resulting from **alternatives** to marriage
2 Threats resulting from the **breakdown** of marriages

### 'Threats' from alternatives to marriage

#### Marriage rates

It is argued that marriage is becoming less popular because the **marriage rate** has declined. However, the decline seems to be due to people delaying marriages rather than not getting married at all, as **the average age** of marriage has been steadily increasing. As **Bernades** (1997) points out, most people do get married at some point in their life.

#### Cohabitation

Cohabitation is increasing. By 2002 over a quarter of non-married people in Britain were cohabiting. However, **Burgoyne and Clark** (1984) found that a significant proportion of their sample thought that cohabitation was a good idea as a prelude to marriage but not as a permanent alternative to marriage.

**Joan Chandler** (1993) takes a different view. She notes that the time couples spend cohabiting is lengthening, and more of them appear to be choosing cohabitation as a long-term alternative to marriage.

The *British and European Social Attitudes Survey* (Barlow et al. 2001) has found that the British population has become increasing accepting of long-term cohabitation and it suggested that marriage would become more of a **lifestyle choice** than a social obligation.

### Single-person households

Another alternative to marriage is to live on your own. Many **single-person households** may be formed as a result of divorce or separation but others may result from a deliberate choice to live alone. Single-person households are becoming more common in Britain.

### Threats resulting from the breakdown of marriages

The second type of threat to contemporary marriage is the apparent rise in marital breakdowns. Marital breakdown can be divided into three main categories:

1 **Divorce** – the legal termination of a marriage.
2 **Separation**, which refers to the physical separation of the spouses.
3 So-called **empty-shell marriages** where the spouses remain living together but their marriage exists in name only.

### Marital breakdown statistics

There was a steady rise in **divorce rates** in modern societies throughout the twentieth century, although the rate appeared to stabilize during the 1990s. According to **Chandler**, approximately 40% of new marriages will end in divorce. The proportion of remarriages has also been rising.

Reliable figures for separation and empty-shell marriages are not available.

### Explanations for marital breakdowns

#### The value of marriage

**Functionalists** such as **Parsons** and **Fletcher** argue that the rise in marital breakdown stems largely from the fact that marriage is increasingly valued. People expect more and demand more from marriage and are more likely to end a relationship which may have been tolerable in the past. The *British Social Attitudes Survey* (2001) has found that people still value marriage but they also see **cohabitation** as a legitimate alternative.

#### Conflict between spouses

The isolation of the nuclear family from wider kin places strain on the marital relationship. **Leach** (1967) suggests that the nuclear family suffers from an **emotional overload** which increases the level of conflict between its members. **Allan and Crow** (2001) suggest that greater **financial independence** for women makes them less willing to accept conflict with their spouse.

### Modernity, freedom and choice

Gibson (1994) claims that the development of **modernity** has put increasing emphasis on the desirability of individual achievement. The ideology of the market emphasizes **consumer choice**, and so, if you are not satisfied with your first choice of partner, you are more likely to leave and try an alternative in the hope of greater personal satisfaction.

### The ease of divorce

It is generally agreed that the **stigma** attached to divorce has been considerably reduced. **Gibson** (1994) believes that **secularization** (the decline of religious beliefs and institutions) has weakened the degree to which religious beliefs can bind a couple together and make divorce less likely.

Changing attitudes to divorce have led to changes in the **law** which have made it easier to obtain a divorce. In Britain, before 1857, a private act of parliament was required to obtain a divorce.

Since 1857 the costs of obtaining a divorce have gone down and the grounds for divorce have been widened. By 1996 there was no need to show that either partner was at fault in order to prove that the marriage had **broken down**. Instead, the partners simply had to assert that the marriage had broken down and undergo a 'period of reflection', normally a year, to consider whether a reconciliation was possible. In 2002 new legislation required spouses to pay a fixed proportion of their income towards childcare costs if they did not have custody of the child or children.

### Conclusion

It is easy to exaggerate the extent to which there has been a retreat from marriage. The socialist feminists **Abbott and Wallace** (1992) recognize the increasing **diversity of family forms** but see the alleged decline of the family and marriage as having been exaggerated for political ends by the **New Right**. **Julia Somerville** (2000) believes that despite 'diversification of family forms and relationships' most people still believe in the value of family life.

## THE FAMILY, POLITICS AND SOCIAL POLICY

Despite the traditional belief that politicians should not interfere in the family, state policies have always had an impact on family life. **Taxation**, **welfare**, **housing** and **education policies** all influence the way in which people organize their domestic life.

Feminists have argued that government policies tend to favour the **traditional nuclear family** with a male breadwinner. **Allan** (1985) argues that much state policy is based on an ideology of the **'normal' family**. Such policies assume that one family member will put primary emphasis on childcare rather than work; that families will usually take care of the elderly, and that wives are economically dependent on their husbands.

**Lorraine Fox Harding** (1996) gives some examples of state policies that favour the traditional family:

- Few council or other public-funded houses have been built to accommodate groups larger than conventional nuclear families.
- Married women can only receive **invalidity pensions** if they can show that their physical condition prevents them from doing housework – a rule that does not apply to men and single women.
- Regulations relating to **maternity leave** and pay reinforce traditional gender roles (despite the introduction of **paternity leave** in 2001).

Not all policies reinforce traditional gender roles. **Fox Harding** points out that in 1991 the House of Lords ruled that men were no longer exempt from being charged with raping their wives.

### New Labour and the family

In general the Blair government's policies have been based around strengthening **traditional families**. However, a number of measures have been taken to help parents combine paid work with domestic responsibilities particularly **Working Families Tax Credits**.

## FAMILIES AND POSTMODERNITY

### Stacey – the postmodern family

**Judith Stacey** (1996) believes that contemporary societies such as the USA have developed the **postmodern family**. She associates changes in the family with a movement away from a single dominant family type and with a greater **variety** in family relationships. Arrangements in the postmodern family are 'diverse, fluid and unresolved'.

The development of the postmodern family has destroyed the idea that the family progresses through a series of logical stages. There can be no assumption that any particular form will become accepted as the best, or normal, type of family. Diversity is here to stay.

### Conclusion

Stacey acknowledges that the postmodern family can create unsettling instability but she generally welcomes it as an opportunity to develop more **egalitarian** family relationships. However, it is questionable to what extent diversity and the postmodern family have become commonplace. It is possible that Stacey exaggerates the extent of change.

## TEST YOUR KNOWLEDGE AND UNDERSTANDING

1 What term best describes the unit of a husband, wife and their dependent offspring?
   a  Symmetrical family
   b  Nuclear family
   c  Universal family
   d  Extended family

2 Three of the following are criticisms of Parsons's view of the family. Which is the odd one out?
   a  Parsons fails to study the relationship between the family and society
   b  Parsons fails to recognize negative aspects of the family
   c  Parsons sees socialization as a one-way process
   d  Parsons ignores variations in family types

3 Which one of the following types of feminism takes into account the variations in women's experiences?
   a  Marxist feminism
   b  Radical feminism
   c  Difference feminism
   d  Socialist feminism

4 Which one of the following perspectives is 'difference feminism' closest to?
   a  Postmodernism
   b  Functionalism
   c  Marxism
   d  Social action theory

5 Which type of family is thought of as typical of pre-industrial societies?
   a  Nuclear family
   b  Classic extended family
   c  Symmetrical family
   d  Agricultural family

6 Which one of the following terms describes the tendency for trends to begin in the middle class and then 'filter' down to other sections of society?
   a  Stratified diffusion
   b  Structural differentiation
   c  Class differentiation
   d  Class structure

7 Three of these are characteristics of the 'cereal-packet image' of the family. Which is the odd one out?
   a  A male breadwinner
   b  A female carer/housewife
   c  Dependent children
   d  Shared domestic roles

8 Which one of the following terms do the Rapoports use to describe family diversity based on the lifestyles of families of different ethnic origins and religious beliefs?
   a  Cohort diversity
   b  Organizational diversity
   c  Cultural diversity
   d  Life-cycle diversity

9 Which one of the following perspectives is most likely to see single-parent families as a problem for society?
   a  Difference feminism
   b  The New Right
   c  Marxist feminism
   d  Functionalism

10 Which one of these terms is used to describe a domestic situation in which the roles of husband and wife are very different?
   a  Conjugal roles
   b  Segregated conjugal roles
   c  Joint conjugal roles
   d  Differentiated roles

11 In Pahl's research, what percentage of couples had a fairly egalitarian system of money management?
   a  Just over 10%
   b  Just over 25%
   c  Just over 50%
   d  Just over 75%

12 Which one of the following is not part of women's triple shift, according to Duncombe and Marsden?
   a  Emotion work
   b  Domestic work
   c  Decision making
   d  Paid employment

13 Three of the following are forms of marital breakdown. Which is the odd one out?
   a  Divorce
   b  Empty-shell marriages
   c  Domestic violence
   d  Separation

14 Three of the following have been suggested as reasons for the increase in the divorce rate. Which is the odd one out?
   a  More is expected of marriage today
   b  The isolation of the nuclear family increases levels of conflict between family members
   c  The stigma attached to divorce has decreased
   d  The rate of remarriage has increased

15 Three of the following reflect a postmodern view of the family. Which is the odd one out?
   a  There is no single dominant family type
   b  There is uncertainty about roles within the family today
   c  The family is progressing through a series of logical stages
   d  There is a lot more choice about how people live their personal lives today

# DEVELOP YOUR ANALYSIS AND EVALUATION SKILLS

## The family is a universal, essential and beneficial social institution.

**Background:** This is advocating a functionalist view of the family, which sees it as present in all societies and essential and beneficial because it performs vital functions. Murdock is a good starting point and Parsons is also important. The short section on the functions of the family is useful as well. There are many ways of criticising the statement using critics of Murdock and Parsons and perspectives which put forward very different views. Both Marxism and feminism see aspects of the family as far from beneficial

| For | Against |
|---|---|
| ■ Murdock (p. 109) | ■ Marxism (p. 110) |
| ■ Parsons (pp. 109–10) | ■ Feminism (p. 110) |
| ■ Fletcher and Parsons (p. 115) | ■ Critics of Murdock (p. 109) |
| | ■ Critics of Parsons (p. 109) |
| | ■ The loss of functions (p. 115) |

**Top tip:** The question of whether the family is universal depends on how you define 'the family'. There is lots of evidence of increased diversity in family types in Britain (pp. 112–14), so you can discuss whether alternatives to conventional nuclear families are good for society or not.

## The conventional nuclear family is dying out in Britain today.

**Background:** This issue is dealt with in several parts of the chapter, particularly those on industrialization, modernization and the family (pp. 111–12), family diversity (pp. 112–14), and marriage and marital breakdown. Recent studies on families and kinship and the dispersed extended and beanpole families suggest something like the nuclear family remains important. However, most of the research on family diversity and evidence of increased family breakdown suggests otherwise. The claim that conventional nuclear families are 'dying out' is rather strong, and you might suggest they are weakening rather than about to disappear.

| For: | Against |
|---|---|
| ■ Theories of diversity (p. 112–14) | ■ McGlone, Willmott and Brannen (partly) (p. 112) |
| ■ Evidence marriage may be in crisis (p. 116–17) | ■ Robert Chester (p. 114) |

**Top tip:** Postmodernism (p. 117) might be useful for suggesting that nuclear families are now just one choice among many.

## The family is still patriarchal.

**Background:** This is clearly a statement that feminists would tend to support. The chapter on sex and gender (chapter 2) is useful for defining and discussing patriarchy (pp. 25–6) and for criticising the concept (p. 26). Radical feminists support this view most strongly, liberal feminists more weakly, and Marxist and socialist feminists partially agree because they see families as both male-dominated and shaped by capitalism. Evidence on conjugal roles suggests some reduction in inequality but would generally support the statement. Postmodernists deny that generalizations such as this are useful, seeing families as different and therefore considering all sweeping statements about them to be invalid.

| For: | Against |
|---|---|
| ■ Radical feminism (strongly) (p. 110) | ■ Functionalism (pp. 109–10) |
| ■ Liberal feminism (weakly) (pp. 110–11) | ■ Postmodernism (p. 117) |
| ■ Marxist/socialist feminism (strongly) (p. 110) | ■ Evidence of reductions in inequality in conjugal roles (p. 115–16) |
| ■ Evidence of continuing inequality in conjugal roles (p. 115–16) | |

**Top tip:** You might consider whether different types of family (pp. 112–14) are equally patriarchal. Lesbian families (p. 111) would seem to be at least one exception.

## AQA-STYLE FAMILIES AND HOUSEHOLDS QUESTION

### AS Unit 1

**Answer all parts of this question**

Total: 60 marks
1 mark = 1.25 minutes

Time allowed: 1 hour 15 minutes

#### ITEM A

As family size has become smaller and the family has seemed to lose its functions, some have argued that the family is dying out. As evidence they put forward the rising divorce rate. It is the increase in single-parent families that has caused most of the concern about the stability of the family. Single-parent families have a great social cost to individuals and financial cost to the state.

#### ITEM B

Increased opportunities for divorce have provided an escape route for many wives. It is not marriage that women resent, as many will re-marry. Rather it is a certain type of marriage they seek to leave. Despite all the so-called advances of recent years, women still work a triple shift.

**Comments on the question**

- A statistical measure that expresses a number as a proportion of a specific population in a given time period

**[a]** What is meant by divorce rate?

[Item A, line 4] [2 marks]

**Advice on preparing your answer**

- The legal termination of a marriage
- You should include the idea of a number per thousand of the married population per year

- This means three-part so you need to identify each aspect
- Don't spend too long – about 5 minutes

**[b]** Explain what is meant by the triple shift.

[Item B, line 6] [4 marks]

- The three elements of the term are explained on pp. 116
- Consider why the word 'shift' is used here. Think of other contexts where the word is used

- Less and you can't score all the marks; more and you are wasting time. They should be made as discrete and separate points
- This means what happens after divorce not what causes a divorce
- This is not quite the same as asking about the effects of divorce, where the focus would be on the individual. The focus here is on the societal level

**[c]** Identify three effects of the rise in the divorce rate. [6 marks]

- You may pick up some ideas from pp. 116–17, although you may have to twist the ideas to fit the question
- Think about the impact on society of increasing numbers of people divorcing. An individual child's low educational achievement becomes a social issue of under-achievement in education

- You must follow the instructions carefully to get full marks. Don't write about two social costs and no financial cost, or vice versa
- Notice the focus of this question. It is not divorce

**[d]** Identify and explain one individual social cost and one financial cost to the state caused by single-parent families.

[8 marks]

- Select an individual cost, see pp. 113–14
- Some of these costs can also be twisted and applied to cover a financial cost

- Consider these qualities in relation to what has been written:
  1 How original or distinctive?
  2 How useful?
  3 How true and accurate?
  4 How complete an account?
  5 How much understanding is shown?
- Plural suggests more than one sociologist
- e.g. universality issue, family structure, roles and functions

**[e]** Examine the contribution of functionalist sociologists to the study of family life. [20 marks]

- You could organize your answer around either of these two parts of the question
- For contributions made, pp. 109–10, 111, 115 and 116
- For points against, pp. 110, 111 and 115 should be used selectively to show up the weaknesses or inadequacy of functionalism in relation to the numbered points opposite

---

- This means within the last fifty years at most, so go no further back than 1952, and exclude historical material
- You don't have to limit yourself to Britain
- The best answers might question what this means

**[f]** Using material from the Items and elsewhere, assess the view that the isolated nuclear family is typical of modern society.

[20 marks]

- This is a functionalist concept, so there could be some overlap with the previous question
- Spend more time on the points against, but still set out the argument for, briefly
- pp. 112–14 are useful to show the diversity of family structures and hence lack of typicality of the nuclear family

# OCR-STYLE FAMILY AND HOUSEHOLDS QUESTION

## AS Unit 2533: Culture and Socialization

**Answer all parts of this question**
Total: 45 marks 1 mark = 1 minute
Time allowed: 45 minutes

### Comments on the question

- Make sure that the examiner can see that you have clearly identified two ways
- No more, no less
- Make sure that you develop explanations of why the two ways identified demonstrate differences across ethnic groups

**[a]** Identify and explain two ways in which household types differ across ethnic groups in the contemporary UK.

[15 marks]

### Advice on preparing your answer

- Make sure that you know what is meant by this concept
- You will find material on p. 114 that will assist you in your response to this question
- Be specific in your identification of particular ethnic groups
- Note that you must not use examples that do not apply to the UK

---

- Describe the view as fully as possible, using supporting evidence
- Consider arguments and evidence that are specifically targeted at the view and/or alternative views on the role of the nuclear family

**[b]** Outline and assess the view that the nuclear family is in decline. [30 marks]

- Remember that this is only one view. You can challenge it
- You should construct an introduction which sets the scene, i.e. identifies the key studies in this debate
- This issue is discussed in the second statement on page 119

# Chapter 9

# POWER, POLITICS AND THE STATE

Textbook pp. 587–683

Specifications

| Specification | Specification details | Coverage |
|---|---|---|
| **AQA** A2: Power and Politics | ■ Explanations of the nature and distribution of power | This issue is discussed throughout the chapter in various contexts. The basic theories are covered on pp. 123–128. |
| | ■ The role of the modern state | Discussion of the role of the state also re-appears throughout the chapter, notably between pp. 123–128. |
| | ■ Different political ideologies and their relationship to political parties | The section on theories of de-alignment (p. 130–1) covers recent shifts in party ideologies in Britain |
| | ■ The nature of, and changes in, different forms of political participation, including voting behaviour | Voting behaviour covered on pp. 129–31. Other forms of participation discussed in context of new social movements (pp. 128–9). |
| | ■ The role of political parties and movements, pressure/interest groups and the mass media in the political process | The role of political parties and pressure groups is a key part of most theories of power (pp. 123–8). There is also a discussion of new social movements (pp. 128–9). |
| **OCR** A2: Power and Control/ Protest and Social Movements | **The context of political action** ■ Defining political action: types of governments, political parties, pressure groups and new social movements | Explanations of key concepts and ideas occur through much of the chapter, particularly between pp. 123–8. New social movements are covered on p. 128–9. |
| | ■ Globalization, global social movements and nationalism | The impact of globalization on politics and the growth of the anti-globalization movement are discussed on pp. 126–9. Nationalism is included in chapter 3 (pp. 38–9). |
| | **The changing patterns of political action** ■ Types of direct action, for example riots, terrorism, demonstrations and strikes | Discussion of the tactics of anti-globalization and other new social movements appears on pp. 128–9. |
| | ■ The relationship between direct action and social class, age, gender, ethnicity, sexuality, disability and nationalism | The characteristics of new social movements are discussed on pp. 128–9. |
| | ■ Explanations of the forms and patterns of political action and how these relate to social structure, economic deprivation, rational responses to problems such as powerlessness and racism, and collective/subcultural identities | Discussion of the forms and patterns of political action among anti-globalization and other new social movements appears on pp. 128–9. Voting behaviour is covered on pp. 129–31. |
| | **Power, culture and identity** ■ Power, authority, legitimacy, ideology and hegemony, and their impacts on the development of new social movements | Power and authority are discussed on p. 123, ideology on pp. 125–6 and hegemony on p. 126. New social movements are covered on pp. 128–9. |
| | ■ Differences and the formation of identities through protest, for example social class, age, gender and ethnic identities | Some coverage of these issues is on pp. 128–9 (see also pp. 175–6). |

For more detailed specification guidance visit **www.haralambosholborn.com**

## DEFINING POWER

A distinction can be made between two types of power:

1 **Authority** is power that is accepted as legitimate – e.g. the power of Parliament to pass laws in a society where citizens accept the political system.
2 **Coercion** is based upon the imposition of power using force, or the threat of force, against people who do not accept it as legitimate.

### Weber – power and types of authority

Max Weber defines power as the ability of people to get their own way despite the opposition of others. He distinguishes three different types of authority:

1 **Charismatic authority** is based upon what are believed to be the special qualities of an individual.
2 **Traditional authority** is based upon a belief in the rightness of accepted customs.
3 **Rational–legal authority** is based on the acceptance of an impersonal set of rules, e.g. a legal system.

These are ideal types (idealized, pure forms of authority) which in reality will tend to be mixed together.

### Lukes – a radical view of power

**Steven Lukes** (1974) provides an alternative, radical view of power. He sees Weber's views as being largely based upon **decision making** (the first face of power). The second face is **non-decision making**, where some issues are prevented from reaching the point where decisions are made. The third face of power is **ideological power**, where people are persuaded to accept the exercise of power over them even when it is against their interests – e.g. women accepting **patriarchal power**.

A problem with this definition is determining what is for or against somebody's interests if it is not based on the opinion of the person concerned.

## THE STATE

### Definitions

Weber defines the state as a body that successfully claims a monopoly on the legitimate use of force in a given territory.

Most sociologists see the state as embracing institutions such as state-run welfare services as well as the criminal justice system, the military and state bureaucracies.

By the twentieth century the world was dominated by nation-states, but in some pre-modern societies, such as the Nuer in Africa, there was no state.

## POWER – A FUNCTIONALIST PERSPECTIVE

■ Talcott Parsons argued that all societies require a **value consensus** based on shared goals.

■ To Parsons, power is used to achieve **collective goals** such as material prosperity.
■ Everybody therefore benefits from the exercise of power (a **variable-sum** view of power). In more conventional views of power, some benefit at the expense of others (a **constant-sum** view of power).
■ **Authority** in society is usually accepted as **legitimate** because it helps to achieve collective goals.

Critics argue that Parsons is wrong to see the exercise of power as benefiting everyone rather than being used to further sectional interests.

## POWER AND THE STATE – A PLURALIST PERSPECTIVE

**Classical pluralists** accept a **Weberian** (constant-sum) definition of power and, unlike Parsons, do not see society as having a value consensus.

They accept that there is some agreement in countries such as the USA about the basic features of the democratic system, but they believe that industrial society is **differentiated** into a plurality of social groups and **sectional interests**.

Divisions are based not only on class, occupation, age, gender, religion and ethnicity, but also on many other specific interests – e.g. whether you own a car, pay a mortgage, use public libraries or have children.

Societies need to prevent a **tyranny of the majority** in which a single interest group always outvotes minorities.

The state is seen as an **honest broker** mediating between different interests and ensuring that no one group becomes dominant. It makes decisions which favour different groups at different times, balancing their interests over extended periods.

**Political parties** are seen as broadly representative since they need to attract sufficient support to be elected. If the existing parties do not represent public interests, new ones emerge.

However, **interest or pressure groups** are needed:

■ To influence governments in the periods between elections.
■ To represent minority interests and ensure that governments take account of all groups in society, not just their own supporters.
■ To increase participation in politics.
■ To represent views on new issues that arise.
■ To respond to changing circumstances.

There are two different types of pressure group:

1 **Protective groups** defend the interests of a particular group in the population – e.g. the British Medical Association (BMA) and doctors.
2 **Promotional groups** are based on causes or issues rather than social groups – e.g. environmental groups. They may have more diverse membership than protective groups.

Pressure groups can try to influence the government in a variety of ways:

- By contributing to party funds – e.g. unions and the Labour Party.
- Through payments – e.g. Mohammed Al-Fayed paying cash to MPs to ask questions in the House of Commons.
- By appealing to public opinion – e.g. rock musicians campaigning for the cancellation of Third World debt.
- Civil disobedience or direct action – e.g. hunt saboteurs.
- By providing expert opinion to the government – e.g. by having seats on government committees or inquiries.

A number of studies have been used to support pluralist views. They have compared government decisions with the wishes of different interest groups. Classic studies by **Dahl** (1961) in the USA, and **Hewitt** (1974) and **Grant and Marsh** (1977) in the UK appear to show that no one sectional interest gets its own way all the time.

The 'New Labour' government of Tony Blair can be seen as balancing business interests (e.g. by allowing private involvement in public services) and worker/union interests (e.g. by introducing minimum wage legislation).

There have been many criticisms of classical pluralism:

1 **Marxists** argue that pluralists fail to take account of the **second face of power**. Radical questions such as real redistribution of wealth never reach the point of decision making.
2 **Westergaard and Resler** (1976) argue that power should be measured in terms of the **consequences of decisions**. Despite lots of legislation designed to help the poor, there has been little real redistribution of wealth in Britain.
3 Some studies – e.g. that of **Marsh and Locksley** (1983) – suggest that business interests have more influence than other groups.
4 Some **promotional groups** seem to have very little influence –e.g. Hugh Ward (1983) argues that anti-nuclear campaigners have had little success.
5 Some interests may be **unrepresented** – e.g. the unemployed lack a protective pressure group.

Some classical pluralists now admit that power may not be as equally distributed as the model originally suggested.

### Elite pluralism

This approach modifies and tries to improve on classical pluralism. Unlike classical pluralists, **elite pluralists** believe that there are some inequalities in power. They acknowledge that there are other faces of power and they see elites – the leaders of interest groups – as more influential than ordinary members.

**Wyn Grant** (1999) believes that, despite changes in pressure group politics, Britain remains largely democratic. The changes include:

- The decline of the influence of the Trade Union Congress (TUC) and Confederation of British Industry (CBI).
- An increase in the number of pressure groups so that most interests are now represented.
- More campaigning directed away from Westminster – e.g. consumer boycotts to put pressure on companies and the increased importance of the European Union and devolved governments.
- Increased use of **direct action** – e.g. by anti-roads protestors.
- More consultation of pressure groups by government, although the insider/outsider distinction remains valid.

Although more realistic than classical pluralism, elite pluralism still ignores the **third face of power** and may underestimate the **inequality of power** in society and the possible use of power by elites to further their own interests.

## ELITE THEORY

Elite theory divides society into a ruling minority and the majority who are ruled. There are different versions of elite theory.

- **Classical elite theory** was developed by the Italians – e.g. Pareto (1848–1923) – in opposition to Marxist theory. Pareto emphasized the importance of the **psychological characteristics** of elites which made them superior to the mass and which allowed them to gain and retain power.
  - **Lions** achieve power through incisive action and the use of force.
  - **Foxes** rule by cunning.

Elites tend to circulate, with lions being replaced by foxes, and foxes then being replaced by lions, and so on.

Pareto can be criticized for simply assuming that elites are superior to the mass, ignoring the differences between political systems, ignoring the importance of wealth, and so on.

- **Modern elite theories** offer more plausible views.

**C. Wright Mills** in the 1950s in the USA argued that there was a power elite which had power through holding key positions (**command posts**) in three institutions:

1 **major corporations**
2 **the military**
3 **the federal government**

The three elites were connected through intermarriage, movement of individuals between elites, a similar educational background and membership of the same prestige clubs.

As a **unified group** they were able to exercise power over a divided and passive mass of the population who took little interest in most political issues.

## Elite self-recruitment in Britain

In Britain, a number of studies have found high levels of **elite self-recruitment** – i.e. most people recruited into elites tend to come from elite backgrounds themselves. There is evidence of cohesion, with people having positions in more than one elite, and elite members having shared educational backgrounds.

George Borthwick *et al.* (1991) examined the educational backgrounds of Conservative MPs in the 1979, 1983 and 1987 elections and found that in 1987 over half had been to public school and 44% had been to Oxford or Cambridge University.

Research by **Phillip Cowley** (2001) into British MPs elected in 2001 found that most Conservative MPs were from private sector occupations with a preponderance from professions such as law, banking and business. Only six of the new MPs elected for the Labour Party were manual workers.

### Evaluation

Although many top positions in Britain and the USA are held by people from elite backgrounds, that does not actually prove that they act to further elite interests rather than those of the mass of the population. There has been little attempt to measure power.

**Marxists** argue that elite theory neglects the importance of **economic power** as opposed to power based on positions held.

## POWER AND THE STATE – MARXIST PERSPECTIVES

- Like elite theory, Marxist theories see power as concentrated in the hands of a minority.
- Unlike elite theory, they see it as concentrated in the hands of a **ruling class** which derives its power from ownership of the means of production.

Marx and Engels argued that the ruling class used their power to **exploit** subordinate classes.

- It was in the interests of the subject classes to overthrow ruling-class power, but the ruling class used the **superstructure** to try to prevent this.
- The **state**, as part of the superstructure, was used to promote ruling-class interests.
- Engels argued that the first societies were **primitive communist** ones, with no state. In primitive communism no **surplus** was produced, so class power could not develop through the accumulation of a surplus, and therefore no state was needed.
- As surplus was produced, wealth was **accumulated**, classes developed and states were born.
- Early states were **oppressive** (e.g. the use of slavery in Ancient Greece and Rome), but democratic states appear to be based on the will of the population.
- Engels believed that in democratic states power stays with the ruling class; such states only create the **illusion of democracy**.

- Corruption and the financial power of capitalists are used to shape state policies in capitalist democracies, ensuring that the state continues to further ruling-class interests.
- In future **communist societies**, based on **communal ownership of the means of production**, the **proletariat** would temporarily take control of the state to defeat the ruling class. Once this was completed, classes would disappear and the state would **'wither away'**.

Marx and Engels describe the state as 'but a committee for managing the affairs of the whole bourgeoisie'. However, Engels accepted that the state could act independently – e.g. when two classes were competing for domination of a society. In some studies Marx showed an awareness of **divisions within states** – e.g. between industrial capitalists and financiers.

Modern Marxists have interpreted the Marxist view of the state in different ways.

**Ralph Miliband** (1969) argues that the state is often the **direct tool of the ruling class**.

- Many of those who occupy top positions in the state come from ruling-class backgrounds and are therefore likely to act to support ruling-class interests.
- Even those from other backgrounds will have to accept ruling-class values to gain positions in the state.
- The protection of **private property** (which serves ruling-class interests) is assumed to be a central role of the state.
- The way in which the state supports private enterprise is **legitimated** through advertising which celebrates the activities of large corporations.

**Nicos Poulantzas** (1969, 1976) criticizes Miliband, arguing that it is not direct interference from the ruling class that makes the state serve ruling-class interests, but the structure of society (a **structuralist approach**).

- As part of the **superstructure**, the state will automatically act to favour the ruling class.
- The state has **relative autonomy** – it has some independence from individual members of the ruling class.
- This allows the state to act in the overall interests of the ruling class rather than being dominated by a single capitalist **faction** (e.g. bankers).
- It also allows the state to make some **concessions** to the working class to defuse their protests and prevent an eventual revolution.
- This **relative autonomy** allows the state to promote the myth that it is acting in the interests of society as a whole.

**Miliband** (1972) criticizes Poulantzas for assuming that the state would act in ruling-class interests without showing how and why. The theory of relative autonomy makes it impossible to prove Poulantzas's theory wrong; whatever the state does can be taken as evidence of ruling-class domination or relative autonomy.

## Evidence to support Marxism

■ **Westergaard and Resler** (1976) argue that power can be measured in terms of **effects** rather than decision-making. Thus, the continued concentration of wealth in the hands of capitalists provides evidence of this group's power.
■ Westergaard and Resler argue that reforms such as the introduction of the **welfare state**, which appear to benefit the working class, have left the basic structures of inequality unchanged.
■ Sociologists such as **Urry** (1973) put forward evidence of non-decision making – e.g. the way in which issues such as replacing capitalism are never considered.
■ Marxists put forward evidence that **ruling-class ideology** makes use of the third (ideological) face of power to support its position.

### Criticisms

Marxist views can be criticized:

1 For failing to explain why the state did not wither away in communist societies such as the Soviet Union.
2 For exaggerating the importance of economic power.
3 For failing to consider other possible sources of power.

## NEO-MARXIST APPROACHES TO POWER AND THE STATE

Neo-Marxist views retain elements of Marxist theory but diverge from orthodox Marxism in a number of ways.

### Gramsci – hegemony and the state

■ Gramsci (1891–1937) argued against **economic determinism** (the theory that the economy determined other aspects of society).
■ He believed that the **superstructure** could influence the **economic infrastructure** as well as *vice versa*.
■ He divided the superstructure into **political society** (essentially the state) and **civil society** (private institutions).
■ To keep control over civil society, the ruling class needed to achieve **hegemony**, or domination, by gaining the consent of the mass of the population.
■ To legitimate their rule, the ruling class might need to make **concessions** to win the support of other classes or class factions.
■ Different sections of the capitalist class needed to be **united**.
■ Ruling-class hegemony was never complete or total. A continuing process was needed to develop and maintain support and legitimate their position.
■ An alliance of groups which dominated society was called a **historic bloc**.
■ Opposition was always likely because people possessed **dual consciousness**. The experience of exploitation and oppression (e.g. at work) tended to make people radical, whereas the ideology promoted by the ruling class tended to make them more conservative.
■ Control over **ideas** was as important in maintaining or overthrowing ruling-class hegemony as was control over the economy.

## Evaluation

Neo-Marxist views avoid the mistake of seeing wealth as the only source of power. However, they provide a less clear theory about the nature of power and do not clearly explain which non-economic factors sometimes take on more importance.

## STATE-CENTRED THEORIES OF POWER

All the previous theories can be seen as **society-centred**: they examine the way in which society shapes the actions of the state. **State-centred** theories see the state as an independent actor, able to exercise power in its own right and pursue its own interests.

**Theda Skocpol** (1985) argues that states have considerable **autonomy**, and their primary aim may be to increase their own power. They have **administrative control** over a territory, the ability to raise taxes and the ability to recruit talented people to work for them.

States such as the communist regimes in China and Russia, and the Napoleonic regime in France, demonstrate the considerable power that states can possess.

### Evaluation

Critics argue that such approaches may **exaggerate state power**. They also point out that some supposedly society-centred approaches recognize that the state has some independent power (e.g. Poulantzas's theory of relative autonomy).

### Noam Chomsky and the power of the US state

Noam Chomsky (1996, 1999, 2000, 2002, 2003) has emphasized the power of the US state and the **economic elites** which he believes dominate government policy.

■ He believes these elites have used the economic power of corporations and the military power of the US state to promote the interests of US capitalism with no regard for **democratic or human rights**
■ Examples include the invasions of Afghanistan and Iraq in the 'War on Terror', the war in Vietnam and support for violent, repressive or undemocratic regimes in Russia, Turkey, Israel, Indonesia and elsewhere.
■ Chomsky believes that **media propaganda** helps to sustain US power.

### Criticism

Chomsky may exaggerate the power of American capitalism and the US state, though he does recognize that other countries and opponents of US capitalism exercise some power.

## GLOBALIZATION AND THE POWER OF THE NATION-STATE

The idea of **globalization** suggests that national boundaries are becoming less important, and that events throughout the world influence what happens in particular societies.

To some theorists of globalization this means that the nation-state is losing its power to non-governmental organizations.

## Ohmae – The Borderless World

Ohmae (1994) argues that there is one giant **inter-linked economy** covering developed and rapidly developing societies.

- This inter-linked economy is dominated by **giant corporations** and is made possible by a rapid growth in **world trade**.
- Improved **communications** make national boundaries unimportant and allow individuals to buy products from anywhere in the world.
- Governments can no longer control economies within **national boundaries** because of the extent of trade across nations.
- **Corporations** can move production easily to cheaper countries; financiers can move money at will around the world.
- Corporations and consumers now have more power than governments.

### Criticisms

Ohmae can be criticized for greatly exaggerating the loss of state power.

- States still have considerable control over **access to their domestic markets** from outside their immediate trading block (e.g. from outside the EC).
- States still largely **monopolize military power**.

## Sklair – The Sociology of the Global System

Sklair (1993, 1995, 2003) believes that states retain some power, but most power now rests with **transnational corporations** (TNCs).

Globalization can be understood in terms of the following spheres and the corresponding transnational practices:

| Sphere | Transnational practice |
|---|---|
| 1 The economic | The transnational corporation |
| 2 The political | The transnational capitalist class |
| 3 The cultural-ideological | The culture-ideology of consumption |

1 Transnational corporations have much more power than consumers because of their control over global capital and resources.
2 The **transnational capitalist class** either rules directly by holding office or uses economic power to prevent states acting against its interests.
3 Most **consumers** are effectively indoctrinated by TNCs into consuming the products produced by them.

However, the global capitalist system creates two crises:

1 The **crisis of class polarization** between rich and poor within and between nations.
2 The crisis of **ecological unsustainability** in which finite resources are used up and the environment is damaged or destroyed.

Globalization is opposed by **anti-global social movements** but Sklair is pessimistic about their chances of challenging the power of TNCs.

Sklair can be **criticized** for exaggerating the power of TNCs and neglecting the influence of finance capital, e.g. banking.

## Hirst and Thompson – questioning globalization

Paul Hirst and Grahame Thompson (1996) are more critical of the theory of globalization.

- They argue that most corporations are still largely based around their home nations and regions, generating most of their profits from the domestic market or the immediate region.
- They admit that states have lost some power, but the fact that states still control territory and regulate populations ensures that they retain much of their power.
- Most individuals still feel part of a particular state and this gives the state some power over them.

## Giddens – globalization and high modernity

Giddens (1990) takes a more balanced approach. He sees globalization in terms of worldwide social relationships linking distant localities and shaping local events. Interaction is stretched across space and time in a process of time–space distanciation. You can interact with someone without being physically near to them or present at the same time (e.g. by using the internet).

There is increasing global competition in business and a world financial market producing a global economy. This restricts nation-state power since nations have to compete to attract inward investment from corporations.

However, nation-states do not lose all their power. They can sometimes mobilize nationalist sentiments and exercise some cultural influence over citizens, and they retain some economic power, but nations need to cooperate to maintain power against transnational corporations and other groups.

### Evaluation

Giddens provides a more balanced view of globalization than Ohmae or Hirst and Thompson.

## Mann – the sources of social power

Mann (1986, 1993) incorporates elements from different theories of power in his general theory.

He stresses that power has always operated across national boundaries through **networks of power**. Power cannot therefore be analysed in terms of its distribution within a particular society.

He argues that there are four main sources of power:

1 **Economic power** (which is important, but it is not the only source of power, as some Marxists believe).
2 **Ideological power** – power over ideas and beliefs.
3 **Military power** – based on physical coercion.
4 **Political power** – exercised by states over citizens.

Power is never monopolized entirely by one group, and changes in society – e.g. technological changes – make the distribution of power unstable.

### Evaluation

Mann's approach shows the dangers of assuming that all power comes from one source and that power relationships are relatively fixed or stable.

## POSTMODERNISM, POLITICS AND NEW SOCIAL MOVEMENTS

Postmodern approaches tend to broaden the definition of politics well beyond the activities of the state and pressure groups.

1 **Jean Baudrillard** (1983) argues that politics has become detached from reality.
   ■ Rather than being concerned with the substance of policy, politics is more concerned with **image**.
   ■ There is no real difference between the main parties – voters have little real choice.
   ■ Politicians have no real power and simply try to maintain the illusion that they do.
   ■ Politics is simply concerned with **simulacra** – signs that have no relationship to reality.

Critics suggest that politicians do make decisions that affect people's lives. Wars, for example, are real, and lead to real people being killed.

2 **Lyotard** (1984) argues that in the postmodern era **metanarratives** (big stories such as political ideologies) have declined in importance.
   ■ People no longer believe in **political ideologies**.
   ■ Politics becomes less about principles and more about **local issues** and the practicality of achieving things.
   ■ Politics simply becomes a series of **language-games** about specialist topics.
   ■ Power is more to do with **knowledge** than state activities.

Lyotard's approach ignores military power and may underestimate the continuing power of nation-states.

3 **Nancy Fraser** (1995) sees politics shifting away from the **public sphere** of the economy and the state, and moving more into the **private sphere**.
   ■ Politics becomes more concerned with debate within groups rather than on a national level.

■ This gives the relatively powerless (such as black women or lesbians) more involvement in politics.
■ Politics is increasingly concerned with the definitions of **issues** rather than control over **resources** such as money.
■ Issues such as gender, sexuality and ethnicity are increasingly important, and a greater **plurality of groups** now has a political voice.

Fraser may exaggerate the degree to which some of the issues she mentions are new on the political agenda. A plurality of groups and issues has had some role in politics for a considerable time.

## NEW SOCIAL MOVEMENTS AND THE NEW POLITICS

Many commentators argue that, as conventional party politics has declined in importance, new social movements have become more important.

### Hallsworth – 'Understanding new social movements'

■ Hallsworth (1994) sees **new social movements** as political movements that have emerged since the 1960s and that challenge the established order of capitalist society.
■ Examples include feminism, environmentalism, anti-racism and anti-nuclear movements.
■ They are based around two types of issue:
   1 The **defence of the natural and social environment** (e.g. the animal rights movement or environmentalism).
   2 Furthering the **rights of marginal groups** (e.g. gay liberation).
■ They have a number of novel features:
   1 They try to extend the definition of what is political to include the **private sphere** (e.g. domestic violence and sexuality).
   2 They tend not to develop **bureaucratic organizations**.
   3 They tend to be **diverse and fragmented** (e.g. feminism).
   4 They do not seek to hold political office themselves and, unlike conventional pressure groups, they are more likely to engage in **direct action**.
   5 They are more concerned with **culture** than with material issues such as living standards.
   6 They tend to be supported by the young, students and those who work in public services (or whose parents do).

To Hallsworth, they are mainly concerned with **post-materialist values** in societies where most people have already attained a reasonable basic living standard.

### Robin Cohen and Shirin M. Rai – Global Social Movements

Cohen and Rai (2000) question whether there is a clear-cut distinction between **old** and **new** social movements. However, they do believe there have been changes with the use of new **tactics** and more use of **modern technology** and shift towards organising on a **global scale**.

There are more **global social movements** because:

1 There are more international organizations.
2 Communication has become easier and cheaper.
3 TNCs have grown in power.
4 Environmental problems have become global in scope.
5 Universal human rights issues have become more prominent.
6 Key values have spread globally.

### Crook, Pakulski and Waters – social movements and postmodernization

Crook, Pakulski and Waters (1992) associate the emergence of new social movements with a **new politics** of **postmodernizing societies**.

■ Old politics was **class-based** and dominated by elites. It was focused on the **state** and seen as separate from everyday life.
■ New politics involves a **volatile electorate** without strong class identities. There is a greater concern with moral issues than with sectional interests, a suspicion of leaders and elites, a move away from concentration on state activities and a **politicization of culture and lifestyle**.
■ The move to the new politics is a result of **class decomposition** (members of the same class become increasingly dissimilar to one another) and social differentiation (those with similar backgrounds develop different lifestyles).
■ The penetration of the **media** into all aspects of life results in a greater focus on the politics of words and images.

#### Evaluation

Crook *et al.* identify some important trends, but they may exaggerate them – e.g. many sociologists deny that there has been a decomposition of classes.

### Giddens – social movements and high modernity

Giddens (1990) examines the relationship between social movements and **high modernity** (he does not believe that we have entered a postmodern age).

■ Giddens sees modernity as characterized by **four institutional dimensions** each of which has corresponding social movements:
1 **Capitalism** produces **labour movements** such as unionism.
2 **Military power** produces **peace movements** opposed to destructive, industrialized warfare.
3 **Surveillance** (the control of information and monitoring of populations) produces **free speech/democratic** movements.
4 **Industrialism** produces **ecological movements**.

■ Globalization produces increased **risks** in terms of ecological damage and military confrontation, and this leads to ecological and peace movements assuming a greater prominence.
■ The emphasis in politics changes, but all these types of movement have existed throughout modernity.

## ANTI-CAPITALISM AND ANTI-GLOBALIZATION

A recent development in social movements is the development of the **anti-capitalist** or **anti-globalization** movement. There were major demonstrations against Western capitalist countries in **Seattle** in 1999 and **Genoa** in 2001. The movement has wide-ranging aims and involves many different groups.

**Alex Callinicos** (2003) sees the anti-capitalist movement as united in opposing problems caused by global capitalism

■ It developed after the collapse of communism leaving **free-market** (or **neo-liberal**) capitalism dominant.
■ It is opposed to the neo-Liberal **Washington consensus** which has tried to spread US style capitalism throughout the world.
■ It is a response to the increased power of TNCs.
■ Specific campaigns, e.g. **Jubilee 2000** opposed to Third World debt and poverty have helped its development.
■ A **financial crisis in East Asia** 1997–8 raised questions about the stability of capitalism.
■ Opposition to US capitalism in underdeveloped countries, e.g. a **peasant's uprising in Mexico** in 1994, have highlighted the problems caused by capitalist policies.
■ In richer countries neo-Liberals have been opposed by workers, e.g. **public sector strikes in France** in 1995.

**Naomi Klein** (2000) has explained the development of anti-capitalism opposed to corporations who rely upon **branding** of products.

■ The logos of companies have become a target of **culture jamming** in which advertisements or **logos** are changed to reveal the negative effects of companies' products and activities.
■ The **Nike swoosh** has been dubbed the 'Swooshsticka' and poor pay in Third World factories producing Nike products has been highlighted.
■ Culture jamming does not challenge capitalist consumer culture as a whole, but a wider movement against capitalist companies, repressive regimes and poor working conditions is developing.

## VOTING BEHAVIOUR

### Patterns of voting 1945–1974

From 1945 to the 1970s there were well-established and fairly predictable voting patterns. There was a fairly clear-cut division between two main parties and two types of policy.

- The **Labour Party** was seen as **left-wing**. It was more likely to support: the redistribution of income and wealth from rich to poor through taxation; high levels of spending on welfare; and state intervention in the economy (e.g. through the nationalization of industries).
- The **Conservative Party** was seen as **right-wing**. It was more likely to support low taxation and the need for inequality and lower levels of spending on welfare, and to oppose nationalization of industries.

**Butler and Stokes** (1974) characterized voting patterns in this era in the following way:

- **Class**, as measured by a person's occupation, exercised a key influence on voting.
- Most voters had a strongly **partisan self-image**, thinking of themselves as Labour or Conservative.
- There were few **floating voters**; most voted consistently for the same party.
- There was a **two-party system**, with most of the working class voting Labour and most of the middle class voting Conservative.
- People were **socialized** by parents and the sorts of schools they attended into supporting particular parties.
- **Third or minor parties** attracted few votes.

Throughout the period there was a small number of **deviant voters** who failed to vote for the party associated with their class. This group influenced election outcomes.

A variety of factors were put forward to explain their deviant voting – e.g. the experience of social mobility, having a partner from a different class background or having parents who voted for different parties.

- Patterns of voting since 1974. A number of commentators believe that voting patterns started to change in the 1970s.
- The influence of **class** on voting started to decline.
- The electorate became more **volatile**, switching votes more often.
- There was a big increase in the number of **deviant voters**.
- The **third party** in British politics (the Liberals, later the SDP/Liberal Alliance and finally the Liberal Democrats) began to attract more support.
- Many argued that the **Labour Party** was in decline, due to a shrinking proportion of the population in working-class, manual jobs.

### Sarlvik and Crewe – partisan dealignment

Sarlvik and Crewe (1983) were leading advocates of the view that major changes were taking place.

- They argued that **partisan dealignment** was taking place. People's sense of attachment to a particular party was weakening rapidly.
- **Class dealignment** was taking place – class was exercising less influence on voting.
- These changes were produced by factors such as the working class buying their own houses and leaving

trade unions, which weakened their working-class attachments.
- Sarlvik and Crewe believed that voting was increasingly shaped by **policy preferences** – people were voting for the parties whose policies they liked rather than the parties they had been brought up to support.

However, critics of Sarlvik and Crewe argued that they exaggerated their case.

### Heath, Jowell and Curtice – the continuing importance of class

Heath, Jowell and Curtice (1985) argued that class continued to exercise a strong influence on voting.

- They supported their claims by adopting a sophisticated **five-class model** instead of what they saw as an over-simplified two-class model (working class and middle class).
- They argued that voters chose more on the basis of the **ideological image** of the party than on specific policies.
- The Labour Party was losing support because its ideological image was too left-wing for many voters, rather than because of changes in society.
- The Liberal/SDP Alliance was gaining support because its image (right-wing on economic issues but liberal on social issues) was close to the ideology supported by increasing numbers of voters.

## COMPETING THEORIES OF VOTING

The **Labour Party** won both the **1997 and 2001** elections with big majorities. The various theories of voting which developed in the debates discussed above can be examined in the light of these results.

1 Dealignment
- **Ivor Crewe and Katrina Thompson** (1999) found evidence of continued **dealignment** with just 16% of voters having **strong party identification** in 1997. Labour had failed to attract a new core of loyal voters from particular social groups. Instead it had gained support from people without strong party loyalty through:
  a **ideological convergence** – moving from left-wing policies to moderate, and,
  b **short-term political factors** such as a buoyant economy.
- However, **Whiteley** *et al.* (2001) found that 65% of respondents were very or fairly **partisan supporters** of a party in the 2001 election although the percentage with any party identification had declined.

2 Class and voting
- **Anthony Heath** and colleagues (Evans, *et al.* 1999) were prepared to admit after the 1997 election that there was a **long-term decline** in the relationship between **class** and **voting**. They attributed this to Labour shifting to the **ideological middle-ground** so that they appealed to both working-class and middle-class voters. However, they believed that class might become more important again if big **ideological divisions** between the parties returned.

■ Both **Pippa Norris** (2001) and **Andrew Russell** (2002) believe evidence from the 2001 election shows that the influence of class is continuing to decline.

**3** Non-class divisions and voting

Sarlvick and Crewe (1983) argued that **non-class factors** such as **trade union membership, housing tenure, public/private sector employment** and **region** were increasingly important in shaping voting. There was little research on issues other than region in the 1997 and 2001 elections, but other non-class factors have been researched.

**a** **Region** – **Curtice and Park** (1997) found that in **1997** the influence of region on voting declined with Labour gaining more votes in the south than the north and more tactical voting. **Norris** (2001) found that in **2001** Labour again increased its vote in the south more than the north weakening regional differences, but the concentration of Conservative votes in the south increased, strengthening regional differences.

**b** **Ethnicity** – **Saggar and Heath** (1999) found that between **1974** and **1997** there were no major changes in the relationship between voting and ethnicity with **Labour** continuing to win a big majority of **ethnic minority votes**. **Russell** (2002) believes similar patterns were repeated in **2001**.

**c** **Gender** – In the 1960s and 1970s **women** were more likely than men to vote **Conservative**. **Pippa Norris (1999) has found that in** Britain and elsewhere the **gender differences** in voting have **declined** with **younger women** less likely to vote for **right-wing parties** such as the Conservatives. This may be due to the influence of **feminism**. **Ludeski** (2001) also found younger women more likely to vote Labour than older women in 2001 and found women more influenced by **policies** rather than **party loyalty** compared to men.

The research therefore suggests that **class** is still of some importance in shaping voting, but it works alongside a range of other factors.

## Policy, ideology and economics

**a** **David Denver** (2002) argues that in **2001 policy preference** had a big influence on the outcome with most voters preferring Labour policies (such as increased spending on public services) to Conservative ones. However, Denver admits overall **party image** might be more important than specific policies.

**b** **Ian Budge** (1999) found **ideological shifts** that might explain recent successes of the Labour Party. Studying election manifestos he found that **Labour** had shifted substantially to the **right** between 1945 and 1997 to occupy the **middle ground** while the **Conservatives** retained distinctly **right-wing policies** in 1997. **Bara and Budge** (2001) found that in 2001 the **Conservative** manifesto remained more **right-wing** than the views of most electors.

– **Ivor Crewe** (1987) argued that people vote for the party that would do most for their own prosperity (**pocket-book voting**).

– **Sanders et al.** (2001) argue that an **image of economic competence** is important if a party is to win elections. In **1997** the **Conservatives lost power** even though the economy was doing well and in **1992** the **Conservatives retained power** despite an economic **recession**. The Conservatives lost in 1997 despite a strong economy because they had lost their reputation for economic competence in 1992 when Britain was forced to withdraw from the **Exchange Rate Mechanism**. They won in 1992 because voters saw **Labour** as **economically incompetent**. Opinion Poll evidence supports the view that voters, subjective view of a party's economic competence shapes voting.

## Conclusion

The evidence suggests that a variety of **social factors** influences how people vote, but does not determine voting. **Voters** make their **own judgements** about the merits of different parties, and parties continually adapt their policies and ideology to try to attract votes.

## TEST YOUR KNOWLEDGE AND UNDERSTANDING

1 Which one of these is an example of the third face of power?
   a A political party refusing to put a controversial motion, put forward by party activists, on to the agenda for a conference
   b The government deciding to pass a new law
   c A man persuading a woman that she should always obey his instructions
   d A school teacher placing a child in detention

2 Which one of these statements about classical pluralism is true?
   a Classical pluralists believe that all members of society share similar interests
   b Classical pluralists believe that it is impossible to prevent a tyranny of the majority
   c Classical pluralists believe that different interests are effectively represented in a democracy
   d Classical pluralists believe that the state acts largely in its own interests

3 Which one of these is an example of a protective pressure group?
   a Greenpeace
   b The National Union of Teachers
   c The RSPCA
   d The Campaign for Nuclear Disarmament

4 Which one of these is a criticism of the pluralist view?
   a Pluralists ignore decision making
   b Pluralists assume that everybody in society shares the same interests
   c Pluralists underestimate the importance of pressure groups
   d Pluralists ignore the second face of power

5 In Marx's theory, the state is seen as:
   a Part of the economic base
   b Part of the superstructure
   c Part of the infrastructure
   d Part of civil society

6 Which of these writers is particularly critical of the exercise of power by the USA?
   a Gramsci
   b Sklair
   c Chomsky
   d Lukes

7 Which of these writers is most sceptical about the theory of globalization?
   a Sklair
   b Ohmae
   c Giddens
   d Hirst and Thompson

8 Which one of these statements about Giddens's discussion of globalization is not true?
   a Giddens sees globalization as destroying the power of the nation-state
   b Giddens sees globalization as involving better communications
   c Giddens sees globalization as partly caused by the increasing power of corporations
   d Giddens believes that globalization can sometimes increase nationalist sentiments

9 Which two of these statements would postmodernists tend to agree with?
   a Power is increasingly related to knowledge
   b Power is increasingly related to image
   c Power is increasingly about money
   d Voters have a real choice in democratic elections

10 Which two of the following does Hallsworth see as characteristic of new social movements?
   a They tend to be concerned with materialistic issues
   b They tend to have bureaucratic organizations
   c They tend to see private life as a political sphere
   d They tend to be concerned with culture

11 According to Naomi Klein culture jamming involves:
   a Interfering with TV and radio broadcasts to combat propaganda
   b Changing society through improvised music
   c Opposing the lifestyle of groups who damage the environment
   d Changing the logos of companies to highlight their harmful activities.

12 Which two of the following are usually seen as left-wing policies?
   a Nationalization of industry
   b Low income tax
   c Cutting spending on welfare
   d Redistributing wealth from the rich to the poor

13 Which two of the following characteristics are associated with Butler and Stokes's analysis of voting from 1945 until the early 1970s?
   a Partisan alignment
   b A strong third party
   c Strong political socialization
   d A volatile electorate

14 Which two of the following elections were won by the Labour Party?
   a 1983
   b 1992
   c 1997
   d 2001

15 Sanders et al believe that British political parties will only succeed in elections if:
   a They have an image as economically competent
   b They have popular policies on health and education
   c They are promising tax cuts
   d They appeal to middle-class voters

## DEVELOP YOUR ANALYSIS AND EVALUATION SKILLS

### *Britain is governed by a ruling class.*

***Background:*** This is clearly stating a Marxist position and you would need to define ruling class and outline the Marxist view. Some Marxists, such as Poulantzas, would agree that the British state serves ruling-class interests, but not that the ruling class governs directly. Sklair would tend to agree with the statement, but sees the ruling class as a transnational capitalist class rather than a class within Britain. Most of the other views in the chapter disagree with the statement, elite theory denying the rulers form a class, pluralists denying any one group monopolizes power, and postmodernists not believing that a ruling class exists. Some theorists of globalization believe the power to control societies largely comes from outside the society, so a ruling class could not govern Britain.

| **For** | **Against** |
| --- | --- |
| ■ Marx and Engels (p. 125) | ■ Elite theory (p. 124–5) |
| ■ Milliband and Westergaard (p. 125–6) | ■ Postmodernists (p. 128) |
| ■ Poulantzas (partially) (p. 125) | ■ Pluralists (p. 123–4) |
| ■ Sklair (partially) (p. 127) | ■ Theorists of globalization such as Ohmae and Giddens (p. 126–7) |

***Top tip:*** The stratification chapter is also useful for this question (see p. 9).

### *Social factors now have little influence on voting behaviour in Britain.*

***Background:*** Early theories of voting (e.g. Butler and Stokes) saw social factors, particularly class, as the key to understanding voting in Britain. The importance of class has long been debated, with many putting an increasing emphasis on other social factors such as region, gender, age and ethnicity. Ivor Crewe has consistently challenged the importance of class, but he has seen other social factors (e.g. union membership, housing tenure ) as increasingly important. Theories emphasizing policy preference, party ideology and images of economic competence all see political factors as more important than social ones.

| **For** | **Against** |
| --- | --- |
| ■ Ivor Crewe (p. 130) | ■ Butler and Stokes (p. 130) |
| ■ Curtice and Park (p. 131) | ■ Heath, Jowell and Curtice (p. 130) |
| ■ Denver (p. 131) | ■ Saggar and Heath (p. 131) |

***Top tip:*** You could use postmodern arguments that social divisions are declining in importance to support this statement (see p. 128).

### *The nation-state is becoming much less important in the arenas of politics and power.*

***Background:*** Most of the older theories of power and the state have tended to focus on power exercised by state, although Marxists have always seen economic power exercised outside the state as crucial. This view has been increasingly challenged by advocates of globalization, those who see new social movements and global social movements as more important than parliamentary politics, and by postmodernists such as Fraser and Crook, Pakulski and Waters, who see politics as shifting away from the public sphere. On the other hand, state-centred theories emphasize the continuing power of the state, and Chomsky's work shows the enormous power of the US state.

| **For** | **Against** |
| --- | --- |
| ■ Postmodernism (p. 129) | ■ Pluralism (p. 123–4) |
| ■ New and global social movements (pp. 128–9) | ■ Elite theory (p. 124–5) |
| ■ Marxist views that emphasize economic power (p. 125–6) | ■ State-centred theories (p. 126) |
| ■ Most theories of globalization (p. 126–7) | ■ Chomsky (in terms of US state power) (p. 126) |

***Top tip:*** Anthony Giddens (p. 128) provides a balanced view that the state retains significant power although it has been reduced by globalization.

## AQA-STYLE POWER AND POLITICS QUESTION

### A2 Unit 4

**Answer all the questions in Part One and one question from Part Two**
Total: 60 marks, 1 mark = 1.5 minute
Time allowed: 1 hour 30 minutes

### ITEM A

In 2000, research from the University of Durham (Who Runs the North East Now?), which focused on regional government, suggested that, despite new institutions, local politics was still the same old story – it was dominated by grey-haired, white men. … The same sort of story emerges nationally.

New legislation in France now requires political parties to put up equal numbers of male and female candidates in all elections. The proportion of women in local councils leapt from 22% to 48% as a result.

Source: adapted from 'In focus: politics – for men', *Sociology Review*, vol. 11, no. 2, November 2001

## Part One

### Comments on the question

- Do exactly as the question asks
- You need to interpret and apply this information
- Don't spend too long on this – about 12 minutes at most
- Just look at Britain

**[a]** Briefly examine two reasons why such legislation [Item A, line 8] might not work in Britain. [8 marks]

### Advice on preparing your answer

- You might consider the following points among others:
  1 Legislation does not change attitudes
  2 Marxist views on cultural hegemony
  3 Those in control might wish to keep power

- No more than 15–20 minutes
- Plural, so look at more than one, which could be organized around:
  1 an age issue
  2 an ethnicity issue
  3 sex/gender issues
- Remember that these stratification issues may be found in any module as a core theme

**[b]** Briefly examine the reasons for the domination of politics by grey-haired, white men. [12 marks]

- The cynicism of youth and lack of political awareness are discussed in chapter 12, p. 173
- Institutional racism (chapter 4, p. 36) or cultural identity might be a good starting point for the ethnicity issue
- Patriarchy (p. 25–6) might be a good starting point for considering the gender issue

## Part Two

- Look at the strengths and weaknesses
- Plural, so you need to consider more than one
- This is one element of the question and refers to the form power takes
- This must be looked at separately; it refers to who has the power
- Usually taken to mean from the second half of the twentieth century
- This section should take the bulk of your time – 50–55 minutes

**Either:**

Assess sociological theories of the nature and distribution of power in modern society.

[40 marks]

- Define the **nature of power** (see p. 123), and remember to look at different ways of measuring power (see p. 123 for ideas) – by decision-making, by non-decision making, by ideology, or by who benefits
- **Distribution of power** – role of the state (p. 123–6); pluralist views (p. 123–4); political parties and pressure groups (p. 123–4); elite theory (p. 124–5); Marxist theory (p. 125–6); role of globalization and transnational corporations (p. 127). You could also consider the position of women, ethnic minorities and the underclass
- You should look for empirical evidence to prove or refute the theories you have discussed

- Look critically at
- Not necessarily political ones; plural, so more than one is expected
- Focus is on changes, so do not lose sight of this
- Only consider theories that suggest that class is less important than sex or ethnicity when you are evaluating
- Ignore anywhere else
- Keep to the time span, i.e. 1970s onwards

**Or:**

Assess the sociological theories that explain the changes in the relationship between social class and voting behaviour in Britain in the last thirty years. [40 marks]

- Butler and Stokes (p. 130) could be the benchmark you use to look at the changes in class alignment
- Reasons for de-alignment:
  1 Policy preferences, p. 131
  2 Volatility, p. 130
  3 Role of ideology, p. 131
- Theories that suggest that class alignment still exists:
  1 Heath, Jowell and Curtice, pp. 130
  2 Marxist theories about false consciousness
- Consider theories that look at women and ethnic minorities as having different interests
- Try to find empirical evidence to prove or refute the various arguments

## OCR-STYLE POWER, POLITICS AND THE STATE QUESTION

### A2 Unit 2536: Power and Control: Protest and New Social Movements

Total: 60 marks 1 mark = 1 minute
Time allowed: 1 hour

#### Comments on the question

- Make sure that you describe this view in a detailed way with supporting evidence
- Look at a range of arguments for and against this point of view
- Make sure that you have a balance, i.e. a similar number of arguments supporting the view and challenging the view

[a] Outline and assess the view that the activities of new social movements aim to challenge the global capitalist order.

[60 marks]

#### Advice on preparing your answer

- Remember that you don't have to accept this view. You can challenge it
- An introduction is necessary to set the scene, i.e. which sociologist or theory takes this position
- The section on pp. 126–8 should be useful in helping you to summarize the key arguments
- Try to finish with an evaluative conclusion based on the evidence presented

# Chapter 10

# WORK, UNEMPLOYMENT AND LEISURE

Textbook pp. 618–689

Textbook pp. 618–689

## Specifications

| Specification | Specification details | Coverage |
|---|---|---|
| **AQA** AS: Work and Leisure | ■ Different theories of the management and organization of work | Different theories such as Marxism and functionalism are covered on pp. 137–9. |
| | ■ Different explanations of the nature and extent of work satisfaction, alienation and conflict at work | Attitudes to work and alienation are discussed on pp. 136–9, issues of conflict and co-operation at work on pp. 139–40. Links in closely with the next specification heading. |
| | ■ The implications of technological changes and their impact on individuals, organizations and society | Covered on pp. 137–9. |
| | ■ Explanations of the causes and effects of unemployment and the problems of measuring it | See the sections on unemployment (pp. 140–1) and the effects of unemployment (pp. 141–2). |
| | ■ Explanation of leisure patterns, and the relationship between leisure, identity and consumption | See the section on leisure (pp. 143–5). |

**Parts of other modules covered**

| | | | |
|---|---|---|---|
| **OCR** A2: Power and Control/Popular Culture | **Leisure and identity** | ■ Patterns and explanations of social class, gender and ethnic differences in consumption; the impact on leisure, lifestyle shopping, and the construction of identity. | ■ These issues are discussed on pp. 143–5. |
| | | ■ Leisure and symbolic work; the activities of individuals and groups in the construction of proto or symbolic communities. | ■ Covered in section on modernity, postmodernity and leisure (pp. 144–5). |
| **OCR** A2: Social Inequality and Difference | | ■ Contemporary workplace inequalities. The impact of changes in the workplace on class, ethnic and gender inequality. | ■ The issue of deskilling is covered on p. 138; flexibility and post-Fordism on p. 138–9. The discussion of 'McJobs' on p. 139 is also important. |

For more detailed specification guidance visit **www.haralambosholborn.com**

## Essential notes

### THE NATURE OF WORK

■ Keith Grint (1991) argues that there is no single, universal definition of work that can be generally applied.

■ Work is **socially defined** within particular societies. For example, although Grint defines housework as work, it is not always defined as such in male-dominated societies.

■ In **pre-industrial societies** work was often regarded as an unfortunate necessity which should be kept to a minimum.

■ Modern, industrial, capitalist societies tend to have more of a **work ethic**, seeing work as necessary and important, and unemployment or idleness as undesirable.

■ **Weber** argued that the modern work ethic stemmed from the **Protestant ethic**, while E.P. **Thompson** (1967) attributed it to **capitalist industrialization** and the need to keep expensive machinery productive.

### WORK AND LEISURE – CONFLICT PERSPECTIVES

#### Marx – alienated labour

■ **Marx** argued that work was the means through which people fulfilled their potential as human beings.

■ In capitalist societies people failed to gain true satisfaction from work.

■ The products produced by workers were reduced to **commodities** to be sold in a market, rather than being an expression of the humanity of those who produced them.

■ Workers were therefore **alienated** from the **products** they produced.

■ Workers also became alienated from the **act of production** – the work itself – because they were forced to work for capitalists to earn a wage. They no longer owned the **means of production** and had to work for those who owned the machinery etc.

■ They were also alienated from **fellow workers**, since each individual was working purely for themselves rather than for the good of the community.

■ Marx saw **wage labour** (work for a wage) as **wage slavery**. The worker was only given part of the value of the products they produced. The rest of it was stolen from them by capitalists, in the form of **surplus value** or profit.

■ Marx thought that the problem of alienated labour could only be overcome through **communism**. In communism the means of production would be communally owned, and people would express their humanity through their work, working for the good of the community as a whole.

Critics have attacked Marx's views:

1 In **communist** countries such as the USSR people still felt alienated from their work.
2 Some Marxists have attacked Marx's work on alienation for being too abstract and philosophical and therefore **unscientific**.

## TECHNOLOGY AND WORK EXPERIENCE

Robert **Blauner** (1964) argued that alienation does not stem from the capitalist system but from the sort of **technology** employed at work.

He defines alienation in terms of:

■ The degree of **control** workers have over work.
■ The amount of **meaning** they find in work.
■ The degree of **social integration** within work.
■ The degree of **involvement** in work.

In terms of these criteria, people who use **craft technology** – such as printers, who use their skill to produce a whole product from start to finish – are not alienated.

On the other hand, workers on **assembly lines** are highly alienated because their jobs are socially isolating and repetitive and require little use of skill or initiative.

However, Blauner believes that **automation** in industries such as the chemical industry will reduce alienation. Machines take over much of the routine work, and workers involved in monitoring, maintenance and repair of machinery have jobs which are not particularly alienating.

Blauner has been criticized for the following reasons:

1 **Marxists** argue that he ignores the sources of alienation in the capitalist system.
2 The interpretation of the **questionnaire data** used by Blauner is open to question.
3 **Grint** (1998) argues that even in assembly-line systems much of the work is away from the assembly line itself, and this work is not alienating.

4 Grint sees Blauner as **sexist**, because Blauner suggested that women lacked the physical stamina to do certain types of work.
5 Nichols and Beynon (1977) found no evidence that levels of alienation had decreased in chemical plants. There was still much routine manual work, and many of those monitoring machines found the work tedious and unsatisfying.
6 Duncan **Gallie** (1978) studied oil refineries in England and France. The French workers were less satisfied than the British ones. This suggested that production technology on its own did not determine the degree of alienation. Instead management style was important. French managers were more autocratic than British ones.

## COMPUTERS, TECHNOLOGY AND CHANGES IN WORK

There is a division between two main approaches in this area:

1 **Technological determinism** assumes that social life is determined by technology.
2 **Social determinism** assumes that cultural and social factors determine the development of technology and the uses to which it is put.

Many argue for an intermediate position between these two extremes.

### Zuboff – In the Age of the Smart Machine

Shoshana **Zuboff** (1988) sees **information technology** as having a big impact on work, but she is not an extreme technological determinist.

She conducted a study of eight organizations, and found that:

■ Manual skills were becoming less important where IT had been introduced.
■ **White-collar** workers increasingly worked at computer terminals rather than interacting with one another, and they therefore felt more isolated.
■ IT was also used to monitor the activities and performance of workers (the **information panopticon**).
■ In some companies IT allowed greater **participation** by ordinary workers – e.g. in contributing ideas – which helped to break down hierarchies.

Zuboff concludes that managers use IT either to '**informate**' a company (spread information to everybody to allow more participation) or to reassert **hierarchical controls**.

### Kling – the consumption of technology

Rob **Kling** (1991, 1992) opposes theories that suggest that technology has a strong influence on work.

■ He argues that technology can be used in many different ways and there is nothing inevitable about its influence on work.

- Using a series of case studies, he shows that technology can be used to increase efficiency, strengthen management control or expand the range of jobs carried out by individual employees.
- The impact of computers is largely shaped by the way in which companies organize access on information systems rather than by the nature of the technology.

### Grint and Woolgar – discourse and computers

Keith **Grint** and Steve **Woolgar** (1992, 1997) argue that the use that is made of information technology is shaped by the **discourse** surrounding it – that is, the way people talk about the technology.

Those who have the **power** to shape the way the technology is talked about and interpreted, shape the sort of use to which it is put.

Critics argue that this view goes too far in attributing no importance to the nature of the technology itself. However people interpret technology, it retains certain **objective capabilities** which limit the uses to which it can be put.

## THE LABOUR PROCESS AND THE DEGRADATION OF WORK

The **labour process** concerns the way in which raw materials are transformed by human labour.

Harry **Braverman** (1974) puts forward a **Marxist** view of the labour process.

- He argues that automation results from attempts to change the labour process in order to increase the **exploitation** of workers.
- He believes that work has been progressively **deskilled** – the amount of skill needed to do jobs has been reduced.
- Deskilling is used so that employers can **control** workers more easily.
- Complex tasks are broken down into many simple operations, reducing the need for workers to use their initiative or skill, and allowing managers to control work more directly.
- **Scientific management**, developed by W. **Taylor** in the early twentieth century, was used to deskill work by analysing it and reducing the 'brain work' needed to carry out tasks.
- Management does make some **concessions** – such as higher wages for a few employees or human relations-style management – to make work more tolerable.
- Braverman claims that deskilling has not just affected manufacturing, but also **clerical work**, and **professional work** such as nursing and teaching.

There have been many responses to Braverman.

- Andrew **Zimbalist** (1979) uses evidence from the printing industry to support Braverman.
- Paul **Thompson** (1983) argues that craft work was never as important as Braverman assumes, and the amount of deskilling has therefore been exaggerated by Braverman.

- Duncan **Gallie** (1994) argues that the expansion of the **service class** has led to an increase in workforce skill. He found that most British employees believe that the amount of skill required in their job has been increasing. **Upskilling** was more common than deskilling, although part-time female workers experienced more deskilling than other groups.
- Craig **Littler** (1983) believes that Braverman exaggerates the influence of scientific management.
- Some **Marxists** argue that methods other than deskilling (such as the use of technology to monitor workers) have become more important in controlling workers.
- Andy **Friedman** (1977) stresses that workers often resist management attempts to impose greater control.
- Braverman fails to define **skill** precisely. Some **feminists** argue that Braverman fails to recognize the amount of skill required in some female jobs.
- Sylvia **Walby** (1986) suggests that unions have protected skill levels in many male jobs, but they have failed to protect or gain proper wages for skilled female workers.

## FLEXIBILITY AND POST-FORDISM

Some sociologists argue that important changes have taken place in work which have led to increased skill requirements rather than deskilling.

**Fordism** (named after Henry Ford) involved the **mass production** of standardized products using relatively unskilled workers on machines dedicated to particular products. Fordist production techniques followed these **assembly-line** production methods.

Some people argue that there has been a shift to **post-Fordism**, or **flexible production**.

- Michael **Piore** (1986) argues that new computer technology makes production more flexible – it is easy to shift to making new products. This enables the production of small batches of specialized products. **Flexible specialization** requires more skilled and versatile workers.
- John **Atkinson** (1985) argues that, from the 1970s, the **flexible firm** developed as a response to economic recession. It involved:

1 **Functional flexibility:** the ability to shift core workers to different tasks.
2 **Numerical flexibility:** the facility to reduce or increase the size of the workforce. Workers were increasingly employed in subcontracted, part-time or temporary jobs rather than full-time permanent ones. These **peripheral workers** needed less skill and had less security than **core workers**.

There have been a number of responses to theories of post-Fordism:

1 Anna **Pollert** (1988) argues that Fordist production methods were never completely dominant in industry, and that Fordist production continues to be common today. She argues that flexibility does not necessarily

increase the skills needed by workers, and she questions whether companies are shifting to peripheral rather than core, full-time workers.

2 Stephen **Wood** (1989), in a study of steel-rolling mills, found that flexibility did not increase skill requirements.

3 **Dex and McCulloch** (1997) studied statistical evidence on the British labour market and found some increase, but only a small one, in the proportions involved in flexible work.

4 Paul **Thompson** (1993) and **Thompson and McHugh** (2002) argue that there has been some move towards greater flexibility, but that the change should not be exaggerated. Workers are expected to perform a greater variety of tasks (**multi-tasking**) but in many workplaces (e.g. McDonald's) each task requires little skill. Often work is simply intensified rather than reskilled.

## RADICAL VIEWS OF CONTEMPORARY WORK

Radical views of contemporary work are critical of the optimistic views about the future of work expressed in post-Fordism.

### George Ritzer – McDonaldization and McJobs

Ritzer (1996, 1998, 2002) believes that the principles on which McDonalds and other fast-food outlets are being run are spreading to other parts of society including work (see p. 217). Ritzer calls work based on these principles **McJobs**.

McJobs have the following features:

■ Work is broken down into simple, **unskilled** tasks.
■ Each task is **timed** and accomplished in as short a time as possible.
■ The work is **predictable** and repetitive.
■ **Computers** are used to monitor workers.
■ Because the work is **dehumanized** there tends to be a high staff turnover even in managerial grades.
■ Work is often **insecure** and low-paid.

Although similar to Braverman, Ritzer's ideas go further because he argues that **managers** have lost power, **consumers** are controlled as well as workers and he sees deskilling and routinization spreading to the **service sector** as well as manufacturing.

**Thompson and McHugh** (2002) believe there is some truth in Ritzer's theory but he exaggerates the spread of McDonaldization and rationalization and underestimates worker resistance.

### Naomi Klein – No Jobs

In *No Logo* (see p. 129) Naomi Klein (2000) discusses the impact on work of global corporation such as *Nike* who rely heavily upon **branding**. Such companies invest much of their money in advertising and other efforts to gain and maintain recognition of their brand,

leaving little money for worker's wages. This has a number of consequences.

■ The corporations increasingly *subcontract* production to the cheapest available suppliers. Many of their products are produced in **free trade zones** in countries such as China and Mexico where wages and working conditions are very poor.
■ Many jobs in manufacturing have shifted from richer to poorer countries where labour costs are cheaper, leading to job losses in richer countries.
■ Where the companies have to employ workers in richer countries, costs are cut through part-time employment and **casualization**, often misleadingly described as 'flexibility'. This has produced increased job insecurity.
■ This has also led to a **polarization** of work in richer countries with a few executives doing very well out of the success of branded, global companies while most employees have seen deterioration in their work.

## CONFLICT AND COOPERATION AT WORK

**Functionalists** such as Talcott Parsons argue that workers and management share **common goals** – i.e. the success of their company. There should therefore be little conflict.

**Pluralists** believe that there are some **differences of interest** between workers and employers (e.g. over wage levels), but there are some **shared interests** as well. For example, workers do not want to increase wages to the extent that they put their company out of business and lose their jobs. According to pluralists, different interests are represented in industrial societies. For example, workers have trade unions to represent them.

**Marxists** argue that workers are exploited under capitalism, through the extraction of surplus value. This provides the potential for **conflict** at work.

The Marxists **Littler and Salaman** (1984) argue that employers tend to deskill and regulate work as much as possible in order to increase profits. However, they have to try to maintain a minimum level of cooperation.

### Strikes

Strikes are one of the most obvious forms of industrial conflict.

■ A **strike** is a stoppage of work by a group of employees.
■ Strike statistics suggest that the strike rate was quite high from 1988 to 1992, but it declined in the later 1990s. From 1997–2001 Britain has had a much lower strike rate than some European countries and overall only just above the average for advanced industrial nations.
■ Strike statistics may not be entirely accurate. They are based on employers' reports (which may underestimate the amount of striking). Definitions of strikes vary from country to country. In Britain, political strikes, strikes involving fewer than ten workers and strikes lasting less than one day are not included.

There appear to have been a number of **phases** of strike activity and trade union development in Britain.

- From the 1950s until the late 1970s there were several periods with high strike rates, and trade unions appeared to have considerable power.
- In 1979, Margaret **Thatcher**, leader of the Conservatives, was elected as prime minister, and she decided to undermine union power by introducing **new laws** which restricted the ability of unions to stage successful strikes.
- According to **Hyman** (1984), these changes led to considerable conflict with unions in the short term, but in the long term they weakened union power.
- Keith **Grint** (1991) argues that **economic changes** (such as high unemployment and low inflation), rather than government policies, are responsible for declining strike rates.
- Peter **Ackers** *et al.* (1996) argue that a variety of changes – e.g. the growth of subcontracting and part-time employment, new management techniques and information technology – have made it difficult for unions to retain the mass loyalty of workers, and this has led to them being more pragmatic.
- The **Labour** government elected in 1997 kept its distance from trade unions (unlike previous Labour governments), but it did introduce some laws that unions approved of (such as the minimum wage).
- Will Hutton (2002) argues that during Labour's second term in office (after 2001) conflict at work was starting to increase again particularly in the **public sector** with wages falling behind those in the **private sector**.

One of the most sophisticated attempts to explain the causes of strikes and other types of industrial conflict was advanced by **Edwards and Scullion** (1982). They examined the relationship between different forms of industrial conflict, including strikes, industrial sabotage, absenteeism, labour turnover, breaches of factory discipline and the withdrawal of cooperation and effort by workers.

They found conflict in all the workplaces they studied, but the nature of the conflict varied:

- Where the management had strong control, absenteeism and labour turnover tended to be high.
- Where workers had a stronger bargaining position, strikes were more common.

## UNEMPLOYMENT

### Unemployment statistics

- Between 1948 and 1966 the official unemployment rate in the UK averaged less than 2% of the workforce.
- In the period between 1975 and 1978 it rose to above 6%.
- Unemployment reached a peak in 1985 and 1986 when 11.8% of the workforce were unemployed.
- Rates then fell until 1992 when another peak of 10.8% was reached.
- Unemployment figures then declined and stood at 5.1% in 2003.

### Official statistics as an overestimation

Although most commentators would accept that official unemployment figures provide a general indication of trends in unemployment, such statistics need to be treated with great caution.

Some critics of the statistics have argued that they exaggerate the amount of unemployment. In the 1980s various Conservatives claimed that up to one million of the 'unemployed' were either working and claiming benefit illegally or not genuinely looking for work.

However, such claims may be exaggerated. **Pahl** (1984), for example, found that the unemployed were no more likely to engage in '**informal work**' than those with paid employment.

### Official statistics as an underestimation

Sociologists usually argue that official statistics underestimate the amount of unemployment rather than exaggerate it.

- Between 1979 and 1987, Margaret Thatcher's Conservative government changed the method of calculating unemployment statistics 19 times, and nearly all of these changes removed substantial numbers from the unemployment register.
- In 1996 unemployment benefit was replaced by the **Jobseeker's Allowance**. **Sweeney and McMahon** (1998) estimated that the associated set of changes removed about 60,000 claimants from the statistics.
- Unemployment figures have been further reduced by various **training schemes**, such as the New Deal which remove young people in particular from the unemployment register.
- Catherine **Barham** (2002) suggests that unemployment figures are reduced by classifying some people who might previously have been defined as unemployed as economically inactive.
- Keith **Grint** (1998) concludes that unemployment figures can be regarded as a **social construction**.

### The social distribution of unemployment

Unemployment is not evenly distributed among groups in the population. Despite the limitations of official figures, it is possible to identify overall patterns.

- **Class** – The lower social classes are the most likely to experience unemployment. There was concern that the recession of the early 1990s was causing unemployment to spread to service-sector jobs, but upper middle-class workers continued to have much lower rates.
- **Gender** – Official figures show higher unemployment rates for men than for women. According to 2002 figures the unemployment rate for men was 5.7% and for women was 4.4%. However, the latter is likely to be an underestimate, as married women can be ineligible for the benefits that would lead to them being registered.
- **Age** – There are higher rates of unemployment for the young, though the unemployment rate for older men sometimes exceeds the national average. Although

**youth unemployment** was seen as a serious issue in the 1980s and 1990s, unemployment is more likely to be a long-term problem for older members of the workforce.
- **Ethnicity** – In general, ethnic minorities suffer from higher rates of unemployment. The rate for Indians and Chinese is closest to the white rate. Unemployment is particularly common among younger members of ethnic minorities and is highest amongst Bangladeshis.
- **Region** – Unemployment tends to be highest in regions that have traditionally relied on the heavier industries; these were badly hit in the recessions of the late 1970s and early 1980s. However, the gap between different regions narrowed in the 1990s, and there were some pockets of relatively high unemployment in areas of the south of England, including London.
- **Disability** – Nearly 60% of those with a 'work-limiting' disability were economically inactive in 1998, with a further 6% unemployed.

Statistically, then, most cases of unemployment would be expected among young, unskilled, male workers living in Northern Ireland, Wales or northern England, particularly among the disabled.

## The causes of unemployment, and government policy

### Technological change and deindustrialization

Recent decades have seen a continuing decline in the importance of **manufacturing industry**, and some commentators have seen these changes as representing a **deindustrialization** of Britain, with serious implications for future unemployment.

**Gill** (1985) has suggested that new technology threatens to reduce the workforce in numerous occupations. The recession of the early 1990s seemed in line with this view, but recovery later in the decade seemed to suggest that a move towards a more service-based economy did not inevitably mean high levels of unemployment.

### Theories of unemployment – market liberal theory

For much of the period since 1945 governments have accepted that they should take responsibility for maintaining low levels of unemployment – an approach based on the ideas of the British economist J.M. **Keynes**.

However, faced with rising inflation as well as rising unemployment, the Conservative government of Margaret Thatcher turned to **market liberal economic theories** which challenged the Keynesian view. These theories emphasized the importance of leaving **market forces** to determine the way the economy developed.

Taxation was reduced, nationalized industries were **privatized** and public support for 'lame duck' industries was withdrawn. It was hoped that unemployment would fall because:

- The costs of employing people would fall as unions lost power.

- Cutting welfare benefits would mean that there would be more incentive to accept low-paid work.

### Evaluation of Conservative policies

**MacInnes** (1987) argues that market liberal policies actually caused unemployment to rise. However, it is possible to argue that some Conservative policies contributed to a fall in unemployment in the late 1990s.

## Marxist theories of unemployment

Marx saw unemployment as resulting from the **capitalist system** itself. He believed that capitalist economies went through cycles. Periods of expansion in which there was full employment were followed by periods of crisis during which unemployment rose. Each successive crisis would be worse than the previous one until eventually the capitalist system would be destroyed.

Capitalism requires workers who can be hired during booms and fired during slumps. Marx refers to the part of the workforce used in this way as the **reserve army of labour**. The unemployed are the victims of the cyclical way in which the capitalist economy works.

### Evaluation of Marxist views

Clearly Marx's predictions of the collapse of capitalism have not come true. Indeed the economic systems of some former communist countries came closer to collapse under communism than those of advanced capitalist countries. However, economic crises continue to hit the capitalist system periodically – e.g. the problems experienced by Japan and other south-east Asian countries in the late 1990s.

## The Labour government and unemployment policies

Despite the Labour Party's traditional commitment to full employment, Tony Blair's government only committed themselves to reducing unemployment rather than eradicating it. They introduced a number of policies, such as the 'New Deal', aimed at encouraging the unemployed back to work and giving employers incentives to take them on. However, from 1999 they also announced they would withdraw benefits from claimants refusing to attend interviews.

# THE EFFECTS OF UNEMPLOYMENT

## The effects on society

The effects of unemployment are usually seen as damaging to society.

- **Sinfield** (1981) identifies four ways in which unemployment reduces quality of life in a society:
  1 Those remaining in work feel less secure and may have their standard of living threatened.
  2 Workers become less willing to leave an unsatisfactory job.

3 The unemployed and those in unsatisfying jobs may scapegoat weaker groups in society, such as married women or ethnic minorities, blaming them for their problems.

4 High unemployment reduces the chance of equality of opportunity being achieved. Employers no longer need to make an effort to recruit from disadvantaged groups.

■ **Lea and Young** (1984) argue that unemployment amongst the young leads to their **marginalization**. This helped to create the **subculture** of despair which led to the urban riots of the 1980s.

■ **Allen and Watson** (1986) point out that a range of social problems have been linked to unemployment but that such problems usually do not have one single, simple cause.

## The personal effects of unemployment

### Health

A 1998 study of England and Wales (reported in Howard, *et al.* 2001) found unemployed men had a 20% higher death rate than employed men.

### Financial effects

Howard *et al.* (2001) report that 77% of people in households where the head of the household or their spouse is unemployed live below the official poverty line.

### Social effects

Fagin and Little (1984) argue that the unemployed lose more than money when they lose their job.

■ Work gives people a **sense of identity** and is a source of relationships outside the family.

■ Work also provides **obligatory activity**. Fagin and Little's study of unemployed men in London revealed that many found it difficult to occupy themselves.

■ Work helps to **structure psychological time**. The men in the study spent more of their time in bed, but their sleep was restless and they felt more tired than they did in paid employment.

■ Work provides opportunities to develop skills and creativity, and it provides a sense of purpose. This **sense of purpose** is lost in times of unemployment.

■ Fagin and Little argue that income from work provides **freedom and control outside work**. It creates the possibility of engaging in leisure activities that cost money.

Such effects can place strain on the personal relationships of the unemployed. **Lampard** (1994) found that marriages were more likely to break up during periods of unemployment.

### Leisure and unemployment

One possible gain from unemployment is an increase in leisure time. However, **Gallie, Gershuny and Vogler** (1994) found that men were slightly more likely to play

and watch sport once they became unemployed, although women were less likely to take part in these activities. Expensive pastimes such as visiting the cinema decreased, while watching television and reading books increased.

## Psychological reactions to unemployment

Research by **Gershuny** (1994) found that the unemployed had poorer psychological health than the employed. However, the psychological well-being of those unemployed who had wide social contacts and felt positive about how they spent their time was better than amongst the employed who did not have these advantages.

## Youth and the effects of unemployment

British governments have devoted significant resources to dealing with youth unemployment. They identify unemployment as a particularly serious problem for the young.

■ This view is supported by **Willis** (1984). He argues that unemployment disrupts the normal **transition to adulthood**. The young unemployed are denied the opportunity to be independent from parents, and often experience long periods of poverty.

■ Not all researchers agree with this view. **Roberts** (1986) accepts that young people do not enjoy unemployment, but he believes that they are better-equipped to deal with it than many older workers, as they have not yet established firm occupational identities.

## Gender and the effects of unemployment

Most research on the effects of unemployment has focused on male unemployment. Traditionally it has been argued that women might be expected to suffer less than men from unemployment because domestic life offers them a sense of identity and purpose.

This view has been challenged. **Henwood and Miles** (1987) found that unemployment was at least as potentially damaging for women as it was for men, and that housewives suffer some of the problems – such as **lack of social contact** – associated with unemployment.

## The effects on communities

**Critcher, Dicks and Waddington** (1992) studied two mining villages in Yorkshire which had experienced pit closures. The closures had significant effects on the local communities.

■ The local economy suffered. Some local shops and services closed.

■ The appearance of the villages declined, and community facilities started to decay.

■ **Informal mechanisms** of social control began to break down. Drug-taking, burglary and other crimes increased.

■ Marriages and family life came under increasing stress.

# LEISURE

The sociology of leisure has only been a major focus of study since the 1970s. Early contributions concentrated on the relationship between leisure and other areas of social life such as work and the family.

## *Parker – the influence of work on leisure*

Stanley **Parker** (1976) defined leisure as the time left over once other obligations have been attended to. Parker argued that leisure activities were closely related to the freedom, **autonomy** (control) and satisfaction people experience at work. He saw the relationship between work and leisure as falling into three main patterns.

1 **The extension pattern** – In this pattern, work extends into leisure: there is no clear dividing line between the two. This pattern is associated with occupations providing **high levels of involvement, autonomy and job satisfaction**. Outside office hours, clients and colleagues are involved in leisure pursuits which allow business and pleasure to be combined.
2 **The neutrality pattern** – In the neutrality pattern, a clear distinction is made between work and leisure. Family life and leisure, rather than work, provide the central interest in life. Occupations typically associated with the neutrality pattern include clerical and semi-skilled manual work, where there are medium to low degrees of autonomy.
3 **The opposition pattern** – Here work is sharply differentiated from leisure. The opposition pattern is associated with jobs that often produce a feeling of hostility towards work. Hours of leisure are long and are used mainly to recover from and compensate for work. Activities include drinking in pubs and working men's clubs. This pattern is associated with **traditional manual work** such as mining and trawling.

## Criticisms of Parker

1 Parker tends to ignore factors other than work which influence leisure patterns. The **Rapoports** (1975), for example, believe that **family lifestyle** is the most important influence on leisure. The leisure pursuits of adolescents tend to be different from those of middle-aged or retired people, for example.
2 **Clarke and Critcher** (1985) point out that Parker's analysis is rather **deterministic**: it does not allow for individual choice in leisure activities and does not account for the wide range of leisure activities engaged in by people who have the same job.
3 Clarke and Critcher also suggest that Parker's work does not deal successfully with the **leisure patterns of women**. He does not examine the influence of housework or the open-ended nature of domestic obligations for many women.

## *Roberts – a pluralist perspective on leisure*

Ken **Roberts** (1978, 1986) stresses the variety of leisure patterns and the range of factors that influence those patterns. He sees leisure as involving individual freedom of choice.

## Social factors and leisure

Unlike Parker, Roberts claims that work has relatively little influence on leisure. Many people do not have paid employment, and, even amongst those who do, **television** takes up the largest single block of leisure time for all occupational groups.

Roberts identifies other social factors that he believes are significant in leisure choices.

- **Family life cycle** is a significant factor. Unmarried people under 30 spend less time watching television and more time socializing than their married counterparts.
- **Gender** is important as women tend to have less leisure time than men.
- Those who stay longer in **education** watch less television and spend more time outside the home with friends.
- Married couples with **joint conjugal roles** tend to engage in home-centred leisure, while those with segregated conjugal roles tend to go out more. (See pp. 115–16 for a discussion of roles in marriage.)

## *Clarke and Critcher – leisure in capitalist Britain*

John **Clarke** and Chas **Critcher** (1985) have developed a **neo-Marxist** approach to leisure. They believe that writers such as Roberts exaggerate the degree of choice involved in leisure. Individual choices are limited by capitalism.

## Capitalism and leisure

Clarke and Critcher claim that capitalism shapes the nature of work and leisure. The development of capitalism removed many of the opportunities for leisure that existed before the Industrial Revolution and created a clear distinction between work and leisure.

The **state** plays a key role in regulating leisure.

- It **licenses** certain leisure activities, such as pubs and clubs, and it censors films and videos.
- It is involved in the **regulation of public space**. The disadvantaged tend to use public spaces for leisure, and this means that the young, ethnic minorities and the working class in general have part of their recreation controlled by the police.
- The state is concerned to prevent **disorderly leisure** which might be a threat to social order. Middle-class tastes are promoted (e.g. the provision of subsidies to opera companies), and working-class leisure patterns are discouraged.

## The commercialization of leisure

Perhaps the most important aspect of leisure under capitalism is the way it has become big business. Large corporations create new products and services and attempt to persuade consumers to purchase them.

However, despite their attempts to establish hegemony (or domination), big business has not always been successful. Clarke and Critcher give the example of **CAMRA** (the Campaign for Real Ale) which has resisted large brewers' attempts to replace natural with keg beers.

### Evaluation of 'class domination' theories

Clarke and Critcher see leisure as being a far more restricted area of social life than Roberts. To Roberts, leisure choices in Britain are as free as can be expected in any society. Companies can only succeed if they provide what consumers want.

Both Roberts and Clarke and Critcher can be accused of **generalizing** about the role of leisure in society and paying too little attention to evidence that may contradict their theories.

## GENDER AND LEISURE

Since the start of the 1980s, feminist sociologists have devoted increasing attention to the relationship between gender and leisure patterns.

### *Statistics*

Government statistics show that in Britain men are more likely than women to take part in most sports and are also more likely to do DIY, while women are much more likely than men to participate in knitting, needlework and dressmaking.

### *Green, Hebron and Woodward – a feminist perspective*

**Green et al.** (1990) studied 700 women in Sheffield, using a range of methods.

### The definition of leisure

- Many of the women interviewed found it hard to separate leisure from other aspects of their lives, but often saw it as a **state of mind**.
- It is much harder for women to forget about work and put aside time for leisure because women tend to have **open-ended domestic responsibilities**.
- Some women with part-time jobs actually saw those jobs as a form of leisure – an opportunity to escape from domestic chores and a chance to socialize.

### Patterns of work and leisure

- Overall, men have more time for leisure than women.
- Leisure for many married women is restricted by financial dependence on their husbands.
- Traditional male attitudes mean that women are often expected to choose their leisure activities from a restricted range of home- and family-based activities.

### Leisure and social control

- Physical violence and sexual attacks outside the home make women afraid to venture out, particularly if they are on their own and it is dark.

- Many leisure venues are dominated by men, and women may feel uncomfortable in them. In Green *et al.*'s study, 80% of women said that they felt uncomfortable in a pub on their own.
- **Ideology** also limits women's behaviour. For example, many mothers feel guilty about leaving their children.
- Most married women took responsibility for the majority of **housework**, often in addition to paid employment. They thus had little time available for leisure.

### Other influences on leisure

The Sheffield study found that a variety of other factors also affected leisure.

- **Class** – women from higher classes have more opportunity to engage in expensive leisure pursuits. They are more likely to participate in sport and keep-fit activities than working-class women.
- **Age, work and domestic situation** – single, young, employed women probably have the most freedom in leisure. They have more financial independence and fewer domestic responsibilities than married women. There are fewer ideological restrictions on their leisure outside the home, and there is no husband to frown on their behaviour.
- **Ethnic group** – ethnic-minority women are subject to **racial** as well as sexual **harassment**, and may be even more unwilling than other women to go out to leisure activities.

Different **cultural traditions** may affect leisure choices. Green *et al.* claim that Asian men are reluctant to encourage women to go out. African-Caribbean women are less restricted in their leisure, which is less home-based than for Asian women, and this encourages independence.

### Conclusion

Although their emphasis is on the constraints on women, Green *et al.* are not entirely pessimistic. They found that women are able to develop and maintain friendships in many unlikely settings, such as outside the school gates and at the shops. They are also slightly more active than men in voluntary organizations and are more likely to attend evening classes.

## MODERNITY, POSTMODERNITY AND LEISURE

A number of sociologists in recent years have argued that we are entering an era of **postmodernity**, and as a result the nature of leisure is changing.

### *Rojek – Decentring leisure*

Chris **Rojek** (1995) argues that leisure needs to be **decentred**. By this he means that leisure should not be seen as a clearly demarcated area of social life which can be studied in its own right. This is because:

- Leisure can best be understood by examining it within the **context** of the society in which it exists.
- In postmodernity the **meaning** of leisure becomes less clear. Leisure overlaps with other areas of social life.
- Rojek identifies some general differences between modern and postmodern leisure.

| Modern leisure | Postmodern leisure |
| --- | --- |
| Work and leisure are two separate areas. | Work and leisure come together – for example, more people work in the leisure industries and experience fun and enjoyment at work. |
| Celebration of the authentic. For example, visiting the Tower of London is superior to visiting a model of it. | Virtual-reality machines, models and representations are fully accepted as valid. |
| People have a strong sense of who they are and engage in leisure pursuits appropriate to their age-group identity. | Age-group identity is no longer a limitation to leisure. Older people might go to night-clubs and rock concerts, and younger people may engage in more sedate pursuits such as golf. |
| There are clear distinctions between different roles and areas of social life – for example, male and female, white and ethnic cultures. | People can pick and choose who they want to be, and leisure plays a central role in identity policies. Your leisure actually creates your identity. |
| There is a sharp distinction between the providers and consumers of leisure. | People cooperate to organize their own leisure. |

### Evaluation of Rojek

Rojek makes very general statements about leisure. As such he exaggerates and simplifies the changes in leisure that he claims have taken place. He provides little evidence to support his arguments.

## Scraton and Bramham – leisure and postmodernity

### Modernity and leisure

In the modern period, the state and voluntary groups became involved in organizing leisure activities that were supposed to benefit individuals and/or society. One focus of the policies was youth – particularly working-class males, who were seen as a **potential social problem**. Youth clubs and the Scouts were designed to keep young people occupied and out of trouble.

The idea of **rational, planned leisure** began to lose influence after the Second World War as society became more diverse and fragmented. These developments heralded changes which some refer to as postmodern leisure.

### Postmodern leisure

Sheila **Scraton** and Peter **Bramham** identify a number of features of postmodern leisure.

1 Postmodern leisure is concerned with **self-indulgence**. You do what you want rather than what others tell you is good for you.
2 Elites can no longer dictate to the masses what is good for them. There is an enormous variety of **subcultural groups** pursuing their own leisure activities, from trainspotting to bungee jumping.
3 Leisure is an expression of the pursuit of a particular **lifestyle**. It is a means to express who you are, rather than a search for relaxation or self-improvement. People's identities become more wrapped up in the consumer goods they buy and their choice of pastimes, rather than in their jobs, families or communities.
4 Postmodernity blurs the distinction between work and leisure. Work increasingly intrudes into the home through emails and fax machines, while work sometimes becomes an extension of leisure activities.
5 Postmodern leisure involves an increasing **concern with the body**. 'Working-out' is all part of the attempt to develop a distinctive lifestyle, body shape and identity.
6 **Nostalgia** becomes important in postmodern leisure because people have lost faith in the future. The heritage industry grows and more people visit places that claim to recreate the past. However, this is often achieved through simulation and virtual reality – what the postmodern writer **Baudrillard** calls simulacra.

## Evaluation of postmodern theories of leisure

**Scraton and Bramham** acknowledge that many of the changes described by postmodernists have taken place. However, they argue that these changes affect some groups more than others.

- **Poorer sections of society** do not have the time or the money to engage in postmodern leisure pursuits.
- Leisure remains **gendered**. Scraton and Bramham point out that video games and virtual reality technology are mostly enjoyed by men.
- **Racism** also restricts leisure activities. Scraton and Bramham quote research which suggests that racism is prevalent in many British sports.

# TEST YOUR KNOWLEDGE AND UNDERSTANDING

**1** According to Grint, work is:
  **a** Activity you get paid for
  **b** Activities other than leisure
  **c** Activities that involve effort
  **d** Activities that a society defines as work

**2** According to Marx, work in capitalist societies produces:
  **a** Boredom
  **b** Alienation
  **c** Anomie
  **d** Egoism

**3** According to Blauner, the degree of alienation experienced by workers is determined by:
  **a** The type of technology being used
  **b** The management techniques being used
  **c** The mental states of the workers
  **d** The nature of the capitalist system

**4** Which of the following writers argues that the discourse surrounding technology shapes the way it influences work?
  **a** Zuboff
  **b** Braverman
  **c** Kling
  **d** Grint and Woolgar

**5** What, according to Harry Braverman, has happened to work in capitalist societies?
  **a** It has been upskilled
  **b** It has been reskilled
  **c** It has become characterized by multi-tasking
  **d** It has been deskilled

**6** The term Fordism refers to:
  **a** The manufacturing of motor cars
  **b** Manufacturing based on mass production
  **c** A management theory
  **d** The use of highly skilled workers

**7** Which one of the following is not a characteristic of post-Fordism?
  **a** The production of small batches
  **b** A heavy reliance upon full-time, permanent workers
  **c** The use of flexible core workers
  **d** The ability to shift production to new products

**8** Which one of the following beliefs is not associated with a market liberal view?
  **a** Cutting welfare benefits will create more incentive to accept lower-paid jobs and will therefore reduce unemployment
  **b** If unions lose power, wage rates will decrease and employers will be able to take on more workers
  **c** Prospects for employment in the long term will be improved if market forces determine the way the economy develops
  **d** Government support for failing industries will reduce unemployment in the long term

**9** Which of these views is not associated with the work of Naomi Klein?
  **a** Jobs in rich countries are increasingly polarized.
  **b** All workers in rich countries are doing poorly.
  **c** Workers are exploited in free trade zones.
  **d** Companies that make extensive use of branding are subcontracting manufacturing to other companies.

**10** Which of the following groups experiences particularly high levels of unemployment?
  **a** Skilled workers.
  **b** The middle-aged.
  **c** Bangladeshis.
  **d** People in Southwest England.

**11** Parker identified three patterns in the relationship between work and leisure. Which of the following is not one of those patterns?
  **a** The oppositional pattern
  **b** The marginal pattern
  **c** The neutrality pattern
  **d** The extension pattern

**12** Which one of the following statements would be most likely to be supported by Clarke and Critcher?
  **a** Leisure is a tool of the capitalist class
  **b** Leisure is central to creating identities in the postmodern world
  **c** There is considerable freedom of choice in the area of leisure activities
  **d** Leisure is a gendered activity

**13** Which one of the following statements would be most likely to be supported by Green *et al.*?
  **a** Leisure is a tool of the capitalist class
  **b** Leisure is central to creating identities in the postmodern world
  **c** There is considerable freedom of choice in the area of leisure activities
  **d** Leisure is a gendered activity

**14** Which one of the following statements would be most likely to be supported by Rojek?
  **a** Leisure is a tool of the capitalist class
  **b** Leisure is central to creating identities in the postmodern world
  **c** There is little freedom of choice in the area of leisure activities
  **d** Leisure is a gendered activity

**15** Which of the following is not a feature of McJobs?
  **a** They are highly skilled
  **b** They are usually insecure
  **c** They are repetitive
  **d** They are predictable

### *Work is becoming more enjoyable for most workers in capitalist societies.*

***Background:*** The Marxist view developed by Braverman clearly contradicts this because it sees work as getting more alienating, and alienating work is not likely to be enjoyable. The idea of McJobs put forward by Ritzer generally supports this position and Naomi Klein also sees work as deteriorating for most workers in both rich and poor capitalist societies. On the other hand, Blauner was much more optimistic about the future of work, and the theory of post-Fordism sees core workers (though not peripheral ones) as experiencing improvements in work. Remember that each of these positions has been criticised.

| *For* | *Against* |
|---|---|
| ■ Blauner (p. 137) | ■ Marx (pp. 136–7) |
| ■ Post-Fordism (pp. 138–9) | ■ Ritzer (p. 139) |
| | ■ Braverman (p. 138) |
| | ■ Klein (p. 139) |

***Top tip:*** Both the optimistic and the pessimistic views of work tend to be rather one-sided and you could comment that most don't take full account of the varied experiences of work both within and between different occupations.

### *The nature of work is largely shaped by technology.*

***Background:*** Technological determinists believe that the nature of work is actually determined by technology. The above statement is weaker than a position of technological determinism, but would still largely be supported by Blauner, who can be seen as a technological determinist. Zuboff supports the statement, as she believes that technology has a big influence on work. On the other hand, there are many critics of this viewpoint covered in the chapter. Marxists, such as Braverman, see the economic system and the desire to control workers as more important than technology. Kling sees the way technology is consumed as more important than the technology itself, and Grint and Woolgar see the discourse surrounding technology as shaping the way it is used. Post-Fordists see wider economic and organizational factors as more important than technology.

| *For* | *Against* |
|---|---|
| ■ Blauner (p. 137) | ■ Braverman (p. 138) |
| ■ Zuboff (p. 137) | ■ Kling (pp. 137–8) |
| | ■ Grint and Woolgar (p. 138) |
| | ■ Post-Fordism (pp. 138–9) |

***Top tip:*** Many of those listed as against this statement would accept that technology has some influence on work, so it is important that you balance the arguments on either side carefully.

### *Leisure today is a lifestyle choice rather than an expression of social background.*

***Background:*** This view is closely related to the postmodern theories of Rojek, and Scraton and Bramham. However, it can also be partially supported with the older pluralist theory of Ken Roberts. This too emphasizes choice but does see social factors as having some influence on leisure. Parker puts forward the strongest arguments that leisure is shaped by a particular social factor (work). Clarke and Critcher strongly argue against this statement by seeing leisure in terms of class domination, while feminists like Green, Hebron and Woodward see leisure as restricted by patriarchal power.

| *For* | *Against* |
|---|---|
| ■ Rojek (pp. 144–5) | ■ Clarke and Critcher (pp. 143–4) |
| ■ Roberts (partly) (p. 143) | ■ Parker (p. 143) |
| ■ Scraton and Bramham (partly) (p. 145) | ■ Green, Hebron and Woodward (p. 144) |

***Top tip:*** Note that Scraton and Bramham outline the postmodern perspective but are not entirely convinced by it themselves and hence give some criticisms.

## AQA-STYLE WORK AND LEISURE QUESTION

### AS Unit 2

**Answer all parts of this question**

Total: 60 marks, 1 mark = 1.25 minutes

Time allowed: 1 hour 15 minutes

### ITEM A

Technology affects work in a number of ways: the physical exertion required, the level of skill, the possibility of interaction with others. Technological determinism argues that machines and how they are organized lead directly to certain types of structures and specific attitudes held by workers.

### ITEM B

There are two main responses to the question 'Why do people work?' The difference is often based on class, with the working class adopting an instrumental view and the middle class a self-actualizing view.

An instrumental view sees work as a means to an end, and so focuses on the need to earn money to support a particular lifestyle. A self-actualizing view sees work as a means of fulfilling human potential and a source of personal satisfaction.

**Comments on the question**

■ The item will help you to interpret the more general meaning of the word

**[a] Explain the meaning of 'determinism'.**

[Item A, line 4] [2 marks]

**Advice on preparing your answer**

■ Read the section in the introduction on positivism (p. 3) to help you
■ Make a general statement from the example in the item

■ Do exactly this, just list them
■ You will not gain marks by saying 'it is too deterministic', as this is tautological. You have to say what this criticism means

**[b] Identify two criticisms of technological determinism as a theory.**

[Item A, lines 3–4] [4 marks]

■ You can apply the criticisms of Blauner's work (p. 137) to answer this question

■ No more, no less!
■ If you know more about factors that make work alienating, turn them round to answer the question set

**[c] Suggest three characteristics of work in industrial societies that may make it fulfilling.** [6 marks]

■ Marx and Blauner (pp. 136–7) describe alienation, which can be turned round to answer this question

■ You must show both skills for both of the motivations in the item

**[d] Identify and explain how the two motivations to work** [Item B, lines 3–4] **might be linked to patterns of leisure.** [8 marks]

■ An application of Parker's theory (p. 143) will provide an answer to this question

- An analysis of the relationship between two variables can be done in a number of ways:
  1 Cause and effect, or effect to cause
  2 A third variable could be the underlying cause of both
  3 There may be an intervening variable that is more important
  4 The relationship may have no causal association
- You might want to define this term

**[e] Examine the relationship between motivation to work and unemployment.**

[20 marks]

- Unemployment as cause of low motivation – Fagin and Little (p. 142)
- Unemployment as effect – New Right/market liberal theory (p. 141) sought to increase incentives to work by cutting benefits
- Physical and mental health may be an intervening variable (p. 142)
- Marxists would see capitalism as the underlying problem that affects both (pp. 136–7)

- Bring in additional information
- Discuss both sides of the argument
- Refers to computerization, therefore the focus should be on more recent studies
- This is the opposite of de-skilling
- You could distinguish between white-collar and manual workers

**[f] Using material from Item B and elsewhere, assess the claim that new technology has led to an upskilling of the workforce.** [20 marks]

- Zuboff and Clarke *et al.* (p. 137) show that this is not a simple relationship
- Kling argues that it is not the technology but how it is used (p. 137–8)
- Older works, e.g. Braverman and Taylor, could be used selectively and more for the later studies they generated (pp. 138)
- Post-Fordism and flexibility and their critics (p. 138–9) will provide further evidence

## OCR-STYLE WORK, UNEMPLOYMENT AND LEISURE QUESTION

### A2 Synoptic Unit 2539: Social Inequality and Difference

**Answer all parts of this question**

Total: 90 marks
1 mark = 1 minute

Time allowed:
1 hour 30 minutes

### ITEM A

The theory of proletarianization suggests that routine white-collar or clerical workers have become part of the proletariat (working class) and can no longer be considered middle-class. Marxist sociologists such as Braverman see such workers as little different from manual workers because they do not own the means of production nor do they perform important social control functions for capitalists. Braverman notes that clerical workers, like skilled manual workers, have been de-skilled, especially by computerization. Clerical work, like factory work, is highly regulated. Clerical tasks have been broken down into simple routines and the office has become like a production line for mental work.

### ITEM B

**Skill characteristics by class (%)**

|  | Lower non-manual (routine clerical) | Skilled manual |
| --- | --- | --- |
| GCSE only required | 61 | 51 |
| No training necessary | 52 | 43 |
| Learnt to do the job in less than a month | 21 | 17 |
| Responsible for the work of others | 22 | 27 |
| Consider job skilled | 68 | 86 |

**Comments on the question**

**Advice on preparing your answer**

[a] Using only Item A, identify two characteristics that routine non-manual workers have in common with manual workers. [6 marks]

- These characteristics should be extracted from Item A
- There is no need to offer any explanation for these characteristics

- The item contains a possible four characteristics from which you only have to choose two

[b] Using Item B only, identify two differences in the skill characteristics of non-manual and manual workers. [6 marks]

- Do not go beyond the item for your answer
- There is no need to offer any explanation for these differences

- Look carefully at how the data are organized
- If you use the data in your response, double-check that you have interpreted it correctly

[c] Identify and explain two ways in which proletarianization can be measured using a questionnaire. [12 marks]

- Don't just compile a list. You must explain how you have broken down the concept and how the questionnaire you have designed measures it
- No more, no less

- Look at the definition and account of proletarianization on p. 11 for ideas on how you might break the concept down into measurable components
- A synoptic question, which wants you to apply your knowledge of methodology to an inequality and difference problem.

[d] Using your wider sociological knowledge, outline the evidence for the view that manual workers experience a greater range of inequalities compared with other social groups. [22 marks]

- A synoptic instruction. As well as using material from this unit for evidence, you should dip into two or three other topics you have covered
- You only have to describe this evidence. There is no need to explain it

- Focus on statistics, trends and sociological studies
- See pp. 8–9 and 12 for evidence relating to this topic area
- Other information can be found in the following topic areas: social stratification (chapter 1), poverty and social exclusion (chapter 4), health, medicine and the body (chapter 5), and education (chapter 11)

[e] Outline and assess the view that the de-skilling of non-manual work has led to changes in class formation and identity. [44 marks]

- Describe the main features of the argument and its supporting evidence
- Examine specific criticism of this position and describe alternative views
- Make sure you discuss both of these separate issues

- Item A might prove useful for your introduction
- See p. 138 for an account of the view

| Specification | Specification details | Coverage |
|---|---|---|
| **AQA** AS: Education | ■ Different explanations of the role of the education system | All the key perspectives, discussed on pp. 152–4 have a view on the role of the education system. |
| | ■ Different explanations of the different educational achievement of social groups by social class, gender and ethnicity | The range of explanations are covered on pp. 156–60. There are separate sections on gender (pp. 160–2) and ethnicity (pp. 162–5). |
| | ■ Relationships and processes within schools, with particular reference to teacher/pupil relationships, pupil subcultures, the hidden curriculum and the organization of teaching and learning | Subcultures and classroom processes can be found in the section on interactionist approaches (pp. 159–60) with additional material in the gender and ethnicity sections (pp. 160–5). The hidden curriculum mentioned explicitly in the section on Bowles and Gintis (p. 153) but the idea is important through much of the chapter. Debates on the organization of teaching and learning covered in sections on streaming/ labelling, gender and ethnicity (pp. 159–165). |
| | ■ The significance of state policies for an understanding of the role, impact and experience of education | Government policies on education are covered on pp. 154–6. |
| **OCR** A2: Power and Control/ Education | **Education, socialization and identity** ■ Education and socialization; the relationship between primary and secondary socialization, cultural transmission and reproduction; values, skills, knowledge and roles | Covered within the context of a discussion of the key theories of education (pp. 152–4). |
| | ■ Institutional processes; classroom knowledge, the hidden curriculum, streaming and labelling | The hidden curriculum is mentioned explicitly in the section on Bowles and Gintis (p. 153) but is important throughout the chapter. Streaming and labelling are covered in the section on interactionist perspectives (pp. 159–60). The sections on gender and ethnicity (pp. 160–5) also contain important material. |
| | **Patterns and trends in educational achievement** ■ Patterns of inequality of educational achievement according to social class, gender and ethnicity | Patterns of class and achievement are described on p. 156, gender and achievement on p. 160 and ethnicity and achievement on pp. 162–3. |
| | ■ Theories and explanations of differential educational achievement eg macro and micro approaches including materialist, culturalist, structuralist and social action theories | These are covered in the sections on differential educational achievement (pp. 156–60), gender and educational achievement (pp. 160–2), and ethnicity and educational achievement (pp. 162–5). |
| | ■ Trends in achievement and participation and the implications for policy and provision | Trends in participation and achievement are discussed in the context of class (p. 156), gender (p. 160) and ethnicity (pp. 162–3). Government policies on education are covered between pp. 154–6. |
| | **Power, control and the relationship between education and the economy** ■ Education and training; the relationship between the academic and the vocational curriculum, the role of educational professionals and the relationship between schooling, employment and the economy | Functionalist, Marxist, Social Democratic and New Right perspectives are important here (pp. 152–6). Also the discussion of Youth Training Schemes (p. 156) and the section on New Labour and post-Fordist perspectives on education (p. 156). |
| | ■ Theories of the transition from school to work eg functionalist, Marxist, feminist and new right theories | These theories are discussed between pp. 154 and 156. |

*continued*

**Parts of other modules covered**

| Specification | Specification details | | Coverage |
|---|---|---|---|
| **OCR** AS: Culture and Socialization/ Youth and Culture | **Youth and schooling** | ■ Experiences of schooling; class, gender and ethnicity. | ■ For class see Willis on p. 154, and Ball on p. 159. For gender see the section on behaviour in the classroom on p. 160, and Francis on p. 161. For ethnicity see pp. 164–5. |
| | | ■ Pro-school and anti-school cultures. | ■ See the discussion of Willis on p. 154. |
| | | ■ Femininity, masculinity and subject choice. | ■ Gender and subject choice is covered on pp. 161–2. |

For more detailed specification guidance visit **www.haralambosholborn.com**

Essential notes

# THE EXPANSION OF BRITISH EDUCATION

Free state education began in 1870. By 1918 school attendance was compulsory up to the age of 14, rising to 16 in 1972. Since then the government has encouraged more people to stay on in post-compulsory education. By 2001 over half of 16–18 year olds were in full-time education in England and Wales and by 2001–2 more than 11% of government spending was on education.

# EDUCATION – A FUNCTIONALIST PERSPECTIVE

Functionalists ask two key questions about education:

1 What are the **functions** for society as a whole?
2 What are the **functional relationships** between education and other parts of the social system?

Functionalists tend to focus on the positive contribution education makes to society.

## Durkheim – education and solidarity

Writing at the end of the nineteenth century, **Durkheim** saw the major function of education as the transmission of society's norms and values.

A vital task for all societies is the welding of a mass of individuals into a united whole – in other words, the creation of **social solidarity**. Education, and in particular the teaching of history, provides this link between the individual and society.

The school is a society in miniature. In school the child learns to interact with other members of the school community and to follow a fixed set of rules. This experience prepares the child for interacting with members of society as an adult and accepting social rules.

Education teaches individuals specific skills which are necessary for their future occupations.

## Criticisms of Durkheim

1 Durkheim assumes that the norms and values promoted in schools are those of society as a whole rather than those of powerful groups.
2 Most contemporary changes in education appear to be aimed at encouraging individual competition and training pupils for particular vocations. It could be argued that the sort of education favoured by Durkheim is not the best preparation for future working life.
3 Hargreaves (1982) believes that most British schools fail to transmit shared values.
4 Unlike Durkheim, other functionalists see competition as a vital aspect of modern societies.

## Parsons – education and universalistic values

**Parsons** argues that school performs three major functions for society:

1 Education acts as a bridge between the family and wider society.

In the family **particularistic** standards apply: children are treated as individuals. In society, however, **universalistic** standards predominate. The individual is judged against standards which apply equally to all members of society.

In the family, status is fixed by birth – it is **ascribed**. However, in society, status is **achieved** (according to occupation, for example) – that is, it is based on **meritocratic** principles.

2 Education helps to ease these transitions. The exam system judges all pupils on merit, and school rules such as wearing uniform are applied to all pupils equally.

| Family | Society |
|---|---|
| Particularistic standards | Universalistic standards |
| Ascribed status | Achieved status |

Education helps to **socialize** young people into the basic values of society.

Schools instil two major **values**:
- The value of achievement
- The value of equality of opportunity

3 Education selects people for their future role in society.

The education system assesses students' abilities so that their talents can be matched to the job for which they are best suited.

## Criticisms of Parsons

1 Parsons fails to consider the diversity of values in modern societies.
2 His view that education works on meritocratic principles is open to question.

### Davis and Moore – education and role allocation

Like Parsons, **Davis and Moore** see education as a means of role allocation. The education system sifts people according to their abilities. The most talented gain high qualifications which lead to functionally important jobs with high rewards.

## Criticisms of Davis and Moore

1 There is only a weak link between educational qualifications and income.
2 Intelligence and ability have only a limited influence on educational achievement.
3 The system of social stratification prevents the education system from grading individuals according to their ability.

## EDUCATION – A CONFLICT PERSPECTIVE

### Bowles and Gintis – schooling in capitalist America

**Bowles and Gintis** (1976) argue that there is a close relationship between social relationships in the workplace and in education. This **correspondence principle** is the key to understanding the working of the education system. Work casts a 'long shadow' over the education system: education operates in the interests of those who control the workforce – the capitalist class.

## The hidden curriculum

Capitalism requires a hard-working, obedient workforce which is too divided to challenge the authority of management. The education system helps to produce a workforce with these qualities through the **hidden curriculum**. The hidden curriculum consists of those things that pupils learn through the experience of attending school rather than through the stated aims of the school. It shapes the workforce in the following ways:

1 It helps to produce a **subservient workforce**. Bowles and Gintis found that students who were more conformist received higher grades than those who were creative and independent.
2 The hidden curriculum encourages an **acceptance of hierarchy**. Teachers give orders, pupils obey. Students have virtually no control over what and how they study. This prepares them for relationships at work where they will also need to defer to authority.
3 Pupils learn to be motivated by **external rewards**. Pupils work only for the qualifications they eventually hope to achieve. There is little satisfaction from school work, as learning is based mostly on the '**jug and mug**' **principle**, where teachers 'pour' their knowledge into students' empty 'mugs'. Work, too, is unsatisfying because it is organized to generate maximum profit rather than with the needs of the worker in mind. Workers, like pupils, are motivated only by external rewards: in their case, pay.
4 School subjects are **fragmented**. Knowledge in schools is packaged into separate subjects with little connection between them. In a similar way, most jobs are broken down into specific tasks carried out by separate individuals. Workers are kept unaware of all parts of the production process, so they remain divided.

## The illusion of equality of opportunity

Bowles and Gintis reject the functionalist view that capitalist societies are **meritocratic**, providing genuine **equality of opportunity**. The children of the wealthy and powerful obtain high qualifications and well-rewarded jobs irrespective of their abilities. The education system disguises this with its myth of meritocracy. Those denied success blame themselves rather than the system. Inequality in society is thus legitimated: it is made to appear fair.

## Evaluation of Bowles and Gintis

1 Bowles and Gintis have been accused of exaggerating the correspondence between work and education. **Brown** et al. (1997), for example, argue that much modern work requires teamwork, while the exam system still stresses individual competition. **Reynolds** (1984) claims that much of the curriculum in British schools is not designed to teach either the skills needed by employers or uncritical passive behaviour.
2 Numerous studies, such as that of **Willis** (1977) (see below), show that many pupils do not accept the hidden curriculum in schools. They have little respect for teachers or school rules.

Bowles and Gintis developed their theory in the 1970s and much has changed since then. However, some developments appear to support their theory:

- The freedom of teachers has been curtailed by the **National Curriculum**.
- Education has become more explicitly designed to meet the **needs of employers** (see pp. 154–6).

## Willis – Learning to Labour

Willis (1977) accepts the Marxist view that education is closely linked to the needs of capitalism, but he does not believe that there is a simple and direct relationship between education and the economy. Willis used a range of **qualitative research** methods, including observation, to study a group of 12 working-class boys during their last year at school and first months at work.

The 12 pupils – the '**lads**' – formed a friendship group with a particular attitude to school. Willis refers to this as a **counter-school culture**. It had the following features:

- The lads felt superior to teachers and conformist pupils who they called 'ear'oles'.
- They saw no value in gaining qualifications.
- Their main objectives were to avoid going to lessons and to do as little work as possible. They entertained themselves by '**having a laff**'. This usually involved misbehaviour.
- The 'lads' found school boring and tried to identify with the adult world by smoking, drinking alcohol and not wearing school uniform.
- The counter-culture was strongly sexist and racist. **Traditional masculinity** was valued and members of ethnic minorities were regarded as inferior.
- Manual labour was seen as more worthy than 'pen-pushing'.

These pupils did not defer to authority, nor were they obedient or docile. They rejected the belief that hard work would lead to success. The 'lads' have very little in common with the sort of conformist pupils described by Bowles and Gintis.

### Shop-floor culture and counter-school culture

When Willis followed the 'lads' into their first jobs he found important similarities between the school counter-culture and the factory **shop-floor culture**:

- Both were racist and sexist.
- Both had no respect for authority.
- Both tried to minimize work and maximize 'having a laff'.
- Both cultures were ways of coping with tedium and oppression.

In their rejection of school the 'lads' partly see through the capitalist system. However, in the end rejecting school merely leads them into some of the most exploitative jobs capitalism has to offer.

### Evaluation of Willis

1 **Gordon** (1984) believes that Willis's study has helped Marxists overcome a tendency to over-simplify the role of education in society.
2 **Blackledge and Hunt** (1985) put forward three criticisms of Willis:
  - His sample is inadequate for generalizing about the role of education in society.

- Willis largely ignores the full range of subcultures within schools. Many pupils fall somewhere in between total conformity and total rejection.
- Willis may have misinterpreted some evidence to fit in with his own views.
3 With the decline in manual work since the period of Willis's research, male working-class attitudes to education may well have become more positive.

## THE NEW RIGHT AND EDUCATIONAL POLICIES IN BRITAIN

**New Right** perspectives influenced the policies introduced by governments throughout the 1980s and 1990s. The key themes of New Right policies were as follows.

1 **Education and economic growth** – Education should largely be concerned with promoting economic growth. Many school-leavers were unemployable because of their lack of skills. A whole range of changes were introduced, such as *YTS* (Youth Training Scheme), a two-year course aimed at combining work experience with education. Training credits, first piloted in 1991, entitled school-leavers to spend a specified sum of money on training.

2 **Competition, choice and standards** – The best method of **raising standards** in education was to introduce market forces and encourage **competition** between educational institutions. Schools that failed to attract students would lose funding and be forced to improve or close.
  - The government laid down a *National Curriculum* which all state school pupils had to follow. Its aim was to ensure that pupils concentrated on what the government saw as key subjects.
  - **Parents** were given the right to send their children to the school of their choice. A policy of open enrolment compelled every school to recruit the maximum number of pupils.
  - Existing schools were allowed to **opt out** of local authority control and instead be funded directly from central government. Opting out created a new category of grant maintained schools. By 1996 these schools were educating about 20% of school pupils.
  - Under the system of **formula funding**, the financing of schools was based on the number of enrolments. This was intended to reward the most successful schools.

3 **Testing and examining** – Parents needed information in order to be able to make informed choices about schools. Increased testing and the publication of results were therefore necessary.
  - **League tables** were introduced to enable easy comparisons between schools to be made.
  - Testing and **attainment targets** were introduced for children of 7, 11, 14 and 16, in the hope that standards would rise as schools competed with each other to reach targets.

4 **Curriculum content** – the New Right and traditionalism. A more business-oriented curriculum was

favoured by the New Right, but at the same time, according to **Ball** (1990), there was an emphasis on retaining **traditional values** and traditional subjects such as Latin and Greek. Social education and multicultural approaches were frowned upon. Initiatives such as **TVEI** (Technical and Vocational Education Initiative) and courses such as **GNVQ** (General National Vocational Qualifications) were introduced to produce young people who had more understanding of work and the economy.

## Critical evaluations of the educational reforms

### Ball, Bowe and Gewirtz – competitive advantage and parental choice

Ball *et al.*'s study attempted to discover the effects that parental choice and the encouragement of competition between schools were having on the education system and particularly on opportunities for different social groups.

### The effects on schools

The study found that the changes were having significant effects on secondary schools.
■ The publication of school league tables meant that schools were keen to attract academically able pupils who would boost their results.
■ Some schools had reintroduced streaming and setting and were directing more resources at pupils who were likely to be successful in tests.
■ As schools have concentrated on the more able pupils, they have paid less attention to those with **special needs**.
■ In an effort to attract more pupils, some schools have taken to publishing glossy brochures, and some have brought in public relations firms. Staff are expected to devote more time and energy to marketing activities such as open evenings. More attention is devoted to the **image of the school**, particularly to making it seem to have a traditional academic focus – for example, by strictly enforcing rules about school uniform.
■ Neighbouring schools have ceased to cooperate with each other, and instead there is 'suspicion and hostility'.

These changes have led to a shift from comprehensive to **market values** in education.

### The education market and degrees of choice

The study argues that three broad groups of parents can be distinguished in terms of their ability to choose between schools.
■ **Privileged/skilled choosers** – These parents spend a lot of time finding out about different schools and evaluating the claims made in their publicity. They often have the money to make choices that will assist their children's education, such as moving house or paying for private education. This group is usually middle-class and some members – such as teachers – benefit from insider knowledge of the education system.

■ **Semi-skilled choosers** – Semi-skilled choosers are just as concerned to get the best possible education for their children but do not have the experience or skill of the privileged choosers. For example, they are more likely to accept rumours and local reputations at face value.
■ **Disconnected choosers** – These parents are not inclined to get involved in the education market. They tend to consider only the two schools closest to their home, often because they do not own a car or have easy access to public transport. They put more emphasis on the happiness of their child than on the academic reputation of the school. Disconnected choosers are likely to be working-class and are more likely to send their children to an under-subscribed school.

Generally, the higher a person's **social class**, the more likely they are to benefit from the best schooling. According to Ball *et al.*'s study, the impression of choice is an illusion. In practice, people's choice is restricted by the limited number of schools available in any area and the class-based nature of the system of choosing.

## The National Curriculum

**Lawton** (1989) identified a number of criticisms of the **National Curriculum**:

1 It was too **bureaucratic**. Many National Curriculum documents were more concerned with controlling teachers than improving standards.
2 It **centralized power** and undermined local democratic control of education.
3 **Private schools** were not subject to the National Curriculum. This meant that only the rich were provided with choice.
4 The content of the National Curriculum was accused of being **traditional and unimaginative** – for example, it was criticized for ignoring political and moral development.
5 Many objected to the publication of test results. Schools that did badly risked losing pupils and going into decline.
6 Some critics worried that all the testing would lead to the **labelling** of some children as failures.

## The National Curriculum and ethnicity

**MacNeil** (1988) argued that the National Curriculum was based on white culture and that it excluded cultural input from ethnic minorities.

■ In **history** the emphasis was on British history and the idea that British colonialism benefited those countries that were colonized.
■ The **language** component of the National Curriculum placed the emphasis on European languages.
■ In **literature** the works of distinguished black writers were ignored in favour of traditional English writers such as Shakespeare.

**Troyna and Carrington** (1990) also point out that religious education had to reflect the dominance of the Christian religion.

## *Youth training schemes*

### Finn – the hidden agenda of YTS

**Finn** (1987) has strongly attacked the new vocationalism involved in the various youth training schemes. He believes that its real objectives were different from those stated:

- The trainees could be used as a source of **cheap labour**.
- The small allowances paid to trainees would depress general **wage levels**.
- The scheme would reduce embarrassing **unemployment statistics**.
- The government hoped that the scheme would **reduce crime** by taking up the free time of young people.

Finn believed that there was no truth in the claim that school-leavers were unemployable. Many school pupils had experience of work through part-time jobs. The real problem was simply lack of jobs.

## 'NEW LABOUR' AND EDUCATIONAL POLICIES IN BRITAIN

The election of '**New Labour**' in 1997 led to some changes in the direction of educational policy.

Some of the new policies were designed to improve standards. For example:

- The government promised to reduce primary school **class sizes** to 30.
- A **literacy hour and a numeracy hour** were introduced in primary schools to ensure that all pupils got a firm grounding in basic skills.
- Ambitious **targets** were set for pupil achievement.
- More emphasis was put on **inspection**.
- In 2000 **Learning and Skills Councils** were set up to oversee and try to raise standards in post-16 education and training.

A number of other policies were designed to reduce inequality of opportunity:

- Extra resources went into **Education Action Zones**. These were established in areas of high deprivation in an attempt to boost educational achievement.
- **Social exclusion units** were introduced to tackle the causes of social exclusion, such as truancy. (See p. 158 on compensatory education.)
- **Grant maintained schools** were abolished. They could no longer act as elite institutions, creaming off the brightest students.
- **The Skills for Life Strategy** was introduced to help adults with literacy and numeracy problems.
- **Higher Education** was expanded to provide opportunities for a higher proportion of the population.

## *Evaluation of New Labour policies*

1 The 1997–2001 Labour government retained some New Right policies such as the importance of consumer choice and competition in raising standards. However, it also attempted to reduce inequalities of opportunity through initiatives such as Education Action Zones.

2 The introduction of **tuition fees** for higher education and the replacement of student grants with loans have been criticized for discouraging those from working-class backgrounds from staying on in education.

3 The New Right has attacked Labour policies by arguing that they have reduced diversity in schooling and are threatening academic excellence by trying to phase out selection. The 2001 Labour government has promised to increase diversity within the comprehensive system.

4 Geoff **Whitty** (2002) argues that New Labour placed too much emphasis on markets in education, and middle class parents were better placed to take advantage of these markets than working class parents.

5 Rob **Strathdee** (2003) believes some progress has been made in developing Vocational Education and Training (VET) but it still largely remains a route into lower paid jobs.

6 Paul **Trowler** (2003) believes that New Labour has exaggerated the power of education to change society, and underestimated the extent to which inequality in society continues to hold back the disadvantaged.

## DIFFERENTIAL EDUCATIONAL ACHIEVEMENT

### *Class and achievement*

The children of parents in higher social classes are more likely to stay on in post-compulsory education, more likely to achieve examination passes when at school and more likely to gain university entrance. These differences were a feature of British education throughout the twentieth century and remain significant today.

- The **Youth Cohort Study** (2002) found that 22% of the children of routine workers, 27% of the children of lower-supervisory workers but 65% of children from higher-professional backgrounds had level 3 (A-level equivalent) qualifications.
- Participation in higher education has been increasing for all social classes. The proportion of those from lower classes participating has risen faster than the proportion of those from higher classes. However, **Gilchrist *et al.*** (2003) found that 63.7% of people aged 21-30 from professional and intermediate backgrounds had achieved HE qualifications compared to just 6.1% of those from unskilled backgrounds.

## INTELLIGENCE, CLASS AND EDUCATIONAL ACHIEVEMENT

The most obvious explanation for differences in educational achievement is the **intelligence** of the individual.

In Britain, the **tripartite system** allocated an individual to one of three types of school largely on the basis of their performance in the eleven-plus intelligence test. There was a strong correlation between results and social class, with middle-class children gaining more places at grammar schools.

## Culture and intelligence

- Many researchers argue that intelligence tests – IQ tests – are biased in favour of the white middle class, since they are largely constructed by members of this group.
- Different social groups have different subcultures and this affects their performance in IQ tests. This means that comparisons between such groups in terms of measured intelligence are invalid.

## Genes and intelligence

There is general agreement that intelligence is due to:

1 The **genes** individuals inherit from their parents
2 The environment in which they grow up and live

Despite objections to their views, some social scientists still argue that genetically-based intelligence accounts for a large part of the difference in educational attainment between social groups.

According to **Hernstein and Murray** (1994), American society is increasingly meritocratic. People's class position is increasingly determined by their intelligence.

## Environment and intelligence

- Research has indicated that a wide range of **environmental factors** – such as motivation, previous experience and education – can affect performance in IQ tests.
- Many researchers now conclude that it is impossible to estimate the proportions of intelligence due to heredity and environment.
- The debate about intelligence is only important if IQ affects educational attainment and level of income. **Bowles and Gintis** (1976) found that IQ was almost irrelevant to educational and economic success. Thus differences in IQ between different social groups may well have little significance.

## David Gillborn and Deborah Youdell – the new IQism

**Gillborn and Youdell** (2001) argue that the idea of 'ability' has now replaced that of intelligence but is used in the same way. Research in two London schools suggested that teachers thought children had largely fixed abilities. They concentrated on children who were borderline for achieving 5 grade Cs in GCSEs because it affected the school's league table results (the **A-C economy**). Black and working class children tended to be perceived as low ability and few were thought to have the potential for 5 GCSEs, so they were held back in the education system.

## CLASS SUBCULTURES AND EDUCATIONAL ACHIEVEMENT

It has been argued that the distinctive norms and values of different social classes affect their educational performance.

## Douglas – The Home and the School

**Douglas's longitudinal study** (1964) related educational attainment to a variety of factors, but the single most important factor was parental interest.

In general, middle-class parents:

- Visited the school more frequently to discuss their children's progress.
- Wanted their children to stay at school beyond the minimum leaving age.
- Gave their children greater attention and stimulus during their early years.

Douglas argued that many differences in educational performance could be traced back to **primary socialization** during the pre-school years.

## Leon Feinstein – parental support and education

**Feinstein** (2003), who has used data from the *National Child Development Study* found that:

- Nursery schooling improved educational achievement if it was a good quality nursery school.
- In most ways the school attended made little difference, but children with average or below average ability did poorly in schools with few children from professional backgrounds.
- Financial deprivation had some effect but this seemed to be largely related to parental interest.
- The most important factor affecting achievement was the extent to which parents encouraged and supported their children.

## Evaluation

The above views which support cultural deprivation theories have been strongly criticized.

**Blackstone and Mortimore** (1994) make the following points:

- The studies are based on teachers' assessments of parental interest. Working-class parents may have less time to visit the school because of the demands of their jobs.
- Working-class parents may be put off visiting the school by the way teachers interact with them.
- More middle-class than working-class children attended a school where there was an established system of parent–school contacts.

## Bernstein – speech patterns

Since speech is an important medium of communication and learning, attainment levels in schools may be related to differences in **speech patterns**. Bernstein (1961, 1970, 1972) distinguished two patterns of speech:

1 **Restricted code** – This is a kind of shorthand speech, which uses short, simple and often unfinished sentences. Users of the code have so much in common that there is no need to make meanings explicit in speech. Meanings are more likely to be conveyed by gesture and tone of voice. Members of the working class are usually limited to the use of the restricted code. *Example: 'She saw it'*
2 **Elaborated code** – This code is characteristic of the middle classes. It fills in the detail and provides the explanations omitted by restricted codes. Anyone can understand elaborated code users in any situation. *Example: 'The young girl saw the ball'*

Bernstein explained the origins of these speech codes in terms of class differences in the family and work situations of the working and middle classes:

■ In middle-class families and in non-manual work, relationships tend to be less rigid, people are treated as individuals and decisions are reached by negotiation.
■ In working-class families and in manual work, relationships are based on a clear hierarchy and little discussion is needed.

Bernstein believed that the middle classes could switch from one code to the other but that the working classes were only able to use the restricted code. As formal education is conducted in terms of an elaborated code, working-class children are placed at a disadvantage.

### Criticisms

**Gaine and George** (1999) attack Bernstein's arguments:

1 Bernstein's distinction between the classes is **over-simplified**. Even if there was a clear working class in the 1960s when Bernstein was writing, this is not the case today.
2 Bernstein produces **little evidence** for his assertions about working- and middle-class family life.

## Cultural deprivation and compensatory education

From the kind of portrayal of working-class life described above, the theory of **cultural deprivation** was developed. This placed the blame for working-class educational failure on the culture of low-income groups.

This led to the idea of **positive discrimination** in favour of culturally deprived children: they must be given extra resources to help them compete on equal terms with other children. This policy is known as compensatory education.

Various schemes of compensatory education have been introduced. The most recent is the introduction of **Education Action Zones** by the Labour government in 1998. These provide extra educational resources in inner-city areas.

### Criticisms of compensatory education

1 The theory of cultural deprivation has been attacked. By placing the blame for failure on the child and his or her background, attention is diverted from the deficiencies of the education system.
2 **Morton and Watson** (1973) argue that compensatory education cannot remove inequality of educational opportunity which is rooted in social inequality in society as a whole.
3 **Whitty** (2002) believes that Education Action Zones do not redistribute sufficient resources to poor areas to make them effective and they neglect poor areas which are not designated zones.

## Bourdieu – cultural capital and differential achievement

The French sociologist **Bourdieu** is strongly influenced by Marxism. He argues that the education system is biased towards the culture of dominant social classes; it devalues the knowledge and skills of the working class.

Bourdieu refers to the dominant culture as **cultural capital** because it can be translated into wealth and power via the education system. Students with upper-class backgrounds have a built-in advantage because they have been socialized into the dominant culture.

The educational attainment of social groups is directly related to the amount of cultural capital they possess. Thus middle-class students have higher success rates than working-class students because middle-class culture is closer to the dominant culture (see pp. 14–15 for further details on Bourdieu).

## Ball, Bowe and Gewirtz – cultural capital and educational choice

The study by **Ball et al.** (see p. 155) was influenced by Bourdieu. It discusses whether the increased emphasis on parental choice and market forces has led to greater equality of opportunity.

## The educational market and middle-class parents

Ball argues that middle-class parents are in a better position than working-class parents to ensure that their children get to the school of their choice. There are a number of reasons for this:

1 Middle-class parents possess cultural capital, which means they have contacts and can 'play the system' to their advantage – for example, by making multiple applications.
2 Middle-class parents have the **'stamina'** to research, visit schools, make appeals and so on.
3 Middle-class parents also possess **material advantages**. They can afford to pay for the transport necessary to send their children to more distant schools; they can move house if necessary to enter the **catchment area** of a desirable school; and they can afford extra tuition and childcare if necessary.

### Working-class and ethnic minority parents

Ball *et al.* did not find that working-class parents were any less interested in their children's education than their middle-class counterparts. However, they did lack the cultural capital and material resources needed to use the system to their advantage.

- Many working-class parents preferred to send their children to the nearest school because of **neighbourhood links**, safety concerns and transport costs.
- Some ethnic minority parents have limited experience of the British educational system and do not feel confident enough about their English language skills to manipulate it.

### Smith and Noble – material factors and British education

Smith and Noble (1995) reassert the importance of **material factors** in influencing class differences in educational achievement:

- **Marketization** is likely to lead to large differences between successful, well-resourced schools in affluent areas and under-subscribed poorly-resourced schools in poor areas.
- Having money allows parents to provide educational toys, books, a healthy diet, more space in the home to do homework, greater opportunities for travel and private tuition.
- To make ends meet, schools are increasingly charging for trips, material and equipment (technically parents are asked for 'voluntary contributions'). Local education authorities are cutting back on free school meal provision and transport costs.

### Cultural or material factors?

Halsey, Heath and Ridge (1980) attempted to measure the importance of cultural and material factors. They distinguished between:

- Family climate – measured in terms of levels of parental education and attitudes to **education.**
- Material circumstances – measured by family income.

The authors found both to be important. Family climate influenced the type of school attended but had little effect on later progress. Material circumstances determined how long children stayed at school.

## EDUCATION – AN INTERACTIONIST PERSPECTIVE

**Interactionists** focus on processes within the education system which result in different levels of achievement. They have researched the details of day-to-day life in schools.

### Labelling and the self-fulfilling prophecy

The **self-fulfilling prophecy** theory argues that predictions made by teachers will tend to make themselves become true. The teacher defines or **labels** the pupil in a particular way, such as 'bright' or 'dull'. The teacher's interaction with pupils will be informed by their labelling of the pupils, and the pupils may respond accordingly, making the label become true: the prophecy is fulfilled.

**Rosenthal and Jacobson** (1968) selected a random sample of pupils in an elementary school in the USA and informed their teachers that these pupils could be expected to show rapid intellectual growth. They tested the IQ of all pupils and re-tested one year later. The sample population showed greater gains in IQ.

Rosenthal and Jacobson claim that the **teachers' expectations** significantly affected their pupils' performance. They speculate that the teachers' encouragement and positive feedback produced a self-fulfilling prophecy.

### Criticisms

1 It has been suggested that the IQ tests used by Rosenthal and Jacobson were of dubious quality and were improperly administered.
2 Some interactionists have recognized that not all pupils will live up to their labels. **Fuller** (1984) found that black girls in a comprehensive school resented the negative stereotypes associated with being both black and female. They felt that people expected them to fail, but they tried to prove them wrong by devoting themselves to their work in order to achieve success. Fuller's work avoids some of the pitfalls of the **deterministic** versions of labelling theory which suggest that failure is inevitable for those with negative labels attached to them.

### Ball – banding at Beachside Comprehensive

**Ball**'s study (1981) examines the organization of a comprehensive school. Pupils were put into one of **three** bands according to information supplied from their primary schools. However, Ball found that, for pupils of similar measured ability, those whose fathers were non-manual workers had the greatest chance of being placed in the top band.

Ball identified the following effects of this banding:

- The behaviour of band two pupils deteriorated.
- Teachers had lower **expectations** of band two pupils. They were directed towards practical subjects and lower-level exams.

### The interactionist approach – an evaluation

#### Advantages

1 It is based on far more detailed empirical evidence than functionalist or Marxist approaches.
2 It shows that educational experiences are not just determined by home background and IQ.
3 **Woods** (1983) claims that the interactionist approach has practical applications. Its insights could help schools to improve teaching and reduce deviance in schools.

## Limitations

1 Many interactionists refer to class differences in education but fail to explain the origins of these differences.
2 Interactionists have been accused of failing to take account of factors outside the school which might influence what happens within education.

## GENDER AND EDUCATIONAL ATTAINMENT

■ By the late 1980s under-achievement by females was attracting more concern than working-class **under-achievement**.
■ At that time females were less likely than males to obtain one or more A-levels and were less likely to go on to higher education.
■ In the mid-1990s there was a sudden reversal. Changes in achievement statistics meant that attention switched to **male under-achievement**.
■ By 2001 47% of females but 37% of males obtained one or more A-levels.
■ In 2001–2 there were 235,000 more females than males in higher education.
■ There is disagreement over whether this change in emphasis due to the under-achievement of males is really justified.

### *Explanations for under-achievement by females*

Most of these explanations are based on the assumption that girls are less successful, and so are more relevant to explaining under-achievement in earlier decades. However, some of the processes described may still be preventing female pupils from achieving their full potential.

### Innate ability

One possible explanation for female under-achievement is that there are differences in **innate ability** between girls and boys.

However, girls actually out-perform boys in IQ tests at young ages. Some researchers have argued that this is because they mature earlier.

In a review of the available evidence, **Trowler** (1995) raises strong doubts about the usefulness of biological explanations of female under-achievement. He points out that:

■ There is very little difference between the IQ scores of boys and girls.
■ Differences in specific abilities might well be a product of social rather than biological differences.

### Early socialization

**Norman** *et al.* (1988) point out that, before children start school, sex **stereotyping** has already begun.

■ Playing with dolls and other types of **toys** that reinforce the stereotype of women as carers may affect girls' educational aspirations.

■ Boys are more likely to be given constructional toys which help develop scientific and mathematical concepts.
■ Gender stereotypes are further reinforced through the **media**.

Girls may come to value education less than boys, as a consequence of early socialization. **Sharpe** (1976) found that the concerns of her sample of working-class girls were 'love, marriage, husbands, children, jobs, and careers, more or less in that order'.

In the 1990s Sharpe (1994) repeated her research and found that girls' priorities had changed, and these changes may well help to explain why girls' educational attainment has improved.

### Socialization in school

**Abraham** (1986) analysed textbooks used in a comprehensive school. He found maths textbooks to be especially male-dominated. Women tended to be shown in **stereotypical roles** such as shopping, while men were typically running businesses.

### Behaviour in the classroom – *self-confidence and criticism*

**Stanworth** (1983) did a study of A-level classes in a further education college. She found that **classroom interaction** disadvantaged girls in the following ways:

■ Teachers found it difficult to remember the girls in their classes.
■ Teachers held stereotypical views of what their female pupils would be doing in the future.
■ Pupils felt that boys received more attention than girls. They were more likely to join in classroom discussion, seek help from the teacher and be asked questions.
■ Girls underestimated their ability and placed themselves below their teacher's ranking.

### *Spender* – Invisible Women

**Spender** (1983) claims that education is largely controlled by men, who use their power to further their own interests.

■ The curriculum favours a male perspective. Women's contributions to human progress are often ignored.
■ Girls receive less attention than boys in the classroom.
■ Boys are often abusive to girls but are not told off.
■ Male dominance in society is the cause of girls' difficulties in education but schools help to reinforce that dominance.

### Criticisms of Stanworth and Spender

**Randall** (1987) criticizes the methods used by Stanworth and Spender. Stanworth's work, for example, was based on interviews rather than direct observation. Therefore it cannot actually establish that teachers are giving less attention to girls. Randall's own research failed to find such a clear-cut bias.

## Becky Francis – girls and achievement

Based both on a review of other research and on her own research **Becky Francis** (2000) makes a number of points about girls and achievement.

- Gender divisions in terms of subject choice are actually getting stronger with fewer women going on to IT and pure science degrees than ten years earlier.
- Although female achievement might have overtaken male achievement, her own research in London found that males still dominate classrooms and get more teacher attention than boys.
- She found boys tended to be disciplined more harshly or frequently than girls, but in the process girls were getting little attention.
- Things had improved since the studies of **Spender and Stanworth** but significant problems remained for females in education.
- Boys also faced problems in the education system.

## GENDER AND SUBJECT CHOICE

Although inequalities of educational achievement between males and females have declined, differences in the subjects studied remain considerable.

The **National Curriculum** limits these differences as school pupils have few options. When choices are available, however, distinct patterns arise.

## Statistics on subject choice

### A level
- Males outnumbered females in business studies, economics, political science, sports and all science and technical subjects apart from biology.
- Females outnumbered males in all other subjects. English, modern languages, psychology and sociology had a particularly high proportion of female entries.

### Degrees
- Males were more likely to gain degrees in physical and mathematical sciences, engineering and technology, and architecture, building and planning.
- In all other areas women predominated and females have overtaken males in obtaining degrees in medicine and dentistry, business and financial studies.
- Men remain dominant in scientific and technical subjects and are more likely than females to obtain PhDs.

## Socialization and subject choice

When choosing which subjects to study, females and males may well be influenced by what they have learned about femininity and masculinity. In her 1970s study **Sharpe** (1976) found that the girls she interviewed rejected jobs such as electricians and driving instructors because they felt that employers and society defined them as 'men's' work. It was therefore no surprise that girls saw little point in opting for typically 'male' subjects.

## Schools and subject choice

**Grafton** (1987) studied a comprehensive school to examine the role of the education system itself in influencing subject choice.

- In the first year the school made it clear that there were only limited places available for members of either sex who wanted to study non-traditional craft subjects. The school made it clear what a 'normal' choice was.
- In the fourth year the timetable was organized in such a way as to limit pupils' choice of non-traditional subjects.
- Tutors were issued with guidelines which required them to discuss non-traditional choices with pupils before allowing them.

Grafton did, however, recognize that factors outside the school were also an important influence.

## Science and gender

**Kelly** (1987) identifies two main reasons why science tends to be seen as masculine:

1 The way science subjects are packaged makes them appear to be boys' subjects. The examples used in textbooks and by teachers tend to be linked to boys' experiences, such as football and cars.
2 Pupils themselves make the greatest contribution to turning science into a boys' subject. Boys dominate classrooms, shouting out answers and grabbing apparatus first.

## Colley – the persistence of gender inequalities in subject choice

**Colley** (1998) reviewed the reasons why gender differences in subject choice persisted in the late 1990s:

1 **Perceptions** of gender roles – despite all the social changes in recent decades, traditional definitions of masculinity and femininity are still widespread.
2 **Subject preferences** and choice – different subjects have different images. Computer studies involves working with machines rather than people, and this gives it a masculine image. The lack of opportunity for group activities and the rather formal way of teaching add to this.
3 **The learning environment** – there is some evidence that girls are more comfortable with scientific and technical subjects when taught in single-sex schools or single-sex classes.

## Reasons for the under-achievement of males

The educational achievement of both males and females has been increasing over recent decades. However, the performance of females has improved faster than that of males. These changes have been interpreted in a number of ways.

### The improved achievement of women

**Mitsos and Browne** (1998) identify five main reasons for the improvement in girls' achievement:

1 The women's movement and **feminism** have raised the expectations and self-esteem of women.
2 Sociologists have drawn attention to some of the disadvantages faced by girls. As a result **equal opportunities** programmes have been developed.
3 The increase in **service sector** and part-time work has opened up employment opportunities for women. There is now more incentive for women to gain educational qualifications.
4 Evidence suggests that girls are more hard-working and motivated than boys. Girls' greater **motivation** and organizational skills may give them a particular advantage in coursework.
5 Girls are estimated to be more **mature** than boys at the age of 16, and consequently take exams more seriously than boys.

## The moral panic about men

**Weiner, Arnot and David** (1997) are sceptical about the sudden discovery of male under-achievement. They make a number of important points:

1 The media see the under-achievement of black and working-class boys as a particular problem because it may lead to the creation of a potentially dangerous '**underclass**'.
2 The differences in subject choice mean that female under-achievement is still characteristic of the higher levels of the education system.
3 The failure to celebrate girls' achievement is part of a '**backlash**' against female success as men feel threatened by the possibility of women becoming equal.

## Reasons for boys' under-achievement

**Mitsos and Browne** accept that boys are under-achieving and suggest the following reasons:

■ Teachers may be less strict with boys, tolerating a lower standard of work and the missing of deadlines.
■ Boys are more likely to disrupt classes. They are more likely to be sent out of the classroom and expelled from school.
■ The culture of masculinity encourages boys to want to appear macho and tough. They are more likely to develop an **anti-school subculture** (see p. 154).
■ The **decline in manual work** may result in working-class boys losing motivation. They see little point in working hard as it will not result in the sort of job they are seeking.
■ Research suggests that boys tend to overestimate their ability. They may become **over-confident** and not work hard enough.
■ Girls may spend their leisure time in ways that complement their education, such as reading and talking.

The ideas of Mitsos and Browne provide some initial suggestions to explain male under-achievement but, as they point out, more research needs to be done in this area.

## Becky Francis – boys and under-achievement

Becky Francis (2000) argues that both boys and girls have problems in the education system. Her research suggests the following reasons for male under-achievement.

■ Boys get more classroom attention but are criticized more by teachers for their behaviour.
■ Unlike the 1970s, boys no longer believe they are more able than girls.
■ Girls are more likely than boys to fit teacher's stereotype of the ideal pupil.
■ Boys are particularly keen not to be regarded as 'swots' or 'nerds' by being seen to be working too hard at school.
■ Most girls in her research have **career aspirations** which require academic success (e.g. ambitions to be a doctor), but professional footballer was the most common career ambition for boys. .
■ Francis concludes that a combination of the career ambitions of girls and the 'culture of laddish masculinity' are the main reasons for females overtaking males in schooling.

# ETHNICITY AND EDUCATIONAL ACHIEVEMENT

## Ethnicity and levels of attainment

Most studies indicate that ethnic minorities tend to do less well than other members of the population. However, this hides important **variations** between and within ethnic groups, with some ethnic minorities being particularly successful.

## The Policy Studies Institute (PSI) survey

The **PSI** *Fourth National Survey of Ethnic Minorities* (Modood *et al.*, 1997) found that the educational qualifications of ethnic minorities had improved considerably since the 1980s.

### Men

■ Chinese, African Asians and Indians were better qualified than whites.
■ Caribbeans, Pakistanis and Bangladeshis were the least well qualified. However, a substantial number of Caribbean men had vocational qualifications.

### Women

■ Women of Indian, African Asian and Chinese origin all had high proportions of advanced qualifications.
■ Caribbean women were more likely to have A-level qualifications than white women.
■ Bangladeshi women were the least well qualified, followed by Pakistani women.

The PSI study also compared the qualifications of those who had been born in Britain, or who were 15 or younger when they migrated, with the qualifications of migrants who came to Britain aged 16 or over:

- There were signs that considerable progress had been made in the educational achievement of Caribbeans.
- Overall, the qualifications of the **second generation** were much better than those of the migrants' generation.
- Bangladeshis and Pakistanis had made least progress and still achieved well below other ethnic groups.

## The achievement of 16-year olds and 18-year olds

1 The **Youth Cohort Study** (2002) found that the proportion of blacks gaining five or more GCSEs has risen as fast as amongst whites, and in all other ethnic groups has risen faster. However, blacks, Pakistanis and Bangladeshis still lagged behind other groups.
2 The **Youth Cohort Study** found that by 2002 black and Indian ethnic groups were more likely than whites to be in full-time education at 18 and were also more likely to be studying for a degree. However, this was not the case for Pakistanis and Bangladeshis.
3 **Gilchrist, Phillips and Ross** (2003) found that, in 2000, ethnic minorities were more likely than whites to go to university, but were also more likely to be concentrated in lower status courses (e.g. in education). Bangladeshi, Turkish and Pakistani students were under-represented at university.

Various attempts have been made to explain differences in educational attainment between ethnic groups.

## Innate ability and attainment

As in the case of class and gender, some commentators have attributed differences in levels of achievement to IQ. **Hernstein and Murray** believe that there is a good case for arguing that differences are genetic. They found that, on average, blacks scored lower in IQ tests than whites.

**Pilkington** (1997) argues against the idea of a genetic basis for IQ differences, for the following reasons:

- It is questionable whether race is a biologically meaningful concept.
- It is also questionable whether IQ tests really measure intelligence.
- Differences in IQ can largely be explained by differences in socio-economic status.

## Cultural and material factors and attainment

### Language

In some Asian households English is not the first language used. The PSI study found that lack of fluency in English was a significant problem for some groups. Amongst men nearly everyone spoke English fluently.

Amongst women about a fifth of Pakistanis and Bangladeshis were not fluent.

- **Driver and Ballard** (1981) found that Asian children for whom English was not their main home language were at least as competent as their classmates by the age of 16.
- The *Swann Report* (1985) found that language was not a significant factor in educational attainment.

### Family life

A number of writers suggest that the nature of family life affects levels of attainment among ethnic minorities.

- It has been suggested that the West Indian population in Britain has a high proportion of **one-parent families** and working women who leave their children without close parental supervision in the early years of their life.
- **Driver and Ballard** (1981) found that South Asian parents have high aspirations for their children's education despite having little formal education themselves.

**Pilkington** (1997) argues that cultural explanations should be treated with caution:

- There are not clear boundaries between ethnic groups.
- There is a great deal of difference within ethnic minority groups.
- There is a danger of **ethnocentrism**, with white commentators criticizing ethnic minority cultures simply because they are different from their own cultures.

However, Pilkington does accept that there are real **cultural differences** between ethnic groups and that these can affect educational achievement. For example, the cohesiveness of some Asian families may assist in the high achievement of some Asian groups.

**Gillborn and Mirza** (2000), on the other hand, believe that African-Caribbean pupils get more encouragement than other groups to stay in education.

**Bhatti** (1999) found in a study of **Asian** parents that they were very concerned about their children's education and many of the girls had ambitious career aspirations. The girls were more likely to leave education because low household income forced them to find paid work than because the family did not value education.

## Social class and attainment

As we saw earlier, class is closely linked to educational attainment, with members of lower social classes gaining fewer qualifications and leaving the education system earlier than higher classes. Poor educational performance by ethnic minorities could be a result of their social class rather then their ethnicity.

Gillborn and Mirza (2000) used data from the **Youth Cohort Study** to show that social class explained some of the differences in achievement between ethnic groups but there were still differences in achievement between children of the same class from different ethnic groups.

## Racism and the education system

### Coard – racism and under-achievement

Perhaps the stongest attack on the British education system's treatment of ethnic minorities has been advanced by Bernard **Coard** (1971). He argues that black children are made to feel inferior because:

- West Indian children are told that their way of speaking is inferior.
- The word 'white' is associated with good, and the word 'black' with evil.
- The content of education tends to ignore black people.
- Attitudes in the classroom are **reinforced** by pupils in the playground where racial abuse and bullying may occur.

Coard believes that this leads to black children developing low self-esteem and low expectations.

### Wright – racism in multi-racial primary schools

**Wright** (1992) studied four multi-racial inner-city primary schools. She found that, although the majority of staff were committed to equality of opportunity, there was still considerable discrimination.

- Asians in primary schools
  - Asian girls received less attention from teachers.
  - Asian customs and traditions were sometimes disapproved of.
- African-Caribbeans in primary schools
  - Teachers expected African-Caribbean pupils to behave badly.
  - African-Caribbean boys received much negative attention from teachers.

## Racism reconsidered

The emphasis on faults in the education system should be treated with some caution.

- Teachers do not necessarily behave in ways that reflect negative stereotypes of ethnic minorities.
- **Taylor** (1981) points out that many teachers are actively concerned to develop a fair policy towards ethnic minority pupils.
- It has been questioned whether black pupils lack self-esteem. The Swann Report (1985) concluded that low self-esteem among ethnic minorities was not widespread.

Recent studies emphasize the variety of ways in which ethnic minorities respond to racism in the education system.

## Mirza – young, female and black

**Mirza** (1992) studied two comprehensive schools in south London.

- The black girls in Mirza's sample did better in exams than black boys and white pupils in the school. She believes that the educational achievements of black women are underestimated.
- Mirza also challenges the **labelling theory** of educational under-achievement. Although there was some evidence of racism among teachers, she denies that this undermined the self-confidence of the black girls. Most girls were concerned with academic success and prepared to work hard.
- Most teachers tried to meet the girls' needs but failed to do so by, for instance, failing to push black pupils hard enough or by patronizing them.

## Mac an Ghaill – ethnic minorities in the sixth form

**Mac an Ghaill** (1992) studied African-Caribbean and Asian students in a sixth-form college in the Midlands. He found that the way students responded to schooling varied considerably and was influenced by their ethnicity, gender and the class composition of their former secondary schools.

All of the ethnic minority students experienced problems in the education system, but they experienced them differently, depending on their gender and ethnic group. Nevertheless, they had all enjoyed some success. They had achieved this through adopting a variety of survival strategies.

- Some of the girls had banded together. They would help each other out with academic work but were less willing to conform to rules about dress, appearance and behaviour in class.
- Some of the other ethnic minority pupils were less hostile to their schools. They tried to become friendly with some teachers while avoiding others who they identified as racist.

The study is important because it shows how class, gender and ethnicity interact within the school system. Like Mirza's study, it also shows that negative labelling does not necessarily lead to academic failure. Although such labelling creates extra barriers, some students are able to overcome them.

## Gillborn, Mirza and Youdell – rationing education

Research by **Gillborn and Mirza** (2000) and **Gillborn and Youdell** (2000) suggests that racism continues to significantly disadvantage ethnic minorities in British education.

**Gillborn and Mirza** found that in some local education authorities ethnic minorities seemed to be particularly disadvantaged, suggesting that those areas had a significant problem with racism.

**Gillborn and Youdell** in a study of two London comprehensives, they found that a system of **educational triage** – in which education was rationed – adversely affected black pupils. Extra help was directed at those who were borderline cases for gaining five GCSEs at grade C. However, many black pupils were considered to have little chance of achieving this standard and were effectively written off, being placed in lower sets or entered for lower tiers of GCSEs. There was a system of racialized expectations in which the behaviour of black pupils was interpreted as threatening, rather than as evidence of wanting to succeed. Unintentional racism therefore held many black pupils back.

## Conclusion

It is probable that many of the factors outlined above work together in producing the lower levels of achievement found in some ethnic minority groups. *The Swann Report* concluded that racial discrimination inside and outside school, along with social deprivation, were probably the main factors.

## Connolly – racism, gender identities and young children

Some recent studies focus more on identity than differential achievement but still have implications for understanding achievement as well.

**Connolly**'s study (1998) of young children in a multi-ethnic inner-city primary school emphasizes the diverse influences on gender in schools. In particular he examines how school relationships are also shaped by ethnicity.

### Black boys

Teachers were more willing to criticize the behaviour of black boys than that of other groups. They felt that some of the black males in the school were in danger of growing up to be violent criminals, and they saw them as a threat to school discipline. However, they also took positive steps to encourage them to participate in school activities such as football.

The boys also brought their own values and attitudes to school, for example those relating to **masculinity**. These also contributed to their identity.

### Black girls

Black girls were also perceived by teachers as potentially disruptive but likely to be good at sports, music and dancing.

### South Asian boys

Some teachers contrasted what they saw as the close and supportive Asian families with the high rates of single parenthood amongst other groups in the area.

South Asian boys tended to be seen as immature rather than seriously deviant.

There was a tendency for other boys who wanted to assert their masculinity to pick on South Asian boys. The South Asian boys had difficulty in gaining status as males. This made it difficult for them to feel confident at school.

### South Asian girls

South Asian girls were seen to be even more obedient and hard-working than South Asian boys, although Connolly's observations showed that their attitude to work was not significantly different from that of other female groups.

South Asian girls had a relatively **low status** among their peers. They were seen as feminine in terms of their passivity and obedience, but they were not seen as potential girlfriends by black and white boys because their culture was considered too alien.

# TEST YOUR KNOWLEDGE AND UNDERSTANDING

1 **Durkheim would probably agree with three of the following statements about education. Which one would he disagree with?**
   a The values promoted by education are the values of powerful groups
   b The school is a society in miniature
   c Education helps create and maintain social solidarity
   d Education makes a positive contribution to society

2 **Which of the following best describes Bowles and Gintis's 'correspondence principle'?**
   a There is a close relationship between ability and achievement
   b There is a close relationship between relationships in the workplace and in education
   c There is a close relationship between relationships in education and in the family
   d There is a close relationship between education and society

3 **Which of the following is not a similarity between shop-floor culture and counter-school culture, according to Willis?**
   a Racism and sexism
   b Refusal to do homework
   c Lack of respect for authority
   d Minimizing work

4 **During the 1980s and 1990s the New Right believed that the best way to raise standards in schools was through which one of the following methods?**
   a Increasing teachers' pay
   b Making more resources available to schools
   c Introducing market forces into education
   d Abolishing private education

5 **What term do Ball et al. use to refer to the group of parents who are least able to take advantage of the education market?**
   a Disconnected choosers
   b Semi-skilled choosers
   c Skilled choosers
   d Excluded choosers

6 **Three of the following statements are criticisms of the National Curriculum. Which is the odd one out?**
   a It is too bureaucratic
   b It centralizes power and undermines local control
   c The content is traditional and unimaginative
   d It allows girls to drop science subjects at an early age

7 **What is the name of the educational initiative introduced by the Labour government of 1997 to boost educational achievement in areas of high deprivation?**
   a Educational Priority Areas
   b Compensatory education
   c Education Action Zones
   d Social exclusion units

8 **Which of these sociologists supports the theory of cultural deprivation?**
   a Leon Feinstein
   b Blackstone and Mortimore
   c Pierre Bourdieu
   d David Gillborn

9 **Which one of the following terms was used by Bernstein to describe the language use of the working class?**
   a Restricted code
   b Shorthand code
   c Elaborated code
   d Implicit code

10 **Which one of the following is an example of the use of cultural capital?**
   a Parents buying a computer for their child to use for school work
   b Parents sending their child to a private school
   c Parents moving house to be near a popular school
   d Parents writing an effective letter to a headteacher so that their child is moved to a set with the best teacher

11 **Which of the following terms is not associated with the work of Gillborn and Youdell?**
   a Educational triage
   b The A-C economy
   c The new IQism
   d The myth of under-achievement

12 **Which one of the following is a criticism of some interactionist approaches to educational achievement?**
   a They are not based on empirical research
   b They are deterministic, assuming that pupils passively accept their labelling
   c They ignore the interaction between teachers and pupils
   d They do not take labelling and the self-fulfilling prophecy into account

13 **Which one of the following statements best describes the changing relationship between gender and achievement?**
   a The achievement of girls has increased but boys' achievement has dropped
   b The achievement of both boys and girls has increased, but girls have improved their educational performance more rapidly
   c The achievement of both genders has remained stable
   d The achievement of both genders has increased at a similar rate

14 **According to Colley, three of the following are factors in explaining why gender differences in subject choice still exist. Which is the odd one out?**
   a Subject preferences and choice
   b The National Curriculum
   c Perceptions of gender roles
   d The learning environment

15 **According to Mitsos and Browne, three of the following are reasons for the improvement in girls' achievement. Which is the odd one out?**
   a There is growing awareness of equal opportunities issues in schools
   b Feminism has raised women's expectations and self-esteem
   c The increase in service sector work has increased employment opportunities for women
   d Girls' IQ scores are higher than boys'

# DEVELOP YOUR ANALYSIS AND EVALUATION SKILLS

## *Cultural factors are largely responsible for working class children under-achieving in the education system.*

**Background:** You might start by noting some evidence that the working class still do relatively poorly in education (see p. 156). Cultural arguments include those of Douglas, Bernstein and Feinstein, but all have been criticized. More sophisticated arguments are partly based on class culture, as in those put forward by Bourdieu, but Bourdieu also holds the education system responsible, as he sees it as biased towards dominant culture. Alternative arguments suggest that material factors are more important or that labelling within schools is largely responsible. The different viewpoints are not mutually exclusive, and you might conclude that a combination of material and cultural factors, and factors inside and outside school, are all significant

| *For* | *Against* |
|-------|-----------|
| ■ Douglas (p. 157) | ■ Criticisms of cultural theories (p. 158) |
| ■ Feinstein (p. 157) | ■ Material theories (pp. 157–8) |
| ■ Bernstein (pp. 157–8) | ■ Interactionist theory (pp. 159–60) |
| ■ Bourdieu (partly) (p. 158) | |

**Top tip:** The study by Ball, Bowe and Gewirtz (pp. 158–9) is useful for illustrating Bourdieu's approach, which suggests how cultural factors are inked to wider class inequality and the operation of the education system.

## *Education serves the interests of the ruling class.*

**Background:** This view is a Marxist one and the clearest supporters are Bowles and Gintis. Willis agrees with this view, although he sees the relationship between education and the ruling class as complex. Finn uses something similar to a Marxist approach when discussing training schemes. Marxism is not without its direct critics (see criticisms on p. 156) and other approaches take a very different view. The New Right deny there is a ruling class (see pp. 154–6) and believe education has failed to produce a suitable workforce. Functionalists, on the other hand, see education as effectively serving the needs of society as a whole.

| *For* | *Against* |
|-------|-----------|
| ■ Bowles and Gintis (p. 153) | ■ Functionalism (pp. 152–15) |
| ■ Willis (p. 154) | ■ The New Right (pp. 154–6) |
| ■ Finn (p. 156) | |

**Top tip:** Much of the research on education suggests that it serves the interests of middle-class children rather well (for example see Ball, Bowe and Gewirtz, pp. 158–9) and doesn't just benefit the ruling class. The working class, however, may miss out on the full benefits.

## *The education of boys is now more of a problem in Britain than the education of girls.*

**Background:** You need to explain the changes in recorded achievement, with girls overtaking boys at all levels of the education system (p. 160). This has led writers like Mitsos and Browne to discuss the reasons for boys' doing less well than girls (though they also believe that improvements by girls are very important). Becky Francis also suggests some problems with the education of boys, however she sees both boys and girls facing some problems. Weiner, Arnot and David see the 'moral panic' about male education as a 'backlash' against female achievement. Colley points that there are still many prestigious subjects that females are unlikely to study.

| *For* | *Against* |
|-------|-----------|
| ■ Statistics on achievement (p. 160) | ■ Weiner, Arnot and David (p. 162) |
| ■ Mitsos and Browne (partly) (p. 161–2) | ■ Colley (p. 161) |
| ■ Francis (partly) (p. 162) | ■ Francis (partly) (p. 162) |

**Top tip:** Connolly's work (p. 165) is useful for showing how gender interacts with class and ethnicity to create educational problems for particular groups of boys and girls.

# AQA-STYLE EDUCATION QUESTION

## AS Unit 2

**Answer all parts of this question**

Total: 60 marks
1 mark = 1.25 minutes

Time allowed: 1 hour 15 minutes

### ITEM A

The government tells us that educational league tables are not just to give parents more information but to spur on low-performing schools. However, some people argue that it is not fair or meaningful to judge a school's performance by its raw results. Research has consistently shown a link between educational achievement and socio-economic status; therefore you have to make allowance for the social circumstances and the language background of the pupils attending a particular school.

### ITEM B

Bowles and Gintis argue that there is a correspondence between school and work. School trains people for work not so much through the formal curriculum of skills and knowledge but through the hidden curriculum which teaches norms, values and beliefs that have a strong influence on pupils' behaviour, making them docile and compliant workers.

---

**Comments on the question**

- Check that you understand the meaning of the phrase in the context of the passage

**[a] Explain what is meant by 'raw results'. [Item A, line 5] [2 marks]**

**Advice on preparing your answer**

- Do not use the words you are being asked to explain
- Always work backwards through the terms, i.e. find another term for 'results', then qualify this by giving a phrase to explain 'raw'

---

- If you fail to read this part of the question you will be giving an answer that is the opposite of what is required
- Your answer here will help you to form the basis of your answer to part [e], so it is a good idea to answer the questions in the examination paper order. This allows you to pick up on helpful clues left by the chief examiner

**[b] Give two factors that affect educational attainment apart from those mentioned in Item A. [4 marks]**

- This does not require any more than a list of two factors, so do not waste your time writing sentences
- Do not use 'class', as this is too similar to socio-economic status
- Gender (pp. 161–2) and ethnicity (pp. 162–5) are the obvious, but not the only, possible answers

---

- There will be 2 marks available for each way you suggest. You cannot make up for any lack of knowledge you might have by writing at length about only two ways

**[c] Suggest three ways in which schools might prepare pupils for work through the hidden curriculum. [6 marks]**

- The item will help to keep you focused if you apply the information given in Item B to actual examples
- Make sure that you give ways that are part of the hidden curriculum (p. 153)

---

- There are two skills to demonstrate here, so you will require a short paragraph for each of two separate ways
- Make sure that your description relates to educational attainment and that it links to the way you have identified

**[d] Identify and describe two ways in which language can affect educational attainment. [8 marks]**

- You could refer to:
  1 Bernstein, pp. 157–8
  2 PSI study, p. 163

- The focus is on change, so don't give a static description at one point in time, although 'no change' is a relevant pattern
- Note the time limit. Reference to patterns under the tripartite system may be inappropriate unless you show that you know this system is still in operation in certain localities

**[e]** Examine the patterns of differential educational attainment during the last 30 years. [20 marks]

- Socio-economic/class patterns (see p. 156)
- Use your answer to part [b] to alert you to other groups
- Gender patterns, p. 160, and subject choice, p. 161
- Ethnicity, pp. 162–3

- You must give knowledge beyond the item
- This tells you to evaluate – if you do not do this you are unlikely to gain more than 7 or 8 marks
- The best answers will pick up specific points of assessment on individual Marxist views as well as offering alternative perspectives as part of a critique
- The plural tells you to write about more than one Marxist view

**[f]** Using material from Item B and elsewhere, assess Marxist views of the role of education in training people for work.

[20 marks]

- Start by interpreting from the item that Bowles and Gintis are Marxist writers
- Develop their analysis by using p. 153
- Go beyond the item by using the work of Finn (p. 156) or Willis (p. 154), thus keeping a tight focus on this issue
- Select ideas from the functionalists (pp. 152–3) as a critique of Marxism, but do not criticize this view as you will be going beyond the requirements of the question

## OCR-STYLE EDUCATION QUESTION

### A2 Unit 2536: Power and Control

Total: 60 marks, 1 mark = 1 minute
Time allowed: 1 hour

**Comments on the question**

- Make sure that you describe the view in a detailed way with supporting evidence
- Look at a range of arguments for and against the point of view
- Make sure that your response is balanced – attempt to minimize personal bias by presenting all sides of the argument objectively and with reasonably equal weight

**[a]** Outline and assess the view that working-class under-achievement is the product of a hidden curriculum. [60 marks]

**Advice on preparing your answer**

- This is an essay question so spend at least 10 minutes planning your response
- Criticisms are offered on p. 153
- An introduction is necessary to set the scene, i.e. to make clear how the concept of the hidden curriculum is defined and which theoretical position is associated with it
- See p. 153 for theoretical accounts of the hidden curriculum
- Try to finish with an evaluative conclusion based on the evidence

Specifications

| Specification | Specification details | | Coverage |
|---|---|---|---|
| **OCR** AS: The Individual and Society | **Introducing the individual and society** | ■ The role of values, norms and the agents of socialization in the formation of culture | These issues are covered in the section on culture and society in the introductory chapter on sociological perspectives (p. 1). Definitions of culture and identity are further discussed on p. 171. Theories of culture can be found on p. 172. |
| | | ■ Learning social roles. How expected patterns of behaviour regulate social life | These issues are covered in the section on culture and society (p. 1). |
| | **Culture and the formation of identities** | ■ The meaning of 'gender identities' The process of gender role socialization | Gender identities are discussed briefly in the context of Bradleys' work on p. 176. More detail can be found in chapter 2, on pp. 24 and 27–28. |
| | | ■ The meaning of 'national' identities. The role of institutions in shaping and reinforcing national identity | National identities are discussed in chapter 3, pp. 38–9. |
| | | ■ The meaning of 'ethnic identities'. Their impact on social behaviour | Ethnic identities are discussed briefly in the context of Bradleys' work on p. 176. There is more detail and specific case studies in chapter 3, pp. 35–6. |
| | | ■ The meaning of 'class identities'. Their impact on social behaviour | Class identities are discussed briefly in the context of Bradleys' work on p. 176. There is more detail in chapter 1 – the upper class on p. 9; the middle classes on pp. 10–12; and the working class on pp. 12–13. |
| | | ■ Contemporary social change and the implications for gender, national, ethnic and class identities | Changing identities are discussed in the section on identity (pp. 174–6). |

**Parts of other modules covered**

| Specification | Specification details | | Coverage |
|---|---|---|---|
| **OCR** AS: Culture and Socialization/ Youth and Culture | **Youth culture and subcultures** | ■ The distinction between youth culture and subcultures; middle-class and working-class subcultures. | Issues surrounding youth culture and subcultures are discussed on pp. 172–3. |
| | **Culture and society** | ■ The significance of class, gender and ethnicity for contemporary youth. | |
| | | ■ Theories of youth subcultures, e.g. Marxism, feminism, postmodernism. | |
| **OCR** A2: Power and Control/Popular Culture | | ■ Defining culture: mass culture, folk culture, high culture, popular culture, global culture, cultural industries and symbolic consumption. | Definitions of culture are discussed on p. 171; theories of culture on p. 172. |
| | | ■ Theoretical approaches to the construction and consumption of culture, e.g. Marxism, varieties of feminism, modernism, post-structuralism and postmodernism. | |

For more detailed specification guidance visit **www.haralambosholborn.com**

# THE DEFINITION OF CULTURE

The word 'culture' has been used in different ways. Jencks (1993) distinguishes four main senses in which the word is now used:

1 Culture can be seen as a quality possessed by individuals who are able to gain the learning and achieve the qualities that are seen as desirable in a cultured human being.
2 The first definition is quite **elitist** as it sees some aspects of what is human as superior to others. The second definition is also elitist but sees certain societies rather than people as superior to others. Some societies are more cultured – in other words more **civilized** – than others.
3 The third definition sees culture as the sum total of all the arts and intellectual work in a society. This is quite a common definition, and culture in this sense is sometimes called high culture.
4 The final definition sees culture as **the whole way of life of a people.** As Linton (1945) puts it, 'The culture of a society is the way of life of its members; the collection of ideas and habits which they learn, share and transmit from generation to generation.'

Most contemporary sociologists adopt the fourth definition. Culture in this sense includes virtually all of the subject matter of sociology.

When the third definition is adopted it is easier to identify a distinct area of study, which includes the sociology of art, music and literature.

## Types of culture

These definitions of culture can be developed by examining the different **types of culture** identified by sociologists.

- **High culture** – High culture usually refers to cultural creations that have a particularly high status – for example, the products of long-established art forms such as opera, theatre and literature. For many who use the term, high culture is seen as superior to lesser forms of culture.
- **Folk culture** – Folk culture refers to the culture of ordinary people, particularly those living in pre-industrial societies. Examples include traditional folk songs and stories that have been handed down from generation to generation.
- **Mass culture** – For its critics, mass culture is seen as less worthy than high culture or folk culture. It is a product of the mass media and includes popular feature films, TV soap operas and pop music. Critics of mass culture (see pp. 173–4) see it as debasing for individuals and destructive for the fabric of society.
- **Popular culture** – The term popular culture is often used in a similar way to the term 'mass culture'. Popular culture includes any cultural products appreciated by large numbers of ordinary people: for example, TV programmes, mass-market films, and popular fiction such as detective stories. While mass culture is usually used as a term of abuse, this is not the case with popular culture. While some do see popular culture as shallow and harmful, others, including some postmodernists, argue that it is just as valid and worthwhile as high culture.
- **Subculture** – The term 'subculture' has been applied to a wide range of groups, including those who live close together and have a shared lifestyle, youth groups who share common musical tastes and enjoy the same leisure activities, ethnic groups, people who share the same religious beliefs, members of the same gang and so on.

Some theorists, particularly functionalists, emphasize the degree to which culture is shared by members of a society. Many other theorists emphasize **cultural pluralism** or subcultural variety in society.

# IDENTITY

## The definition of identity

**Identity** refers to the sense that someone has of who they are, of what is most important about them. Important sources of identity are likely to include nationality, ethnicity, sexuality, gender and class.

- **Personal identity** refers to how a person thinks about themselves.
- **Social identity** refers to how they are perceived by others.

Personal and social identity do not necessarily match. A person perceived by others to be male may see themselves as a woman trapped in a man's body.

## The importance of identity

The concept of identity has become increasingly important in sociology. In the past, people's identities were seen as fairly stable, widely shared and based on one or two key variables such as **class and nationality**. More recent **postmodern theories** of identity have suggested that people's identities can frequently change and may contain considerable contradictions. For example, the meaning of 'masculine' and 'feminine' has become much less clearcut.

According to postmodernists:

- People actively create their own identities.
- People have a great deal of choice about what social groups to join.
- Through shopping and other forms of consumption people can shape and change their identities.

To some writers, individuals no longer have a stable sense of identity at all – their identities are **fragmented** (see p. 176).

# IDENTITY AND CULTURE

The concept of identity is closely related to the concept of culture. Identities can be formed through the cultures and subcultures to which people belong. However, different theories see the relationship between culture and identity in rather different ways.

- Theories such as functionalism and Marxism see identity as originating in a fairly straightforward way from involvement in particular cultures and subcultures, e.g. people living in Britain would be expected to have a strong sense of British identity.
- Theories influenced by postmodernism stress the diversity of ways in which, for example, British people from different ethnic or national origins interpret British identity.

## Culture – functionalist perspectives

**Durkheim** (1903) believed that a **shared culture** is necessary if a society is to run smoothly. This shared culture is passed down from generation to generation and exists over and above the wishes and choices of individuals. People must conform to the culture of their society if they are to avoid the risk of punishment.

- To **Parsons** (1951) society is not possible without a shared culture. It allows people to communicate and to work towards shared goals.
- **Parsons and Bales** (1955) argue that culture is passed on to children through **socialization**, particularly through primary socialization in the family (see p. 109).
- Parsons and Durkheim generally saw culture as slow to change although they believed that major changes in culture do occur as societies evolve.

### Evaluation

Parsons has often been accused of exaggerating both the extent to which contemporary societies possess a common culture, and the extent to which people conform to the culture into which they are socialized.

Parsons did acknowledge that everybody did not share an identical culture. However, contemporary societies may possess such cultural diversity that they raise questions about how much culture needs to be shared. In Britain, for example, there is a great deal of ethnic, religious and regional diversity, yet British society continues to function. It may be that functionalist views are more applicable to **traditional societies**.

## Marxist theories of culture and identity

**Marx** claimed that in class-stratified societies culture can be seen as little more than **ruling-class ideology**. It is simply an expression of the distorted view of the world advanced by the dominant class. Contemporary Marxists have developed theories of institutions such as the mass media along these lines (see p. 182–3).

- One interpretation of Marx sees the working class as suffering from **false class consciousness** – its beliefs and culture shaped by the ruling class.
- Other interpretations see the working class and other cultures as possessing some independence from ruling-class domination.

## Neo-Marxist theories of culture

**Neo-Marxist** approaches have been significantly influenced by Marxism, but all tend to argue that culture has considerable independence from economic influences, and that there is no straightforward correspondence between class and culture.

The Birmingham Centre for Contemporary Cultural Studies (CCCS) extended the study of culture to an examination of youth cultures. They draw extensively on the writings of the Italian Marxist, **Antonio Gramsci** (1971) who argued that dominant ideology could always be opposed and that ideological domination – what he called **hegemony** – is never complete.

## Youth subcultures

To the CCCS, **youth subcultures** often represent creative attempts to win space from dominant cultures. Youth cultures create their own distinctive styles of dress and music and these represent an attempt to 'solve', in an imaginary way, the problems faced by youth. The example of **Teddy boys** can illustrate these arguments.

### Jefferson – Teddy boys

**Jefferson** (1976) argues that the youth culture of Teddy boys (or Teds) represented an attempt to recreate a sense of **working-class community** which came under threat in the post-war period from urban redevelopment and growing **affluence** (wealth) in some sections of the working class.

Some unskilled working-class youth responded by forming groups in which members had a strong sense of loyalty and were willing to fight over their territory. Their style of dress incorporated Edwardian-style jackets, bootlace ties and suede shoes. Jefferson sees aspects of this style as part of an attempt to buy status:

- Edwardian-style jackets were originally worn by upper-class 'dandies', and by wearing them the Teds hoped that some of the status of this group would rub off on them.
- Bootlace ties appeared to come from Western films where they were worn by the 'slick city gambler' who was forced to live by his wits. Like their counterparts in the Westerns, the Teddy boys felt themselves to be outsiders who needed to live by their wits.

By adopting these styles, working-class youth can at least feel that they are doing something to protect their territory, gain **status** and recreate community.

### Evaluation

Neo-Marxist theories such as those of the CCCS tend to fall between two stools:

- To conventional Marxists they fail to fully acknowledge the importance of the economy in shaping culture.
- To postmodernists they fail to fully accept the freedom that people have to invent cultures.

## Hebdige – Subculture: The Meaning of Style

**Hebdige** (1979) uses some Marxist ideas in his analysis of youth subcultures but is also influenced by **semiotics** – the study of the meaning of symbols and signs.

■ Each subculture develops its own style by taking everyday objects and transforming their meaning. This new 'secret' meaning expresses, in code, a form of **resistance** to subordination. Punks, for instance, transformed the meaning of safety pins and ripped jeans.

■ Each subculture is **spectacular**: it creates a spectacle and intends to get noticed.

Hebdige contrasts mod and skinhead subcultures. **Skinheads**' appearance was a kind of exaggerated version of the working-class manual labourer and expressed the image of the 'hard' working-class man. **Mods**, on the other hand, adopted a more respectable appearance which reflected aspirations to be upwardly mobile and join the middle class. However, despite their respectable suits, their style reflected a love of 'cellar clubs, discotheques, boutiques and record shops' which was outside the conventional middle-class world.

Hebdige also analyses black British subcultures. First-generation migrants adopted smart and conventional dress which reflected their aspirations to succeed in Britain. By the 1970s, the disappointments that stemmed from racism and high levels of unemployment began to be expressed in the style of **Rastafarians**. British Rastafarians expressed their alienation from British culture by adopting simple clothes with an African feel. The key themes of Rastafarian style were resistance to the dominance of white culture and the expression of black identity.

### Evaluation

1 Hebdige's work is only as good as his interpretations. However, there is no evidence that members of the youth subcultures he writes about saw their own subculture in the same way as Hebdige. This lack of empirical evidence could be seen as a limitation of his work.

2 For postmodernists Hebdige is wrong to assume that it is possible to attribute any one meaning to a subculture. Rather, it is open to a variety of interpretations each of which is equally valid.

### Grossberg – The Deconstruction of Youth

Grossberg's (1994) discussion of the changing meaning of youth is influenced by **post-structuralism**. This approach argues that our identity is created by our involvement with particular discourses – particular ways of thinking and talking about something.

To Grossberg, if people come to think of 'youth' in a particular way, then people who think of themselves as young will tend to act in ways that are consistent with this view.

Grossberg outlines three main phases in the development of youth discourses:

1 Following the Industrial Revolution, discourses about young people were concerned with the ideas of adulthood and **childhood** rather than youth. Childhood was seen as a time of innocence. Children were protected and kept away from work until they were deemed old enough to become adults and leave school.

2 After the Second World War the idea of **youth** as a **transitional period** between childhood and adulthood became important. Youth was seen as 'on the one hand, a time of fun, a time in which one could take risks, and, on the other hand, a potential threat'. During this period youth created its own cultures, particularly those related to rock and roll. Young people took the new discourse of youth and used it to create their own culture.

3 From the late 1970s young people lost some of their rebellion and replaced it with **cynicism**. They lost the desire to celebrate youth in its own right and became more obsessed with becoming part of the adult world. Political activities were superseded by hanging around in shopping malls.

Grossberg attributes this change in the meaning of youth to the way in which adults have helped to shift the discourse of youth. Adults are increasingly unwilling to give up their idea of themselves as youthful, redefining it as an attitude of mind rather than simply an age. Also, many aspects of youth culture have become incorporated into adult-controlled institutions. Rock music is frequently used in advertising, for example.

### Evaluation

The emphasis on **language** of post-structuralists such as Grossberg leads them to neglect material reality. Marxists would argue that **material wealth** has just as much influence on society as discourses or ways of talking about things. In the end it is **capitalists** who have the **power** to determine which records, clothes and so on are available to young people.

## MASS CULTURE

In 1950s America there was considerable concern about the impact of what was called **mass culture**. As individuals had more and more free time, the **mass media** stepped in to fill people's spare time with undemanding entertainment such as soap operas, popular films and magazines.

**Macdonald** (1957) saw no merit in mass culture. He believed it had nothing of significance to say and was designed to appeal to the lowest common denominator. He argued that mass culture was actually undermining the fabric of society because people were losing their involvement in social groups and becoming isolated individuals.

### Strinati – a critique of mass culture theory

**Strinati** (1995) attacks mass culture theory on a number of grounds:

1 The consumers of mass culture are not a **passive** 'mass' of people. They are discriminating and reject many products which they find insufficiently interesting or entertaining.

2 It is not the case that all popular culture is **homogeneous** (the same). In reality there is a wide variety of styles. Popular music, for example, includes 'rap', jazz, heavy metal and so on.

3 It is not possible to distinguish a superior '**folk culture**' from an inferior mass culture. Folk, blues and country music, for example, have all been influenced by a range of musical traditions.

4 There is no clear distinction between mass culture and **high culture**. Strinati gives the examples of jazz music, the films of Alfred Hitchcock and rock-and-roll records which have attained the status of classics.

## MODERNITY, POSTMODERNITY AND CULTURE

### Strinati – postmodernism and popular culture

Strinati (1995) describes how theories of postmodernism explain popular culture.

### The main features of postmodernism

1 'The breakdown of the distinction between culture and society.' Society has become '**media-saturated**' and this means that the media are extremely powerful. They become so all-consuming that they actually create our sense of reality.

2 'An emphasis on **style** at the expense of substance.' Products become popular because they have designer labels rather than because they are useful. Surface qualities assume more importance than anything deeper.

3 There is a 'breakdown of the distinction between art and popular culture'. Elements of what used to be thought of as 'high culture' become incorporated into popular culture – the pop artist Andy **Warhol**, for example, produced a print consisting of thirty representations of the Mona Lisa. Unlike the critics of mass culture (see p. 173), postmodernists see no reason to be unhappy about this: they welcome the fun and variety of postmodern culture.

4 The development of '**confusions over time and space**'. Rapid travel and instantaneous communications lead to confusions over time and space. The media make it possible to witness events on the other side of the globe almost as if you were there. Theme parks recreate the past and try to create the future; while some films and novels deliberately avoid following a storyline from start to finish.

5 Finally, postmodern culture involves 'the decline of **metanarratives**'. It involves a decline in faith in any absolute claim to knowledge, such as religion, science and Marxism. It denies that there is any sense of progress in history. Everything is equally valid and the search for truth is pointless and dangerous.

### Reasons for the emergence of postmodernism

Strinati identifies three main reasons for the emergence of postmodernism:

1 Advanced capitalist societies emphasize **consumerism**. A more affluent population with more leisure time needs to be entertained and persuaded to spend money. The media is central to these processes and so media images come to dominate society.

2 New **middle-class occupations**, such as design, marketing, advertising and creative jobs in the various media, involve persuading people about the importance of taste. Once persuaded, people seek guidance on taste issues from the media. Other occupations – such as teaching and therapy – promote the idea that lifestyle is important, and so people are encouraged to consume the goods and services required for their favoured lifestyle.

3 There has been a gradual disappearance of identities based on such things as class, local communities and religion. People's identities become more personal and individual and constructed by the media.

### An evaluation of postmodern theories of culture

Strinati raises a number of problems with postmodern theories:

1 Postmodernists exaggerate the importance of the mass media. There is no reason to think that people cannot distinguish between image and reality. Few people actually believe that characters in soap operas are real, for example.

2 People do not buy products just because of their image or the designer label attached to them; they also buy them because they are useful. What is more, not all members of society have a culture that attaches importance to the image of products.

3 Postmodernism is itself a 'metanarrative' so this undermines the claim that metanarratives are in decline.

4 Some people have less opportunity than others to experience changes in concepts of time and space. Poorer people do not have access to computer or satellite technology or jet travel. What is more, there are no studies that show that people actually are confused about space and time.

5 Generally people still find it possible to distinguish between what they consider art and what they see as popular culture. Strinati believes that postmodernists simply create their own hierarchy of taste, placing their own favourite cultural products at the top.

6 The impact of postmodernism on popular culture has been exaggerated. Strinati focuses on films and points out that many of the supposed postmodern aspects of contemporary cinema are nothing new. Also, many films regarded as postmodern still have strong narratives (storylines).

## IDENTITY

Richard **Jenkins** argues that social identity is 'our understanding of who we are and of who other people are, and, reciprocally, other people's understanding of themselves and of others'. Identity involves making comparisons between people and establishing similarities and differences between them. Those who are believed to be similar share an identity.

### Kath Woodward – the formation of identities

Woodward (2000) discusses three central questions about the formation of identities.

1 **To what extent do we shape our own identities?** Identity is partly subjective but also partly external and dependent on the judgement of others. You may choose to support a football team but it is more difficult to make a personal decision about your gender identity. You may regard yourself as a man but everybody else might see you as a woman. Thus identity is formed through a combination of **individual agency** and **structural constraints**.

2 **How are identities formed?** Woodward draws on the work of three key writers.
- Mead argued that human development involves imagining the way others see us. Thus our identity is linked to the external identity others give us.
- Goffman saw the social world as rather like a play. Individuals put on a performance for others to convince them about who they are. Through presenting yourself in particular roles the individual develops identities.
- Freud believed that childhood experiences, often unconscious, were vital for the development of identities in adulthood, particularly gender and sexual identities.

3 **Are there particular uncertainties about identity in contemporary Britain?** Woodward believes that there is evidence of greater uncertainty over identities. She suggests a number of reasons.
- Heavy manufacturing industry has declined, **undermining traditional masculine identities** based on being the family breadwinner with a job for life.
- The increased employment of married women has created uncertainty about gender roles, particularly the role of housewife.
- **Family roles are changing** with the increase in divorce and single parenthood. New reproductive technologies are threatening old biological 'certainties'.
- **New social movements** have developed, for example the women's movement, movements for gay and lesbian rights and the environment. These have encouraged positive identification.
- Certainty about **national identity** has been reduced. Britain is increasingly multicultural and there is an increasing emphasis on local and regional identities.
- The growth of **consumer culture** increases people's choices about identity. People can express identity through what they buy, for example their clothes and jewellery. They can even alter their bodies through cosmetic surgery or visiting the gym.

### *Stuart Hall*

According to **Hall** (1992) contemporary societies are increasingly characterized by the existence of **fractured identities**. People no longer possess a single, unified concept of who they are. This fragmentation of identity has a number of sources.

### Modernity and change

The pace of change has increased in 'late-modern' societies and this makes it difficult for people to retain a unified identity.

### New social movements

In the past, social class provided something of a 'master identity'. However, in the 1960s and 1970s people began to organize around issues other than class. **New social movements** developed based around issues such as gender, ethnicity and the environment.

With the rise of new social movements, identity itself became a political issue. Identity politics emphasizes the importance of hearing the voices of oppressed groups such as gays and lesbians, black women, the disabled and so on.

### Globalization

The ease with which people move around the world, improvements in communications and the global marketing of styles and images can lead to a **'cultural supermarket effect'**. People can choose from a wide range of identities, adopting the values and lifestyles of any group they choose.

On the other hand, global consumerism can also lead to increased similarity, as products such as Coca-Cola can be found anywhere.

### *Globalization and different sources of identity*

In modern societies nationality was an important source of identity. **National identity** was used to create a sense of solidarity among citizens of different classes, ethnic origins and so on. With globalization this is not so easy. Hall identifies three responses:

1 In some places people have tried to reaffirm national identity as a **defensive mechanism**. They have perceived a threat to their national identity from immigration for example.
2 The first reaction is characteristic of ethnic majorities. But **ethnic minorities** sometimes react in defensive ways as well. In response to racism and exclusion, ethnic minorities have sometimes placed a renewed emphasis on their ethnic identities and culture.
3 A third reaction is the construction of new identities. A British example is the construction of a **'black' identity**, embracing British African-Caribbeans and Asians. In this case identity becomes hybrid, mixing more than one existing identity into a new identity.

The first two responses to globalization have had the effect of reviving ethnicity as a source of identity, often in opposition to existing nationalism. In several parts of the world ethnic groups have demanded their own nation-states as bigger nation-states (such as the USSR and Yugoslavia) have broken up. This has led to considerable violence and even civil war.

Hall sees this **nationalism** as a worrying trend. He argues that the idea of **ethnic purity** is largely a myth as nearly all populations come from a variety of ethnic backgrounds.

## Bradley – fractured identities

**Bradley** (1997) attempts to pull together classical and postmodern sociological approaches in understanding the relationship between identity and inequality.

## Three levels of identity

Bradley believes that it is useful to think of identity as working at three levels:

1 **Passive identities** – these are identities which have the potential to become important but largely lie dormant. Bradley sees class identity in this way. Most British people accept that class inequalities exist but do not see themselves as a member of a class most of the time. However, circumstances could change.
2 **Active identities** – these are identities which individuals are conscious of and which provide a base for their actions.
3 **Politicized identities** – these are formed through campaigns highlighting the importance of a particular identity and using it as a basis for organizing **collective action**. For example, feminists succeeded in turning gender into a politicized identity in the 1970s and 1980s.

Bradley accepts that postmodernists have a point in arguing that there is a good deal of choice over identity and that identities are becoming more fragmented. However, she still sees identities as rooted in membership of social groups.

Bradley examines four aspects of inequality: class, gender, 'race'/ethnicity and age, although she does recognize other important social divisions such as sexuality and disability.

## Class and identity

Bradley does not see class as the strongest source of identity in contemporary Britain. She sees it as a passive form of identity, partly because it is less visible in the everyday world than age, 'race'/ethnicity and gender. However, she notes that inequality is increasing and that this creates the potential for class to be an increasingly important source of identity.

## Gender and identity

Bradley notes the move away from theories such as radical feminism which saw women as a single group, towards theories which see women (and men) as being fragmented into different groups. She believes that both types of theory are important, and that common experience of sexism provides a basis for a shared identity for women.

However, not all women experience disadvantage to the same extent or in the same ways. **Black feminists**, for example, have suggested that the family is experienced differently by white and black women.

To Bradley, gender is a very important source of identity in contemporary Britain. It is also an active, politicized identity for women as a result of feminism.

## 'Race'/ethnicity and identity

Like gender, 'race'/ethnicity has become a more important source of identity in Britain than class and is more likely to produce active and politicized identities. Sometimes this is due to the visibility of skin colour but this is not always the case. The violence in the former Yugoslavia occurred between white ethnic groups, for example.

The importance of 'race'/ethnicity depends on how it is used politically to mobilize groups and provide them with a sense of belonging. The identity of a British Muslim has assumed more importance than other potential identities as a result of the revival of Islam as a world religion.

For dominant ethnic groups, ethnic identity is rather less politicized but can become more politicized in certain situations. In Britain, **Scottish** and **Welsh** ethnic identities are more active and politicized than English identity, but an **English identity** can become important in some contexts (such as sporting events).

## Age and identity

Age is an important source of identity for individuals but it is not usually a politicized identity. This is because people move through different age groups and know they will not stay in one group for ever. Also, the most disadvantaged groups are the young and the old, and they have little in common.

Some aspects of **youth culture** express a sense of conflict with adults and have helped age to become a more active identity. There are also some examples of age becoming a politicized identity, such as the coalition of youth groups that opposed the Criminal Justice Bill in the 1990s, and the activities of the Grey Panthers in America who have campaigned for the rights of the elderly.

## Conclusion

Bradley concludes that stratification systems and identities are becoming both polarized and fragmented.

- **Polarization** – there are increasing differences between the rich and poor and young and old. There is also some polarization between ethnic groups, particularly with the re-emergence of nationalist and fascist organizations.
- **Fragmentation** – there is fragmentation and division in each of the categories above. As a result, people in contemporary societies tend to have fractured identities. They lack an identity that overrides all others.

# TEST YOUR KNOWLEDGE AND UNDERSTANDING

1 Which one of the following definitions of culture is used by most sociologists?
a The sum total of all the arts and intellectual work in a society
b The whole way of life of a people
c A quality possessed by individuals who are particularly civilized
d A quality possessed by societies that are more civilized than others

2 Which term best describes the culture of ordinary people, particularly those living in traditional societies?
a Popular culture
b High culture
c Folk culture
d Subculture

3 Which perspective emphasizes the degree to which culture is shared?
a Functionalism
b Marxism
c Postmodernism
d Interactionism

4 Three of these statements would be supported by most postmodernists. Which is the odd one out?
a People shape and change their identities through shopping and other forms of consumption
b People have a great deal of choice about their identities
c People's identities are strongly shaped by their socialization
d People actively create their own identities

5 Three of these statements are reasons given by Strinati for the growth of postmodernism. Which is the odd one out?
a There is a growing gap between the wealthy and the poor
b The more affluent population has more leisure time and so the media become more important
c People are encouraged to consume the goods and services required for their favoured lifestyle
d People's identities are less based on class, local communities and religion. They are now more personal and constructed by the media

6 Three of these statements would be supported by most functionalists. Which is the odd one out?
a Cultural diversity is characteristic of all societies
b A shared culture is necessary for society to run smoothly
c Culture is passed on to children through socialization
d Culture is generally slow to change

7 Which one of the following statements best describes the CCCS's analysis of youth subcultures?
a Youth subcultures represent an attempt to win space from dominant cultures
b Youth subcultures represent the diversity of young people's experience in contemporary societies
c Youth subcultures are little more than delinquency
d Youth subcultures are simply part of ruling-class ideology

8 Which one of the following terms is used to describe the method of analysing symbols and signs used by Hebdige in his study of youth subcultures?
a Postmodernism
b Semiotics
c Neo-Marxism
d Content analysis

9 Three of the following are criticisms of mass culture theory. Which is the odd one out?
a The consumers of mass culture are not a passive mass of people
b It is possible to distinguish between mass culture and high culture
c It is not the case that all popular culture is homogeneous
d It is not possible to distinguish between a superior folk culture and an inferior mass culture

10 What sort of identities does Hall claim are characteristic of late-modern societies?
a Cultural identities
b Social identities
c Fractured identities
d National identities

11 What term do postmodernists use to describe theories that claim they have access to absolute knowledge about the world?
a Structuralism
b Metanarratives
c Social action theory
d Religions

12 Three of these statements are criticisms of postmodern theories of culture. Which is the odd one out?
a Postmodernists exaggerate the importance of the mass media
b People do not buy products just because of their label or image
c The majority of people can distinguish between art and popular culture
d Globalization is breaking down national boundaries

13 According to Hall, what has been the most significant factor in causing national identity to decline in importance?
a A decrease in the importance of social class
b Globalization
c English sports teams failing in recent years
d The influence of ethnic minorities

14 What term best describes mixing more than one identity to create a new one?
a Diversity
b Hybridization
c Globalization
d Ethnic minority

15 Which one of the following is a definition of Bradley's 'active identities'?
a Identities which have the potential to become important
b Identities which are used as the basis for organizing collective action
c Identities which have been created as a result of postmodernity
d Identities which individuals are conscious of and which provide a basis for their actions

## DEVELOP YOUR ANALYSIS AND EVALUATION SKILLS

### *Culture is shared by members of a society.*

*Background:* This view is a central characteristic of functionalist approaches. They believe that society is not possible without some sort of consensus over values. Marxists see this consensus as an illusion, providing a smokescreen for continuing class inequality and exploitation. Postmodernists emphasize the diversity of cultures and identities in contemporary Britain.

| *For* | *Against* |
|---|---|
| Functionalist approaches such as: | ■ Marx (p. 172) |
| ■ Durkheim (p. 172) | ■ Neo Marxist subcultural approaches (pp. 172–3) |
| ■ Parsons (p. 172) | ■ Postmodern approaches (pp. 174–6) |

*Top tip:* Culture has been defined in a number of ways (see p. 171) and a brief discussion of these differences will be useful. Examples of cultural diversity in Britain (see chapter 3, p. 35) will also assist evaluation.

### *Mass culture has a dangerous effect on society.*

*Background:* A definition of mass culture can be found on p. 173. Note its similarity to the term 'popular culture'. Negative views, such as those of Macdonald, were particularly popular during the 1950s when there was considerable concern about the impact of the mass media on society. Postmodernists tend to celebrate popular culture and deny any distinction between high and popular culture.

| *For* | *Against* |
|---|---|
| ■ Macdonald (p. 173) | ■ Strinati (pp. 173–4) |
| | ■ Postmodernism (p. 174) |

*Top tip:* Be careful to discuss the definition of 'mass culture'. Make sure you identify the views of those such as Macdonald as deriving from some time ago, although bear in mind that there is still concern about popular culture 'dumbing down' British culture.

### *Youth subcultures are ways of resisting dominant ideology.*

*Background:* A definition of subculture can be found on p. 171. The view here represents the starting point of analyses of youth subcultures by the Birmingham Centre for Contemporary Culture (see p. 172). Their work represents a neo-Marxist position.

| *For* | *Against* |
|---|---|
| ■ Jefferson on 'Teddyboys' (p. 172) | ■ Evaluation of neo-Marxist views (p. 173) |
| ■ Hebdidge on 'mods' (pp. 172–3) | ■ Evaluation of Hebdidge (p. 173) |
| ■ Gilroy (in chapter 6) (p. 84) | |

*Top tip:* Remember that most young people are not members of subcultures. Subcultural theory concentrates on very small groups of unrepresentative young people.

# AQA-STYLE CULTURE AND IDENTITY QUESTIONS (FROM A RANGE OF MODULES)

The AQA specification examines this area as a theme underlying all topics in sociology.
The questions that follow are taken from a variety of modules to show how the
information in this chapter can contribute to answers for the examination.

## Family and Households, AS Unit 1

**Comments on the question**

- Look at both sides and provide evidence where possible
- This is about a stage in the life cycle; it is not a question about socialization

[a] Examine the view that childhood is a social construction.

[20 marks]

**Advice on preparing your answer**

- This has a particular meaning, i.e. that 'childhood' means different things at different times and in different places
- Grossberg (p. 173) would be a useful starting point

## Mass Media, AS Unit 1

- You must look at both sides and come to a conclusion based on the evidence you use
- This is a problematic concept
- Do not repeat the question as an introduction; it is better to start by defining the key terms

[b] Evaluate the claim that the mass media have created a mass culture society. [20 marks]

- Marxist theories, p. 172
- Mass culture, pp. 173–4
- Critiques of this approach pp. 173–4
- Pluralist theory as an alternative, chapter 13, pp. 182
- The section on postmodernism (p. 174) needs to be used selectively for its focus on the mass media

## Crime and Deviance, A2 Unit 6 Synoptic Paper

- This term can mean a variety of things:
  1 Does it explain the cause?
  2 Does it explain the effect?
  3 Can it be operationalized?
  4 Is it valid?
  5 Is it reliable?
  6 What are its strengths?
  7 What are its weaknesses?
  8 Does it provide policy solutions?

[c] Assess the usefulness of the concept of subculture to an explanation of deviant groups. [40 marks]

- Choose the most appropriate issues from the list opposite to apply to this question
- The term is explained on p. 171
- Neo-Marxist studies (pp. 172–3) provide useful illustrative material
- Other relevant material is in chapter 6

## World Sociology, A2 Unit 4

- Make sure that you understand this term
- Use the three terms as the organizing principle for your answer
- You will have to do additional reading on this topic to enable you to answer this question fully

[c] 'Globalization has changed the cultural, political and economic relationships between societies.' Explain and discuss this statement. [40 marks]

- The cultural supermarket effect, hybrid identities (pp. 175–6) and popular culture (p. 171) can be applied to this part of the question
- National identities and politicized identities (pp. 38, 39 and 174–6) can be applied here
- Ideas of consumerism could be used as a starting point

# OCR-STYLE CULTURE AND IDENTITY QUESTION

## A2 Unit 2533: Culture and Socialization: Youth and Culture

**Answer both parts of the question**
Total: 45 marks, 1 mark = 1 minute
Time allowed: 45 minutes

**Comments on the question**

- Make sure that the examiner can see that you have clearly identified two characteristics
- No more, no less
- Make sure that you develop an explanation of why these two characteristics are unique to youth culture and not found in mainstream culture

**[a]** Identify and explain two characteristics of youth cultures that distinguish them from mainstream culture.

[15 marks]

**Advice on preparing your answer**

- You will find material on pp. 172–3 that will assist you in answering this question

- Describe the view as fully as possible, using supporting evidence
- Make sure that you consider arguments and evidence against the view and/or alternative view(s)
- Aim for balance –don't make the mistake of focusing on one theory or youth culture at the expense of others

**[b]** Outline and assess the view that deviant youth subcultures were formed in order to resist and shock dominant social groups.

[30 marks]

- Remember that this is only one view. You can challenge it if you want
- Information about deviant youth subcultures can be found on pp. 172–3
- Your introduction should briefly define concepts such as youth culture and dominant groups, and terms such as 'resist' and 'shock'
- Some criticisms can also be found here

## Specifications

| Specification | Specification details | | Coverage |
|---|---|---|---|
| **AQA** AS: Mass Media | | ■ Different explanations of the relationship between ownership and control of the mass media | Pluralist, Marxist and neo-Marxist theories are covered on pp. 182–3. |
| | | ■ Different explanations of the relationship between the mass media and ideology | The concept of ideology is explained in relation to the media in the sections on pluralist and Marxist theories (pp. 182–4). |
| | | ■ Different explanations of the processes of selection and presentation of media content | The theory of cultural hegemony is relevant here (p. 183). Also important are the organizational factors affecting the selection and presentation of media output (p. 184). |
| | | ■ The role of the mass media in representations of age, social class, ethnicity, gender, sexuality and disability | Media representations are discussed in the section on the role and influence of the media: images and social groups (pp. 185–8). |
| | | ■ Different explanations of the relationship between the mass media and their audiences | Covered in the section on the role and influence of the media: audiences and their responses (pp. 185–8). |
| **OCR** AS: Culture and Socialization/ Mass Media | **Media institutions** | ■ Trends in the ownership and control of the mass media | Discussed in the context of Marxist theories (pp. 182–3). |
| | | ■ The relationship between ownership, control and production: the influence of proprietors and professionals | The influence of proprietors is covered on pp. 182–3, professionals on p. 184. |
| | | ■ Ownership and trends in production and consumption (eg internet, cable TV); the implications for state regulation | Trends in consumption described on pp. 185–8, ownership on pp. 182–3. |
| | **Content and representation in the mass media** | ■ The role of media professionals in constructing the news and moral panics | See the section on organizational factors (p. 184). |
| | | ■ Media stereotypes; gender, ethnicity and class | Media representations of gender, ethnicity and class are discussed on pp. 185–7. |
| | | ■ Theories of media content e.g. pluralism, Marxism and postmodernism | Pluralist and Marxist theories are discussed on pp. 182–3, postmodernism and the media on p. 185. |
| | **The effects of the mass media** | ■ The effects of the mass media on audiences | Media effects are covered in the section on the role and influence of the media: audience responses (pp. 184–5). |
| | | ■ Media effects and the implications for censorship | The idea that the media may have damaging and dangerous effects is linked to the 'hypodermic syringe model'. Alternative views are presented on pp. 184–5. |
| | | ■ Mass communications and globalization | Increasingly global patterns of ownership are discussed on pp. 182–3. Globalization is discussed in the context of postmodernism on p. 185. |

For more detailed specification guidance visit **www.haralambosholborn.com**

# INTRODUCTION: UNDERSTANDING THE 'MASS MEDIA'

It is possible to distinguish between:

1 The **mass media** where a message is conveyed from one point to a large number of other points.
2 **Interactive media** where some limited communications back from the points receiving the messages is possible.
3 **Interpersonal media** where messages are conveyed between single points, e.g. text messaging between individuals.
4 **Network media** where messages can be conveyed in any direction.

**New Media** refers to media utilising ICT (information and communications technology) such as the internet and digital multi-channel TV. New media are spreading rapidly, e.g. in 2003 43% of people in the UK had internet access.

Although the mass media communicate the same message to large numbers of people it should not be assumed that the message is always **interpreted** in the same way by all those receiving it.

■ The audience should not necessarily be seen as one 'mass'. Audiences vary – e.g. according to **class**, **gender**, **ethnicity** and **region**.
■ **Postmodernists** emphasize that media messages are **polysemic** – they can be interpreted in very different ways by different individuals.

# ROLE AND INFLUENCE OF THE MEDIA: STRUCTURE AND CONTENT

## Pluralist theories

Pluralists are sympathetic to the media and see them as acting in a responsible way and reflecting the wishes and interests of their audiences.

■ To pluralists, society consists of many different groups with **diverse interests**.
■ Each group has roughly equal **access to power**.
■ The mass media reflect this **diversity** in what they cover.
■ The media operate in the **public interest**.
■ The media follow **public opinion** rather than shape it.

### An illustration

In their book *Personal Influence*, **Katz and Lazarsfeld** (1955) studied the media's influence on political opinion in the USA in the 1940s. They found that:

■ People had different amounts of **exposure** to the media.
■ Different media had different **degrees of influence** (TV could be more powerful than newspapers when using images).
■ The **content** of the messages determined whether they had much effect.

■ People tended to accept messages that supported **existing prejudices** and reject those that contradicted them.
■ Messages were mediated by **opinion leaders** and did not directly influence people's attitudes or how they voted.

There are a number of criticisms of pluralism:

1 **Philo** (1986) argues that pluralism may be an **ideological justification** for the media, put forward by those who work in the media industry.
2 **Blumler and Gurevitch** (1995) argue that journalists and politicians have a shared culture. Under the **lobby system**, journalists rely on politicians for information and will tend to present the politicians' view of the world.
3 The pluralist model assumes that the content of the media is diverse, rather than providing evidence that it is.
4 The 2003 attack on Iraq shows that diverse viewpoints are not always available. Around 500 journalists were **embedded** with coalition troops making it difficult to report impartially.

## Marxist theories

■ Marxists see the **ownership or control** of the media by a capitalist ruling class as the key to understanding the mass media.
■ The media transmit the ideas of the **ruling class**.
■ The ruling class use the media to promote their products, to make a **profit** and to persuade people to accept the capitalist system.
■ The ruling class largely own the **means of production** (e.g. TV stations, newspapers, publishers), and huge corporations dominate the media. There is evidence of increased **monopolization**, as a few big companies such as News Corporation gain domination of the media market. This can be achieved through:
1 **Levels of expenditure**: which ensure that only the biggest corporations can produce blockbuster films such as *Titanic* and **economies of scale** which means that vast amounts of merchandise can be produced at low cost.
2 **Synergy**: in which a single product such as a film can be used as the basis for other media products (e.g. computer games and soundtracks).
3 **Branding**: in which financial muscle is used to market branded products to make them appeal to consumers.
4 **Globalization**: this involves selling products worldwide, e.g. Rupert Murdoch claims his News Corporation satellite and TV channels reach three quarters of the world's population.

There are four major trends in media ownership in recent decades.

1 **Concentration** – According to Bagdikian (1997), the US media were controlled by 50 corporations in the 1980s,

but just 10 in 1997. In 2000 Time Warner and the internet company America Online (AOL) merged, creating an enormous media corporation.

2 **Growth** – Big media companies are constantly taking over smaller ones to grow. In 1998 America Online (AOL) took over Netscape and in 2000 bought Time Warner.

3 **Integration** – Different parts of the media have become united in single companies. For example Viacom is involved in television, publishing, video and the internet.

4 **Globalization** – Viacom owns many local companies such as MTV India, MTV Southeast Asia and MTV Nordic to distribute its products throughout the world.

To most Marxists the **logic of capitalism** dictates the content and effects of the mass media.

■ The poor and powerless have little money to spend buying media products so their interests are largely ignored.

■ Poor consumers bring in little **advertising revenue**.

■ **Bagdikian** (1997) argues that news that is of interest to capitalists (e.g. stock market news) gets plenty of coverage. Negative news about capitalism (e.g. the living standards of the poor) gets little coverage.

Another strand of Marxism emphasizes **direct interference** in the content of the media by owners. For example, editors of newspapers owned by Rupert Murdoch have told stories of him ringing up to direct the content of the front page.

## Criticisms

Marxist perspectives have been criticized:

1 They may underestimate the importance of **state regulation** – e.g. of the BBC.

2 To pluralists, the media must respond to **audience preferences** if they are to survive. Capitalists need to serve audiences to make a profit.

3 **Anti-establishment programmes** do get made – e.g. *The Simpsons* with its negative portrayal of family life.

4 **Postmodernists** deny that power is concentrated in the hands of the rich.

5 The public can use the media to oppose the policies of giant corporations (e.g. public media pressure persuaded Shell not to dump the Brent Spar oil rig at sea).

## Neo-Marxist theories: cultural hegemony

Neo-Marxist approaches put less emphasis than Marxism on direct control by capitalists, or the way in which the logic of capitalist competition shapes the media.

They argue that it is the dominance of ruling-class culture (**cultural hegemony**) that shapes the media.

There are competing views within the media, but **ruling-class ideology** becomes the main influence on how people understand and make sense of the social world.

### Hall and cultural hegemony

Stuart Hall (1995) argues that the way in which the media classify the world assumes a **basic consensus** about how the world works, and this dominant view is taken for granted.

For example, the media assume that wage demands cause inflation (rather than, say, profiteering by companies).

There is no conspiracy to manipulate the meanings of the media, simply a widespread acceptance of certain ways of seeing the world.

### Discourse analysis

**Discourse analysis** examines the connections between power and how certain ways of thinking about certain types of event come to be accepted.

For example, **Norman Fairclough** (1995) argues that the television programme *Crimewatch* operates to **legitimate** the role of the police and to encourage the public to believe that they can work with the police in combating crime. It contradicts images of the police as corrupt, inept, etc.

However, discourse analysis represents only one person's analysis; other viewers might 'read' the message of *Crimewatch* differently.

## The Glasgow Media Group and cultural hegemony

The Glasgow Media Group has done a variety of research supporting the **cultural hegemony model**.

It argues that **connotative codes** (which evoke attitudes and emotions) are used. For example, in industrial disputes, **negative words** (such as 'threat' and 'demand') are used to describe strikers, while more positive words (such as 'offer') are used to describe management. This evokes sympathy for managers and hostility towards strikers.

■ Certain **visual angles** (e.g. filming from behind police lines in picket-line clashes) encourage identification with the police viewpoint.

■ Media professionals **set the agenda** for news stories and take a pro-establishment stance (e.g. looking at effects rather than causes of strikes).

■ 'Extremist' political views are treated unsympathetically.

Recent work by the Glasgow Media Group accepts that cultural hegemony is not complete.

■ Some **journalists** (e.g. Jonathan Dimbleby) challenge establishment views.

■ Audience research shows that audiences do not always believe media messages.

■ There is an element of **interaction** between broadcasters and audiences, and audience reaction can change the views and actions of programme makers (as well as broadcasters influencing audiences). Audiences are not just passive. This process is called a **circuit of communication**. In the circuit of communication, production, content and the reception of messages all influence each other.

## Organizational factors

Media professions and organizations may have a direct effect on media content.

**Galtung and Ruge** (1965) identify criteria that journalists are taught to value in stories. These are:

- **Frequency** (short-lived events are preferred).
- **Threshold** (more intense events are preferred).
- **Unambiguity** (especially events that fit into an established story type).
- **Meaningfulness** (relevance to the audience).
- **Unexpectedness** (unexpected events are preferred).
- **Elite nations** in the story are preferred.
- **Elite individuals** in the story are preferred.
- Reference to **individuals** makes a story more newsworthy.
- **Bad news** is more newsworthy than good news.

**Boyd-Barrett** (1995) criticizes Galtung and Ruge, pointing out that they fail to explain where journalistic values come from, and they ignore structural factors and cultural hegemony (see above).

**Grossberg** *et al.* (1998) identify **production processes** as important (e.g. using official sources such as the police for information and comment). The use of such sources biases media content towards powerful social groups.

## ROLE AND INFLUENCE OF THE MEDIA: AUDIENCES AND THEIR RESPONSES

## 1 *The hypodermic model*

The hypodermic model assumes that media messages are directly **injected** into audiences as if by a syringe. The media can act like a drug or narcotic, directly changing behaviour.

This process was demonstrated by **Bandura, Ross and Ross** (1963), who conducted psychological experiments which showed that boys would imitate aggression in films they had watched (**social learning theory**).

The hypodermic model has been criticized because:

1 **Audiences** are very diverse and react in different ways.
2 **Long-term effects** may differ from short-term ones.
3 It ignores the different **uses** audiences make of the media – e.g. TV programmes may only be used as background noise.
4 It ignores other media effects – e.g. watching violent films as an **outlet** for aggression rather than a cause of it.

Nevertheless many politicians and other commentators are still influenced by the hypodermic model

## 2 *The two-step flow model*

**Merton** (1946) and **Katz and Lazarsfeld** (1955) argued that media effects may not be direct, but that messages are interpreted by key individuals who then influence others.

- Step 1 – the media message reaches the audience.

- Step 2 – the message is interpreted by the audience and it influences them.

**Social interaction** is an important element of step 2. **Opinion leaders** interpret messages for others and shape what influence the messages might have.

A study by **Livingstone and Bovill** (2001) supported the two-step flow model analysing media use by children and young people. **Peer groups** spent large amounts of time discussing media (especially TV) and this influenced the way that programmes were interpreted.

**The multi-step flow model** refines the two-step flow model by recognizing that there may be several stages in the interpretation of media messages. For example, **Dorothy Hobson** (1990) shows how discussions about soap operas at work may change people's interpretation of them.

The two-step flow model has been **criticized**.

It is argued that there may be no dominant opinion leaders or **consensus** about the meaning of media messages and it ignores the possibility that the meaning of media messages might be **imposed by the powerful**.

## 3 *The uses and gratifications model*

This model is based on the idea that people use the media in a variety of ways. **McQuail** (1972) suggests four possible uses:

1 **Diversion or escape**.
2 **Personal relationships** (e.g. feeling part of a soap opera community).
3 **Personal identity** (confirming or weakening the sense of who we are by using certain media messages).
4 **Surveillance** (finding out what is going on).

The uses made of the media may vary according to **age**, **gender**, etc.

This model has been **criticized**:

1 It fails to explain why people use the media in different ways.
2 It ignores the possibility that the media can create people's needs.
3 It focuses on individuals rather than social, cultural and structural factors.

## 4 *The interpretative model*

In the interpretative model, the audience filters messages, ignoring, rejecting, accepting or reinterpreting them.

**Fiske** (1988) uses the idea of **intertexuality** – relating different texts/contexts to one another, e.g. relating soap operas to your own life or relating interviews with actors to performance in a film.

Audience members can move between different levels of involvement in watching TV: **engagement**, **detachment** and **referential** (relating events to one's own experiences).

Buckingham (1993) uses the idea of **media literacy**. Degree of knowledge and understanding of the media affects the depth of people's interpretation of the media. The more sophisticated viewers can understand the codes or rhetoric of TV language and the meanings that can be inferred from the way programmes are produced.

There are **criticisms** of the interpretative model:

1 It may underestimate the power of media messages and how strongly they can be reinforced.
2 It is an **individualistic** approach, which neglects the role of subcultures in shaping interpretations.

## 5 *The structured interpretation model*

This model argues that audiences do interpret the meaning of the media, but there is a **preferred reading**, influenced by the way in which the message is encoded. However, researchers need to be aware that different subcultures (class, gender, ethnicity, age, religion, etc.) will tend to interpret the messages in different ways.

For example, **David Morley** (1980) showed how the audience of *Nationwide* interpreted a story differently:

■ **Trade unionists** saw it as biased towards management.
■ **Managers** accepted the news coverage as unbiased.
■ **Middle-class students** saw the programme as superficial.
■ **Black, mainly working-class students** saw it as boring.

Thus the media can be read/interpreted in many different ways (they are **polysemic**). Different groups bring different languages, concepts and assumptions to interpreting messages.

There are a number of **criticisms** of this approach.

Some sociologists (e.g. **postmodernists**) deny that social groups have such a strong influence on interpretations of the media.

## 6 *Audience reception and postmodernity*

Postmodernists adopt views that question the idea of 'the audience' as conceived in other approaches.

**Baudrillard** (1988) argues that **media-saturated societies** have produced **hyperreality**, in which objectivity breaks down and images can be interpreted in many ways, even by the same people at different times.

**Turkle** (1996) sees TV as part of the postmodern culture of **simulation** – we identify more with the fictional life of TV than we do with real life.

■ We treat media messages as if they were real – e.g. real Cheers bars have opened.
■ The distinction between image and reality breaks down. People no longer search for the real meaning of media messages but use media images in the playful creation of different **identities**.
■ The media become part of **lifestyle** rather than conveyors of information.

Critics have attacked postmodernism:

1 **Webster** (1999) argues that:
   ■ The **social context** still influences the way in which the mass media are used and interpreted.
   ■ You still need to look at who creates the media information and for what purposes (as **Marxists**, for example, would argue).
2 **Lerner** (1994) argues that postmodernism obscures **inequality** and prevents attempts to improve the world.

## ROLE AND INFLUENCE OF THE MEDIA: IMAGES AND SOCIAL GROUPS

Media messages can be seen as passing through four stages:

1 Formulation
2 Message content – the 'text'
3 Audience reception
4 Effects of message

These stages can be applied to different social groups.

### *Gender*

#### Formulation

Most media workers are women, but **Croteau and Hoynes** (2001) found that in the USA in the mid-1990s women made up only 6% of top newspaper managers and wrote 20% of TV news reports.

**Radical feminists** argue that **patriarchal domination** means that male perceptions of women dominate the media. 'Women's issues' – e.g. sexual harassment, police attitudes to rape, problems of childcare – get little attention.

#### Message content

Generally males outnumber females in all TV programme types – e.g. there is a ratio of seven males to three females in some soaps, there are few women in cartoons and there are three all-male ads for every one all-female ad.

However, the portrayal of women is changing e.g. The role of *Buffy the Vampire Slayer* is quite different to roles in earlier decades and in Bond films women have become increasingly strong and resourceful. But:

■ Old films and TV programmes with stereotypical female and male roles are recycled on cable and satellite.
■ Different parts of the media tend to portray gender in different ways. **Provenzo** (1991) found that computer games normally portray women as passive, young and attractive, whereas men are 'macho'.
■ News presenters are more likely to be female than in the past, but they are generally young and attractive and **Ross** (2002) argues that they are used to make news more human and watchable. 'Fanciable' news readers are used as **sex objects** despite the seriousness of the news.

- **Gauntlett** (2002) found that women's magazines still emphasize personal beauty and sex, while men's lifestyle magazines such as *FHM* and *Maxim* reassert traditional masculine values.
- **ICT**-based new media offer a vast range of representations of men and women, but women tend to be portrayed as sex objects in the widely available **pornography**.

## Audience reception

Recent **radical feminists** argue that women are active interpreters of messages, and they may reject stereotypical and **patriarchal messages**.

- **Ang** (1985) argues that women may get pleasure from soap operas like Dallas and are not just the passive victims of stereotyping.
- **Skirrow** (1986) uses the concept of **gender valence** – the relationship between gender identities and technology. Women reject video games because they are part of a technology associated with male power.
- **Turkle** (1988) argues that women reject computers because they do not want a close relationship with a machine.
- **Livingstone and Bovill** (2001) found girls are more likely to read books than boys who are more likely to have computers in their bedrooms. Games consoles are very important in boys' culture although there is evidence that differences between the sexes are decreasing
- **Gray** (1987) argues that telephones are a more female technology because they allow human contact.
- **Lewis** (1990) argues that music videos have a male gender valence because they are based on male adolescence – rebelliousness, sexual promiscuity and female conquest. However, girl bands, which encourage female friendship and solidarity, may be changing this.
- The **postmodernist Hermes** (1995) argues that some women find women's magazines educative and relaxing. She stresses that the way in which these magazines are used by women can change.

(See also the discussion of class and audience reception, below.)

## Media effects

To those using the **hypodermic model** (e.g. Provenzo), the media socialize women to be dependent and men to be dominant.

- **Frueh and McGhee** (in Tuchman, 1978) claimed that heavy TV viewing amongst US children correlated with traditional **sex-role stereotyping**.
- **Beuf** (1974) argues that children model themselves on **TV role models**, and this leads many girls to abandon their ambitions before they reach the age of 6. The media also make females concerned about their body image and the need to get and keep a man.
- To **socialist feminists**, such as Kath **Davies** (1987), the media encourage women to accept **patriarchal capitalism**.

- Angela **McRobbie** (1991) uses a **cultural hegemony** approach, suggesting that an interest in make-up and appearance becomes taken for granted in girls' magazines.
- **Liberal feminists** find evidence of **sex-role stereotyping** in the media and then assume that it influences behaviour. However, Gaye **Tuchman** (1978) accepts that images may change with time, although media images tend to lag behind changes in society.

## *Ethnicity*

### Formulation

Although there are many black and Asian television presenters in the UK, there are few people from ethnic minorities in senior management positions.

### Message content

Representations of ethnicity are varied. Some are very sympathetic to ethnic minority worldviews (e.g. Asian TV programmes and films), and some 'white establishment' programmes are quite sympathetic.

However, there is also evidence of **stereotyping**.

- Tabloid newspapers tend to portray ethnic minorities as a **threat**.
- TV tends to portray ethnic minorities in a **restricted range of roles**. The Broadcasting Standards Commission (1999) has found that black people tend to be portrayed in arts, media, entertainment, health and caring, sports and police roles, and Asians in arts, media, entertainment, health and caring and student roles. There are few portrayals of minorities in roles such as legal professionals.
- **Sarita Malik** (2002) believes there is a **racialized regime of representation** within which black people are portrayed as having different experiences from other groups. 'Whiteness' is portrayed as the norm.
- Newer studies emphasize the beliefs media messages appeal to, rather than relying simply on content analysis. **Cottle** (2000) suggests that coverage of ethnic minorities that emphasizes **multiculturalism** reinforces stereotypes of ethnic minorities as the 'other'.

### Audience reception

Research suggests that the interpretation of representations of ethnicity can be quite varied. The **Broadcasting Standards Commission** (Fletcher, 2003) found that some saw representation of ethnic minorities as **stereotypical** or **tokenistic** while others saw it as positive.

**Karen Ross** (2000) used focus groups of people from different ethnic minority groups. She found that they believed that the media portrayed individual ethnic groups in a rather stereotypical way. Each group was portrayed as **homogeneous**. For example, 'blackness' was emphasized more than differences between individual black people.

**Gillespie** (1995) studied 14–18-year-old Punjabis in Southall, London.

- They used the media to define their own ethnicity, comparing themselves to characters in Indian 'soaps' such as the *Mahabharata* and non-Asian soaps such as *Neighbours*.
- They reflect on cultural differences between themselves and others, and dream of aspects of American culture, but recognize that their culture is different.
- They develop a hybrid national and cultural identity, combining elements of Islam and Westernization.
- This leads to some critical evaluation of their parents' culture.

## Media effects

- Van Dijk (1991) argues that newspapers have a major impact in developing a perception of immigration as a problem. He uses a hypodermic model, arguing that this perception may lead to racist attacks etc.
- Hartmann and Husband (1974) studied the impact of media messages in different areas. In areas with a large Asian population (e.g. the West Midlands), race relations were seen as less of a threat than in areas with few Asians (e.g. Glasgow).

Factors such as class and gender also influence the degree to which media reporting of ethnicity will affect the audience.

## *Class*

### Formulation

Most people in senior positions in the media are of middle-class origin.

### Message content

Glennon and Butsch (1982) studied class lifestyles in family contexts on US TV and found that:

- Working-class families are under-represented.
- Two-thirds of programmes had managers or proprietors as heads of household.
- Only 4% had blue-collar heads of household.
- Middle-class parents are usually portrayed as good at dealing with problems.
- Working-class fathers are often portrayed as figures of fun.

The Glasgow Media Group (see p. 183) have found that the working class are often associated with 'trouble'.

### Audience reception

Ann Gray (1992) conducted a study of women from different classes and their use of TV and video.

- Lower social classes both used and accepted TV and video more than higher classes.
- Higher classes were more anxious about children using TV.
- Context (i.e. who you watched TV with) was important to viewing.

- Men enjoyed current affairs, documentaries and sport more than women.
- Men tended to control viewing more than women.
- In the highest classes, both men and women valued 'quality' 'classics' and disliked 'popular' 'trash' genres.
- In lower classes, women liked 'soppy', 'fantasy' and 'soft' genres; men preferred 'hard', 'tough' and 'factual' genres.
- In all classes, men preferred 'heroic', 'public', 'societal' and 'physical' programmes; women preferred 'romantic', 'domestic', 'familial' and 'emotional' programmes.

## *Age*

### Formulation

Media workers in senior positions tend to be older than those in junior ones.

### Message content

- According to Pearson (1983), adolescents have long been portrayed as a problem by the media. There has been a long-standing myth of a golden age when youth was less troublesome (usually twenty years previously), but there have always been problem groups of youths (Victorian hooligans, Teds in the 1950s, Travellers today).
- Amongst older age groups, Sontag (1978) finds a double standard: women have to match up to a youthful ideal, men do not.
- Lambert *et al.* (1984) found that on British TV people over the age of 60 did appear – usually portrayed as politicians, business people, experts, etc. – but they were almost exclusively men.
- Biggs (1993) found that soap operas were dominated by middle-aged/older people. Sit-coms tended to present stereotypes of the old as enfeebled, forgetful or cantankerous. Biggs found that although there was little concern on TV about the problems of age, some more positive images of the elderly were coming through.
- Signorelli (1989) analysed 14,000 US TV characters and found that the very young and the very old were under-represented. Older characters were less likely to be represented as 'good' but also less likely to be involved in violence.
- There is some favourable treatment of older people. Dail (1988) claims that they often have a positive image in soap operas; and Featherstone and Hepworth (1995) show how, in a growing market, magazines like *Retirement Choice* generally present more positive images.

### Audience reception

Gunter and McAleer (1997) found that the young (aged 4–24) watch less TV (2.8 hours per day) than older people.

- Those with access to more media watched less TV, and TV did not seem to displace other activities.
- For older viewers, TV was a comfort and company; and for those who did not get out much it offered 'virtual mobility'.

David **Buckingham** (1993) has examined whether children are less **media literate** and more 'taken in' by media messages than adults.

- He found that most children were aware of the purpose of advertising. They were sometimes critical of the quality of what was being sold and cynical about 'free' gifts.
- Some were '**wise consumers**', trying out advertised toys before purchase. Less of a hypodermic effect and more of a **uses and gratifications** effect was found – e.g. they used adverts to generate lists of requests for Christmas presents, but were realistic about what parents could afford.

Buckingham found children to be active interpreters but he also notes that:

- They were enthusiastic about watching adverts.
- They did not always view adverts critically.
- The interviews may not have revealed the extent to which children accepted adverts.

## Media effects

- **Hebdige** (1988) argues that the media structure the way in which the young perceive society. Youth subcultures are based partly on these perceptions but also on the reality of situations. Hebdige, as a **neo-Marxist**, sees the media as absorbing and neutralizing rebellious youth subcultures – e.g. by marketing **signs** of **youth culture** as mass-market products.
- **Gillespie** (see pp. 186–7), as a **postmodernist**, sees youth as more empowered.

## *Disability*

### Formulation

Few senior people in the media are disabled.

## Message content

The **Broadcasting Standards Commission** (1999) found that:

- Disabled people appeared in 7% of TV programmes but only accounted for 0.7% of all those who spoke.
- There were three disabled males to every disabled female.
- Only one in ten were both ethnic minority members and disabled.

**Longmore** (1987) found that disabled people/disability were commonly portrayed in the following ways:

- as an emblem of **evil**
- as **monsters**
- as the loss of one's humanity
- as compensated for by **substitute gifts** (e.g. the blind having special powers)
- as leading to **courage** or achievement against the odds
- as a **sexual menace**

**Cumberbatch and Negrine** (1992) suggest that the disabled are often seen as the objects of **pity** or charity, but rarely as a normal part of life. Disability is normally portrayed as their key characteristic.

## Audience reception

**Cumberbatch and Negrine** found that people with disabilities, or those in close contact with disabled people, were less likely to accept media portrayal of disability.

## Media effects

**Cumberbatch and Negrine** found that for those without close contact with disabled people, disability is seen as a **problem**. This may make it difficult for disabled people to be integrated into everyday life. However, Cumberbatch and Negrine conclude that more than changes in media coverage are needed to improve the lot of the disabled.

# TEST YOUR KNOWLEDGE AND UNDERSTANDING

1 **Which two of the following statements would be supported by pluralists?**
   a The media act in the public interest
   b The media tend to produce stereotypical views of women
   c The media tend to have a conservative bias
   d Fairness and balance are important features of the media

2 **Which one of these statements could not be used as a criticism of pluralist theory?**
   a Pluralists fail to take account of the fact that consumers have choice in the media output they consume
   b Pluralists ignore the influence of owners on the content of the media
   c Pluralists fail to take account of how the lobby system shapes the content of the media
   d Pluralism ignores the possibility that the state can shape the content of the media

3 **From a Marxist point of view, the mass media can best be described as part of:**
   a The economic base
   b The superstructure
   c The means of production
   d Humanity's species being

4 **Which one of these statements best describes the neo-Marxist views of Stuart Hall?**
   a The media never include anti-establishment views
   b The media tend to assume a basic consensus in society
   c The media are shaped by a conspiracy against the working class
   d The media are fair and balanced

5 **The group that developed the cultural hegemony model is the:**
   a Edinburgh Media Group
   b The Aberdeen Media Group
   c The Dundee Media Group
   d The Glasgow Media Group

6 **Which one of these is not a reason why cultural hegemony is never complete?**
   a Audiences do not always believe media messages
   b Some journalists attack establishment views
   c Audiences have some influence on programme makers
   d The variety of messages conveyed by the media is always strictly limited

7 **The idea that the media directly shape the behaviour of the audience is called:**
   a The hypothetical model
   b The hypodermic model
   c The injection model
   d The drug model

8 **In the two-step flow model, which one of the following intervenes between the audience and the interpretation of the message?**
   a Opinion leaders
   b Gate-keepers
   c Audience preconceptions
   d Editors

9 **The interpretative model can be criticized for which one of the following reasons?**
   a It neglects the influence of membership of social groups on the audience
   b It exaggerates the power of the media
   c It puts too little emphasis on the differences between the ways in which individuals 'read' the media
   d It assumes that people copy what they see in the media

10 **Which two of the following are findings from the research of Livingstone and Bovill?**
   a Girls spend more time reading than boys
   b Games consoles are very important in boys' culture
   c There is no significant difference in the reading habits of bioys and girls
   d Girls now use computers as much as boys

11 **According to postmodernists, media messages are increasingly used:**
   a To access information
   b To create identities
   c To strengthen political ideologies
   d To help people make rational choices

12 **An example of gender valence is:**
   a Women watching soap operas because they are interested in family life
   b Few women using video games because the technology is seen as masculine
   c Women discussing media programmes with other women
   d Women arguing with men over the content of the media

13 **According to the Broadcasting Standards Commission, which one of these is not a role in which ethnic minority groups are frequently seen in the media?**
   a Legal professional
   b Sportsperson
   c Entertainer
   d Worker in the health and caring professions

14 **According to Gillespie, young Asians use the media in a way that:**
   a Encourages them to reject Asian culture and identity
   b Encourages them to accept Asian culture and identity
   c Encourages them to develop a hybrid culture and identity
   d Has no effect on their culture and identity

15 **According to Karen Ross:**
   a Ethnic groups tend to be portrayed as being homogeneous
   b There is now over-representation of ethnic groups on television
   c The media emphasizes the differences within each ethnic groups
   d Ethnic groups are portrayed accurately in the mass media

## DEVELOP YOUR ANALYSIS AND EVALUATION SKILLS

### The mass media are dominated by capitalist interests.

***Background:*** This statement reflects Marxist views on the media. Some versions of Marxism see direct interference by media moguls as crucial, while others stress the logic of capitalism more, but both would agree with this statement. Neo-Marxist theorists of cultural hegemony largely agree, but would qualify the statement, arguing that capitalist domination is not complete. Pluralists disagree with the statement, arguing that the media reflect the interests and wishes of audiences rather than those of capitalists and some sociologists believe that organizational factors influence the media more than capitalism.

| *Yes* | *No* |
|---|---|
| ■ Conventional Marxism (p. 182)<br>■ Logic of capitalism Marxism (p. 183)<br>■ Neo-Marxism (p. 183) | ■ Pluralism (p. 182)<br>■ Organisational factors (p. 184) |

***Top tip:*** Postmodernists (p. 185) also strongly disagree with this statement arguing that the media are an integral part of society and peoples' lifestyle and they deny that Marxism can explain the role or content of the media.

### The portrayal of disadvantaged groups in the media is no longer stereotypical.

***Background:*** You can discuss such groups as women, ethnic minorities, the young, the old, the disabled and the working class. Much of the evidence does suggest that there has been a change in media portrayal away from crude stereotypes, but if you look carefully some stereotyping is still present. Some of the findings are contradictory and it may be difficult to reach a single conclusion about all groups in every part of the media. The following are examples of studies supporting the different viewpoints and other studies could be included as well.

| *Yes* | *No* |
|---|---|
| ■ Gauntlett (p. 186)<br>■ Broadcasting Standards Commission (p. 186)<br>■ Longmore (p. 188)<br>■ Glennon and Butsch (p. 187) | ■ Examples of non-stereotypical female roles (pp. 185–6)<br>■ Dail (p. 187)<br>■ Featherstone and Hepworth (p. 187) |

***Top tip:*** Gillespie's study (pp. 186–7) suggests that there are now quite diverse portrayals of ethnic minorities which are interpreted in a variety of ways.

### The mass media have little effect on society because the audience interprets the messages in very different ways.

***Background:*** This statement supports the view that interpretations of the media are polysemic. It is certainly supported by postmodernists and to a certain extent by the interpretative, structured interpretation, uses and gratifications and two-step flow approaches. All of these believe that any effects of the media are indirect and mediated by individual and social interpretations of messages. The hypodermic model sees the effects of the media and gives little thought to the possibility of different interpretations. This is largely discredited but the hegemonic model suggests that certain types of message are so dominant in the media that these viewpoints come to dominate others.

| *Yes* | *No* |
|---|---|
| ■ Two-step flow model (p. 184)<br>■ Postmodernism (p. 185)<br>■ Interpretative model (p. 184)<br>■ Structured interpretation approach (p. 185)<br>■ Uses and gratifications approach (p. 184) | ■ Hypodermic model (p. 184)<br>■ Neo-Marxism and cultural hegemony (p. 183) |

***Top tip:*** The sections on audience reception for different minority groups are useful for discussing this issue.

# AQA-STYLE MASS MEDIA QUESTION

## AS Unit 1

**Answer all parts of this question**

Total: 60 marks
1 mark = 1.25 minutes

Time allowed:
1 hour 15 minutes

### ITEM A

We found that television and press reporting of mental illness often focused on violent incidents. People who worked in the area of mental health tended to discount this media view, yet we found some cases where the fear generated by media accounts overwhelmed direct experience. One young woman was afraid of her non-violent elderly patients because of what she had seen on television.

Source: adapted from Greg Philo, 'Media effects and the active audience', *Sociology Review*, vol. 10, no. 3, February 2001

### ITEM B

When strikes are reported, although both sides are usually presented, a system of agenda setting and gatekeeping tends to ensure that the views of the owners and managers are heard more clearly than those of the strikers. Thus cultural hegemony is maintained.

---

**Comments on the question**

- Only 2 marks so keep this brief
- This provides the context in which to locate your answer

**[a] Explain what is meant by cultural hegemony.**

[Item B, line 5] [2 marks]

**Advice on preparing your answer**

- See p. 183 for help if you do not understand this term

---

- No more, no less
- Only look at journalists, not other media personnel
- See p. 842 of the textbook for a definition

**[b] Suggest two ways in which journalists might act as gatekeepers.**

[Item B, line 3] [4 marks]

- Some of the criteria listed on p. 184 may help you to answer this

---

- This requires only a list; you are not required to discuss them
- Only do what you are asked to do
- Item A can be interpreted to give one way

**[c] Identify three ways in which people might be influenced by the output of the mass media.**

[6 marks]

- A selection from the following could be used:
  1 Stereotyping of ethnic minorities, p. 186
  2 Labelling of women, pp. 185–6
  3 Advertising
  4 Behaviour changing/social learning theory, p. 184

- To demonstrate both skills you will need more than a list
- It means what it says, so only do two
- Only look at owners, not other media personnel

**[d]** Identify and briefly describe two criticisms of the view that the owners of the mass media control its output.

[8 marks]

- The most obvious criticisms come from pluralists (p. 182) and postmodernists (p. 183)

- This means look at both sides of the argument
- The best answers might distinguish between these two processes
- Make sure that you know what these are – remember your culture and identity core theme

**[e]** Assess the view that the mass media create and perpetuate stereotypes. [20 marks]

- The section on gender, age and ethnicity (pp. 185–7) will be useful here
- Look for empirical evidence to back up your arguments
- You might use these processes to help you reach a conclusion; e.g. 'the media perpetuate but do not create the stereotypes'

- This means you need to look at arguments against the theory as well as at evidence that supports it
- How far does it explain all or any aspects of the media's influence?
- This is the focus of the question. Make sure that you apply your material to this issue

**[f]** Using material from the items and elsewhere, examine the usefulness of the uses and gratifications model as an explanation of the influence of the mass media on the audience. [20 marks]

- See p. 184 for an account of this model
- Criticisms are offered on p. 184
- Alternative explanations can be found on pp. 184–5. These need to be used selectively and applied to the focus in a critical way

## OCR-STYLE COMMUNICATION AND THE MEDIA QUESTION

### AS Unit 2533: Culture and Socialization

**Answer both parts of this question**
Total: 45 marks, 1 mark = 1 minute
Time allowed: 45 minutes

### Comments on the question

- Identify – do this clearly so that the examiner can see two points
- No more, no less
- Explain with reference to empirical studies, or illustrate with conceptual examples
- Resist the temptation to be assertive or commonsensical

**[a]** Identify and explain two ways in which mass media representations of ethnic minorities may affect audiences.

[15 marks]

### Advice on preparing your answer

The section on ethnicity (pp. 186–7) will be useful here
- The way the media report on particular social groups
- If possible, be specific about ethnic minority groups
- Think about behaviour or attitudes

---

- This means describe the argument in the question
- This means look at the critique of this view and if possible consider alternative points of view
- This is the focus of the question – make sure that you apply your material (e.g. empirical studies, evidence, etc.) to it
- Begin by outlining and discussing this particular theory

**[b]** Outline and assess the view that the relationship between the media and the audience is more complex than that indicated by the hypodermic syringe model of media effects [30 marks]

- See p. 184 for an account of this model
- A critique is offered on p. 184
- A selection of other models and empirical studies could be used. Choose three or four from:
  1 Two-step flow model, p. 184
  2 Multi-step flow model, p. 184
  3 Uses and gratifications model, p. 184
  4 David Buckingham, p. 188
  5 Interpretative model, p. 184–5
  6 Structured interpretation model, p. 185
  7 Postmodernism, p. 185

Specifications

| Specification | Specification details | Coverage |
|---|---|---|
| **AQA** AS: Sociological Methods | ■ The different quantitative and qualitative methods and sources of data, including questionnaires, interviews, observation techniques and experiments, and documents and official statistics | The main methods and sources of data are covered between p. 199 and p. 206. |
| | ■ The distinctions between primary and secondary data, and between quantitative and qualitative data | These definitions are included in the introductory part of the chapter on p. 196. |
| | ■ The relationship between positivism, intepretivism and sociological methods | Positivist methodology is covered on p. 196 and interpretive methodology on p. 197. |
| | ■ The theoretical, practical and ethical considerations influencing the choice of topic, choice of method(s) and the conduct of research | Choice of topic is discussed on p. 199 and choice of method on pp. 199–200. Sampling is covered on p. 200 and piloting on p. 201. |
| | ■ The nature of social facts and the strengths and limitations of different sources of data and methods of research | Social facts are defined on p. 196. Each source of data is evaluated between pp. 201–5. |
| **AQA** A2: Theory and Methods | *Candidates should examine the following areas in addition to the material studied at AS level* | |
| | ■ Consensus, conflict, structural and social action theories | These theories are covered on pp. 2–3 and then in more depth in chapter 15. |
| | ■ The concepts of modernity and post-modernity in relation to sociological theory | See the section on the development of human societies (pp. 1–2). There is more detail in chapter 15 on pp. 218–20. |
| | ■ The nature of 'science' and the extent to which sociology may be regarded as scientific | See the section on sociology and science (p. 206). |
| | ■ The relationship between theory and methods | This relationship is the focus of pp. 196–7. The study of suicide (pp. 197–8) is a good example of relevant debates. |
| | ■ Debates about subjectivity, objectivity and value freedom | See the final section of this chapter on methodology and values (p. 207). |
| | ■ The relationship between sociology and social policy | This relationship is explored in a variety of chapters in the book, for example chapter 4 (p. 53), chapter 6 (pp. 80–83) and chapter 11 (pp. 154–6). |
| **OCR** AS: Sociological Research Skills | **Basic concepts in research design** ■ Reliability, validity, representativeness and generalization | These concepts are explained on pp. 199–200. |
| | ■ Identifying causes and effects | Correlation and causation are covered on pp. 196–7. |
| | ■ Ethics in the research process | The ethical implications of methods are covered as part of the discussion of sources of data (pp. 199–204). The feminist approach to interviewing is also relevant (pp. 198–9). |
| | **Aspects of data collection** ■ Sampling; populations and response rates | Sampling issues are discussed on p. 200. |
| | ■ Collecting primary data. Quantitative and qualitative approaches. Piloting, surveys, questionnaires, interviews and observation | Primary methods are covered between pp. 199–203. |
| | ■ Sources of secondary data. Documents; libraries, official sources and the internet | Secondary sources are covered between pp. 203–5. |

*continued*

| Specification | Specification details | Coverage |
|---|---|---|
| **OCR** AS: Sociological Research Skills *continued* | **Interpreting and evaluating data**<br>■ Interpreting and evaluating quantitative data. Tables and graphs | Quantitative approaches are discussed on pp. 196, 197 and 199–206. The sociology of suicide (pp. 197–8) is a good example of the interpretation of quantitative data. |
| | ■ Interpreting and evaluating qualitative data | Qualitative approaches are discussed on pp. 197–206. The sociology of suicide (pp. 197–8) is a good example of the interpretation of qualitative data. |
| | ■ Interpreting and evaluating documents, official statistics and other secondary sources | The sociology of suicide (pp. 197–8) is also a good example of the interpretation of official statistics. For other secondary sources, see pp. 203–5. |
| | ■ Reporting research results | Some approaches believe that the reporting of research should have particular purposes. An example is feminist methodology (pp. 198–9). |
| **OCR** A2: Applied Sociological Research Skills | **Research design and sociological theory**<br>■ Generating research questions or hypotheses: reviewing the field and the theoretical background | Choice of issues to research is discussed on p. 199, quantitative approaches to starting research on pp. 196–7. The sociology of suicide (pp. 197–8) is a good example of how different starting points affect conclusions. |
| | ■ Operationalising concepts and categories (e.g. 'race', 'ethnicity' 'class' 'gender' 'attitudes') | The process of operationalising concepts is explained on p. 201. |
| | ■ Research design. Generalization, reliability and representativeness. The role of piloting. Sample design | Research design is covered on pp. 199–200, piloting on p. 201 and sample design on p. 200. |
| | ■ Ethical issues in research design | The ethical implications of methods are covered in the discussion of sources of data (pp. 199–200). The feminist approach to interviewing is also relevant (pp. 198–9). |
| | **Techniques of data collection**<br>■ Ethical and safety issues in negotiating access and conducting research | The discussion of participant observation (pp. 202–3) is relevant here. |
| | ■ Quantitative and qualitative techniques of collecting and recording data. Questionnaires, interviews, participant and non-participant observation, use of secondary sources | Covered on pp. 199–206. |
| | ■ The context of data collection. Validity, researcher effect, observer bias, intercultural issues (e.g. gender, race, class etc.) | Validity is explained on pp. 199–200, researcher effect and intercultural issues in the context of interviewing on p. 202 and observer bias on p. 203. Postmodernist criticisms of conventional research are also relevant here (p. 207). |
| | **Interpreting, evaluating and reporting data**<br>■ Quantitative analysis. The meaning of tables and graphs. Trends, similarities and differences | Quantitative approaches are discussed on pp. 196–7, 201, 203–4. The sociology of suicide (pp. 195–6) is a good example of the interpretation of quantitative data. |
| | ■ Qualitative analysis. Interpreting and coding qualitative data. Interpretive bias and 'standpoint' research (e.g. feminist perspectives) | Qualitative approaches are discussed on pp. 194–5, 199, 201–2. The sociology of suicide (pp. 197–8) is a good example of the interpretation of qualitative as well as quantitative data. In terms of 'standpoint' research, feminist research methods are covered on pp. 198–9. |
| | ■ Reporting research. Conventions, referencing and transparency in reporting the research process. The reflexive researcher. Accountability to research participants. | The section on feminist methodology (pp. 198–9) has implications for the accountability of the researcher to participants. |

# INTRODUCTION

Methodology is concerned both with **research methods** and with the **philosophies** underlying them. It tries to establish accepted ways of getting the best possible data about the social world.

Broadly, some sociologists support using **scientific methods** and **quantitative data**, while others see such methods as inappropriate in the study of human society and prefer **qualitative data**.

Newer approaches include:

■ **Feminism** – which is a branch of critical social science concerned with the liberation of women.
■ **Postmodernism** – which rejects the idea that you can discover the truth about society.

# 'SCIENTIFIC' QUANTITATIVE METHODOLOGY

## Positivism

**Positivism** is an early influential approach, advocated by **Auguste Comte** (1986, first published 1840s) and **Emile Durkheim** (1897), which suggests that sociology can be scientific.

Positivism argues that:

1 There are **objective social facts** about the social world.
2 These facts can be expressed in **statistics**.
3 You can look for **correlations** (patterns in which two or more things tend to occur together).
4 Correlations may represent **causal relationships** (one thing causing another).
5 **Multivariate analysis** (analysing the importance of many different possible causes) can help you to find what the true causes of things are.
6 It is possible to discover **laws** of human behaviour – causes of behaviour which are true for all humans everywhere and throughout history.
7 Human behaviour is shaped by **external stimuli** (things that happen to us) rather than **internal stimuli** (what goes on in the human mind).
8 To be scientific you should only study what you can **observe**. It is therefore unscientific to study people's **emotions**, **meanings** or **motives**, which are internal to the unobservable mind.

## Popper – falsification and deduction

An alternative approach which says that sociology can be scientific is put forward by **Popper** (1959).

Popper argues that you cannot ever be sure that you have found the truth. What is considered true today may be disproved tomorrow.

A scientific theory is one that can be tested. From the theory you can **deduce** hypotheses and make precise **predictions**. If repeatedly tested and found to be

correct, a theory may be provisionally accepted, but there is always the possibility that it will be proved wrong (or falsified) in the future.

**Scientific theories** are ones that make precise predictions. Popper regards some sociology (such as **Marxism**) as unscientific because the predictions are not precise enough.

Popper uses a **deductive approach**: you deduce hypotheses from a theory and check that they are correct.

## Experiments

Many sciences make use of experiments. In experiments theories can be tested in precise conditions controlled by the researcher.

Experiments involve trying to **isolate** the effects of **independent variables** (possible causes) on a **dependent variable** (the thing to be explained). A **control** (in which everything is held constant) and an **experiment** (in which one independent variable is changed) are compared, allowing scientists to find precise causes. Experiments can be **replicated** (reproduced exactly) to test the **reliability** of findings.

However, sociologists rarely use **laboratory experiments** because:

■ Laboratories are **unnatural settings** and people may not behave normally.
■ It is **impractical** to conduct laboratory experiments on large numbers of people or over long periods.

## Field experiments

**Field experiments** take place outside the laboratory in **natural settings**.

Examples include **Rosenthal and Jacobson** (1968) on labelling in education (see p. 159) and **Brown and Gay** (1985) on racial discrimination by employers (p. 39).

Field experiments avoid unnatural laboratory situations, but it is difficult to control variables, and if those being studied are aware of the experiment, this may alter their behaviour (the **Hawthorne Effect**). If subjects are unaware that they are being studied, this raises ethical issues.

## The comparative method

This involves using the same logic as the experiment, but using events that have already taken place rather than creating artificial situations. Social groups, times or places are systematically compared to try to **isolate variables**.

The comparative method has been very widely used. Examples include **Durkheim** on suicide (see p. 197), **Weber** on the Protestant ethic (see p. 95) and Marx on social change (see pp. 215–16).

It is more difficult to isolate variables than in controlled experiments, but the comparative method is based upon **real social events** and is the only systematic way to study long-term or wide-scale social change. It is central to sociology.

# INTERPRETIVE AND QUALITATIVE METHODOLOGY

Qualitative data usually take the form of words. Compared to statistics, qualitative data tend to be richer and to have more depth.

## The interpretive approach

- **Interpretivists** usually advocate the use of **qualitative data** to interpret social action, with an emphasis on the meanings and motives of actors.
- Interpretivists often see sociology as different from the **natural sciences** in that it requires the understanding of **meaningful behaviour** by humans.
- From this viewpoint, people do not simply react to **external stimuli** but interpret the meaning of stimuli before reacting. An understanding is therefore required of people's unobservable subjective states, which cannot be reduced to statistical data.

There are several different interpretivist approaches.

**1 Weber**
Weber (1948) sees sociology as the study of **social action** (or meaningful behaviour).
- This requires understanding or *verstehen*.
- You need to **understand** why people behave in particular ways. For example, in *The Protestant Ethic* and the *Spirit of Capitalism* (1958) Weber tries to understand why Calvinists reinvested their money and became early capitalists.

**2 Symbolic interactionism**
- Symbolic interactionists see individuals as possessing a **self-concept** or image of themselves.
- This is largely shaped through the reactions of others to the person.
- Herbert **Blumer** (1962) argues that sociologists need to understand the viewpoint of the people whose behaviour they are trying to understand. They cannot do this simply by using statistical data.
- **Interactionists** prefer methods such as in-depth interviews and participant observation.
- **Labelling theory** is the best-known version of interactionism.

**3 Phenomenology**
- Phenomenologists go further than other interpretivist approaches, rejecting the idea that **causal explanations** are possible.
- To them the social world has to be **classified** before it can be measured. Classifications (e.g. whether an act is suicide, or whether somebody is a criminal) depend upon the judgements of individuals.
- These judgements reflect the **common sense** and **stereotypes** of individuals rather than some objective system.

- Since there is no way of choosing between classification systems, no hard facts can be produced, so **causal explanations** are not possible.
- Phenomenologists try to understand the classifications people use to give order and meaning to the social world.
- Cicourel's (1976) study of juvenile justice is an example.

# THE SOCIOLOGY OF SUICIDE

This topic provides a good illustration of different research strategies.

## Durkheim

Durkheim (1897) tried to show that suicide was not just a product of individual psychology and that **positivist methods** could be used to study it and explain the suicide rate.

He showed that suicide rates varied fairly consistently. High suicide rates were **correlated** with:

- Protestants rather than Catholics or Jews.
- Married people rather than single people.
- Parents rather than the childless.
- Political stability and peace rather than political upheaval and war.

From the statistical patterns, Durkheim claimed to have found four types of suicide:

1 **Egoistic suicide** was caused by **insufficient integration** into social groups (e.g. Protestants had less connection to their church than Catholics).
2 **Anomic suicide** resulted from **too little regulation** in industrial societies at times when rapid social change disrupted traditional norms (e.g. both economic booms and depression led to a rise in suicide rates).
3 **Altruistic suicide** resulted from **too much integration** in non-industrial societies (e.g. the practice of suttee – Hindu widows throwing themselves on their husbands' funeral pyres).
4 **Fatalistic suicide** resulted from **too much regulation** in non-industrial societies (e.g. the suicide of slaves).

Despite his association with positivism, Durkheim used elements of a **realist** approach in looking for **unobservable structures** underlying suicide rates.

### Responses to Durkheim

- **Positivists** have generally supported the principles on which his work was based but have modified details.
- **Halbwachs** (1930) argued that Durkheim overestimated the importance of religion. Halbwachs himself found that living in urban areas was an important factor correlated with high suicide rates.
- **Gibbs and Martin** (1964) tried to define integration in a more precise way than Durkheim, by using the concept of status integration.

## *Interpretive theories of suicide*

### J.D. Douglas

**Douglas** (1967) points out that suicide statistics are based on coroners' **interpretations** and **negotiations** between the parties involved. The relatives/friends of an individual might persuade the coroner not to record a death as suicide.

Douglas believes that there are different types of suicide based on their **social meanings**. There are different meanings in different societies – e.g. in Innuit society, elderly Eskimos were expected to kill themselves in times of food shortage.

**Case studies** are needed to find the different social meanings of suicide, such as transformation of the soul, transformation of the self, a search for sympathy or a means of revenge.

### Jean Baechler

**Baechler** (1979) develops Douglas's approach, defining suicides in terms of the types of solution they offer to different types of situation:
1 **Escapist suicides** involve fleeing from an intolerable situation.
2 **Aggressive suicides** are used to harm others.
3 **Oblative suicides** are used to obtain something that is desired (e.g. saving another or getting to heaven).
4 **Ludic suicides** involve taking risks for excitement or as an ordeal.

## *Criticisms of interpretive theories*

A problem with interpretive theories is that the categories used to classify suicides are simply a matter of the researcher's judgement.

### J. Maxwell Atkinson

**Atkinson** (1978) develops a **phenomenological** view. He believes that it is impossible for coroners or researchers to objectively classify suicides. The facts are simply a social construction.

From studies of coroners' courts he finds that four factors shape the commonsense theories of coroners:
1 The presence of a suicide note is taken to indicate suicidal intent.
2 Some types of death (e.g. hanging) are seen as more likely to be suicide.
3 Location and circumstances are important.
4 Evidence of depression or particular difficulties tends to encourage suicide verdicts.

When positivists study suicide statistics, all they uncover are the **commonsense theories** of coroners – for example, a tendency to record the deaths of depressed or lonely people as suicides.

**Critics** of phenomenology, such as **Barry Hindess** (1973), point out that the logic of this view can be turned against phenomenologists' own theories of how deaths are categorized as suicides – i.e. they are no more than their own interpretations and cannot be supported by objective data.

### *Steve Taylor*

**Taylor** (1982, 1989, 1990) tries to move beyond positivism and phenomenology using a **realist approach**.

He agrees with phenomenologists that certain factors influence coroners. From a study of deaths on the London underground he found that evidence of **social failure** or **social disgrace** tended to lead to suicide verdicts.

However, Taylor claimed that evidence from case studies revealed underlying patterns of suicide.

Suicides could be seen as one of four types, based on a person's **certainty** or **uncertainty** about **themselves** or **others**:
1 **Submissive** suicide involves certainty that your life is over, e.g. a terminal illness.
2 **Thanatation** involves uncertainty about yourself and whether you should live, e.g. playing Russian roulette.
3 **Sacrifice** involves certainty that others have made your life unbearable, e.g. rejection by a lover.
4 **Appeal** suicide involves uncertainty about others, e.g. suicidal behaviour which may win back a lover if they save you from death.

Taylor explains some variations in suicide – for example, why some suicide attempts are more serious than others – but his theory is hard to test and relies upon the interpretation of sometimes limited secondary data.

## QUANTITATIVE AND QUALITATIVE METHODOLOGY

**Ray Pawson** (1989) points out that in practice most sociologists use both **qualitative and quantitative data**:
- Most **positivists** use some **interpretation** in their research (e.g. Durkheim), and most interpretivists use some numbers (e.g. Cicourel).
- Disputes between positivists and anti-positivists have become less common in sociology.
- New philosophies of science (e.g. **realism**) move beyond old approaches.

## FEMINIST METHODOLOGY

Feminists such as **Abbott and Wallace** (1997) criticize 'malestream research' (male-dominated mainstream research) for:
1 Researching only men and using **male-only samples**.
2 Ignoring 'women's issues' such as housework.
3 Neglecting **sex and gender as variables**.

However, there is increasing attention to women and gender in sociology, and research is becoming less dominated by the 'malestream'.

## Feminist research methods

Ann **Oakley** (1981) argues that in a **masculine** approach to **interviewing**:

- There is an emphasis on **objectivity** and detachment.
- **Interviewees** are manipulated as sources of data and have an entirely passive role.
- The emphasis is on **reliability**.

Oakley believes that in a **feminist approach** to interviewing:

- The interviewer should be willing to answer questions and provide helpful information to respondents.
- Research should be **collaborative**. You should always gain consent and even help out those being interviewed.
- Interviewees can help improve the **validity** of the results by becoming increasingly **reflective** about their own lives.

Oakley uses this approach in her study of **childbirth**.

**Pawson** (1992) has criticized Oakley for simply adopting the techniques of unstructured interviewing. However, Oakley's approach has novel features, such as advising and helping the interviewees (which other theorists see as unduly influencing those being studied).

## Feminist standpoint epistemology

**Feminist standpoint epistemology** argues that women have a unique insight into the social world by virtue of being an **oppressed group**.

Some standpoint feminists, such as Stanley and Wise (1990), believe that you should examine a plurality of women's viewpoints (e.g. women of different ethnic groups).

Critics such as **Pawson** suggest that:

1 Some feminist researchers will not accept the viewpoints of women they disagree with (such as those who don't think they are oppressed).
2 Standpoint epistemology neglects the **oppressors** (usually men) and therefore makes it difficult to understand how oppression comes about.
3 It can be **relativistic**, i.e. accepting a variety of women's viewpoints as valid without any way of distinguishing between more and less useful ones.

## POSTMODERN METHODOLOGY

- **Epistemological postmodernists** reject the idea that any research procedure can produce a single 'true' description of the world.
- **Lyotard** (1984) sees all knowledge as **story-telling**, with no way of distinguishing between true and untrue stories.
- **Postmodern ethnography** allows us to collect different people's stories.
- Some postmodernists are simply concerned to reveal the contradictions in other sociological theories, using the technique of deconstruction.

## Evaluation

Many critics regard postmodernism as too **relativistic** (knowledge simply depends on your point of view). They point out that postmodern 'stories' about the social world cannot be shown to be better than any other stories.

**Mats Alvesson** (2002) believes that postmodern methodology can be used to refine traditional methodology rather than to reject it altogether. For example, he believes that you cannot take data from interviews at face value and as the 'truth'. People's stated beliefs can be challenged to see if they really hold them. This can form the basis of reflexive pragmatism – the researcher produces the best data they can without seeing it as absolutely true.

## THE RESEARCH PROCESS

To start research, sociologists have to select an **area to study**. This may be influenced by:

- The **values and beliefs** of the researcher (e.g. Paul Heelas sees the New Age as a significant phenomenon see p. 98).
- Developments in the subject and the desire to follow fashion or advance your career.
- Developments in the social world (e.g. the emergence of fundamentalist religion).
- Government policies (e.g. research into marketization in education).
- The availability of research **funds.**
- **Practicalities** such as time, money and access.

## PRIMARY SOURCES

**Primary sources** are data collected by sociologists themselves. **Secondary sources** are pre-existing sources of data.

## Choosing a primary research method

Like choosing a topic, the choice of method may be influenced by factors such as **funding** (it is usually easier to get funding for quantitative studies).

The **nature of the topic** may make particular methods more appropriate, and the **approach of the researcher** (e.g. **positivist** or **interpretivist**) will influence the choice.

Also important are questions of:

- **Reliability** – whether another researcher using the same procedure would obtain the same results. Quantitative methods are sometimes seen as more reliable.
- **Validity** – whether the data produce a true reflection of social reality. Some see qualitative data as offering a more valid picture of social reality.

According to **Alan Bryman** (2001) there are four types of validity:

- **Measurement validity** (or construct validity) concerns whether something really measures what it claims (e.g. whether IQ tests measure intelligence).

- **Internal validity** concerns whether a causal relationship is real or not.
- **External validity** concerns whether results can be generalized.
- **Ecological validity** concerns the issue of whether social science theories hold true in everyday settings.
- **Practicality** – particularly issues of time, money, sample size and access

## Choosing a sample

A **sample** is a part of a larger population, often chosen as a **cross-section** of the larger group.

Sampling is used in order to **generalize** about the larger **population** (to make statements about a group bigger than the one actually studied).

- The **population** is the total group the researcher is interested in.
- The **sampling unit** is the individual thing or person in that population.
- The **sampling frame** is a list of all those in the population (e.g. the electoral register is a sampling frame of those eligible to vote). There is no comprehensive sampling frame of everyone in Britain, but the Postcode Address File is often used (e.g. it is used by the British Crime Survey).

There are a variety of ways of producing a sample.

## Random sampling

In this approach every **sampling unit** has an **equal chance of being chosen**. It relies upon statistical probability to ensure a representative sample, so a large sample is needed to give a high chance of representativeness.

## Stratified random sampling

To ensure **representativeness**, the population is divided into groups according to important variables such as class, gender and ethnicity, and the sample is then chosen in the same proportions as their preponderance in the population. This method ensures a good cross-section and requires a smaller sample than random sampling, but it is only possible with a **sampling frame** containing all the relevant information about members of the population.

## Quota sampling

In this method **quotas** are established which determine how many people with particular characteristics are studied. Once a quota is filled no more people in that category are studied. It is useful if the proportions of different types of people in a population are known and if there is no suitable sampling frame. It is often used in **opinion polls** and it is generally quicker and cheaper than random sampling.

However, the results may be distorted if, for example, the researcher questions people in one particular

place at a particular time, since the sample will not then be representative. Also, people may be unwilling to reveal personal details to see if they fit into a quota category, and there may be practical difficulties finding members of particular quota groups.

## Multi-stage sampling

This involves getting a sample of a sample – e.g. a sample of voters in a sample of constituencies. It can save time and money but it makes a sample less genuinely representative.

## Snowballing

In snowballing, a member of a sample puts the researcher in touch with other potential members of the sample. It is useful for studying groups who cannot be easily located, but the networks connecting them make it less than representative.

## Non-representative sampling

This occurs when members of a sample are picked because or despite them being **untypical** or to study specific characteristics. It is used:

- To **falsify** a general theory by looking for exceptions to a rule (e.g. Oakley on gender roles, see p. 24).
- To find the **key informants** who can provide most information about an area of social life.
- In a **convenience sample** to make use of the easiest sample to access.

## Case studies

Case studies involve the study of a **single example** of something. They can be used:

- To develop a comprehensive understanding of something by studying it in depth (e.g. Pryce' study of St Paul's, Bristol, see p. 35).
- To develop a general theoretical approach by **falsifying a theory** (e.g. Gough's study of the Nayar, falsifying Murdock's theory that the family is universal, see p. 109).
- To develop typologies (e.g. Douglas's typology of the social meanings of suicide, see p. 198).
- To generate new hypotheses.

A problem with case studies is that you cannot **generalize** from them. Bryman (1988) suggests that this can be overcome through **multiple case studies** (e.g. Edwards and Scullion compared industrial relations in several British factories (1982)). However, it can be difficult to compare the findings of case studies carried out by different researchers.

## Life histories

A life history is a case study of **one person's life**. An example is **Thomas and Znaniecki's** (1919) study of Jenny, an ageing woman.

Plummer (1982) suggests that they are useful for helping you to understand the world from an individual's point of view. They provide rich detail and can help to generate hypotheses.

Some **feminists**, such as **Mies** (1993), think that life histories can be used to help women understand their own situation and perhaps change their lives – e.g. life histories discussing domestic violence may help a woman decide to leave a violent partner.

**Postmodernists** sometimes use case studies to explore the increased fluidity and variation in peoples' experiences (e.g. Stacey's (1996) study of family life, see p. 117).

## Pilot studies

Pilot studies are small-scale preliminary studies carried out before a bigger study to improve, help to design, or test the feasibility of proposed research.

They can be used:

■ To test how useful and unambiguous interview questions are (e.g. **Young and Willmott**, see p. 112).
■ To develop ways to gain the cooperation of respondents.
■ To develop research skills.
■ To decide whether or not to proceed with research.

## Social surveys

Social surveys are **large-scale** studies which collect standardized data about large groups, often using questionnaires.

■ **Factual surveys** collect descriptive information (e.g. David Gordon *et al.* on poverty (2000)).
■ **Attitude surveys** examine subjective opinions (e.g. opinion polls).
■ **Explanatory surveys** test theories or produce hypotheses (e.g. Marshall *et al.*'s study of class (1988)).

## Questionnaires

Questionnaires consist of written questions.

■ When administered by an interviewer, a questionnaire becomes a **structured interview**. This allows clarification of questions but introduces the possibility of **interviewer bias**.
■ **Postal questionnaires** avoid interviewer bias but have low response rates.
■ **Telephone questionnaires** tend to result in unrepresentative samples.

Questionnaires involve **operationalizing concepts**, i.e. turning concepts – such as alienation and class consciousness – into questions.

Questions may be **open-ended** or **fixed-choice**:

■ **Open-ended questions** may give more valid data, as respondents can say what is important to them and express it in their own words. However, the data are difficult to quantify, and interpretation is required when using the data. Coding of the answers (putting them into categories) distorts the actual replies given by respondents by linking responses that are not identical.
■ **Fixed-choice questions** are easy to classify and quantify, but respondents are limited to using the concepts and categories predetermined by researchers. The answers may be reliable but lack some validity.

Questionnaire data are often analysed using **multivariate analysis** and statistical techniques.

### The advantages of questionnaires

1 Large amounts of data can be collected quickly.
2 There is little personal involvement by researchers.
3 **Access** to subjects is easy.
4 It is easy to **quantify** the results, find **correlations** and use **multivariate analysis** to look for causes.
5 **Positivists** see differences in answers as reflecting real differences since everyone responds to the same stimuli.
6 **Comparative analysis** and **replication** (repeating the questionnaire) are easy, making the results reliable.
7 A **large, geographically dispersed sample** can be used, increasing the representativeness of the data and the ability to generalize.
8 To **positivists**, the statistical patterns revealed can be used to develop new theories; and questionnaires can be devised to test existing theories.
9 **Non-positivists** see questionnaires as useful for collecting straightforward, **descriptive data**.

### The disadvantages of questionnaires

**Interpretive sociologists** question the use of questionnaires, while **phenomenologists** reject them altogether.

1 Different answers may not reflect real differences between respondents since they may **interpret** questions differently.
2 In designing questionnaires, researchers assume they know what is important, and therefore it is difficult to develop novel **hypotheses**.
3 The **operationalization** of concepts distorts the social world by shaping concepts in line with researchers' rather than respondents' meanings.
4 The **validity** of the data may be undermined by deliberate lying, faulty memory or respondents not fully understanding their own motivations. People may not act in line with questionnaire answers. For example, La Pierre (1934) found that US hoteliers were racist when replying to questionnaires but not when faced with real situations.
5 Researchers are distant from their subjects, making it difficult to understand the social world from their viewpoint. **Interaction** cannot be understood through questionnaires. To **feminist** researchers, questionnaires preclude the possibility of subjects evaluating the research.
6 The coding of open-ended data distorts the distinct answers given by individuals.

Most sociologists accept that surveys are useful for collecting factual or **descriptive data**, but there is more controversy over their use in **explanatory studies**.

## Interviews

- **Structured interviews** are questionnaires administered by a researcher.
- **Unstructured interviews** do not have preset questions but are more like a conversation.
- Many interviews are **partly structured**, with some preset questions, or the researcher has a list of topics to cover. Some interviews allow prompts where interviewers can clarify questions or stimulate responses.

There are different interviewing styles:

- Most interviews are **non-directive** – they try to avoid influencing the interviewee, in order to increase the objectivity of the research.
- **Becker** (1970) suggests that more **aggressive interviewing** is useful for some topics, e.g. hidden racist feelings may be revealed through confrontation.
- Some **feminists** believe that interviewees should be **collaborators** in the research.
- **Group interviews** are sometimes used to put respondents at ease or to make respondents more **reflective** and more likely to open up as a result of interaction between interviewees.
- **Focus groups** are a type of group interview often used by political parties, which in **Bryman's** words (2001) emphasize the 'joint construction of meaning'.

## Advantages of interviews

A variety of sociologists use interviews. They may not be ideal for **positivists** or **interpretivists**, but are useful to both.

1 **Quantitative researchers** prefer interviews to participant observation – because **larger samples** can be used, **statistical data** can be produced with the **coding of** questions, and the research can be **replicated** to increase **reliability**.
2 **Qualitative researchers** prefer interviews to questionnaires because concepts can be clarified, and there is more opportunity for respondents to express ideas in their own way, say what is important to them and explore issues in depth.
3 However, the main advantages are **practicality** and **flexibility**. Interviews can examine past, present or future behaviour, subjective states, opinions, attitudes or simple factual information. They can be as in-depth or as superficial as the researcher wants.
4 Interviews are useful for studying groups who might not return questionnaires or consent to participant observation (e.g. **Laurie Taylor's** study of professional criminals (1984)).
5 To **feminists**, interviews have theoretical advantages since they provide space for **critical reflection** and **interaction** between interviewer and interviewee.

## The disadvantages of interviews

1 As with questionnaires, the **validity** of interview data may be affected by respondents being untruthful, having faulty memory or not fully understanding their own behaviour. People may have reinterpreted past events in the light of later experience (e.g. David Matza's delinquents disapproved of delinquent behaviour (1964)).
2 The presence of the researcher may influence answers (**interviewer bias**). **Labov** (1973) found that the 'race' of the interviewer affected young black children in speech tests. Interviewers might consciously or unconsciously lead respondents towards preferred answers.
3 Social factors such as ethnicity may influence the sort of answers members of different social groups are willing to give.

## Conclusion

Despite their imperfections, the practicality and flexibility of interviews make them attractive to researchers using different theoretical perspectives, and they are widely used. **Hammersley and Gomm** (2004) believe that interview data should be handled carefully but remains useful when combined with other methods.

## Observation and participant observation

Observation is used by a variety of sociologists.

- **Positivists** see observation as essential.
- **Interpretive sociologists** tend to particularly support **participant observation**, in which the researcher becomes part of the social life being studied.
- **Ethnography** is the study of a way of life and often uses participant observation.

### Joining the group, collecting and recording the data

**Overt participant observers** are open about doing research. This is advocated because:

- It is regarded as unethical to mislead subjects.
- It allows the observer to ask questions.
- The observer can retain some **detachment**.

However:

- The observer may influence the subjects' behaviour if they know they are being observed.
- In **covert participant observation**, the researcher does not reveal that they are doing research. This is advocated because:
- Respondents may act more naturally.
- Some groups would not allow an overt observer.
- The observer becomes fully engaged with the group.

However:

- Some regard it as **unethical** to lie.
- It may be difficult to opt out of illegal/immoral activities.
- The observer may 'go native' and lose objectivity.

**Recording data** from participant observation can be a problem, as the use of cameras/tape recorders may not be possible. Researchers usually write up field notes when they can, but they may forget things or be highly selective about what they do record.

## The advantages of participant observation

1 Researchers are less likely than in other methods to impose their own **concepts, structures and preconceptions** on the data.
2 They may gain answers to questions which they hadn't anticipated (e.g. Whyte, 1955).
3 It is difficult for respondents to lie or mislead.
4 For these reasons many see participant observation as having a high degree of **validity**.
5 **Symbolic interactionists** support participant observation because it allows an understanding of the subjective viewpoints of individuals and the processes of **interaction** in which people's **meanings, motives and self-concepts** constantly change. It therefore avoids a static picture of social life.
6 The researcher understands subjects better because they experience some of the same things.
7 It provides **in-depth** studies which can be useful both for developing new theories and for falsifying existing ones.

## The limitations and disadvantages of participant observation

1 It can be **time-consuming** and **expensive** for the researcher.
2 The researcher is limited to studying a small number of people in a single place.
3 It will be impossible to join some groups to carry out observation.
4 Researchers' lives may be disrupted, they may need to do illegal/immoral things or they may face dangers.
5 Samples may be too small for **generalizations**.
6 Studies **cannot be replicated**, so the results may be **unreliable**, and comparisons difficult.
7 The interpretations are rather subjective as the researcher has to be very selective about what is reported.
8 The presence of the researcher will change group behaviour and affect the **validity** of the data.
9 To **positivists** it is an **unsystematic, subjective and unscientific** method.

## Conclusion

Participant observation is the only research method that gets very close to real social life, but it is rather subjective. It is strong on **validity** but weak on **reliability**.

## *Postmodern ethnography*

Postmodern ethnographers do not believe that an objective description of social life is possible.

**Tyler** (1986) sees postmodern ethnography as designed to **stimulate the imagination**, like a work of literature. He believes that ethnography should simply be used to record the viewpoints of the many different groups in society. The researcher has no special ability to interpret the accounts of subjects.

Critics argue that this approach is too **relativistic** – ethnography becomes similar to fiction with no special claim to describe a real world.

## *Longitudinal research*

Longitudinal research or panel studies follow a group of people over an extended period, using periodic data collection.

Examples include **J.W.B. Douglas's** (1964) study of home life and education, the *Child Health and Education Survey* and the *British Household Panel Survey* used by **Berthoud and Gershunny** (2000) in the study of family life.

They are usually **large-scale quantitative** studies, but participant observation can also be longitudinal.

## Advantages of longitudinal research

1 People don't have to report on events retrospectively so problems of faulty memory or reinterpretation of events are reduced.
2 It can be used to examine a large number of **variables**.

## Disadvantages of longitudinal research

1 The size of the participating **sample** may drop over time, affecting the **reliability** of findings.
2 Whatever method is used will have limitations.
3 Taking part in the study might affect subjects' behaviour.

# SECONDARY SOURCES

**Secondary sources** are data that have already been produced – by, for example, the government, companies, or individuals (personal documents).

Existing sociological studies become secondary sources when used by other sociologists.

- They can be **quantitative** (e.g. government statistics) or **qualitative** (e.g. letters and diaries).
- They can be **historical** or **contemporary**.

Secondary sources are used for **practical** reasons. They save time and money and may include data that are beyond the scope of sociologists to collect (e.g. census data). They allow the study of societies in the past for which it is impossible to produce primary sources.

## *Official statistics*

**Government statistics** cover a wide range of topics including demography (census statistics), crime, employment and unemployment, industrial relations, educational achievement, family life (e.g. divorce statistics), household composition data, and so on. The government conducts statistical surveys such as the *General Household Survey* and the *British Crime Survey*, and since 1801 it has carried out a census every decade.

Such sources are invaluable because they are easily accessible and much more thorough than any data sociologists could produce. The census is the only survey that tries to include the whole of the population, and participation is legally compulsory.

However there are different views on statistics.

■ Some **positivists** such as **Durkheim** (1970) have seen official statistics as both valid and reliable (e.g. his study of suicide).

However, many official statistics are highly **unreliable** – for example, many crimes are not reported, to not or recorded by the police (see pp. 76–7).

■ Some sociologists believe that it is possible to produce **valid** and **reliable** statistics. For example, they believe that reliable **crime** statistics can be produced using surveys.
  – **Self-report studies** are questionnaires which ask people if they have committed crimes (e.g. West and Farrington's study of delinquency (1973)).
  – **Victim studies** ask people if they have been the victims of crime (e.g. the government's *British Crime Survey*).

However, such studies may not be entirely **reliable**, due to factors such as non-response and the limitations of sampling.

■ Some argue that the results are **invalid**. **Box** (1981) argues that in self-report studies people may lie, hide or exaggerate crimes. The total number of crimes recorded in studies depends on the willingness and ability of respondents to be honest, and the interpretation of the researcher as to whether a crime has taken place.

## A phenomenological view

**Phenomenologists** regard all crime statistics as invalid. They are simply the product of the categorization procedures used to produce them. For example, **Maxwell Atkinson** (1978) sees suicide statistics as the product of coroners' **taken-for-granted assumptions** about the sort of people who commit suicide. To **Cicourel** (1976), all statistics are based on subjective classifications.

## A conflict view

**Conflict theorists** see statistics as the product of **inequalities in power**. To **Miles and Irvine** (1979), government statistics are not lies, but the collection procedures and definitions are manipulated by governments. Examples include frequent redefinitions of unemployment which reduce official unemployment figures and the manipulation of data on NHS hospital waiting lists by removing people who have missed appointments for an operation. Some poverty statistics are no longer published.

Some conflict theorists question the categories used in statistics. For example, the Marxist **Theo Nichols** (1996) argues that official definitions of social class ignore the existence of wealth inequalities. From this point of view, statistics reflect **ideological frameworks** which in turn reflect **power inequalities** rather than individuals' assumptions.

## Historical sources

These are vital for studying **long-term social changes**.

**Peter Laslett** (1972, 1977) used parish records and **Michael Anderson** (1971) used census data to show that industrialization led to an increase in extended family households in Britain (see p. 112).

Parliamentary investigations, diaries, letters, autobiographies, speeches and mass media reports are all useful sources.

However, **statistical sources** suffer from the same possible problems of reliability and validity as contemporary statistics. Qualitative sources reflect the subjective views of those who produced them. Sometimes this is nevertheless useful – for example, when studying the effects of religious beliefs on the development of capitalism.

## Life documents

These are documents created by individuals which record **subjective** states. They include diaries, letters, photos, biographies, memoirs, suicide notes, films, pictures etc.

**Thomas and Znaniecki** (1919) used letters and statements to study Polish peasants who emigrated to the USA. However, **Plummer** (1982) argues that personal documents are rarely used by contemporary sociologists because:

■ Surviving documents may not be representative.
■ They are open to differing **interpretations**.
■ They are highly **subjective** – the same events discussed in a document such as a diary might be described very differently by someone else involved.
■ The content may be influenced by the identity of the person or people intended to read the document.
■ Private diaries, not intended to be read by others, overcome the above problem, but few are available to researchers.

However, **Plummer** believes that life documents are still very useful because:

■ They allow insights into people's subjective states.
■ **Symbolic interactionists** see them as revealing the **personal meanings and self-concepts** which they see as shaping behaviour.

## The mass media and content analysis

The mass media may be **unreliable** for providing factual information, but they may be the objects of study. Some researchers see such studies as useful for revealing the **ideological frameworks** of those who produce the mass media. This is important because of the influence of the media.

Pawson (1995) describes different ways of analysing the content of the mass media:

1 Formal content analysis involves classifying and counting content. For example, **Lobban** (1974) and later **Best** (1993) counted the appearances of girls and boys in different **gender roles** in children's books.

This technique is reliable but it involves inferring the meaning of the text from numbers alone.

2 **Thematic analysis** examines a topic and looks for the messages that lie behind the coverage. For example, Soothill and Walby (1991) found that newspaper coverage of rape emphasized the pathological nature of individual rapists and largely ignored rapes by partners and friends.

However, such studies rarely use representative samples and don't examine the impact of the messages on the audience.

3 Textual analysis involves the detailed analysis of small pieces of text. For example, the **Glasgow Media Group** looked at the words used to describe managers and strikers.

However, this relies heavily on the researcher's interpretation and may therefore be unreliable.

4 **Audience analysis** examines how the audience interprets the messages of the media – e.g. **Morley's** (1980) study of responses to *Nationwide*.

However, the honesty and openness of respondents may be questionable, and such studies cannot reveal long-term effects of media messages.

### Assessing secondary sources

John **Scott** (1990a, 1990b) argues that the following criteria can be used to assess secondary sources:

### Authenticity

- **Soundness** concerns whether the document is complete and **reliable**.
- **Authorship** concerns whether it was written by the claimed author.

### Credibility

- **Sincerity** concerns whether the author intended to provide a true account or was trying to mislead the readers.
- **Accuracy** concerns whether the author is able to be truthful, e.g. whether faulty memory might affect accuracy.

### Representativeness

This concerns whether the documents are typical or **representative** of what is being studied.

- **Survival**, or lack of it, may mean that representative documents do not exist.
- **Availability**, or lack of it, may mean that researchers cannot gain access to representative samples even where they have survived.

### Meaning

- **Literal understanding** involves being able to read, decipher or translate the content.
- **Interpretative understanding** involves interpreting what the document signifies, and there may be very different possible interpretations.

**Stuart Stein** (2002) identifies particular problems in using the **internet** as a secondary source. Unlike published sources there are no editorial or review processes, which are designed to ensure the **reliability** and **validity** of the data. Consequently, data needs to be used with caution particularly in relation to the **identity**, **credibility** and **authority** of the author(s).

## TRIANGULATION

**Bryman** (1988) argues that most sociologists use a mixture of **quantitative** and **qualitative** sources. Sociologists as far back as **Weber** have combined methods

Examples include:

- **Eileen Barker's** (1984) study of the Moonies which used observation, questionnaires and interviews.
- The use of statistical computer programmes to analyse ethnography.
- **Winlow's** (2001) study of 'bouncers' in Sunderland which used participant observation, interviews and secondary sources.

Martyn **Hammersley** (1996 in Bryman 2001) distinguishes three ways of combining methods:

- **Triangulation** in which findings are cross-checked using a variety of methods. (The term triangulation is often used to refer to combining methods whatever the purpose).
- **Facilitation** in which one method is used to assist or develop the use of another method.
- **Complementarity** in which different methods are combined to dovetail different aspects of an investigation.

**Bryman** (2001) identifies ten uses of **multi-strategy research**.

1 **Triangulation** to check the reliability of data produced using different methods.
2 **Qualitative** research facilitating quantitative research, e.g. by designing questionnaire questions.
3 Quantitative research facilitating **qualitative** research, e.g. by helping to identify people for a sample.
4 Filling in the **gaps** where the main research method cannot produce all the necessary data.
5 Using some methods to study **static** features of social life and others to study **processual** features, ie. changes.
6 Using different methods to obtain different **perspectives** from research subjects.
7 Using different methods to help to **generalize**.
8 Using **qualitative research** to understand the relationship between variables revealed in the quantitative research.
9 Studying different aspects of a phenomenon.
10 Solving a **puzzle** by using a different method to that initially used.

Bryman sees multi-strategy research as very useful in that the limitations and disadvantages of each individual research method can be partially overcome.

# SOCIOLOGY AND SCIENCE

## Scientific methodology

**Positivists** see sociology as a **science** based on the use of **objective observation**, **statistics**, a search for **correlations**, **causal relationships** and **laws** (see p. 196).

**Popper** (1959) sees science as based on **falsifiable** theories which make **precise predictions**. He regards some sociology, such as **Marxism**, as **non-scientific** (see p. 196).

Both see a scientific methodology as **desirable**. **Positivists** see science as producing **objective truth**, while **Popper** sees science as getting as close as possible to the truth, since it is always possible that a theory will be **falsified** in the future.

**Phenomenologists** reject the idea of a scientific sociology because:

1 The social world cannot be **objectively classified and measured**; classification reflects the subjective categories and interpretations of individuals.
2 Sociologists can only study the way classifications are made; they cannot discover some underlying **objective truth**.

## The social context of science

Some sociologists argue that science does not follow any single methodology. It takes place in a **social context** and often does not involve an objective search for truth.

**Kaplan** (1964) distinguishes:

1 **Reconstructed logics** (the methods scientists claim to use).
2 **Logics in use** (the actual methods they use).

**Michael Lynch** (1983) illustrates this by showing how scientists studying rats' brains ignored slides that contradicted their theories, dismissing them as **artefacts** (or mistakes produced during the laboratory procedures). Scientists look for evidence to confirm theories, ignoring evidence that might falsify them.

**Roger Gomm** (1982) argues that **Darwin's** theory of evolution was accepted because the social context of Victorian Britain, with its **laissez-faire capitalism**, welcomed the ideas of natural selection and **survival of the fittest**. Opposition to revolution encouraged acceptance of evolutionary theory, and evolutionary thinking allowed Victorian Britons to see themselves as superior to the people in conquered colonies. Lack of fossil evidence of evolution was ignored because of the social context.

## Kuhn – paradigms and scientific revolutions

**Kuhn** (1962) argues that scientific communities develop a commitment to a particular paradigm – a set of shared beliefs about some aspect of the physical world: how it works, how to study it and how to interpret evidence. A paradigm provides the complete framework within which scientists operate. Ideas from outside the paradigm are normally dismissed.

During a **scientific revolution**, however, anomalies, which the paradigm cannot explain, come to the fore. One paradigm is rejected and replaced by another, and science returns to its **normal state** in which the paradigm is not open to question. An example is the move from **Newtonian** to **Einsteinian** physics.

From this point of view, sociology can be seen as **pre-scientific** because there are a variety of **paradigms** (or **perspectives**), such as **feminism**, **Marxism**, **postmodernism**, etc.

It may not be **desirable** for sociology to become scientific, in Kuhn's sense, because the **conflict between perspectives** is a critical element of sociology.

**Anderson, Hughes and Sharrock** (1986) criticize Kuhn for underestimating the extent of disagreement between scientists, and question whether his approach has much relevance to sociology.

## The realist view of science

Realists such as **Roy Bhaskar** (1979) and **Andrew Sayer** (1984) believe that it is both **possible and desirable** for sociology to be **scientific**. They see **physical and social sciences** as similar.

Sayer argues that some sciences have **closed systems** in which all **variables** can be measured. However, many sciences are **open** – all **variables** cannot be measured and **precise predictions** cannot be made (e.g. **seismology** and **meteorology**). Sayer therefore rejects **Popper's** view that a scientific theory must make **precise predictions**.

Sayer believes that sociology is scientific but societies are **complex open systems**, making it impossible to make precise predictions.

**Keat and Urry** (1982) argue that some sciences deal with things that cannot be directly **observed** – e.g. sub-atomic particles, continental drift and magnetic fields. They therefore reject the **positivist view** that science confines itself to studying the **observable**. They argue that sociology can still be seen as scientific if it studies unobservable meanings and motives.

Realists believe that scientists try to discover the **underlying structures and processes** that cause observable events (e.g. evolution). Sociologists try to do exactly the same, looking for **social structures** (e.g. in Marxism the economic base and superstructure and social classes) and **processes** (e.g. capital accumulation). **Realists** therefore argue that much **sociology** is **scientific**.

# METHODOLOGY AND VALUES

There are different views on whether sociology is or can be **objective** or **value-free**.

- Bierstedt (1963) defines objectivity in terms of investigators not being influenced by their own beliefs.
- **Comte, Durkheim and Marx** all thought they were **objective and scientific**.
- **Weber** argued that the actual **selection of a topic** for research was bound to be influenced by values, but that the research itself could be value-free.

However, many sociologists who considered their work value-free have been accused of being **value-laden**:

- **Functionalists** have been seen as having a **conservative bias** in stressing the usefulness of institutions.
- **Durkheim's** values are revealed in his opposition to inherited wealth.
- **Marx** was committed to **revolutionary politics**.
- **Weber's** values influenced his view that **bureaucracy** could stifle human freedom.

## Can values be eradicated from sociology?

- As Weber suggested, values are bound to influence what topics sociologists think are important enough to study.
- Sociologists' values may also influence which **aspects of a topic** they study. **Gouldner** (1971) argues that all sociologists make **domain assumptions** – e.g. about whether humans are **rational** or **irrational**, whether society is essentially stable or unstable, etc.
- All research is **selective** – e.g. what questions are included in a questionnaire or what aspects of a social setting an observer takes note of – and **values** may influence the selection process.

- All research involves some degree of **interpretation** which may be influenced by values. For example, **interpretive sociologists** see questionnaires as distorting the real nature of the social world in line with the researcher's assumptions and values. **Positivists** see participant observation research as based on the subjective and value-laden perceptions of interpretive researchers.

**Phillips** (1973) concludes that values influence the choice of topic and the methods and sources of data used in research.

In 'Anti-minotaur', **Gouldner** argues that fact and value cannot be separated in sociology, just as the bull and human in a **minotaur** cannot be separated. **Gouldner** thinks that sociologists should bring their values into the open so that others are aware of any possible bias.

To many **postmodernists**, knowledge is simply the reflection of the values of the social groups that create the knowledge.

However, other sociologists argue that sociology is not simply an expression of people's values. **Carspecken** (1996) argues that there is a **real, objective social world**, and this makes it possible to reject some claims about the truth which do not fit reality. Thus, while values will always influence sociology, research can show that some theories are more supported by evidence than others.

This view is also supported by the **realist theory of science**.

## TEST YOUR KNOWLEDGE AND UNDERSTANDING

1 **Which two of these statements would positivists agree with?**
   a Human behaviour is shaped by external stimuli
   b Human behaviour is unpredictable
   c There are no such things as social facts
   d Sociology should be scientific

2 **Which one of these statements would Popper agree with?**
   a No theory can be seen as definitively true as it may be proved wrong in the future
   b Scientists can discover the absolute truth
   c All sociology is scientific
   d It is not desirable for sociology to be scientific

3 **Which one of these statements is true?**
   a Phenomenologists do not believe it is possible to objectively classify the social world
   b Symbolic interactionists believe it is impossible to explain human behaviour
   c Weber believes there are no facts about social life
   d Herbert Blumer does not believe that you can understand the viewpoint of other human beings

4 **Which of Durkheim's types of suicide results from a lack of regulation in a rapidly changing society?**
   a Altruistic suicide
   b Anomic suicide
   c Fatalistic suicide
   d Egoistic suicide

5 **Which one of these approaches does Oakley advocate in feminist research?**
   a Researchers should be objective
   b Researchers should be collaborative
   c Researchers should keep their distance from subjects
   d Researchers should put reliability before validity

6 **The type of sampling in which every member of the relevant population has an equal chance of being selected is called:**
   a Random sampling
   b Snowball sampling
   c Quota sampling
   d Stratified sampling

7 **Which one of these statements is false?**
   a Telephone surveys tend not to be representative of the whole population
   b Postal questionnaires avoid interviewer bias
   c Postal questionnaires usually have a high response rate
   d Fixed-choice questions make it easy to quantify data from questionnaires

8 **Which one of the following would not be an example of interviewer bias?**
   a The interviewee forgets some information
   b The interviewee is influenced by the gender of the interviewer
   c The interviewee gives the answer they believe the interviewer would most like to hear
   d The interviewer unintentionally puts ideas into the interviewee's head

9 **Which two of these statements are correct?**
   a Interviews are one of the most flexible research methods
   b Positivists believe that unstructured interviews provide the most reliable data
   c Interviews are only used by interpretivist sociologists
   d Interviews generally use larger samples than participant observation

10 **Postmodern ethnography can be criticized because:**
   a It cannot be used to study historical societies
   b It is too relativistic
   c It doesn't allow you to understand the world from the viewpoint of those being studied
   d It requires specialist training for researchers

11 **Which of these is not a secondary source?**
   a Official statistics
   b A personal diary
   c An interview
   d A government report

12 **Conflict theorists tend to see official statistics as:**
   a A reliable and valid representation of social life
   b Based on the personal opinions of officials
   c Reflecting ideological frameworks
   d Of little interest to sociologists

13 **Triangulation refers to:**
   a Research where three respondents are used
   b A type of longitudinal study
   c The process of interpreting qualitative data
   d The use of several research methods in one study to check the data

14 **Realists believe that:**
   a It is possible and desirable for sociology to be scientific
   b It is possible but undesirable for sociology to be scientific
   c It is impossible but desirable for sociology to be scientific
   d Sociologists have nothing to learn from scientists

15 **Which one of these perspectives has often been seen as reflecting conservative values?**
   a Feminism
   b Weberian sociology
   c Functionalism
   d Interactionism

## DEVELOP YOUR ANALYSIS AND EVALUATION SKILLS

### *It is both desirable and possible for sociology to be scientific and objective.*

***Background:*** This view was originally supported by positivists, but was attacked by phenomenologists and interpretivists generally. Most of the classical sociologists (e.g. Marx, Durkheim, Comte) thought that their approaches to sociology were scientific and objective. However, they have been attacked both for putting forward value-laden theories, and by Gouldner, who does not believe value-freedom is possible. From Thomas Kuhn's viewpoint, sociology is not scientific because a single paradigm is not accepted by all. Popper thinks much sociology is not objective and scientific, although it is possible for it to become so if it sticks to precise predictions. Critical realists would agree with this statement because they do not believe that precise prediction is necessary to be scientific.

| ***For*** | ***Against*** |
|---|---|
| ■ Positivism (p. 196) | ■ Kuhn (p. 206) |
| ■ Popper (p. 196) | ■ Phenomenology (p. 197) |
| ■ Realism (p. 206) | ■ Interpretitive sociology (p. 197) |
| ■ Marx (pp. 215–16) | ■ Arguments it is impossible to be value-free (p. 207) |
| ■ Durkheim Comte (p. 196) | ■ Gouldner (p. 207) |

***Top tip:*** Weber (p. 207) is useful for arguing you cannot be value-free in selecting topics for research, but after that value-freedom is possible and desirable.

### *All research methods have their uses, especially when combined together.*

***Background:*** This is a view put forward by Weber originally, but which rather fell out of favour when positivists, phenomenologists, and interpretivists argued for quantitative or qualitative methods to be superior. Both the advocates of quantitative and those of qualitative approaches exaggerated their case, and in practice most sociologists do use a full range of methods. All research methods have particular advantages (as well as disadvantages) and sociologists such as Bryman believe that triangulation and other forms of methodological pluralism are the way forward.

| ***For*** | ***Against*** |
|---|---|
| ■ Triangulation (pp. 205–6) | ■ Positivism (p. 196) |
| ■ Weber (p. 197) | ■ Phenomenology (p. 197) |
| ■ The material which shows all methods have their limitations (pp. 199–203) | ■ Interpretivist sociology (p. 197) |

***Top tip:*** Bryman believes that most sociologists use a mixture of methods (p. 205).

### *Secondary sources tend to be unreliable and invalid and are therefore of little use to sociologists.*

***Background:*** Reliability and validity (pp. 199–200) need to be defined to answer this question, and what is meant by secondary sources also needs to be explained (pp. 203). Different sociologists tend to see different types of secondary data as reliable and valid. Foe example, positivists tend to favour official statistics (though Marxists and interpretivists see them as invalid), while interpretivists see life documents as largely valid (but positivists do not). All secondary sources have problems attached to them and there might be particular biases built in, but the same is true of primary sources. Secondary sources are the only option for historical sociology and when sociologists can't afford to collect their own data, so they are certainly of some use to sociologists.

| ***For*** | ***Against*** |
|---|---|
| ■ Positivist views on life documents (p. 204) | ■ Positivist views on statistics (p. 204) |
| ■ Interpretivist, phenomenological and conflict views on statistics (p. 204) | ■ Interpretivist views on life documents (p. 204) |
| | ■ Arguments that secondary sources generally are useful (pp. 203–205) |

***Top tip:*** John Scott's work (p. 205) is useful for showing the caution needed with the use of secondary sources, but also for suggesting that they can be very useful when used with care.

# AQA-STYLE METHODS QUESTION

**AS Unit 3**

| | |
|---|---|
| **Answer all parts of this question**<br><br>Total: 60 marks<br>1 mark = 1 minute<br><br>Time allowed:<br>1 hour | **ITEM A** – Official Statistics<br><br>**Governmental surveys**  **Registration data**<br>*Snapshots of society*   *Continuous collection of data*<br>■ Population census    ■ Births, marriages & deaths<br>■ General Household Survey  ■ Divorces<br>■ Mortality & Morbidity   ■ Business accounts<br>■ British Crime Survey   ■ Unemployment<br>■ Family Expenditure Survey  ■ Crime<br>              ■ Child abuse<br><br>Source: adapted from Lawson, Jones and Moores, *Advanced Sociology through Diagrams*, Oxford University Press, 2000 |

**ITEM B**

After long years of rejection, happy days are here again for researchers in the social sciences. In Whitehall the search is for 'evidence', but Government largesse does not come free. 'Too often in the past, policy has not been informed by good research, but too many academics want to address issues other than those that are central to the political and policy debate.' But academic social scientists worry that 'evidence led' may mean, 'what we want for our own political purposes'. What was that adage about pipers and tunes?

Source: adapted from David Walker, 'You find the evidence, we'll pick the policy', *Guardian*, 15 February 2000

---

**Comments on the question**

■ Interpret the meaning from the item
■ Check its appropriateness by testing it in the original context

**[a] What do sociologists mean by 'evidence led'?**

[Item B, line 8] [2 marks]

**Advice on preparing your answer**

■ Basing conclusions on the evidence, or facts found after investigation or research

■ You should pick out features that distinguish these sources
■ Note: in this context they are both secondary sources, so this cannot be used as a difference

**[b] Explain the difference between Crime Statistics and the British Crime Survey.** [4 marks]

■ Use the information from the item to help you
■ See p. 76 for more detail

■ Concentrate on the statistics mentioned. Think about how and why births are registered, compared to crime or child abuse which may never be uncovered

**[c] Explain why the statistics for births are likely to be more accurate than for crime or child abuse.**

[6 marks]

■ Think of the legal obligation to register births. Look at pp. 76–7 and see if you can twist this to make an answer here

■ Just two!
■ Notice the negative here. Give reasons for not using opinion polls
■ This should take you no longer than 8 minutes

**[d]** Identify and explain two objections that could be made to the use of opinion polls in sociological research.

[8 marks]

■ Look at the section on surveys and questionnaires, p. 201, and see if you can use this material in answering parts of this question

■ You should consider issues of reliability and validity
■ Look at the advantages and disadvantages
■ Concentrate on the ones in Item A
■ i.e. not to those people who collected them in the first place

**[e]** Using material with which you are familiar, examine the usefulness of Governmental Official Statistics to sociologists doing research. [20 marks]

■ This is the positivist/anti positivist, quantitative versus qualitative debate
■ Look at pp. 197 and 203–204 for the positivist points and pp. 198 and 202 for the anti-positivist points

■ This means that you do not have to limit your answer to secondary sources
■ Look at both sides and come to a conclusion
■ The planning rather than the actual carrying out of the research

**[f]** Using material from the items and elsewhere, assess the importance of various factors that might affect research design. [20 marks]

■ Use the three types of factors – practical, theoretical and ethical – as your organizing principle. This will help you to make an assessment
■ See pp. 199–200 for help

# OCR-STYLE METHODOLOGY QUESTION

## A2 Unit 2537: Applied Sociological

**Research Skills**

**Answer all parts of this question**

Total: 60 marks
1 mark = 1 minute

Time allowed:
1 hour 30 minutes

### ITEM A

The Making of Men by Mac an Ghaill was an ethnographic study of 'Parnell School', an 11–18 comprehensive school in an inner-city area of the Midlands characterized by high unemployment and poverty. Mac an Ghaill collected research data over a four-year period whilst employed as a teacher at the school. He mainly observed school life and wrote down his observations on a daily basis. He also encouraged some students to keep diaries and to design questionnaires focused on issues that they thought were important. Moreover he carried out formal and informal group and individual interviews with both pupils and teachers.

Part of his research focused on a group of lads he labelled the 'Macho Lads', who belonged to an anti-school subculture which actively resisted the authority of the school and teachers in an exaggerated masculine way. Mac an Ghaill concluded that their resistance was understandable and rational because the lads realized that they were likely to face a future of unemployment, youth training and social exclusion. As Mac an Ghaill says of these lads, 'they're more straight-forward than those half hippie middle-class kids. You can be sure that none of them with all their connections will end up on a training scheme or on the dole.'

### ITEM B

The National Union of Teachers requires quantitative and qualitative data to discover the levels of stress that teachers in secondary schools face. You have been asked to design a proposal which will target an appropriate sample of secondary schools and teachers.

---

**Comments on the question**

- There is no need to explain why particular types of method are used
- No more, no less

**[a]** Using only Item A, identify one quantitative and one qualitative method used in this study. [6 marks]

**Advice on preparing your answer**

- The item identifies six methods but you only need to mention two

- Make sure that the examiner can clearly see two separate strengths identified with explanations

**[b]** Identify and explain two strengths of triangulation. [8 marks]

- See pp. 205–6 for an account of this approach

- Describe only, don't offer an explanation
- Note that the focus is on the research findings, not the research methods
- There is no need to use material outside of this item

**[c]** Summarize what the research findings in Item A tell us about some working-class boys' attitudes towards education. [10 marks]

- Don't copy the item word for word. Attempt to put it into your own words

- Note the focus on the process of the research
- Describe all stages of the research – e.g. choice of method, access issues, sampling, operationalization, ethical issues, etc.
- You must link the research process to the research context outlined in Item B

**[d]** Outline and explain the research process you would adopt in collecting quantitative data on the experiences of secondary school teachers. [Item B]

[14 marks]

- Think carefully about your choice of method. It has got to be practical
- The sample size is going to rule out straight away some methods
- The fact that the research is sponsored by the NUT means that there is access to a sampling frame, which should bring to mind the possibility of using a questionnaire
- See the section on questionnaires on p. 201, and think about which strengths are appropriate to this research context
- See the section on sampling techniques on p. 199. Which is the most appropriate and why?

- You need to anticipate certain types of problems relating to all aspects of the research process
- You must suggest some possible ways of dealing with these problems

**[e]** Assess the potential weaknesses of your research proposal, briefly explaining how you intend to overcome them. [22 marks]

- For example, look at the weaknesses of questionnaires (see p. 201). Which of these could be related to this research context?
- Look through this section for ideas on how you might deal with potential problems. In particular, you should examine the section on triangulation and methodological pluralism (pp. 205–6)
- You will need to address theoretical issues to get near the top of the highest mark band (see pp. 196–7)

## Specifications

An understanding of the major sociological perspectives is important across all aspects of both AQA and OCR specifications, especially at A2 level.

**Parts of modules covered** (NB *Socialization, culture and identity* is a theme running through the AQA specification)

| Specification | Specification details | Coverage |
|---|---|---|
| **AQA** A2: Theory and Methods | ■ Consensus, conflict, structural and social action theories. | ■ Consensus approaches are covered in the section on functionalism (pp. 214–15); conflict approaches on pp. 215–16. Social action theories are discussed on pp. 216–18. The difference between structural and social action theories is explained on p. 214, and an evaluation of that distinction can be found on p. 218. |
| | ■ The concepts of modernity and post-modernity in relation to sociological theory. | ■ These issues are discussed on pp. 218–220. |

For more detailed specification guidance visit **www.haralambosholborn.com**

## Essential notes

## INTRODUCTION

### Structural versus social action theories

There are two main types of sociological theory:

1 **Structural** or **macro** perspectives examine the way in which society as a whole fits together. Examples include Marxism and functionalism. They tend to see human activity as a product of social structure.
2 **Social action**, **interpretive** or **micro perspectives** examine smaller groups of people in society and are concerned with the subjective states of individuals. They tend to see society as a product of human activity. Examples include symbolic interactionism and Weber's theory of social action.

However, many theories do not fit neatly into one category or the other, there are variations within perspectives and some perspectives and individual studies combine elements of both approaches. For example, **Weber** used both **structural** and **social action** perspectives in his general approach, and postmodernism cannot be readily categorized in terms of these concepts.

## FUNCTIONALISM

■ Functionalism views society as a **system** with interconnected parts.
■ Early functionalists used a **biological analogy**, comparing parts of society to parts of the human body (e.g. the government was compared to the brain).
■ In terms of this analogy, both humans and societies have certain basic needs (or **functional prerequisites**) that must be met if they are to survive.
■ Social **institutions** are held to meet these basic needs (e.g. families provide socialization which helps meet a basic need for a common culture).
■ Institutions are studied by identifying the way in which they contribute to meeting needs.
■ The **function** of an institution is seen in terms of its contribution to the survival of the whole (i.e. society).
■ Some functionalists accept that there may be aspects of society which are **dysfunctional** – which prevent it from operating smoothly – but they generally pay little attention to them.
■ Functionalism has been accused of having a **conservative ideology**. It tends to support preservation of the status quo, since anything that persists in society is seen as providing a useful function.

### Emile Durkheim

■ Durkheim believed that people were constrained by **social facts**: ways of acting, thinking and feeling in a society.
■ Shared **moral codes** shaped individual consciousnesses.
■ Social facts were caused by other social facts (e.g. the influence of religion on suicide rates) but could also be explained in terms of the **functions** they performed for society.
■ Parts of society would only persist if they served useful functions.
■ Societies needed a **collective conscience**, or shared morality, in order to function successfully.

- Modern industrial societies could be disrupted by the existence of **anomie** (normlessness) and **egoism** (where individuals are not integrated into social groups). Both of these stemmed from a **complex division of labour**. People did specialist jobs, and this weakened solidarity in society.

## Talcott Parsons

- Parsons believed that all societies needed a **value consensus** based upon shared goals.
- Societies developed **rules** based upon this value consensus and **norms** about how people should behave, which fitted in with the overall goals.
- When individuals are **socialized** to accept the values, goals and norms, and where this works smoothly, social equilibrium is achieved.
- Parsons saw society as a **system** with four basic needs or **functional prerequisites**:
  1 **Adaptation** – the need for an economic system to ensure the survival of members of society.
  2 **Goal attainment** – the need to set goals, a function primarily carried out by the government.
  3 **Integration** – the need to control conflict, a function carried out by the legal system.
  4 **Pattern maintenance** – the maintenance of values, achieved largely through education, religion and family life.
- Parsons saw change in terms of a shift in values from **pattern variables A** to **pattern variables B**. Under the former, status was based on ascription, and people were treated as specific individuals. Under the latter, in modern societies status is based upon **achievement**, and individuals are judged according to impartial universalistic standards (e.g. exam systems).
- Social change also involves the development of specialist institutions, such as those of the welfare state – a process called **structural differentiation**.

## Robert K. Merton

- Merton was a functionalist, but he accepted that societies did not always work smoothly.
- He argued that parts of society could be **dysfunctional** and might prevent society from running smoothly.

## Functionalism – a critique

1 Functionalism has been accused of being **teleological** – that is, it confuses cause and effect. The functions of an institution are the effects it has rather than the reasons why it exists.
2 Functionalism assumes, without putting forward evidence, that a **value consensus** exists, and it ignores conflict and diversity in society.
3 Functionalism is too **deterministic**. It sees human behaviour as shaped by the needs of the social system, and makes no allowance for the fact that individuals have choices about how they behave.
4 **Alvin Gouldner** (1971) argues that functionalism ignores the extent to which people are coerced in society to do things they do not wish to do.

5 **Lockwood** (1970) argues that functionalism ignores conflicts of interest between groups, which tend to destabilize social systems.
6 **Jonathon Turner** and **Alexandra Maryanski** (1979) argue that functionalism remains useful for understanding social structures and how they influence behaviour, although it does have many flaws.

## CONFLICT PERSPECTIVES

Conflict perspectives take many forms – e.g. **Marxism**, **feminism**, **anti-racism** – but all agree that there are different groups in society with conflicting interests.

## Marxism

- Karl Marx saw history in terms of conflict between **social classes**.
- Marxism is based upon a philosophy of **dialectical materialism**: the idea that history proceeds through the clash of material forces, particularly classes.
- Marx saw human society as based upon work and the production of goods. Hence he argued that society had a **material base**.
- In the earliest stages of history, under **primitive communism**, there was no economic surplus and no private wealth, so classes did not exist.
- As some individuals began to **accumulate wealth** (e.g. herds of animals), and passed it down to their children, classes emerged.
- Power tended to be monopolized by a **ruling-class** minority (those who owned the **means of production**) who dominated a subject-class majority.
- This caused tension and provided the potential for conflict.
- The ruling class used their control over institutions such as religion to justify or **legitimate** their position and persuade the subject class that they were not being exploited.
- Humans became increasingly **alienated** from their true selves and their true interests. Religion was a form of alienation, since people created in their minds a non-existent alien being which then controlled their behaviour.
- In capitalist societies, where people worked for wages, and companies made profits, workers were alienated from their work. They were alienated because they worked for other people, lacked control over their work and did not own the products they produced.
- An end to alienation and exploitation could only be achieved in a **communist society** in which there was no private property. Instead there would be communal ownership of the means of production. There would be no classes and therefore no exploitation. Instead of working for others to make a profit, people would work for the good of the society as a whole.
- All societies apart from communist ones have two main classes: the owners of the means of production (the **ruling class**) and the non-owners of the means of production (the **subject class**).

- The **means of production** are those things that are necessary to produce other things, such as **land**, **capital**, **raw materials**, **machinery** and **labour power**.
- In **capitalist societies**, the ruling class or **bourgeoisie** owned **capital** (money used to finance production), while the **subject class**, or **proletariat**, owned only **labour power** which they had to sell to the bourgeoisie.
- The bourgeoisie used the superstructure – the non-economic parts of society such as education, religion and the state – to stabilize society.
- They encouraged the development of **false class consciousness** whereby people saw society as fair and just.
- Eventually the proletariat (or working class) would become aware that they were being exploited, and they would develop **class consciousness** (an awareness of their true class interests).
- The proletariat would be increasingly **exploited**, they would suffer from slumps in the capitalist system and they would become aware of increasing inequality between themselves and the bourgeoisie.
- They would organize themselves into trade unions, political parties and revolutionary movements, overthrow capitalism and establish a **communist society**.

## Marxism – a critique

1 Critics have argued that as capitalism has developed, class consciousness has reduced rather than increased.
2 Communist societies did not end inequality and exploitation, and they tended to be unpopular and to restrict individual **liberty**. By the early 1990s most communist regimes had collapsed.
3 Marxism seems to exaggerate the importance of economic factors, ignoring the influence of **ideas** and **culture** (e.g. **Weber**'s Protestant ethic theory).
4 Marxism has been accused of **economic determinism** – seeing individuals' behaviour as determined by the economic system and neglecting the extent to which individuals have free choice.
5 Marxism emphasizes **class** differences and pays too little attention to gender, ethnicity, sexuality, age, lifestyle, etc.
6 Defenders of Marxism argue that it is not truly an **economically deterministic** theory. Marx emphasized that individuals and groups had to make their own history, but the economic structure determined the context in which that process took place.

## Neo-Marxism

Neo-Marxists are strongly influenced by Marx but reject one or more aspects of his work.

**Antonio Gramsci** is one example. Gramsci suggested that ownership of the means of production was not enough to win ruling-class control. It needed to make **alliances** with other classes and make some real **concessions** in order to attain hegemony (political domination).

Gramsci saw aspects of the **superstructure** as having some independence from the ruling class. (See p. 126 for a detailed description of Gramsci.)

Neo-Marxists tend to place more emphasis on **cultural** and **ideological factors** than Marx himself did. In doing so they rather water down the ability of Marxism to explain how society works in economic terms.

## Conflict theory

Conflict theories emphasize the importance of conflict between different groups in society, but they do not place emphasis on class alone.

Conflict may take place between **occupational groupings**, **men** and **women**, **ethnic** or **religious** groups, **age** groups, **heterosexuals** and **homosexuals**, the **disabled** and **able-bodied**, and so on.

**Weber**'s views on **class**, **status** and **parties** (see p. 8) illustrate aspects of conflict theory.

# SOCIAL ACTION AND INTERPRETIVE PERSPECTIVES

- Some of these approaches deny the existence of a clear social structure that tends to direct individual behaviour.
- Some accept the existence of a structure but see it as shaped by individuals.

## Max Weber

Weber combined a consideration of **social structure** (e.g. classes, status groups and bureaucracies) with a concern with **social action**.

He described sociology as the study of **social action** – which he defines as any intentional, meaningful behaviour which takes account of the existence of other people.

Explaining social action requires *Verstehen*, or understanding. You need to **understand** what actions mean to people – e.g. it is possible to understand that a woodcutter with a piece of wood and an axe is chopping wood. But you also need to understand the motive behind an action.

An example is the **Protestant ethic** study (see p. 95), in which Weber discusses the meaning of Protestantism to some of its followers and their motives for working hard to reinvest money.

Weber accepts the existence of institutions such as **bureaucracies**, but he sees them as consisting of individuals carrying out social actions.

- Bureaucracies are organizations with sets of **rules** and **hierarchical relationships** (e.g. the civil service or large corporations).
- In bureaucracies individuals carry out **rational social action**: social action intended to achieve particular goals, such as increasing the profits of a company.

Weber saw the modern world as increasingly governed by rational social action (or the process of **rationaliza-**

tion). **Pre-modern societies** were regulated more by **traditional social action**: people behaved in certain ways because people had long behaved in those ways.

In modern societies governed by rational social action there was far more scope for innovation, but to some extent bureaucracies with strict rules stifled individual creativity.

Weber was neither a **materialist** (like Marx) who believed that material forces shaped history, nor an **idealist** who believed that ideas shaped history. Instead, Weber believed that both materialism and idealism played a part in explaining human history. For example, the development of capitalism required both the right material conditions and the religious ideas of Protestantism.

## Weber – a critique

1 Weber has been criticized by **Lee and Newby** (1983) as a **methodological individualist** – somebody who reduces everything to the actions of individuals and ignores how social structure shapes society.
2 To the extent that Weber does deal with social structure, what he says seems to contradict some of his ideas on the importance of individual social action.
3 **Postmodernists** deny that the contemporary social world is increasingly characterized by rationalization.

## George Ritzer – the McDonaldization of society

Ritzer (1996) supports Weber's view that capitalist societies would drive towards bureaucratic organization and rationalization in the pursuit of profit .

He sees McDonalds as representing a contemporary and extreme form of **bureaucratization**. He sees McDonalds as based on the following principles:

1 **Efficiency** – the 'optimum method in getting from one point to another' is achieved using the principles of conveyor belts to feed people as rapidly as possible.
2 **Calculability** – involves measuring all products precisely.
3 **Predictability** is achieved by standardizing the physical environment and ways of operating in all McDonalds.
4 **Control** involves providing precise directions to workers and monitoring them, and customers are controlled through the use of drive-throughs and security guards.

According to Ritzer McDonaldization has spread to many other areas of social life including the film industry, education, employment and shopping malls.

However, Ritzer believes that the effects of McDonaldization can be counter-productive and **irrational**. The negative effects can include:

- Long queues
- Customers doing their own unpaid work (clearing tables)
- **Dehumanization**
- Unhealthy food
- Stifling imagination and creativity

Although Ritzer is pessimistic about the future he believes individuals can **resist** and slow down the spread of McDonaldization particularly through the way they act as consumers.

# SYMBOLIC INTERACTIONISM

## George Herbert Mead

- Mead is usually seen as the founder of **symbolic interactionism**.
- Human behaviour is social because people interact in terms of **symbols**.
- Symbols (e.g. words or flags) stand for other objects and imply certain behaviour – e.g. the symbol 'chair' implies an object that you can sit on.
- Humans do not have **instincts**, and thus they need symbols in order to survive and interact. For example, they need symbols for different plants which indicate whether they are edible or poisonous.
- Meanings and symbols are largely shared by members of society.
- In order to understand the behaviour of others, it is necessary to take the role of the other: i.e. imagine that you are them in order to try to understand the reasons for their behaviour.
- Individuals have a **self** – an image of what sort of person they are. This largely reflects how other people react to them. By taking the role of the other (imagining how others see us) we build up a **self-concept**. For example, we come to see ourselves as brave or cowardly, hard or soft.
- Society has a culture and a plurality of **social roles** – e.g. the roles of husband and wife. These roles imply certain behaviours, but the roles are flexible and can change. For example, there is considerable leeway in how people carry out different family roles.

## Herbert Blumer

Other interactionists, such as Herbert Blumer, have developed Mead's approach.

- Blumer emphasizes that people do not react automatically to **external stimuli** but **interpret their meaning** before reacting (e.g. interpreting the meaning of a red light before deciding how to react to it).
- Meanings develop during interaction and are not fixed.
- **Rules** and **structures** restrict social action and shape the interpretation of meaning to some extent, but they are never absolutely rigid and fixed.

## Symbolic interactionism – a critique

1 Interactionists fail to explain where the **norms** which partly shape behaviour come from.
2 They may underestimate the degree to which human behaviour is **constrained**.
3 They neglect the role of **structural factors** – such as the unequal distribution of power and the existence of inequality – in shaping human societies.

## PHENOMENOLOGY

Phenomenology is a European philosophy. Like other social action approaches it is concerned with **subjective meanings**, but unlike them it denies that you can produce **causal explanations** of human behaviour.

- According to its founder, **Husserl**, individuals organize chaotic sensory experience into phenomena.
- **Phenomena** are things which are held to have characteristics in common – e.g. the category 'dog' includes a range of animals with particular characteristics.
- The emphasis is on the subjective nature of the **categorization**. Although a real world exists, how it is categorized is a matter of human choice rather than an objective process.
- The purpose of phenomenology is to understand the **essence of phenomena** – the essential characteristics which lead to something being placed in a particular category.
- An example of phenomenology is **Atkinson's** work on **suicide**, which looks at why certain events are categorized as suicides, rather than looking at the causes of suicide (see p. 198).

## UNITING STRUCTURAL AND SOCIAL ACTION APPROACHES

As discussed, there are two main approaches in sociology:

1 **Structural approaches** (which emphasize how social structures shape social action).
2 **Social action approaches** (which emphasize how social groups produce society through their actions).

Sociologists have increasingly tried to combine these two approaches.

In The *Sociological Imagination*, C. **Wright Mills** (1959) suggested that you needed to understand how the larger historical scene affected individuals.

### Giddens – the theory of structuration

Anthony Giddens advocates **structuration** theory. He sees **structure** and **action** as two sides of the same coin.

- Structures make social action possible, but social actions create the structures.
- Giddens calls this the **duality of structure**.
- This can be illustrated by language. Grammar is the structure of language, but individuals create the structure by talking and writing in ways that follow grammatical rules. If people start to use language in a different way, then grammatical rules will change. However, people can only use language and understand each other because there is some grammatical structure.

- In the same way, societal structures and institutions are **reproduced** through people's actions, but if their actions change, the structures and institutions change.

Critics of Giddens, such as **Margaret Archer** (1982), argue that he puts too much emphasis on people's ability to change society by acting differently, and he underestimates the **constraints** under which people operate.

## MODERNITY, POSTMODERNITY AND POSTMODERNISM

It is possible to distinguish two types of theoretical approach within sociology:

1 **Modern theories** – such as those of **Durkheim**, **Marx** and **Weber** – argue that the objective truth about society can be discovered.
2 **Postmodernism**, on the other hand, argues against the idea of **objective truth**.

Some sociologists distinguish different eras in human development and argue that there has been a move from **modernity** to **postmodernity**, although others dispute this.

### Modernity

Many sociologists have distinguished between **pre-modern** and **modern societies**. The change is often associated with industrialization.

- **Marx**, **Weber**, **Durkheim** and most classic sociologists saw the development of modernity as **progress**.
- The **Enlightenment** (an eighteenth-century intellectual movement) is often seen as the starting point of modernity. The Enlightenment rejected the idea that thinking should be limited by **religious beliefs** and **tradition** and argued that humans could work out the best way to organize societies for themselves.
- **Weber** in particular saw the change to modernity in terms of the triumph of **scientific rationality** over **superstition**, **tradition** and **religious faith**.

### Postmodern theories

Postmodern theorists reject the idea that human society can be perfected through rational thought; they reject the idea that **grand theories** can discover the truth.

Postmodernism first developed in architecture. It rejected modern concrete, steel and glass tower blocks, which some modern architects saw as the solution to the problem of accommodating people.

Postmodern architecture uses a greater variety of styles and uses the architecture of earlier eras rather than just using modern materials and designs.

There are two particularly influential postmodern theorists: **Lyotard** and **Baudrillard**.

## Lyotard – postmodernism and knowledge

Jean-François Lyotard is a French social theorist.

■ Lyotard argues that the move to postmodern culture started in the 1950s.
■ It involves changes in **language-games**.
■ Pre-industrial societies had a language-game based on **narrative**. Narrators of stories have **legitimacy** because of who they are (e.g. their position within a tribe).
■ With the Enlightenment, **denotative language-games** became dominant. In these, statements are judged in terms of abstract standards of proof, deriving from science.
■ Science itself is based upon **metanarratives** – big stories which give meaning to other narratives. Metanarratives behind science see progress through science and conquering nature as possible. Such metanarratives influenced events such as the French Revolution and helped to make **Marxism** popular in the twentieth century.
■ Postmodernism leads to '**incredulity towards metanarratives**'. The metanarratives of the twentieth century failed to solve the world's problems and in fact made things worse. For example, Marxism led to tyranny in the communist USSR. People no longer believe in a simple recipe for progress.
■ In postmodernism, denotative language-games are replaced by **technical language-games**. These are not judged by standards of truth, but by standards of usefulness.
■ Postmodern society is based upon producing **saleable, useful** knowledge rather than searching for eternal truths.
■ Postmodern society is more **diverse, pluralistic and tolerant** than modern societies in which doctrinaire metanarratives dominated.

## Lyotard – a critique

1 Critics argue that Lyotard's theory is itself a sweeping metanarrative about the development of society.
2 He advances little evidence to support his theory.
3 The **Marxist Terry Eagleton** sees **Lyotard's** theory as justification for uncontrolled **capitalism** which puts profit before human well-being.

## Baudrillard – Simulations

Like Lyotard, Baudrillard sees society as moving through several stages.

He argues that Marxists are wrong to see contemporary society as based on the production of **material goods**. The economy is increasingly based on the production and sale of **signs** and **images** – e.g. the image of pop stars is what sells rather than the content of their records.

Signs have developed through four stages:

1 Signs are a **reflection of a basic reality**.
2 Signs become a **distortion of reality**.
3 Signs disguise the **absence of reality** (e.g. images of a non-existent God).
4 Signs bear no relation to any reality – signs become **simulacra**.

Examples of simulacra are:

■ Disneyland, which reproduces imaginary worlds such as 'Future World'.
■ The mummy of Rameses II, which was transformed by attempts to preserve it.
■ Los Angeles, which Baudrillard sees as an 'immense script ... a perpetual motion picture'.

Baudrillard believes that **politics** has imploded into a **meaningless exchange of signs** in which politicians have no real power. People become trapped in a situation where image and reality cannot be separated, particularly through watching TV.

## Baudrillard – a critique

1 Baudrillard's arguments are highly abstract and not based on systematic research.
2 **David Harvey** (1990) suggests that the decisions made by politicians make a real difference to people's lives.
3 Baudrillard makes absurd statements such as claiming that the first Gulf War was simply a series of images on TV screens.

## Greg Philo and David Miller – a critique of postmodernism

**Philo and Miller** (2001) make a number of criticisms of postmodernism.

■ It encourages **political apathy**, as it denies the existence of an objective reality that social scientists can analyse.
■ The emphasis on language detracts attention from real social problems.
■ Postmodernism fails to challenge distorted or misleading images of reality presented by the media – e.g. about the Israeli-Palestinian conflict.
■ Postmodernism ignores the growing inequalities of wealth and income, the growing power of corporations and the increasing influence of **market forces** on social life.
■ Philo and Miller believe that the growth of **consumerism** and the fragmentation of **styles** does not represent the development of a new type of society.

## Harvey – Marxism and postmodernity

Harvey accepts that we are moving towards a **postmodern era**, but he rejects postmodern theory. He believes that modern theories such as Marxism can be used to understand and explain postmodernity.

■ He emphasizes the role of the **economy** in changing society.
■ He accepts that images have become more important but sees this as part of capitalists' attempts to maintain and increase **profit**.

- He argues that the **economic crisis** of the 1970s (which followed a rise in oil prices) made it difficult to make profits out of mass production.
- Firms moved towards a system of **flexible accumulation**, in which there are frequent shifts in consumer demand and the products produced by firms.
- Capitalism increasingly turns **cultural products** (such as fashion, music and art) into commodities to be bought and sold.
- **Time and space** become **compressed**, as people can travel and communicate more easily, and products from around the world become available in local stores.
- This produces unsettled, rapidly changing cultures.
- There is a process of **globalization** in which governments lose some power to control events in their own territory.

Harvey therefore accepts that there is a move towards postmodernity but believes that this can be understood in terms of modern social theory. He also believes that the planned improvement of society is still possible.

# MODERN THEORIES OF SOCIETY AND THE SOCIOLOGY OF MODERNITY

Numerous sociologists reject postmodern theories and argue that societies can be understood, explained and improved. **Anthony Giddens** is one example.

- Giddens believes that societies have entered an era of **high modernity**.
- Despite important changes, such as **globalization**, key features of modern societies remain.
- In particular, societies are still based upon the modern characteristic of **reflexivity**.
- Reflexivity involves people reflecting upon the world and thinking about acting differently in the future to improve things.
- People increasingly reflect upon all aspects of their lives and consider changing them.
- This makes contemporary culture increasingly unsettled and changeable. This is not, however, a feature of **postmodernity** but an extension and development of a key feature of **modernity**.

# TEST YOUR KNOWLEDGE AND UNDERSTANDING

1 **Which two of the following are structural perspectives?**
   a Functionalism
   b Marxism
   c Symbolic interactionism
   d Weber's theory of social action

2 **Functionalism is often seen as having:**
   a A conservative ideology
   b A liberal ideology
   c A radical ideology
   d An anarchistic ideology

3 **According to Durkheim, which two of the following are problems of societies with a complex division of labour?**
   a Fatalism
   b Anomie
   c Egoism
   d Social facts

4 **Dialectical materialism means:**
   a The existence of conflict
   b The study of socialization
   c The clash of material forces such as classes
   d The economic foundations of society

5 **In Weber's sociology, Verstehen means:**
   a Social action
   b Structure
   c Meaning
   d Understanding

6 **Weber thought that modern societies were dominated by:**
   a Traditional social action
   b Charisma
   c Rational social action
   d Idealism

7 **Herbert Blumer believes that:**
   a There are no rules in society
   b Rules are fixed and inflexible
   c Rules exist but are flexible
   d Modern societies are increasingly dominated by rules

8 **In phenomenology, phenomena are:**
   a Things which belong in the same category
   b Amazing social events
   c The basic rules of society
   d Causal explanations

9 **In interaction, when you try to understand the viewpoint of somebody else, you:**
   a Take the role of the other
   b Step into somebody's shoes
   c Engage in empathy
   d Use telepathy

10 **The intellectual movement which gave rise to modernity is known as:**
   a The Awakening
   b The Rebirth
   c The Illumination
   d The Enlightenment

11 **According to Baudrillard, postmodern society is based on:**
   a Materialism
   b The production and sale of signs
   c Art
   d Language-games

12 **David Harvey:**
   a Accepts that truth about society cannot be found
   b Rejects the idea that postmodernity has arrived
   c Advocates a theory of high modernity
   d Thinks that postmodernity can be understood using a modern theory

13 **According to Giddens, reflexivity means:**
   a Greater flexibility
   b Automatic reaction
   c Reflection and planning future actions
   d Insensitivity to other cultures

14 **The sociological theory that puts most emphasis on materialism is:**
   a Interactionism
   b Marxism
   c Functionalism
   d Postmodernism

15 **The sociological theory that denies the existence of facts about society is:**
   a Marxism
   b Weberian theory
   c Phenomenology
   d Giddens's theory

## DEVELOP YOUR ANALYSIS AND EVALUATION SKILLS

### Structural perspectives are superior to interpretative perspectives.

**Background:** Structural perspectives include Marxism and functionalism and perhaps some versions of feminism (particularly Marxist feminism and approaches which see patriarchy as a structure). They sees society as having a structure which shapes action. Interpretative perspectives include interactionism and phenomenology and postmodernism is critical of structural approaches. Although both approaches have their advocates, it can be argued that they look at different aspects of society and are stronger when combined than when used in isolation.

| For | Against |
| --- | --- |
| ■ Marxism (pp. 215-16) | ■ Symbolic interactionism (pp. 217–18) |
| ■ Functionalism (pp. 214–15) | ■ Phenomenology and ethnomethodology (p. 218) |
| ■ Marxist/functionalist feminism (p. 24) | ■ Most types of postmodernism (pp. 218–20) |
| ■ Other feminisms (e.g., Walby) (pp. 25–6) | |

**Top tip:** Giddens (p. 218) and Weber (pp. 216–17) both advocate combining structural and interpretative approaches and many types of neo-Marxism combine elements of both as well (p. 216).

### We now live in postmodern societies.

**Background:** You need to discuss the differences between modern and postmodern societies to answer this (see pp. 1–2) and between postmodernity and postmodernism (p. 218). Marxism and functionalism are seen as modern theories which would oppose this claim, while Weber saw societies as becoming modern with greater bureaucratization and rationalization. This could be illustrated with Ritzer's work (p. 217). Postmodernists such as Baudrillard and Lyotard would clearly agree with this statement, but remember there are criticisms of their views. You could look at the arguments on both sides in some of the other chapters on issues such as popular culture (chapter 12, p. 174), religion (chapter 7), and 'race' ethnicity and nationality (chapter 3, p. 39).

| For | Against |
| --- | --- |
| ■ Baudrillard (p. 219) | ■ Marxism (pp. 215–16) |
| ■ Lyotard (p. 219) | ■ Functionalism (pp. 214–5) |
| ■ Postmodern feminism (p. 26) | ■ Weber (pp. 216–17) |

**Top tip:** Giddens (p. 218) is useful for accepting some aspects of postmodernism but arguing for the idea of high-modernity, which does not see societies as having moved fully into postmodernity yet.

### Marxists place too much emphasis on classes and material factors.

**Background:** It is worth looking at the materialist basis of Marxism in some detail in discussing this statement, with a discussion of issues such as dialectical materialism, and alienation (pp. 136–7). Some neo-Marxists (such as Gramsci, p. 126) would agree with this view up to a point, but remember there are many interpretations of Marx and not all see him as an economic determinist. You can contrast materialism with idealism and a useful issue to illustrate this is Weber's protestant ethic theory (see pp. 95–6). Weber certainly thought Marx was too much of a materialist and most postmodernists and symbolic interactionists would also be critical of materialism.

| For | Against |
| --- | --- |
| ■ Weber (pp. 216–17) | ■ Marx (pp. 215–16) |
| ■ Symbolic interactionism (pp. 217–18) | |
| ■ Postmodernism (pp. 218–19) | |
| ■ Some neo-Marxists (p. 216) | |

**Top tip:** Although he writes about postmodernity, David Harvey (pp. 219–20) is still essentially a Marxist and uses materialism to understand changes in contemporary societies.

# AQA-STYLE THEORY AND METHODS QUESTION

## A2 Unit 5

Total: 60 marks
1 mark –
1.5 minutes

Time allowed:
1 hour 30 minutes

### ITEM A

For her coursework project, an A-level sociology student decided to investigate the relationship between school size and pupil performance. She hypothesized that smaller schools would gain better A-level results than larger schools. She took her data from the Department of Education school league tables published annually in a national newspaper. When she saw how many schools there were, she decided to limit her analysis to one local authority area.

The results looked like this:

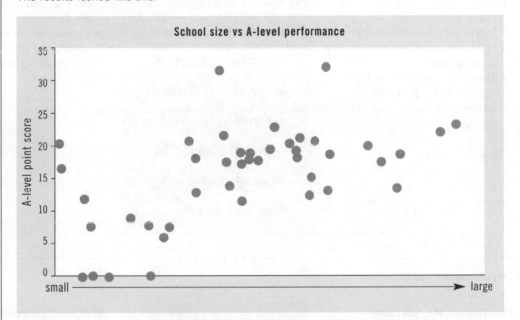

As part of the evaluation of the project, the student wrote that she would have liked to follow up her study by interviewing two headteachers, of a small and a large secondary school, to explore with them the associations she was investigating.

### Comments on the question

- Check that you understand this term which is an important concept when carrying out quantitative research

**[a]** Suggest one way that school size might be operationalized in the project in Item A. [2 marks]

### Advice on preparing your answer

- The meaning can be found in chapter 14 (p. 199). Apply this understanding to your own knowledge of schools

- This is the prediction she made at the beginning of the study about what she was expecting to find (see Popper, chapter 14, p. 194)
- Do not forget to answer this part of the question. It will carry most marks

**[b]** Was her hypothesis confirmed or rejected by the findings? Explain the reason for your answer. [4 marks]

- Before you interpret the results in the item, look at causality (chapter 14, p. 194). This will help you to understand the different types of relationships that might exist

- You need to select one (see chapter 14, p. 200)
- The marks will be awarded here, not for your selection of a type of interview

**[c]** What type of interview would you use for the follow-up study?

Give three reasons for your choice. [6 marks]

- To help you make a logical analysis that you can apply to this research problem, read chapter 14, p. 200 on interviewing, and p. 203–4 on triangulation

- This is an important distinction that you should be able to make and use appropriately:
  1 Practical problems will apply to all researchers regardless of their perspective
  2 Theoretical problems will be specific to one group of sociologists

**[d]** Identify and explain one practical and one theoretical problem of using official statistics reported in the press as a source of data for the research project in Item A. [8 marks]

- Distinguish the theoretical from the practical problems, which are discussed in chapter 14, p. 197
- Choose only one of each and explain the problem in the context of the research described in the item

---

## SECTION B

**Answer one question from this section**

**Comments on the question**

- A balanced response is required that recognizes that this is not the only or necessarily the best approach to sociology
- This tells you to explore the link between methods and theory

**Either:**

Assess the view that the 'social world has to be studied and explained from the actor's point of view'. [40 marks]

**Advice on preparing your answer**

- Identify the theoretical position in the question as interactionist
- Develop and explain this theory using pp. 215–16
- Offer a critique of the theory (pp. 215–16)
- Alternative theoretical perspectives can offer a different view: functionalism (pp. 212–13); Marxism (pp. 213–14)
- A conclusion could be drawn from the work of Giddens (p. 216)

- You will need to distinguish between these two terms
- Your answer should be reasonably balanced between the two elements of the question

**Or:**

Examine the concepts of modernity and postmodernity in relation to sociological theory. [40 marks]

- Explain the meaning of the terms (p. 216)
- Describe the essential features of each (pp. 216–17), using at least one named writer for each concept
- Make appropriate critical comments throughout your answer (pp. 216–17)

# OCR-STYLE SOCIOLOGICAL THEORY QUESTION

## A2 Unit 2536: Power and Control: Popular Culture

Total: 60 marks, 1 mark = 1 minute
Time allowed: 1 hour

### Comments on the question

- Make sure that you describe both views in a detailed way with supporting evidence
- Look at a range of arguments for and against both theoretical positions
- It is important to be balanced. Try to give equal weighting to both theoretical positions

**[a]** Outline and assess modernist and postmodernist theories of culture and consumption.

[60 marks]

### Advice on preparing your answer

- This is an essay question so spend at least 10 minutes planning your response
- Construct an introduction which briefly and clearly explains the concepts used in the question
- The sections on pp. 171–4 offer accounts of both the modernist and postmodernist positions
- Try to finish with an evaluative conclusion based on the available evidence

# ANSWERS

**Introduction** (p. 4)
1c, 2b, 3d, 4a, 5a, 6a&c, 7a, 8c, 9b, 10d, 11d, 12c, 13d, 14b, 15b

**Chapter 1** (p. 18)
1c, 2c, 3a, 4a&d, 5c, 6c&d, 7c, 8c&d, 9a, 10a, 11c, 12d, 13c&d, 14b, 15b&c

**Chapter 2** (p. 29)
1a&b, 2c&d, 3a, 4b, 5c, 6b&c, 7c, 8c, 9b, 10c&d, 11a, 12d, 13d, 14b, 15a&c

**Chapter 3** (p. 41)
1b, 2d, 3b, 4a, 5c&d, 6b&d, 7b, 8c, 9b, 10c, 11d, 12a, 13c, 14b, 15b

**Chapter 4** (p. 54)
1a, 2b, 3d, 4a, 5d, 6b, 7d, 8c, 9b, 10a&c, 11c, 12c, 13b, 14d, 15a&c

**Chapter 5** (p. 68)
1c, 2d, 3a, 4b, 5b, 6a, 7d, 8c, 9a, 10c, 11c, 12d, 13c, 14b, 15d

**Chapter 6** (p. 88)
1d, 2c, 3a, 4c, 5b, 6a, 7a, 8b, 9d, 10a, 11b, 12c, 13b, 14c, 15c

**Chapter 7** (p. 104)
1c, 2c, 3c, 4a, 5a, 6a, 7a, 8c, 9b, 10d, 11b, 12b, 13b, 14b, 15a

**Chapter 8** (p. 118)
1b, 2b, 3c, 4a, 5b, 6a, 7d, 8c, 9b, 10b, 11b, 12c, 13c, 14d, 15c

**Chapter 9** (p. 132)
1c, 2c, 3c, 4d, 5b, 6c, 7d, 8a, 9a&b, 10c&d, 11d, 12a&d, 13a&c, 14c&d, 15a

**Chapter 10** (p. 146)
1d, 2b, 3a, 4d, 5d, 6b, 7b, 8d, 9b, 10c, 11b, 12a, 13d, 14b, 15a

**Chapter 11** (p. 166)
1a, 2b, 3b, 4c, 5a, 6d, 7c, 8a, 9a, 10d, 11d, 12b, 13b, 14b, 15d

**Chapter 12** (p. 177)
1b, 2c, 3a, 4c, 5a, 6a, 7b, 8b, 9b, 10c, 11a, 12d, 13b, 14b, 15d

**Chapter 13** (p. 189)
1a&d, 2a, 3b, 4b, 5d, 6d, 7b, 8a, 9a, 10a&b, 11b, 12b, 13a, 14c, 15a

**Chapter 14** (p. 208)
1a&d, 2a, 3a, 4b, 5b, 6a, 7c, 8a, 9a&d, 10b, 11c, 12c, 13d, 14a, 15c

**Chapter 15** (p. 221)
1a&b, 2a, 3b&c, 4c, 5d, 6c, 7c, 8a, 9a, 10d, 11b, 12d, 13c, 14b, 15c

# INDEX